AF291932

Migrants shaping Europe, past and present

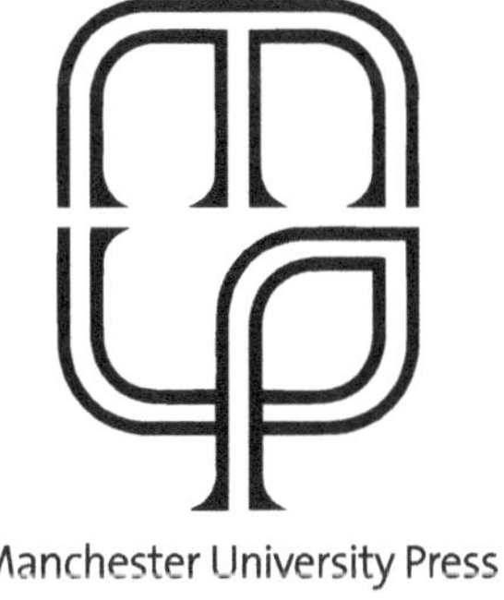

Manchester University Press

Migrants shaping Europe, past and present

Multilingual literatures, arts, and cultures

Edited by Helen Solterer and Vincent Joos

MANCHESTER UNIVERSITY PRESS

Publication of this open monograph was the result of Duke University's participation in TOME (Toward an Open Monograph Ecosystem), a collaboration of the Association of American Universities, the Association of University Presses, and the Association of Research Libraries. TOME aims to expand the reach of long-form humanities and social science scholarship including digital scholarship. Additionally, the program looks to ensure the sustainability of university press monograph publishing by supporting the highest quality scholarship and promoting a new ecology of scholarly publishing in which authors' institutions bear the publication costs. Funding from Duke University Libraries made it possible to open this publication to the world.

Published by Manchester University Press
Oxford Road, Manchester M13 9PL

www.manchesteruniversitypress.co.uk

British Library Cataloguing-in-Publication Data
A catalogue record for this book is available from the British Library

ISBN   978 1 5261 6616 6 hardback

First published 2022

Typeset
by New Best-set Typesetters Ltd

For Kevin, compañero de viaje,
& those North Carolinians at work who are not from around here

In memory of Sandu Talpău

Contents

Contributors

James S. Amelang, Universidad Autónoma de Madrid

Tenley Bick, Florida State University

Vincent Joos, Florida State University

Akash Kumar, University of California, Berkeley

Eric Leleu, independent photographer

Pedro M. P. Raposo, Academy of Natural Sciences

Raquel Salvatella de Prada, Duke University

Helen Solterer, Duke University

Anna Tybinko, Duke University

Saskia Ziolkowski, Duke University

In Transit Collective: Ellen Raimond, Marianne Wardle, Elvira Vilches, Alán José, Pedro Lasch, Raquel Salvatella de Prada, Shreya Hurli, Helen Solterer, Duke University

Acknowledgments

This book is a collective response to one international challenge confronting us, devised during another.

It, too, is a survivor, making its way through a global pandemic, and a local hurricane. Its appearance, at last, would be unthinkable without the support and stick-to-it-ness of many.

Thanks go first to Duke colleagues, who supported it generously over the years: Gennifer Weisenfeld as Dean of the Humanities; Giovanni Zanalda, Director of the Center of International Studies; Sarah Schroth as Director of the Nasher Museum; and Martin Eisner and Richard Rosa, as Chairs of the Department of Romance Studies.

The Trent Foundation awarded funding at a pivotal time as the project began to take shape.

Colleagues at Duke Libraries helped to sustain it in vital ways; Meg Brown giving it more of a public face; Dave Hansen and Haley Walton, advocates for its open access.

Elvira Vilches and Alán José were the rarest of collaborators at an early stage; their commitment to the comparative character of the project ensuring its ongoing life.

Emilie Picherot never failed to share her expertise in Arabic, on the streets of Paris, as in libraries in France.

The students in seminars energized it with their own thinking, translations, and questions, especially Sophie Caplin, Susan Yun, and Cole Zaharris.

The anonymous readers of the manuscript gave us commentaries that helped to strengthen the book, and make it even more responsive to the challenge of migration in our times.

During the COVID-19 winter of 2020 and the summer of 2021, Shreya Hurli was an indispensable ally, proving what steady, shared work can accomplish.

Bryant Holsenbeck, in her inimitable artist-activist's style, helped me to understand fully what it takes to make something new with many creative people.

My first and last thanks go to the contributors. With all the challenges of our COVID-19 years together, they remained committed to their work and our endeavor. A force for good in our world. Vincent Joos and Saskia Ziolkowski made an improbable proposition take real shape at last: a gift. In the ninth hour, Victoria George contributed more to completing this book than the index she prepared.

H. S.

First, my thanks go to Helen Solterer, who initiated this project long before I came on board as a co-editor. With a true interdisciplinary and collective spirit, and during trying times, Helen kept the project moving in new, creative, and exciting directions. I am grateful for her mentoring and her infinite patience. I want to thank Townsend Middleton and all my colleagues at the University of North Carolina at Chapel Hill who continue to support and fuel my work on European and US immigration.

Carolina Sanchez Boe's engaged scholarship on immigration is a model of grounded activism. I am grateful for her invaluable feedback and advice.

Martin Munro and Racha Sattati, from the Winthrop King Institute for Contemporary French and Francophone Studies at Florida State University have been generous with their time and support. Many thanks to Preston McLane and to the team of the Florida State University Museum of Fine Arts for supporting our collective work.

A heartfelt thank you to all the contributors. Their vision and open-mindedness made this project not only possible, but also urgent and important.

V. J.

Helen Solterer & Vincent Joos
Durham, North Carolina; Tallahassee, Florida

Introduction

Helen Solterer and Vincent Joos

This comparative volume advances an argument about the sustained contribution of migrants to Europe's literatures, social cultures, and arts.

Firstly, those named most often by others as "migrants" do not represent a sudden, unprecedented crisis, as pundits and politicians continue to claim, with successive waves of migration. Instead, people arriving in the Spanish enclaves in Morocco, landing on the Italian islands of Sicily and Lampedusa, held up on the French coast of the Channel – and drowning in increasing numbers – are the latest generations of *migrantes, migranti, migrants* to participate in European life. They stand in a long line, heirs of the perennial presence of those who started their lives "elsewhere," who were forced to move or chose to do so, all of them learning to live in several languages.

This volume breaks with the notion of a current-day migration emergency to show, secondly, that what we pragmatically call "Europe" has never been bounded by the seas that surround it (Abulafia, 2019). Peoples have regularly been crossing the Mediterranean in the south, travelling through the continent, traversing the Channel in the north. This circulation of men, women, and children, the movement of inventive ideas they bring with them is far from exceptional – it is the lifeblood of culture. Contributors to the volume counter the perception of crisis by conceiving of a cultural history of the European continent as one time-honored site of significant movements of peoples.

Thirdly, these many displaced and dispossessed peoples, known and unknown, have shaped European cultures in a major way over many centuries. "Europe" is no less in motion than those identified as migrants (Guénoun, 2000: 17). At the heart of the book is the argument that migrants are fundamental actors in the historical making of that "work in progress" that is Europe – in what they do and what they express, and in how they are represented by writers and artists of many stripes. To make this argument, contributors work with the arts and sciences of migration, together with oral accounts of migrants. Across several languages and materials, they show both the fatal and fruitful consequences of this mass movement.

Contributors to this volume take a very long critical view. Already by the fifteenth century, world historians argue, the peoples of three continents, Africa, Europe, and Asia, had become inter-connected, their movements more common than not. (Hoerder, 2015: 6; 2002; Phillips 1994). Displaced by warring political powers, brought by force in servitude from other lands, travelling as merchants, or moved by a taste for adventure, early modern peoples around the European continent can as likely be identified as migrants as those we encounter today. In the Mediterranean south, multiple holy wars of Islamic caliphates and Christian kingdoms, as well as civil wars among city-states on the Italian peninsula, displaced thousands of individuals, including those who wrote inventively about what they lost. In the north of the continent as well, struggles between competing dynasties starting in the fourteenth century rousted thousands more out of their lands, including a number who expressed the shock of their dispossession in poetry and drawing. In the north and south, as across the continent, huge numbers of premodern peoples took to the roads over land and water – a phenomenon that merits being interpreted in its full cultural implications.

The question of premodern migrants is being taken up again by historians investigating urban and civic culture (Rubin, 2020: 19–21). This research zeroes in on many more types of passers-through, especially women workers, and builds on the work of earlier generations. Social historian Henri Pirenne argued that "the city is the creation of those who migrated toward it. It has been made from without and not from within" (Pirenne, 1914: 502).[1] Pirenne was investigating his own well-surveyed terrain of multilingual port cities in the north such as Ghent and Antwerp, as well as those in the south, Venice and Genoa. The hundred-year-old Pirenne thesis, however surpassed, did demonstrate the vital, engaging involvement of migrants in the labor force and urban life, whether they came from the land's end of Brittany or the other extreme limit of the European continent in the east. It is a thesis, too, that leads some contributors to argue in a social and economic vein, following Pirenne, that in this way "Europe 'colonized' itself thanks to the increase in inhabitants," those who had come from outside the walls of cities and far beyond as well.[2]

This question of premodern migrants is also inflected by the cultures of slavery. Researchers are beginning to reconsider the serf vs. enslaved comparison that has long limited thinking about such peoples in European societies (Rio in Ismard et al. 2021: 101–8). Their investigations are extending progressively in zones around the Mediterranean, in its port cities, as much as in the Atlantic (Barker, 2019: 3; McKee, 2014). They, too, draw on the work of historian-writers from two generations ago. Iris Origo, for example, brought to light a forgotten episode in history, one of Armenians and Africans, among others, moved against their will to work in Tuscan households during the fourteenth and fifteenth centuries.[3] Origo pioneered the abiding problem of enslavement as a necessary direction for tracking migration historically along one of its southern routes.

When we pose the question of migrating peoples around Europe in modern times, it is not surprising, then, how inextricably bound up this is with colonial histories. In an edited volume entitled *Les Mondes de l'esclavage* (*The Worlds of Slavery*), scholars show that slavery has an immense structural power and contributes to the institution of new forms of coerced labor outside of the slavery regime itself, and this beyond the Atlantic world (Ismard et al. 2021). Here, contributors tackle several histories of colonial ideologies and practices that tell us much about who has migrated and why. They analyze the process of colonization that has undergirded immigration and its present-day state management. Some contributors examine this process in the terms of social practices aimed at controlling human relations, as well as of production. Others reckon with a colonial imprint on people's ways of thinking and writing, the ways writers and critics challenge – and surpass – that legacy too. In studying various migrant cultures, literatures, and arts in post-colonial regimes, they take up ethnic, racial, and religious categories used to stigmatize migrants.[4] Within these formidable constraints, contributors also examine how people take hold of every medium available to represent the condition of migrants to critique the political powers enforcing their lives, and to express imaginatively other ways of living. They turn also to those artists whose work is created to protest the ways anti-immigrant figures are inculcated. In sum, the volume's authors regard those peoples displaced as a consequence of colonial legacies as prime movers and shakers of culture; rooted communities are, in fact, the exception in the Maghreb, North Africa, for example, as Julia Clancy-Smith argues (2011: 21).

With this historical understanding, contributors conceptualize "migrants" in a new way. In order to identify their contributions to cultures, literatures, and arts, they work to establish their sizeable presence in European history. Who are premodern migrants? This is a question still rarely pursued about those forced to move onto and around the continent during the fourteenth century. How are groups identified during the fifteenth century, as well as the sixteenth and seventeenth, periods conventionally cast as the early, defining eras of imperial and colonial expansion in Africa, as in the Americas? The terms used to identify "migrants" at the time are configured principally through stories of banishment and exile. Peoples are perceived as *personae non gratae*, divested of their humanity. To gauge the implications of names means considering many groups as migrants, and foregrounding individuals whose social circumstances characterize them in this way.

Several contributors pursue the work of reconceptualizing premodern peoples as "migrants." They place groups who are defined by ethnicities, separated by religion, and identified by language, at the core of their investigations. They examine the part these migrants play in Europe's early modern conflicted history, the formative influence of what they write – and what is written about them – on conceptions of literature. Other contributors who study contemporary circumstances take up the figures that stigmatize migrants – outsiders at the origin of crisis – as well as the myths of European prosperity awaiting them. They work to undo these distorted pictures, analyzing the range of anti-immigrant discourses and practices around specific events of dispossession and routes of migration. For example, even if states like France prevent certain migrants from participating in the social culture of Europe by refusing their asylum claims, by incarcerating them, or by pushing them away from urban centers, migrants make a forceful intervention in the continent's cultural and political make-up. Artists from the world-over have been collaborating with migrants to depict the conditions in tent camps, but also the rich lives, hopes, and aspirations of people stuck at borders, in Calais, among others (Miyamoto and Ruiz, 2021; Agier, 2018). Contributors, then, also focus on writers and artists who create an alternate point of view on the migrant condition. They track what Dominic Thomas (2012) names "new grammars of migration" and how these grammars restructure political practices towards migrants. They pursue the ways that migrants interact with Spanish, Italian, and French vernaculars, and enter into cultures in Europe through various networks and local organizations who engage with them.

Culture, language, art at stake

In all these ways, this history of migration around Europe is a specifically socio-cultural one. It involves the growing and changing ensemble of representations, in speech, writing, visual arts, and other objects that people create in search of a sense of self, and a social commons in which they participate. We understand culture in the elementary sense that art critic Georges Didi-Huberman uses when he considers migration; it's a process of imagining one another through dialogue (Didi-Huberman and Giannari, 2017: 61). Words and images are the raw material, and what takes shape is less artifact or product than something dynamic. Contributors take culture as a social and aesthetic activity of making, one pursued by migrants along their way, as by those who witness them, and represent their lives in an act of support. In the line of writer John Berger and photographer Jean Mohr who made the first concerted effort to think of migrants around Europe with critical imagination, we work together across verbal and visual media (Berger and Mohr, 1975: 96).

Our investigations concentrate on three related cases. Each one is articulated, first, through language. We delimit areas by three Romance vernaculars: Italian, French, and Spanish. All three languages issue from an imperial language of enormous influence, a Latin imposed under Roman rule. Their shared lexicon bears the traces of uprooting peoples from their places and propelling many of them as servants and enslaved peoples into the unknown – into unfamiliar countries, as well as alien tongues.[5] Those who used any one of the three vernaculars were also familiar with other major languages – Arabic being one prime example. For those who practiced the early forms of Romance languages, it is difficult to imagine how they spoke and wrote without registering their multilingual environs. In our investigations of premodern cultures, we see how migrants are compelled by force of circumstance to "move around" several vernaculars. Because they changed places, and inhabited different countries, they lived and worked in the presence of a variety of languages. Suzanne Akbari and Karla Mallette's collective of critics traverse a "sea of languages" in thirteenth- and fourteenth-century Mediterranean cultures: Arabic with Spanish and Italian – and the Ur-mother tongue, Latin, which Mallette plumbs deeply; Sharon Kinoshita gives attention to the many multilingual resonances in French in Cyprus at the eastern periphery (Mallette, 2021; Akbari and Mallette, 2013; Kinoshita, 2020; and Ruiz, 2017: 166). Alison Cornish reminds us that a common "Romance" parlance among writers of the pedigree of Bruno Latini and Dante was also used by merchants for pragmatic reasons (Cornish, 2006: 310).[6] In the north of the European continent, at much the same time, we can track a similar and widespread multilingual practice: French vying and converging with English and Flemish, as Jonathan Hsy and Ardis Butterfield demonstrate (Hsy, 2017; Butterfield, 2009).

In twentieth-century cultures around Europe, speakers and writers who need to work across Romance vernaculars and the Semitic languages of Arabic, Amharic, Tigrinya, and Hebrew are prevalent, as they are in current times. Indeed, this modern-day version of the transfer of language and knowledge, *translatio linguae et studii* through the enforced transfer of political power, the *translatio imperii*, explains much about the acculturation of migrants. Those who are forced to move by the march of European empires, whether the Spanish one in North Africa, the French in the Maghreb and *Francafrique*, and the Italian in Libya and East Africa, find themselves obliged to speak and write otherwise. Our contributors turn their attention to the choices migrants make: how they respond to the necessity to communicate in the Romance languages of their supplementary cultures. Yet contributors also address how pragmatic – and ingenious – migrants are when it comes to expression. Whether they enter into Italian, French, or Spanish, each vernacular can become for them a *lingua franca*. In our analysis, each offers independent ways for people to express themselves and to create despite the considerable constraints of their circumstances.

Fiction is one principal use of language that we examine. The writer Juan Goytisolo, who insisted on recognizing such multilingual, multi-ethnic histories in his to-ing and fro-ing between Morocco and Spain, captures the imaginative potential of this verbal expression in the novel *Reivindicación del conde don Julián* (*Count Julian*, 1970). "Ever on the move," he writes in Spanish, "my only sustenance your nourishing language."[7] What is a useful tool is also a sustaining life force of sorts. Goytisolo is referring to the power that language confers to create figures and give free voice. Here it is his character talking, Count Julian of Ceuta, fashioned out of the eighth-century historical person, and made notorious by legend for enabling Tariq ibn Ziyad's Muslim warriors to invade Visigothic Spain. Goytisolo's Julian, who speaks Arabic-Castilian, gives voice to the human right of movement in speech and representation. This movement that individual speakers exercise and authors practice is one baseline of our thinking, and a subject that several contributors debate.

In all three of our chosen cases, Italian and French, as well as Spanish, contributors are alert to migrants' expressiveness, those who adopt new languages in daily interaction, those who make them their own opportunistically, in inventive writing. That is why contributors also entertain the dynamic mixing of vernaculars. Somali and Arabic resonate in migrants' speech and writing with Italian; so does French with Flemish, Kurdish, and Mandarin, and Spanish with Arabic. These are all examples of Europe's languages, and they take shape in art too. Franco-Lebanese graphic writer Zeina Abirached imagines this linguistic mix in images: "ever since my childhood I've been knitting a language made of two delicate and precious threads" ("*Je tricote depuis l'enfance une langue constituée de deux fils fragiles et précieux*") (Abirached, 2015: 96–7).

Images offer a further medium for analyzing our three cases. Whether in textile, video, or sculpture, they prove equally crucial in determining what migrants invent from their experience and how they are represented. Today's ubiquitous image-making medium of photography allows us to follow people over huge distances by land and sea, over years. Photographs are themselves a form of transport, Berger remarks, two generations ago (Berger and Mohr, 1975: 17). Today's digital photography massively develops this mobility of image; it increases the ease and speed of making images that seem to award us even personal contact with those in transit. Since the controversial "Dublin" law in the European Union requiring migrants to seek asylum in the first country in which they arrive, these easily-made images can also prove a dangerous impediment to freedom of movement; if smartphone images are captured by authorities in Europe, they are used to justify detaining migrants against their will, in the country where they are first photographed, and deporting them. Contributors working on Spanish, French, and Italian fronts, mindful of these risks, still turn to photographs in order to chronicle migrants' ways of living. They are careful to avoid the type of photograph that could identify individual migrants. When photographer Eric Leleu takes portraits of migrants along the Channel coast, for example, he does so when people cover their faces. Such carefully constructed images can nonetheless document something of the views of migrants passing through or blocked in camps today.

In our work, time-honored images of drawing and painting, as well as those of printing with engraved metal and woodcuts, join those of contemporary artists. Contributors embrace these media in order to see how early modern visual cultures depict migrants around Europe. The language of images provides clues about how and when peoples were stigmatized, about what they saw. Fifteenth-century manuscript illumination in the French-speaking north that depict numerous besieged cities represent groups stripped and exposed, visually debasing them as inferior. Painter Joachim Patinir details brutal scenes in the countryside, people fleeing their houses set on fire, scenes that could easily represent the wars in his early modern Flanders as a background for his biblical subject, the Holy Family in Flight from Egypt (Vergain, 2007). The fine arts of seventeenth-century Spanish courts are also telling. They include a drawing of Vicente Carducho, several large canvases of Vicent Mestre and Pere Oromig figuring crowds of Spanish Muslims gathered at the docks of port cities, on the verge of banishment from their homes, and expulsion from their own culture. Other contributors examine early maps and instruments. The rich traditions of Islamic sciences in the twelfth century offer material for exploring how precisely people's movements were plotted and facilitated.

Migrating in Spanish, Italian, French

The first case that the volume investigates, the Spanish one, brings us to a major interface of African and European continents. *Bāb al-Magrib*, "Gateway of the West" in Arabic, and *Estrecho de Gibraltar*, the "Strait" in Spanish, name the passageway between the Iberian peninsula and North Africa where people cross through the port city of Ceuta.[8] During early modern times, the traffic back and forth in this area was intense and violent: from Muslim conquerors of Hispania, to Christian crusaders facing off with the Almohad caliphate in the Maghreb, from uneasy cohabitation of three different communities to the State-sponsored expulsion of Spanish Muslims that James Amelang examines in this volume.[9] His work reconceives those known as Moriscos, as migrants. Amelang reviews ways to discover how they understood their plight, what happened after they were deported. The successive movements of peoples that resulted also typifies the area today. Thousands of Moroccans who continue to cross the Strait to work in Spain nourish contemporary Spanish Islamic cultures. When we consider this movement of people in socio-cultural terms, we approach what are destructive and fruitful transactions linguistically. Author and critic Abdelfattah Kilito represents this process wryly: "I speak every language, but in Arabic" (Kilito [2013], 2018). Writing this in French, Kilito acknowledges how languages acquired by force of colonial circumstance can also be transformed by every speaker. He captures the conflictual and creative energy of the multilingual situation familiar to many inhabiting both Magrebi and European cultures. The *Diario de un ilegal* (*Diary of a Clandestine Migrant*, 1999), which Moroccan journalist Rachid Nini wrote in Arabic, with an eye to its Castilian translation exemplifies this process. Anna Tybinko pursues this writer's bilingual ways of representing Moroccan migrants, addressing Maghrebi audiences and crossing into his host's language, confronting Spanish readers with precarious migrants working in their midst.

The second, Italian case marks another "Southern" interface between Africa and Europe.[10] It, too, brings us into an area characterized by deep interaction of Romance vernaculars and Arabic, issuing from the eleventh-century Norman invasion that forced Muslims to flee (Baby-Collin et al, 2021; Carpentieri and Symes 2020; Grévin, 2010). Akash Kumar contributes to the argument for the formative Arabo-Islamic literary culture of Sicily by way of Ibn Hamdîs' poetry lamenting his lost home. Studying the place of these Sicilian odes, the *Siqilliyat*, in an Italian literary tradition brings Kumar to weigh the repercussions of identifying Ibn Hamdîs as kin to another poet in exile, Dante. Today's migrant writers in Italy draw on a further range of language, the result of more recent, twentieth-century colonial occupations, yet no less part of the cultures of this country. Arabic is still influential; so are Somali, Amharic, and Tigrinya, the vernaculars of East Africa in Somalia, Ethiopia, and Eritrea, which Mussolini had attempted to claim for Fascist Italy. To account for the range of expressiveness of Italian writers means turning to all those who have "come home" from such former colonies, to consider their work as integral to Italian culture. A recent anthology of refugee stories co-edited by author Igiaba Scego and the UN Refugee Agency, examined by Saskia Ziolkowski, epitomizes the generative energy of this fiction, infused with African traditions. Artists working in stone and other materials also exemplify such transformations of Italian cultures. In Tenley Bick's view, the sculpted Gate of Europe that an artist erected on the island of Lampedusa provides a powerful social act of art-making; so does the lesser known intervention of another artist who walls up the Gate as a critique of the Italian welcome to migrants.

The French case, finally, takes us the farthest north in our investigation, to the Channel coast. This area too was invaded and occupied – constituted by a cavalcade of rival dynastic powers beginning in the fourteenth century. The French–English conflict is well-known; yet later early modern wars involving the Spanish Hapsburgs, and implicating Flemish, Genoese, and Turkish peoples, make this area a particularly crucial test case. Calais is the focus of analysis (Sanyal, 2017).[11] In this port city, the stand-off today between the French government backed by the European Union, and England Brexiting away, leads contributors to begin constructing the multilingual and multi-cultural history of the "North-Pas-de-Calais" area (Babels, 2017). First, Helen Solterer reconceptualizes Calais during the so-called Hundred Years' War in the fourteenth–fifteenth centuries as a site of forced migration. She makes this critical step by studying the idea of the enclave. Working with fiction about the premodern city under siege, and today's Calais harassed and hunkered down, she examines the imaginative territory that writers create for migrants and their communities. Vincent Joos takes another important step by investigating Chinese laborers brought to Calais during World War I. His inquiry, coupled with Eric Leleu's photography of the French area, devotes critical attention to one of the least-recognized groups of migrants in France and Europe.

By focusing work on these three cases, in Spanish, Italian, and French, we are drawing another map for the cultural history of migration around Europe. Contributors are introducing a less familiar human geography of Arab, African, and Asian peoples, both in early modern times and in the twentieth century. This socio-cultural map is given shape by the imagination, and is humanized by a greater range of peoples and their expressiveness. Contributors detail it through many types of fiction, visual arts, and material objects. The map that comes into view does not coincide fully with the one that traces migrant routes around Europe today – from the Middle East, the Turkish and Greek Mediterranean through the Balkans, as much as from the Maghreb, East and West Africa, northwards. Instead, mapping our socio-cultural history charts the movements of migrants in the way writers and artists represent them. This cartography in Italian, French, Spanish, we contend, bears as great a social force and cultural significance as the more familiar maps of migrant routes.

In this map, various focal points epitomize that force: Ceuta/Melilla for the Spanish case, Sicily/Lampedusa for the Italian, and Calais for the French. All three are known as chief chokepoints for people moving today from the global South to the north.[12] In our view, they are equally important points of entry into the history of migrant peoples around Europe. They function as powerful sites of imagination in premodern times. Furthermore, our cases highlight a significant and rich linguistic range. Even as we write in English, our comparative inquiry is articulated through other languages that bespeak major areas of migration.[13] The three cases extend the debate about migration beyond the British empire and its Globish. The chapters advance a socio-cultural history of migration that argues for a wider and influential multilingualism.

Interpreting migration

Investigating an ensemble of words, images, and things on a large scale, over many centuries and kilometers, is our chosen method for changing not only the conception of migrants, but also the ways they are perceived as "others."[14] As writer Hisham Matar observes: "Only inside a book or in front of a painting can one truly be let into another's perspective" (Matar, 2019: 36–7). He came to this insight as he spent hours looking at Lorenzetti's fourteenth-century fresco, *Buon Governo* (*Good Government*), in Siena. It was forged through his efforts to make sense of having to flee Libya where Khaddafi's regime murdered his dissident father, and to come to London and New York where he makes his life writing. This coming-into-awareness becomes a basic principle in his work. It happens through his attentiveness to words and images, to ancient Bedouin poetry and Manet's painting, as his memoir, *The Return*, composed in his second language, makes clear.

Attentiveness to words and images means more than decoding and analyzing cultural artifacts. Becoming aware of someone else's perspective demands a form of radical empathy. As the historians Michelle Caswell and Marika Cifor write, radical empathy assumes "that we are inextricably bound to each other through relationships, that we live in complex relations to each other infused with power differences and inequities, and that we care about each other's well-being" (Caswell and Cifor, 2016: 31). The premodern lay people, poets, and artists who appear in this volume are not considered as distant others expelled or trapped, but as human beings who experience and narrate (im)mobility, as human beings who *feel* the nostalgia, the uneasiness, and sometimes the relief brought by moving "elsewhere." As such, those migrating around premodern Europe are akin to today's migrants, who are too often accounted for in dehumanizing quantitative forms.

By thinking historically across languages, by taking into account human geography and its political evolution, contributors dislocate European immigration and investigate peoples' movements in a non-teleological framework. The cultural history of migration we are composing responds to the habit of foreshortening its length and limiting it to twentieth-century examples.[15] Alongside dynamic migrant cultures around Europe from the history of present times or "living" memory, we place others from early, and modern eras.[16] This longue durée cultural history does not, however, aim for any comprehensive sweep. Composed case by case, it confronts in several specific ways the claims of culture wars that are over-simplifying public debates about present-day immigration in Europe.

Diptych-triptych

The chapters are organized according to Romance language, in diptychs or triptychs. We use this ancient design that creates pairs or trios to provide a critical frame of comparison for our three cases. Each diptych juxtaposes a chapter on early modern migrant cultures with another on its contemporary ones. In this way, it heightens relations and contrasts within each case. What emerges is less a continuity of migrant cultures than their inter-relations. Structures common to the history of migrant cultures in Spanish, Italian, and French come to the fore, as well as connections *between* these cases.

The three diptychs set into relief a new, historically grounded conception of "migrants." Recognizing the early modern Moriscos in the Spanish kingdom, or Dante, figurehead of an Italian tradition, as a migrant writer, or the multitudes sent into flight by the Hundred Years' War in the French kingdom, including poet Eustache Deschamps, fundamentally changes the critical perception of the cultures of migration. It also enriches the understanding of contemporary migrants: those Magrebi who cross into Spain now and write about their itinerancy; those bringing out the Somali and Libyan character of Italian literature and art today; those who labored around Calais a hundred years ago. This reconceptualization extends the timeline of migration around Europe. The implications for European literatures, social cultures, and the arts are profound: for the ethnic mix of culture in Spanish; for the literary crowns in Italian; for the multi-cultural matrix in French.

The opening diptych that frames the whole collection of chapters introduces the argument for the decisive participation of migrants in European cultures by examining material culture. Pedro Raposo takes up a scientific instrument, the astrolabe made and used throughout the Islamic world from at least the seventh century onwards. His chapter introduces a premodern history that tracks the widespread movement and interaction of peoples across North Africa and the European continent which created a rich, common culture, however vigorously it was contested and fought over. His men of science from premodern Islamic Europe exemplify those people on the move in the Mediterranean whom Fernand Braudel described as "indispensable

… who often brought with them new techniques, no less indispensable than their persons to urban life" (Braudel, 1976: 306). Raposo also addresses the ongoing work of shaping the public perception of such an object through museum exhibits.

In the final chapters, we return to artwork, to contemporary pieces of Raquel Salvatella de Prada, Barthélémy Toguo, Annette Messager, and Pedro Lasch.[17] Their work, juxtaposed with the premodern Catalan atlas and Jacques Callot's etchings reconfigure our vision of migration around Europe.[18] They bring the historical work of the volume to a culminating point and complete the final diptych with original pieces on today's migrant cultures. From Ceuta/Melilla to Calais, along paths of West Africans and others moving through the global South, they invite us to visualize the arts of migration in an expansive way.

Notes

1 In the introduction to the reissue of one of Pirenne's major works, *Medieval Cities*, Michael McCormick underlines the value of Pirenne's thesis for the "long, deep history of globalization" (Pirenne [1925], 2014: xxiii–iv).

2 "Just about the year 1000 there began a period of reclamation which was to continue, with steady increase, up to the end of the twelfth century. Europe 'colonized' herself" (Pirenne, [1925] 2014: 81).

3 Origo (1955). Sally McKee places Origo's work in the context of current research on medieval enslaved peoples (McKee, 2014: 285–6).

4 Some contributors are alert to the ways Cedric J. Robinson analyzes these categories in historical perspective (Robinson, 2020: 22–4). See also historian El Hamel (2013). On perceptions in premodern Europe, see Phillips (2017); on racializing tropes in the premodern Magreb, see al Azmeh (1992).

5 Erich Auerbach, in the vanguard generation of philologists, explored this history ([1949] 1961: 15–19).

6 See also Eisner (2020) on vernacularization.

7 Goytisolo, Lane, trans. (1989: 104).

8 On Ceuta, see Fuchs and Liang (2011: 264–5) and Hirsch and Pontin (2009: 94). On the Arabo-Islamic understanding of these contact zones between dar-es-Islam and "Unbeliever" or enemy zones, see Brauer (1995): 11–15.

9 Brann (2021) studies the challenge of taking the full measure of Muslim and Jewish traditions during this period. Gilbert (2020) provides the social history of Arabic translation that is the frame for some of the Moriscos.

10 On migrants attempting to make it to Europe through this crossing, see Proglio et al. (2018). On the rescue operations on the high seas given the Italian government's restrictive measures, see accounts by our colleagues at Duke, Hardt and Mezzadra (2020).

11 For the visual arts of contemporary Calais, see Hicks and Mallet (2019), following their exhibit at the Pitts River Museum (2019), and Mendel (2017); and on the

photography of laborers struggling on the international waters offshore, *Calais vu par Allan Sekula, Deep Six / Passer au bleu* (2000); and Van Gelder (2015). Two artists of note working in Calais today are Agathe Verschaffel, Jank, and their exhibition/installation, "TransPORTs – Calais vue du port," Musée des beaux arts, Calais, December 2016–March 2017.

12 Thomas Nail underscores the importance of specific sites in changing perceptions (Nail, 2015: 5).

13 See Chedgzoy et al. (2018). This collection is entirely devoted to English-speaking Britain. One contemporary comparative project of note is Abderrezak (2016).

14 Homi Bhabha gives a trenchant rationale of the particular methods of humanities; see his Introduction to Sorensen (2018: 10). Cox et al. (2020) is a powerful example recently published. See also Boucheron (2017). Khanmohamadi (2013) represents the ethnographic approach in the humanities focused on premodern cultures.

15 See also De Vivo (2015: 419); Duclassen and Duclassen (2012).

16 On the history of present times, see Passerini et al. (2020): 2–3.

17 The work of Salvatella de Prada, Toguo, and Lasch stands in sharp contrast and opposition to the practices of art plunder. Toguo's *New World Climax* woodcuts were the subject of students' research projects over several years at Duke University and benefitted from his first-time visit to the American South. It is important to note that none of the other [premodern] art objects installed were involved in any such incidents of plunder.

18 The installations of this work at the Nasher Museum, Duke University, are among several recent pioneering exhibits that bring into view these vibrant migrant cultures in some of its historical depth. See also Berzock (2019).

References

Abderrezak, Hakim (2016) *Ex-Centric Migrations: Europe and the Maghreb in Mediterranean Cinema, Literature, and Music.* Bloomington: University of Indiana Press.

Abirached, Zeina (2015) *Le Piano Oriental.* Paris: Presses Casterman.

Abulafia, David (2019) *The Boundless Sea: A Human History of the Oceans.* Oxford: Oxford University Press.

Agier, Michel (2018) *La Jungle de Calais.* Paris: Universitaires de France.

Akbari, Suzanne Conklin and Karla Mallette (2013) *A Sea of Languages: Rethinking the Arabic Role in Medieval Literary History.* Toronto: University of Toronto Press.

Auerbach, Erich (1949) *Introduction à la philologie des langues romanes.* Frankfurt am Main: V. Klostermann. (1961) *Introduction to Romance Languages and Literatures.* Daniels, Guy, trans. New York: Capricorn Books [pref. March 1948].

al Azmeh, Aziz (1992) "Barbarians in Arab Eyes," *Past and Present* 134, pp. 3–18.

Babels (2017) *De Lesbos à Calais, comment Europe fabrique des camps.* Bouagga, Yasmine, ed. Paris: Le Passager clandestin.

Baby-Collin, Virginie, Sophie Bouffier and Stéphane Mourlane, eds (2021) *Atlas des migrations en Méditerranée: de l'Antiquité à nos jours.* Arles: Actes Sud.

Barker, Hannah (2019) *That Most Precious Merchandise: The Mediterranean Trade in Black Sea Slaves, 1260–1500*. Philadelphia: University of Pennsylvania Press.

Berger, John and Jean Mohr (1975) *A Seventh Man: A Book of Words and Images about the Experience of Migrant Workers in Europe*. London: Verso.

Boucheron, Patrick, ed. (2017) *Migrations, réfugiés, exil*. Paris: Odile Jacob.

Brann, Ross (2021) *Iberian Moorings: Al Andalus, Sefarad, and the Tropes of Exceptionalism*. Philadelphia: University of Pennsylvania Press.

Braudel, Fernand (1976) *The Mediterranean and the Mediterranean World in the Age of Philip II*. Siân Reynolds, trans. New York: Harper and Row.

Brauer, Ralph (1995) "Boundaries and Frontiers in Medieval Muslim Geography," *Transactions of the American Philosophical Society* 85, pp. 1–73.

Butterfield, Ardis (2009) *The Familiar Enemy: Chaucer, Language and the Nation in the Hundred Years War*. Oxford: Oxford University Press.

Calais vu par Allan Sekula, Deep Six / Passer au bleu (2000) Calais: Musée des Beaux Arts et de la Dentelle de Calais.

Carpentieri, Nicola and Carol Symes, eds (2020) *Medieval Sicily, al-Andalus, and the Magrib: Writing in Times of Turmoil*. Leeds: Arc Humanities Press.

Caswell, Michelle and Marika Cifor (2016) "From Human Rights to Feminist Ethics: Radical Empathy in the Archives," *Archivaria* 81, pp. 23–43.

Chedgzoy, Kate, Elsbeth Graham, Katharine Hodgkin, and Ramona Wray (2018) "Memory and the Early Modern," *Memory Studies* 11, 1 (January).

Clancy-Smith, Julia (2011) *Mediterraneans: North Africa and Europe in the Age of Migrations, 1800–1900*. Berkeley: University of California Press.

Cornish, Alison (2006) "Translatio Galliae: Effects of Early Franco-Italian Literary Exchange," *Romanic Review* 97, 3–4, pp. 309–30.

Cox, Emma, Sam Durrant, David Farrier, Lyndsey Stonebridge, and Agnes Woolley, eds (2020) *Refugee Imaginaries: Research across the Humanities*. Edinburgh: Edinburgh University Press.

De Vivo, Filippo (2015) "Crossroads Regions: The Mediterranean," in *Cambridge World History*, vol. VI, *The Construction of a Global World, 1400–1800 CE*, part I, Foundations. Jerry H. Bentley, Subray Subrahmanyam, and Merry Wiesner-Hanks, eds. Cambridge: Cambridge University Press, pp. 415–444.

Didi-Huberman, Georges and Niki Giannari (2017) *Passer quoiqu'il en coûte*. Paris: Minuit.

Duclassen, Ian and Leo Duclassen (2012) "European Migration History," in *Routledge International Handbook of Migration Studies*. Steven J. Gold and Stephanie J. Nawyn, eds. New York: Routledge, pp. 52–63.

Eisner, Martin (2020) "Vernacularization and World Literature: The Language of Women in the World of God," in *A Companion to World Literature*. Ken Seigneurie, ed. Vol. 2. Hoboken, NJ: Wiley, pp. 1–7.

El Hamel, Chouki (2013) *Black Morocco: A History of Slavery, Race, and Islam*. Cambridge: Cambridge University Press.

Fuchs, Barbara and Yuen-Gen Liang (2011) "A Forgotten Empire: The Spanish–North African Borderlands," *Journal of Spanish Cultural Studies* 12, 3, pp. 261–273.

Gilbert, Claire M. (2020) *In Good Faith: Arabic Translation and Translators in Early Modern Spain*. Philadelphia: University of Pennsylvania Press.

Goytisolo, Juan ([1989] 2011) *Count Julian*. Helen Lane, trans. London: Serpent's Tail.

Grévin, Benoît, ed. (2010) *Maghreb-Italie: Des Passeurs médiévaux à l'orientalisme (XIIIe-milieu XXe siècle)*. Rome: École française de Rome.

Guénoun, Denis (2000) *Hypothèses sur l'Europe: un essai de philosophie*. Paris: Circé. [(2013) *About Europe: Philosophical Hypotheses*. Irizarrry, Christine, trans. Stanford. Stanford University Press.]

Hardt, Michael and Sandro Mezzadra (2020) "Introduction: Migrant Projects of Freedom," *South Atlantic Quarterly* 11, 1, pp. 168–75.

Hicks, Dan and Sarah Mallet (2019) *Lande: The Calais "Jungle" and Beyond*. Bristol: Bristol University Press.

Hirsch, Bertrand and Yann Potin (2009) "Le Continent détourné: frontières et mobilité des mondes africains," in Patrick Boucheron, Julien Loiseau, Yann Potin, and Pierre Monnet, eds. *Le Monde au XVe siècle*. Paris: Fayard, pp. 84–113.

Hoerder, Dirk (2002) "Judaeo-Christian-Islamic Mediterranean World up to the 1500s," in *Cultures in Contact: World Migrations in the Second Millenium*. 2nd edition. Durham, NC: Duke University Press, pp. 23–53.

— (2015) "Global migrations," in *Cambridge World History*, vol. VI, part 2, Patterns of Change. Jerry H. Bentley, Subray Subrahmanyam, and Merry Wiesner-Hanks, eds. Cambridge: Cambridge University Press, pp. 3–28.

Hsy, Jonathan (2017) *Trading Tongues: Merchants, Multilingualism, Medieval Literature*. Columbus: Ohio State University Press.

Ismard, Paulin, et al., eds. (2021) *Les Mondes de l'esclavage*. Paris: Seuil.

Khanmohamadi, Shirin A. (2013) *In Light of Another World: European Ethnography in the Middle Ages*. Philadelphia: University of Pennsylvania Press.

Kilito, Abdelfattah (2013) *Je parle toutes les langues, mais en arabe*. Arles: Sinbad-Actes Sud. [(2018) *Hablo todas las lenguas, pero en árabe*. Cerezales, Marta, trans. Santander: El Desvelo Ediciones].

Kinoshita, Sharon (2020) "Marco Polo and the World Empire of Letters," in the *Wiley-Blackwell Companion to World Literature*, Ken Seigneurie, ed.vol. 2, 601CE to 1450. Oxford: Wiley-Blackwell, pp. 1039–50.

Mallette, Karla (2021) *Lives of the Great Languages: Arabic and Latin in the Medieval Mediterranean*. Chicago: University of Chicago Press.

Matar, Hisham (2019) *A Month in Siena*. New York: Random House.

McKee, Sally (2014) "Slavery," in *The Oxford Handbook of Women and Gender in the Middle Ages*. Oxford: Oxford University Press, pp. 281–94.

Mendel, Gideon (2017) *Dzhangal*. London: GOST.

Miyamoto, Bénédicte and Marie Ruiz (2021) *Art and Migration: Revisioning the Border of Community*. Manchester: Manchester University Press.

Nail, Thomas (2015) *The Figure of the Migrant*. Stanford: Stanford University Press.

Origo, Iris (1955) "The Domestic Enemy: Eastern Slaves in Tuscany in the Fourteenth and Fifteenth Centuries," *Speculum* 30, 3 (July), pp. 321–66.

Passerini, Luisa, Milica Trakilović and Gabriele Proglio, eds (2020) *The Mobility of Memory, Migrations and Diasporas across European Borders*. London: Berghahn Books.

Phillips, Seymour (1994) "The Medieval Background," *Europeans on the Move*. Nicolas Canny, ed. Oxford: Clarendon Press, pp. 9–25.

— (2017) "Outer World of the European Middle Ages," in *European Ethnographies: European Perceptions of the World Beyond*. James Muldoon, Felipe Fernández-Armest and Joan-Pau Rubiés, eds. London: Routledge, pp. 4–45.

Pirenne, Henri (1914) "The Stages in the Social History of Capitalism," *American Historical Review* 3 (April), pp. 494–515.

— ([1925] 2014) *Medieval Cities: Their Origins and the Revival of Trade*. Frank D. Halsey, trans. Princeton: Princeton University Press.

Proglio, Gabriele and Laura Odasso, eds (2018) *Border Lampedusa: Subjectivity, Visibility and Memory in Stories of Land and Sea*. New York: Palgrave.

Robinson, Cedric J. ([1983] 2020) *Black Marxism: The Making of the Radical Black Tradition, Revised and Updated Third Edition*. Chapel Hill: University of North Carolina Press.

Rubin, Miri (2020) *Cities of Strangers: Making Lives in Medieval Europe*. Cambridge, Cambridge University Press.

Ruiz, Teofilo F. (2017) *The Western Mediterranean and the World 400 CE to the Present*, Hoboken NJ: Wiley-Blackwell.

Sanyal, Debarati (2017 [reprinted 2020]) "Calais: Refugees, Biopolitics, and the Arts of Resistance," *Representations* 139, pp. 1–33.

Sorensen, Diana, ed. (2018) *Territories and Trajectories*. Durham, NC: Duke University Press.

Thomas, Dominic (2012) "Into the Jungle: Migration and Grammar in the New Europe," in Multilingual Europe, Multilingual Europeans. *European Studies* vol. 29, pp. 267–84.

Van Gelder, Hilde, ed. (2015) *Ship of Fools / The Dockers' Museum*. Leuven: Leuven University Press.

Vergain, Alejandro, ed. (2007) *Patinir, Catalogue Raisonné*. Madrid: Prado.

PART I

A premodern cultural history

1

The astrolabe: from "mathematical jewel" to cultural connector

Pedro M. P. Raposo

Introduction: a "mathematical jewel"

On March 21, 1930, readers of the *Belvidere Daily Republican*, a local newspaper from Belvidere, Illinois, were presented with a short note titled "400 Years Old." Prominently illustrating the note was a photograph of the astronomer Philip Fox (1878–1944) staging an observation with a large antique astronomical instrument (Figure 1.1). The caption read "Professor Fox, chief of the Adler Planetarium at Chicago, using an astrolabe, an instrument to tell latitude, longitude, and time of the day from the sun, which was made in England in the year 1500 and is still workable. It has been acquired for the collection of astronomical and navigational instruments of the planetarium" (*Belvidere Daily Republican*, March 21, 1930).[1]

The instrument, a planispheric astrolabe,[2] was part of a lot containing roughly 500 instruments, which benefactor Max Adler (1866–1952) and Philip Fox had secured for the Adler Planetarium from Anton W. M. Mensing (1866–1936), a Dutch antiques dealer based in Amsterdam. Though sold and shipped from the Netherlands, the so-called Mensing collection included scientific instruments originating in places as varied as the already mentioned England plus Germany, Italy, France, and other European countries, as well as North Africa, the Middle East, and the Indian subcontinent. The bulk of the collection as such had previously traveled from France. It was amassed by the Paris-based collector and dealer Raoul Heillbroner, then sequestered by the French government during the Great War (Heilbronner was German, and thus regarded as foe), and finally purchased by Mensing, for most of it to end up in Chicago.

The acquisition of the Mensing collection established the core of the holdings of the Adler Planetarium, which opened to the public on May 12, 1930, becoming the first institution of its kind in the Western Hemisphere (Raposo, 2019; Taub, 2005). The Mensing collection was used to seal the character of the Planetarium as a proper museum of astronomy, which was

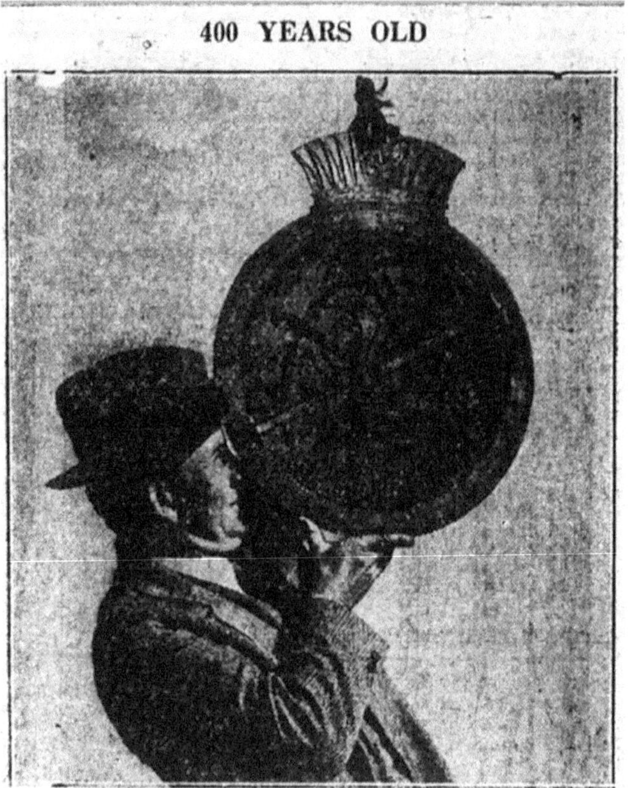

Figure 1.1 Philip Fox holding an astrolabe in the *Belvidere Daily Republican*, March 21, 1930. Adler Planetarium Collections.

further stressed in its original designation, "Adler Planetarium and Astronomical Museum."[3] In Fox's own words, the Planetarium was "in reality an Astronomical Museum in which the Planetarium instrument [a Zeiss Mk II planetarium projector] is the principal exhibit" (Fox, 1935: 6).

The choice of an astrolabe for the photograph printed in the *Belvidere Daily Republican* was an apt one. The instrument had long been symbolic of astronomy and of the mastery of this science, due, to a significant extent, to its complexity, comprehensiveness, and versatility.

In its most common form, the astrolabe is at once an analog computer and an observing imstrument shent. Its main components are the mater or main body, the throne, the rete (which is a map of the sky), the rule, the alidade, and several plates (each individual plate also being called a tympan), as well as a pin that serves as the axis of the instrument, and the so-called horse, which keeps the various parts together (van Cleempoel, 2005; Webster and Webster, 1998; Turner, 1985) (Figures 1.2 and 1.3).

The rete, the plates, the rule, and the horse are to be found on what is normally referred to as the front side of the instrument, which is used for calculations. The front side consists essentially of a projection of the celestial sphere through the method of stereographic projection, resulting in a functional model of the sky. Each instrument typically comes with a set of interchangeable plates containing coordinate grids projected for different latitudes (with each side of an individual plate normally corresponding to a different latitude). Since the plates are interchangeable, the instrument can in principle be used for an array of latitudes.

The astrolabe could be employed in a number of different operations (Evans, 1998), such as finding the time for observations of the sun or the stars, calculating the time of sunrise or sunset for a given date, or, in the case of certain instruments from the Islamic world, finding daily times of prayer and the qibla (the direction to Mecca), which further made the astrolabe particularly relevant for Islamic culture. The instrument was also used in connection with astrology and medicine (Schmidl, 2018), and applied to surveying work. Users of the astrolabe would have included astronomers,

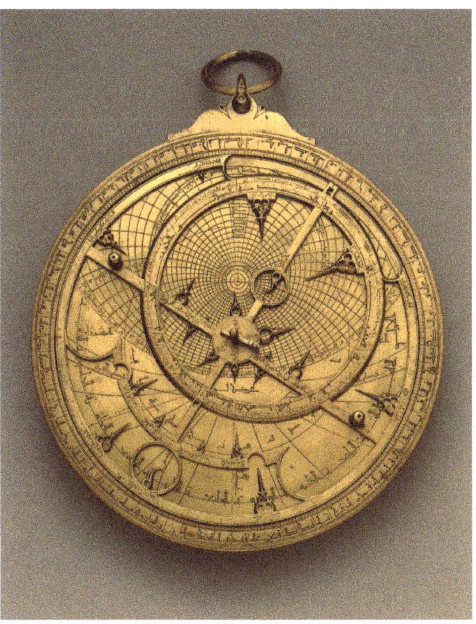

Figures 1.2 Front of an astrolabe by Muhammad ibn al-Fattuhal-Khama'iri, Seville, Spain, Adler Planetarium Collections, M-35.

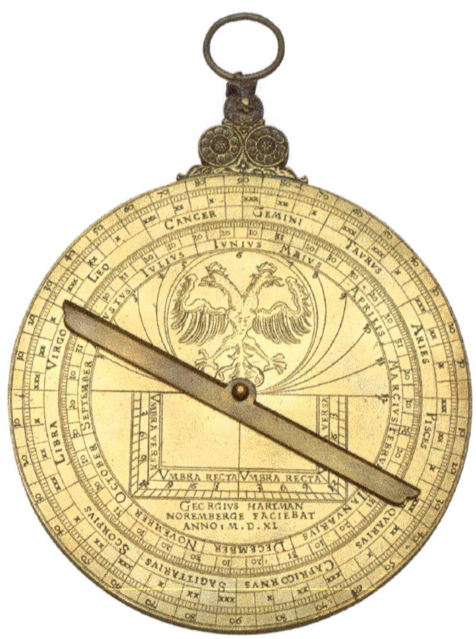

Figure 1.3 Back of an astrolabe by Georg Hartmann, Nuremberg, Germany, 1540, Adler Planetarium Collections, M-22.

astrologers, religious officials, civil servants, physicians, and surveyors (Schechner, 1998).

The back of the astrolabe was typically used to observe the altitude of the sun or a given star above the horizon. It included a moving alidade with sights for that purpose. It additionally contained features that provided elements for calculations (such as the position of the sun in the ecliptic for a given date, thus sparing the user from consulting a table) or that were suited for particular operations (for example, a shadow square, which could be used by a surveyor to determine the height of a building or the depth of a well).

The astrolabe has a long history whose details are not totally clear, and which remains a rich and compelling research topic that has been approached in recent years from a number of different angles (King, 2018, 2004–2005, 1987; Rodriguez-Arribas, Burnett, and Ackermann, 2017; Bennett and Strano, 2014; Eagleton, 2007; Newberry et al., 2006; van Cleempoel, 2005; Webster and Webster, 1998; Schechner, 2008, 1998; Turner, 1985). But one thing is for sure: its history is one of far-reaching movements of knowledge, people, and objects. The basic underlying concepts of the astrolabe seemed to have emerged by the second century BC in Ancient Greece. The earliest known treatises on the construction and use of the instrument date from the third century AD. It likely started to be regularly made and used in the Middle East from the seventh century onwards, with the oldest surviving instrument dating from the ninth century. Knowledge of the instrument traveled from the Middle East through North Africa into Europe via Al-Andalus (the Iberian Peninsula). A European tradition of astrolabe-making started to take shape beginning in the thirteenth century. By the mid-sixteenth century, the astrolabe was losing ground in western Europe to newer, simpler, and more specialized instruments. At the same time, knowledge of the instrument had traveled further east into the area under the influence of the Mughal Empire, with Lahore (in modern Pakistan) emerging as a center of fine instrument making (Sarma, 2020; Newberry et al., 2006). Astrolabes continued to be produced and used in areas under the influence of Islam well into the nineteenth century.

From the late nineteenth century onwards, the astrolabe was increasingly regarded in western Europe as a symbol of the scientific prowess of ages past. Concomitantly, it became an emblem for the connoisseurship of those very few able fully to grasp the subtleties of this complex apparatus, and, importantly, literally to put their hands on surviving examples. The photograph published in the *Belvidere Daily Republican* placed Fox in that selective group. It was also a statement of the character of the new planetarium led by Fox as a proper museum, one centered on a newfangled machine (the Zeiss opto-mechanical projector) capable of recreating the heavens and its motions indoors, but which was also home to a splendid collection of scientific relics "400 years old" or more. And the instrument chosen for the photograph was not just any historical example of the astrolabe. It was an exceptionally large instrument materializing a concept for a universal astrolabe (that is, an astrolabe that can in principle be used at any latitude without the need to change latitude plates) presented by the mathematician John Blagrave (1561–1611) under the suggestive designation of "Mathematical Jewel" (Webster and Webster, 1998). Fox used this expression in his guide of the Adler Planetarium and its collections to refer to the astrolabe in more general terms: "The Arabs certainly appreciated it, preserved, and perfected it, a Mathematical Jewel" (Fox, 1935: 35).

Curating and displaying the astrolabe

With the acquisition of the Mensing collection, the Adler Planetarium joined a group of emerging science museums that to this day house the largest collections of astrolabes in the world, all of which started to evolve significantly around the same time in the 1930s. The other members of this group include, in the United States, the Smithsonian National Museum of American History, and on the other side of the Atlantic, the National Maritime Museum (now part of the Royal Museums, Greenwich), the History of Science Museum in Oxford, and the Museo Galileo in Florence. Adding to these institutions, the British Museum also houses a significant collection of astrolabes.

By the late nineteenth century, astrolabes were increasingly coming into the hands of Western dealers and collectors. The examples originating from the Islamic world exerted a particular appeal on philologists, since deciphering their predominantly Arabic inscriptions required linguistic and philological skills that were the province of a select few. Adding to its fundamental geometrical complexity and its artistic qualities, this further contributed to accentuating the perceived "exotic" character of the astrolabe, making it symbolic of a sort of scientific orientalism.

Even to learned enthusiasts such as Philip Fox, there were barriers to fully deciphering the details of such pieces, as he admitted in his guide to the Adler Planetarium (Fox, 1935). A detailed description of all the astrolabes and related instruments from the Islamic world in the Adler's collections was only published several decades later (Pingree, 2009). The catalog, simply titled *Eastern Astrolabes*, was prepared by the historian of ancient mathematics David Pingree (1933–2005). Pingree's catalog was decades in the making, and constituted the second in a planned series of volumes covering the entirety of the Adler's collection of scientific instruments. The first volume, co-authored by Roderick Webster and Marjorie Webster and published in 1998, is titled *Western Astrolabes* (Webster and Webster, 1998). That the first two volumes in the series were dedicated to astrolabes is telling of the high status that these instruments held in the perceived hierarchy of the strengths and worth of the collections of the Adler Planetarium.

The separation of Western and Eastern astrolabes echoes a curatorial approach established in the first major modern study dedicated to the instrument: *The Astrolabes of the World*, authored by the Oxford scholar Robert Gunther (1869–1940) and published in 1932 (Gunther, 1932). This seminal work covered the roughly 300 historical astrolabes that were known at the time to be in museum and private collections. Gunther's main organization criterion was, in his own words, "topographical," meaning geographical. *The Astrolabes of the World* is thus presented in two volumes, respectively covering Eastern and Western instruments. This division is understandable taking into account the differences in style, particular features, and above all language that are usually evident between the two groups, whose efficient study and cataloging also requires distinctive skill sets, as already pointed out. But Gunther's approach also contributed to the establishment of a conceptual East–West divide that would influence the scholarship and curation of the astrolabe for decades to come.

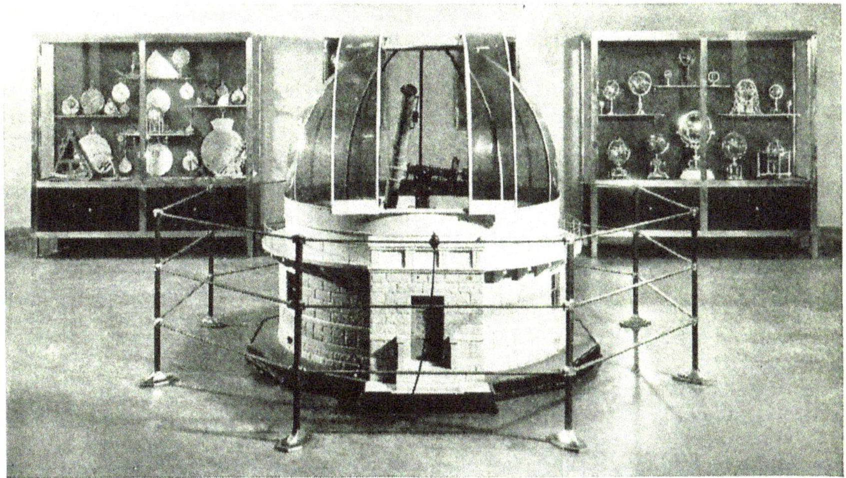

Figure 1.4 The original astrolabe display at the Adler Planetarium (cabinet on the left). Note the Blagrave astrolabe featuring prominently. Fox (1935), Adler Planetarium Library.

This distinction was not so evident in the early museum displays of the Adler Planetarium, in which both Western and Eastern astrolabes gained a prominent place from day one. Several astrolabes of different origins were presented in a cabinet together with other historical items (Figure 1.4) bearing some connection, even if remote, with the astrolabe, in order to emphasize the relations between this encompassing instrument and an array of other astronomical and mathematical devices. Detached from the original contexts of their production, use, and circulation, which were not mentioned in the display, here the instruments served mainly to illustrate a genealogical succession of observing and measuring devices used in astronomy and related sciences, in accordance with a positivist concept of a universal science progressing linearly towards ever greater exactness and overarching truths. This was further reinforced by the placement of the astrolabe cabinet close to a model of a modern astronomical observatory. Additionally, two transparencies of astronomical photographs taken with some of the largest telescopes available at the time separated the astrolabe cabinet from an armillary sphere[4] display. Although that aspect would probably escape most visitors, the juxtaposition of astrolabes with several other devices also served to emphasize the versatility of the astrolabe, which could, in principle, be used for operations similar to those for which the other (simpler and more specialized) instruments were eventually designed and produced.

The comprehensiveness of the astrolabe as a material compendium of astronomical knowledge and as a multi-purpose instrument is a central element of its persisting allure, which Gunther summarized thus: "[the astrolabe] is the result of a combination of many discoveries and inventions. It is a product of the human mind acting simultaneously in several directions, which, aided by the mechanical skill of generations of instrument makers, has created a new organ by means of which previously laborious operations have been simplified and new paths have been cleared for future progress" (Gunther, 1932: vi).

The versatility of the astrolabe is often used nowadays to introduce the instrument to non-expert audiences, by comparing it to a tablet or a smartphone on the grounds of the multitude of different apps that typically populate such devices, adding to the fact that these modern technologies are also used for obtaining basic utilitarian information such as the time of day (Poppick, 2017). The analogy is obviously anachronistic and problematic, one of its many flipsides being that an artifact as complex, exquisite, and certainly expensive as the astrolabe would be accessible only to a very few. But the same analogy is also telling of how the astrolabe resonates with modern notions and expectations regarding the power of science and technology to understand and predict natural phenomena, yield devices capable of solving a vast array of problems at once, and bring at least some degree of order and harmony into daily life. It equally speaks to an enduring fascination with the ability of peoples from ages past to conceive and produce complex devices.

Though that fascination may rely on a well-informed appreciation of history, it can also be tied to misconceptions about the past (particularly the Middle Ages) and prejudices about the willingness and disposition of non-Western peoples to engage with techno-scientific endeavors. And this can easily lead to regard realizations such as the astrolabe as an exceptional accomplishment in a general picture of backwardness. Gunther seems to have espoused such views in his seminal catalog, as he noted that the functions of the astrolabe included "keeping alive through barbarous ages the fundamental truths of Astronomy" (Gunther, 1932, vol. I: vi). Philip Fox's remark "the Arabs certainly appreciated it, preserved, and perfected it" (Fox, 1935: 35) is ambiguous; if on the one hand he extolls the contribution of Arab peoples to the development of the instrument, on the other hand he seems to single that out as an exception.

In recent decades the historiography of science has increasingly addressed and recognized the importance of Islamic peoples and cultures, especially in the Middle East, in preserving and expanding on the knowledge of astronomy, mathematics, and other fields during the Middle Ages and beyond, thus helping set the foundations for the emergence of modern science. This contradicts deeply ingrained misconceptions about the Middle Ages as a period of intellectual backwardness, as well as narratives of modern science as an essentially Western endeavor. The proper inclusion of the contributions of peoples from the Islamic world in such narratives becomes even more important when one takes into account the debates around the presentation of Islamic culture, and particularly Islamic art in museums (Norton-Wright, 2019; Bier, 2017; Junod et al., 2013). These debates and the lines of inquiry they have fostered, which are closely related to the idea of decolonizing the museum, have developed in the last two decades in response to growing misrepresentations of Muslims in Western media prompted by 9/11 and additionally fueled by news of the alleged migrant crisis, with a particularly strong expression in the Mediterranean region.

While there is a general consensus around the idea that museums can play a relevant role in counteracting negative representations of Islam by carefully presenting the art and culture of Muslims, the proper ways of doing so are a contentious matter. A particularly relevant point in such discussions is that an overarching definition of Islamic art is probably untenable, and certain to remain a contentious matter, as it would have to encompass a great variety of aesthetic sensibilities corresponding to distinct cultural and geographical contexts. In a similar vein, these lines of inquiry have also evinced the importance of integrating different Islamic voices into museum displays and narratives, in order to avoid artificial identitary constructions centered on the often misguiding idea of "community." The latter might, in fact, reinforce deeply engrained notions of the "other," instead of highlighting what people of different origins, faiths, and cultures have in common (Shatanawi, 2012).

As far as science and technology are concerned, another problematic issue is how to properly present contributions from the Islamic world without slipping into the exaggerations and distortions of narratives suggesting that modern science, and by association contemporary techno-scientific societies at large, are fundamentally shaped by inventions and discoveries originally emanating from the Islamic world. This was particularly evident in the popular travelling exhibit "1001 Inventions: Discover the Golden Age of Muslim Civilization" and its accompanying book (Al-Hassani, 2012).[5] They extolled science and technology in the Islamic world and their purported impact on contemporary life by favoring profiles of geniuses, a recurrent use of superlatives (such as "the first," "the greatest," etc.), and stories of groundbreaking discoveries and inventions neatly located in space and time, and ascribed to particular individuals (mostly men). These are precisely the sort of tropes on which positivist, Western-centric narratives of science have thrived in the first place, and which continue to pervade public discourses about science and technology.

The exhibition and the book motivated a scholarly response in the shape of an edited volume, suggestively titled *1001 Distortions* (Brentjes, Edis, and Richter-Bernburg, 2016), which, interestingly, comes with a cover showing a distorted astrolabe. Seeking to address the more general issue of how to present the history of science in non-Western cultures, the volume brings together various contributions that pinpoint the historiographic shortcomings of "1001 Inventions." It also presents various takes on the issue of how to better place the contributions of the Islamic world into global narratives of science and technology, while acknowledging that certain claims relating to the history of science and technology have been used to belittle the intellectual and cultural acumen of Muslims. The history of science and technology therefore constitutes another arena where prejudice against Muslims must be tackled, although not at the cost of historical rigor.

The volume includes one chapter dedicated to the astrolabe (Schmidl, 2016), which, however, remains predominantly descriptive in its scope and content. As an instrument whose basic concept and design circulated through, and was adapted and expanded upon in varied geographical and cultural spaces, the astrolabe provides a case in point as regards the narrative balance between the specific contexts of its production and use, and a broader picture of knowledge evolving through processes of displacement and circulation (Raposo et al., 2014; Golinski, [1998] 2005; Livingstone, 2003; Latour, 1988). These two complementary dimensions of scientific knowledge reflect important developments in the historiography of science over the last three decades or so. On the one hand, the so-called "material," "spatial," and geographical" turns led to favoring nuanced historical narratives highlighting the material culture of science and the particular geographical and spatial contexts of knowledge production, often at the cost of losing the bigger picture by opting instead for the narrrower confines of a so-called micro-history. On the other hand, a growing focus on circulation has sought to take advantage of the contextual richness provided by such historiographical angles, while placing the emphasis on the movement of ideas, people, and knowledge between different spaces as an integral part of knowledge production itself.

In 1998 the Adler Planetarium opened an exhibition titled "The Universe in Your Hands," which after some minor changes and updates over the years has remained one the Planetarium's permanent displays of scientific instruments, now under the title "Astronomy in Culture." The exhibition offers a compromise between antiquarianism and some elements akin to the newer historiographic angles outlined above. As far as astrolabes are concerned, the more traditional, "antiquarian" approach is evident in a display that presents examples of both Western and Islamic astrolabes selected mainly on the grounds of their perceived value as the "jewels" of the collection, and thematically displayed by "materials," "decorations," the "rete," and "great makers."

A more nuanced take on the instrument comes across in a display that recreates the layout of a medieval classroom, in which astrolabes and other instruments are placed in the broader context of medieval science and learning. Even more significant is a display with a map that highlights the contributions of scholars and instrument makers from the Islamic world, placing particular examples of astrolabes in the respective places where they were made (Figure 1.5). The display is intended to show how the movement of knowledge about the astrolabe, and more generally how astronomy through regions under the influence of Islam, contributed to the development of this discipline and to paving the ground for the emergence of modern science. The display sits next to an interactive module that explains how to find the qibla using an astrolabe.

It must be noted that addressing the functionality of scientific instruments in museum displays is a complex issue, and the astrolabe presents a particularly challenging case given its intricacy and the many steps that are usually required to efficiently perform even a simple operation such as finding the

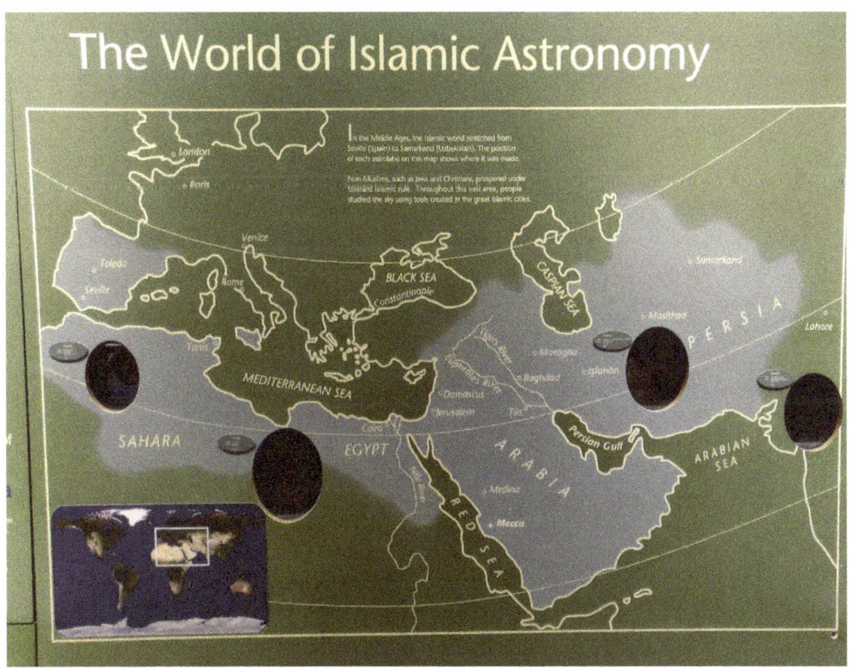

Figure 1.5 Display in the "Astronomy in Culture" exhibition at the Adler Planetarium.

time from observations of the sun or stars. In this regard, the effectiveness of this and other interactive components of the exhibition have proved to be limited. But there are deeper conceptual issues that must also be noted here. Though the map display shown in figure 1.5 evinces the area around the Mediterranean as a wide space of circulation, the directions of the movements of knowledge, people, and instruments associated with the astrolabe are not made explicit. Moreover, the use of "The World of Islamic Astronomy" as a title for the display denotes an enduring influence of the East–West divide, with astronomy and its geographical space of circulation in the Islamic world being presented as standing apart from modern Western science. Additionally, at least three major traditions in astrolabe making can be identified in the Islamic world, each with its own geographical settings: the Maghribi astrolabes, produced in Northwestern Africa and Al-Andalus (that is, the part of the Iberian Peninsula that was under the influence of Islam); the Mashriqi instruments, made in the Middle West, West Asia, and South Asia, in areas that are nowadays part of countries such as Iraq, Iran, and Syria; and the instruments originating from regions that were under the Mughal empire and are now part of India and Pakistan. Not only the display with the map is focused solely on the Maghrib and the Mashriq, reflecting a chronological focus on the Middle Ages, as the cultural nuances of these different geographical areas during that period are overlooked. At best, very attentive visitors will notice some differences between the instruments corresponding to those different areas and make sense of their chronological order if they read the labels.

Some attempts are made in adjoining displays to establish connections between Islamic astrolabes and the adoption of the instrument into medieval Europe, and more generally between the contributions of astronomers from the Islamic world and modern science, but the divide clearly prevails. It is further reinforced by the "antiquarian" astrolabe display mentioned above, where, despite the inclusion of astrolabes of varied origins, only two European instrument makers are highlighted under "Great Makers": the French Jean Fusoris (c. 1365–1436) and the German Georg Hartmann (1489–1564). The medieval classroom space also fails to highlight how the astronomy and mathematics taught in European medieval universities was in significant debt to contributions from scholars and texts from the Islamic world.

New pathways for presenting the astrolabe in a museum context

While this chapter was being written, discussions were under way at the Adler Planetarium towards the renewal of these displays, which is certain not only to address the aforementioned issues on the grounds of relevant scholarship in history of science, but also to be informed by recent developments and debates on the presentation of these instruments, and more generally of Islamic art in culture in art museums. Two cases in point are the exhibitions "In Transit: Arts & Migration Around Europe" (Duke University/Nasher Museum of Art, 2018), and "Caravans of Gold, Fragments in Time: Art, Culture, and Exchange Across Medieval Saharan Africa" (Northwestern University/Block Museum of Art, 2019),[6] both featuring astrolabes loaned from the Adler's collections.

The instruments presented in "Caravans ..." are a universal astrolabe made in the thirteenth century in North Africa or Spain, plus an instrument by Muhammad ibn al-Fattuhal-Khama'iri dating to 1236–1237 and made in Seville, Spain. Both instruments are thus part of the Maghribi tradition. "Caravans ..." places them in the context of the medieval Saharan trade and its significance as regards the movement of people, culture, and religious beliefs through West Africa, the Middle East, North Africa, and Europe from the eighth to sixteenth centuries. The exhibition as a whole ultimately aims to explore the global impact of these movements (Berzock, 2019). "Caravans ..." has several points of resonance with "In Transit," but the latter entailed a bolder move, using art to reframe the purported global refugee crisis – with the use of the word "crisis" in this context resonating with ideas of invasion and an associated, impending catastrophe. "In Transit" engaged with the issues surrounding the displacement of refugees, while focusing on two major zones of migration: "Northern Europe, from the region around Calais, Flanders and the Low Countries, and Southern Europe, from Islamic Spain to the African Maghreb" (https://intransitduke.org, accessed October, 24 2020). Two astrolabes from the collections of the Adler Planetarium were also put on display: the aforementioned Maghribi astrolabe by Muhammad ibn al-Fattuhal-Khama'iri featured in "Caravans ...," and an astrolabe comprising printed parts (the plates and back of the mater) assembled with wooden components (mater, throne, and rete), and completed with metal implements. The printed parts were originally engraved and printed by Philippe Danfrie in Paris in 1584 (on the basis of a previous version from 1578, which was corrected to reflect the new Gregorian calendar) and reissued in 1622 by Jehan Moreau (Karr-Schmidt, 2011; Webster and Webster, 1998).

The two instruments were used to illustrate the circulation of the basic concept and design of the astrolabe between North Africa and Europe, thus accentuating how past migrations promoted the circulation and growth of knowledge. There is no evidence to support the often mentioned but misguided idea that planispheric astrolabes were used for navigation (King, 2018).[7] But besides the movements of knowledge that are a crucial part of its history, the astrolabe does entail other aspects resonant with the processes of placement, displacement, and relocation that lie at the heart of human migrations, since it is fitted to be adapted to different latitudes, or in the case of universal astrolabes, to be used at any latitude.

It is also interesting to note the differences in materials between the two astrolabes presented in "In Transit." While the fine Al-Andalus astrolabe is made of brass, as was typical, the French integrates paper, wooden, and metal components. Printed astrolabes, of which very few assembled examples survive, started to be produced in Europe in the sixteenth century during the rise of Western print culture, as a way of exploring new niche markets for an instrument that was traditionally accessible and affordable only to a very few (Karr-Schmidt, 2011). Our historical understanding of the astrolabe as a material artifact is constrained by the extant instruments, which are mostly brass devices. This comes as no surprise, since those were naturally more likely to survive than any counterparts made of feebler materials, which would also be perceived as being less valuable. European printed astrolabes are not necessarily the only alternatives to metal instruments that ever existed. Nevertheless, they hint at the creative power of displacement and relocation, showing how the old astrolabe gained new material forms through its encounter with the emergent European print culture.

As could be expected from an exhibit project where art is used to approach a contemporary subject, the aesthetics of the astrolabe was a central element for its inclusion in "In Transit". But here the astrolabe's exquisite aesthetic appeal acquires new meanings. Particularly relevant in this regard was the placement of the Al-Andalus astrolabe next to the "New World Climax" prints of Barthélémy Toguo (Figure 1.6), and between the pages of the late fourteenth-century Catalan Atlas of Abraham Cresques. While Toguo's prints highlight the humanity of migrants from Western Africa seeking entry and legal status upon arriving in Europe, the atlas plots the world from the Mediterranean south to the north of the European continent, that is, the geographical space at the core of the origins, development, and circulation of the astrolabe. Viewers are thus invited to think of the astrolabe as part of a long human chain of cultural, scientific, and artistic developments that links diverse peoples, places, and cultures, but along which barriers continually arise.

The astrolabe thus emerges as a cultural connector. In that regard, the lead image chosen by the History of Science Museum to present the Oxford-Multaka project on its website is very telling. This project aims to "use museum and collections as a 'meeting point' ['Multaka' in Arabic] for bringing people together" (www.hsm.ox.ac.uk/multaka-oxford, accessed October 24, 2020). It engages volunteers with researching and presenting the collection of Islamic scientific instruments at the History of Science Museum and the textiles collection from the Arab World at the Pitt Rivers

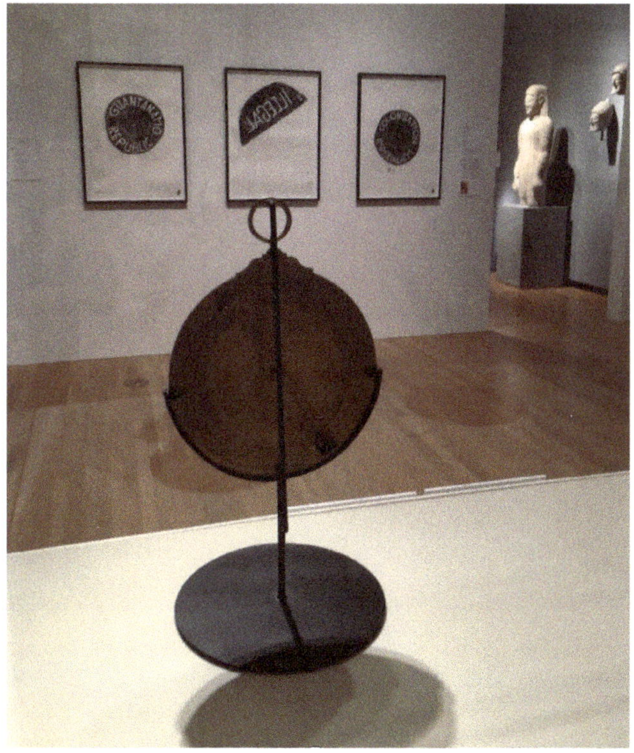

Figure 1.6 Astrolabe by Muhammad ibn al-Fattuhal-Khama'iri, Seville, Spain, 1236–37, Adler Planetarium Collections M-35; sitting across three woodcuts from the series "New World Climax" by Barthélémy Toguo (2011), in the "In Transit" installation at the Nasher Museum of Art, Duke University, 2018. Photo: Christopher Helms, with permission from Duke University/Nasher Museum of Art.

Museum. The image, in which a volunteer holds a cardboard replica of an astrolabe while in interaction with an audience in a museum gallery (presumably next to displays containing actual instruments), is representative not only of the aims of the project, but also of how the astrolabe can be efficiently reframed as a centerpiece in cultural dialogues and exchanges, beyond the confines of traditional scholarship and curatorial practice.

Also during the writing of this chapter – and in the context of a global pandemic that forced many institutions, including the Adler Planetarium, to temporarily close its doors to the public – the Adler undertook a first exploratory project towards newer approaches to presenting the objects in its collections that relate to astronomy in the Islamic world. In April 2021,

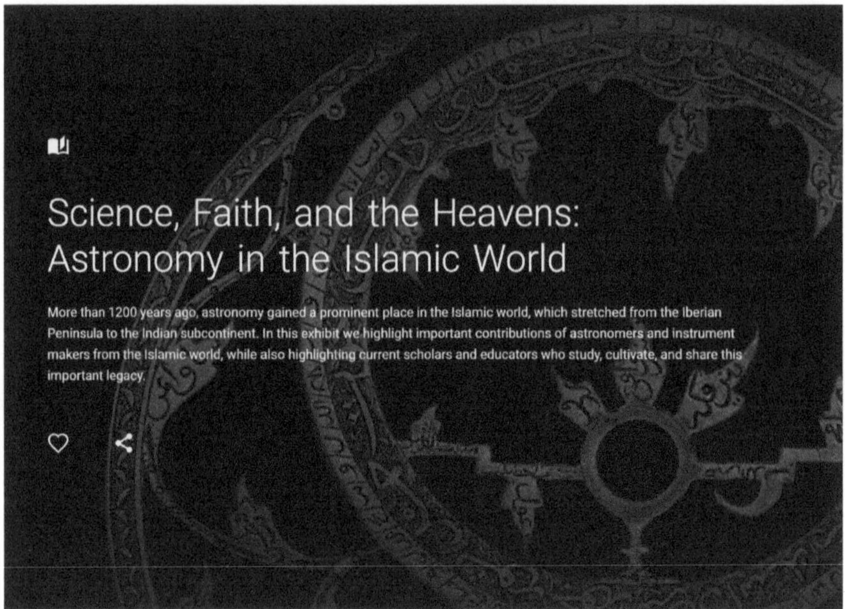

Figure 1.7 Opening page of the Adler Planetarium's digital exhibition on Google Arts & Culture platform, "Science, Faith, and the Heavens," launched in April 2017 (Adler Planetarium/Google Arts & Culture). The exhibition is accessible through https://artsandculture.google.com/partner/adler-planetarium (accessed July 31, 2021).

the digital exhibition "Science, Faith, and the Heavens" was launched on the Google Arts & Culture platform (Figure 1.7).

Counting on the guest curation of an expert on astronomical instruments and practices in the Islamic world, and combining images of Adler artifacts with those of objects, manuscripts, and other items from additional collections, the exhibit seeks to capture how the practice of astronomy, as well as its visual and material cultures, connected with religion, aesthetics, and broader cultural features in different historical and geographical contexts falling under the encompassing concept of an Islamic world. The exhibition is equally intended to convey a notion of how the movement of people and knowledge shaped astronomy in this space. It also counted on several guests with varied backgrounds, including scholars, students, and museum guides and volunteers, who were invited to contribute with their own thoughts and impressions as to the significance of this cultural legacy, and one personal favorite historical item they found representative of it. The exhibition was thus intended to give room to a multitude of voices as opposed to a single, overarching curatorial direction. It will not come as a surprise that astrolabes feature prominently in the exhibit and were picked up by several of the featured guests as their favorite objects.

Concluding remarks

Between the photo of Philip Fox proudly simulating an astronomical observation with the "Mathematical Jewel" and the image of the Multaka project volunteer holding a cardboard astrolabe, or the featured guests of the "Science, Faith, and the Heavens" exhibition citing particular examples as their favorite object and explaining why there is a long path of changing curatorial attitudes and conceptions about the role for museums and their collections in broader society. An exquisite and arcane scientific relic, the astrolabe is thus reframed as a conversation piece for intercultural dialogue. This by no means implies that it will cease to be regarded as a "mathematical jewel." In fact, it is the combined allure of its aesthetic appeal and technical complexity that keeps on attracting the attention of scholars as well as museum curators, stakeholders, and audiences. Together with a long history representative of how the movement of people, ideas, and objects shapes the development of knowledge, aesthetics, culture, and ultimately the whole world, those qualities of the astrolabe put it in a good stead to function as a cultural connector.

The astrolabe entails a remarkable potential to attract and intrigue varied audiences coming from different cultural backgrounds. But it is also a multi-layered device (literally and figuratively) whose multitude of dimensions and meanings is difficult, if not impossible, to efficiently address in a single display, exhibition, or museum program. A focus on aesthetics will divert attention from the rich technical and scientific content of the instrument. On the other hand, the complexity of the latter might also put many visitors off. In this regard, the smartphone analogy becomes acceptable if used, not as a technical metaphor establishing misleading, anachronistic parallels between devices of a very different nature and scope, but as a starting point to explore how people from all walks of life and provenances have sought to understand celestial cycles, develop tools to make sense of time and space, and overall to seek to bring order and harmony into their lives. The astrolabe is not the smartphone of the Middle Ages, nor are our tablets the astrolabes of our age. But all these devices speak of science (in the broad sense of pursuing a systematic understanding of natural phenomena) and technology as fundamental human pursuits that are by no means exclusive to the modern era or to a particular group of people.

Such an approach provides a way of highlighting commonalities between diverse peoples and their cultures, but in order to be effective, it must not be forgotten that each astrolabe corresponds to a specific historical context, and that the same instrument may well have crossed varied cultural spaces before landing in a museum or private collection. There is no such thing as "the" Eastern or "the" Western astrolabe, convenient as such categories might be as top-level organizers for scholarship and curatorial work on the instrument. The astrolabe can only function effectively as a cultural connector if used to highlight the various cultures and historical periods that intertwine during its long history, beyond reductionist dualisms such as East–West.

The astrolabe can be an effective point of entry into past cultures of knowledge, on which it can help shed light. But one must not be blinded by the astrolabe. Instead of being singled out as treasures from the past, astrolabes will be better presented in the context of the other devices, technologies, scientific ideas, spiritual practices, and artistic sensibilities espoused by the people who produced and might have used this particular instrument. This will be essential to circumventing any idea that the astrolabe was an exceptional realization among a supposed backdrop of backwardness. Similary, exaggeration must be avoided. And just as museums with relevant Islamic art collections are recognizing the importance of collecting works by contemporary Muslim artists, it is important that narratives of science centered on the astrolabe and their connection with the Islamic world acknowledge that the contributions of Muslims are not only to be found in a distant past. Together with people of all provenances, they have continued to make modern science and technology thrive as part of vast international networks of researchers and scholars empowered by the movement of people across institutions, countries, and continents. Anachronisms and direct parallels with the scientific and technological practices of ages past are certainly also to be avoided here, but so are any notions pretending that the role of Muslims in making science and technology advance is confined to the past.

While its history lends itself to grand narratives of movement and displacement as engines of scientific and technical knowledge, the astrolabe is, after all, just a detail – even if a highly significant and particurlaly alluring one – in a much broader picture of how those movements have shaped the techno-scientific societies of the modern world.

Acknowledgments

I would like to thank Helen Solterer and Ellen Raimond for sharing their insights on the "In Transit" project and installation, and Taha Yasin Arslan, Vincent Joos, James Amelang, Saskia Ziolkowski, and the anonymous readers from Manchester University Press for their comments on earlier versions of this chapter.

Notes

1 It must be noted that the description is not accurate in its reference to the instrument being used to determine longitude, though latitude could in principle be found using an astrolabe (even if the device was not designed for that particular purpose). However, determining the time from the stars or the sun was definitely among the primary functions of this versatile instrument. See below for further technical information.

2 Astrolabes can take the form of planispheric, spherical, and linear instruments. Additionally, there is the mariner's astrolabe, an instrument bearing similarities to the planispheric astrolabe but much simpler, which was used from the late fifteenth century onwards for the purpose of determining latitude at sea. There is also the so-called Danjon astrolabe, a modern device conceived by the French astronomer André-Louis Danjon (1890–1967) for the study of latitude variations. In the remainder of this chapter, unless otherwise stated, the word "astrolabe" is used to refer specifically to the planispheric astrolabe.

3 It was later renamed Adler Planetarium and Astronomy Museum, and is now simply Adler Planetarium.

4 An armillary sphere is formed by a framework of rings representing imaginary celestial circles that help make sense of the celestial motions. The astrolabe is, to a great extent, an armillary sphere projected onto a plane.

5 The organization behind the exhibit and the book is called 1001 Inventions, and uses the motto "Discover a Golden Age – Inspire a Better Future" (www.1001inventions.com, accessed July 31, 2021).

6 The exhibition is a travelling show, having also been presented at the Aga Khan Museum in Toronto. It was installed at the National Museum of African Art in Washington, DC as this chapter was being written.

7 As mentioned in note 2, a similar but much simpler instrument called a mariner's astrolabe was used in oceanic navigation during the late fifteenth and the mid-sixteenth centuries, which possibly contributes to the confusion.

References

Al-Hassani, S. T. S. (2012). *1001 Inventions: The Enduring Legacy of Muslim Civilization. Official Companion to the 1001 Inventions Exhibition*, 3rd edition. National Geographic, 2012.

Belvidere Daily Republican, March 21, 1930.

Bennett, J. and Strano, G. (2014). "The So-Called 'Chaucer Astrolabe' from the Keoliker Collection: An Account of the Instrument and its Place in the Tradition of Chaucer-Type Astrolabes," *Nuncius* 29(1), pp. 179–229.

Berzock, K. B. (ed.) (2019). *Caravans of Gold, Fragments in Time: Art, Culture, and Exchange Across Medieval Saharan Africa*. Chicago and New Jersey: The Block Museum and Princeton University Press.

Bier, C. (2017). "Reframing Islamic Art for the 21st Century," *Horizons in Humanities and Social Sciences* 2(2), pp. 1–25.

Block Museum of Art, www.blockmuseum.northwestern.edu/exhibitions/2019/caravans-of-gold,-fragments-in-time-art,-culture,-and-exchange-across-medieval-saharan-africa.html (accessed October 24, 2020).

Brentjes, S., Edis, T., and Richter-Bernburg, L. (eds) (2016). *1001 Distortions: How (Not) to Narrate History of Science, Medicine, and Technology in Non-Western Cultures.* Würzburg: Ergon Verlag, 2016.

Eagleton, C. (2007). "Chaucer's Own Astrolabe: Text, Image, and Object," *Studies in History and Philosophy of Science* 38(2), pp. 303–26.

Evans, J. (1998). *The History and Practice of Ancient Astronomy.* New York, Oxford: Oxford University Press.

Fox, P. (1935). *Adler Planetarium and Astronomical Museum: An Account of the Optical Planetarium and a Brief Guide to the Museum.* Chicago: The Lakeside Press, R. R. Donnelley & Sons Co.

Golinski, J. ([1998] 2005). *Making Natural Knowledge: Constructivism and the History of Science.* Chicago, London: The University of Chicago Press.

Gunther, R. T. (1932). *The Astrolabes of the World, based upon the series of instruments in the Lewis Evans collection in the old Ashmolean Museum at Oxford, with notes on astrolabes in the collections of the British Museum, Science Museum, Sir J. Findlay, Mr. S. V. Hoffman, the Mensing Collection, and in other public and private collections.* Vol. 1: The Eastern Astrolabes. Oxford: Oxford University Press.

Junod, B., Khalil, G., Weber, S., and Wolf, G. (eds) (2013). *Islamic Art and the Museum: Approaches to Art and Archeology of the Muslim World in the Twenty-First Century.* London: Saqi Books.

Karr-Schmidt, S. (2011). *Altered and Adorned: Using Renaissance Prints in Daily Life.* New Haven and London: Art Institute of Chicago and Yale University Press.

King, D. (1987). *Astronomical Instruments.* London: Variorum Reprints.

King, D. (2004–2005). *In Synchrony with the Heavens: Studies in Astronomical Timekeeping and Instrumentation in Medieval Islamic Civilization.* Leiden, Boston: Brill.

King, D. (2018). "The Astrolabe," https://davidaking.academia.edu/research# (accessed October 24, 2020).

Latour, Bruno (1988). *Science in Action: How to Follow Scientists and Engineers through Society.* Cambridge, MA: Harvard University Press.

Livingstone, D. (2003). *Putting Science in its Place: Geographies of Scientific Knowledge.* Chicago, London: University of Chicago Press.

Newberry, B. D., Notis, M. R., Stephenson, B., Cargill, C. S., and Stephenson, G. B. (2006). "The Astrolabe Craftsmen of Lahore and Early Brass Metallurgy," *Annals of Science* 63(2), pp. 201–13.

Norton-Wright, J. (ed.) (2019). *Curating Islamic Art Worldwide: From Malacca to Manchester.* Cham: Springer/Palgrave.

Pingree, D. (2009). *Eastern Astrolabes.* Chicago: Adler Planetarium and Astronomical Museum.

Poppick, L. (2017). "The Story of the Astrolabe, the Original Smartphone," www.smithsonianmag.com/innovation/astrolabe-original-smartphone-180961981/ (accessed October 23, 2020).

Raposo, P. M. P. (2019). "Astronomy Between Solemnity and Spectacle: The Adler Planetarium and the Century of Progress fair in Chicago, 1933–34," in Beretta, M., Canadelli, E., and Ronzon, L. (eds), *Behind the Exhibit: Displaying Science and Technology at World's Fairs and Museums in the Twentieth Century*. Washington, DC: Smithsonian Institution Scholarly Press, pp. 89–110.

Raposo, P. M. P., Simões, A., Patiniotis, M., and Bertomeu-Sanchez, J. (2014). "Moving Localities and Creative Circulation: Travels as knowledge production in 18th century Europe," *Centaurus* 56(3), pp. 167–88.

Rodriguez-Arribas, J., Burnett, C., and Ackermann, S. (2017). "Astrolabes in Medieval Cultures," *Medieval Encounters*, special issue 23(1–5), pp. 1–478.

Sarma, S. R. "A Descriptive Catalogue of Indian Astronomical Instruments," https://srsarma.in/catalogue.php (accessed October 24, 2020).

Schechner, S. J. (1998). "Astrolabes: A Cross Cultural and Social Perspective," in Webster, R., and Webster, M., *Western Astrolabes*. Chicago: Adler Planetarium and Astronomy Museum, pp. 2–25.

Schechner, S. J. (2008). "Astrolabes and Medieval Travel," in *The Art, Science, and Technology of Medieval Travel*. Ashgate: Aldershot, pp. 181–210.

Schmidl, P. G. (2016). "'Mirror of the Stars': The Astrolabe and What it Tells About Pre-Modern Astronomy," in Brentjes, S., Edis, T., and Richter-Bernburg, L. (eds) (2016), *1001 Distortions: How (Not) to Narrate History of Science, Medicine, and Technology in Non-Western Cultures*. Würzburg: Ergon Verlag, pp. 173–87.

Schmidl, P. G. (2018). "Using Astrolabes for Astrological Purposes: The Earliest Evidence Revisited," in Dunn, R., Ackermann, S., and Strano, G. (eds), *Heaven and Earth United, Leiden: Instruments in Astrological Contexts, Brill.

Shatanawi, M. (2012). "Engaging Islam: Working with Muslim Communities in a Multicultural Society," *Curator: The Museum Journal* 55(1), pp. 65–79.

Taub, L. (2005). "'Canned astronomy' versus Cultural Credibility: The Acquisition of the Mensing Collection by the Adler Planetarium," *Journal of the History of Collections* 7(2), pp. 243–50.

Turner, A. J. (1985). *The Time Museum, Vol. 1: Time Measuring Instruments, Part 1 – Astrolabes, Astrolabe Related Instruments*. Rockford: The Time Museum.

van Cleempoel, K. (2005). *Astrolabes at Greenwich, A Catalogue of the Astrolabes in the National Maritime Museum*. New York: Oxford University Press and the National Maritime Museum.

Webster, R., and Webster, M. (1998). *Western Astrolabes*, Chicago: Adler Planetarium and Astronomy Museum.

PART II

Migrating in Spanish

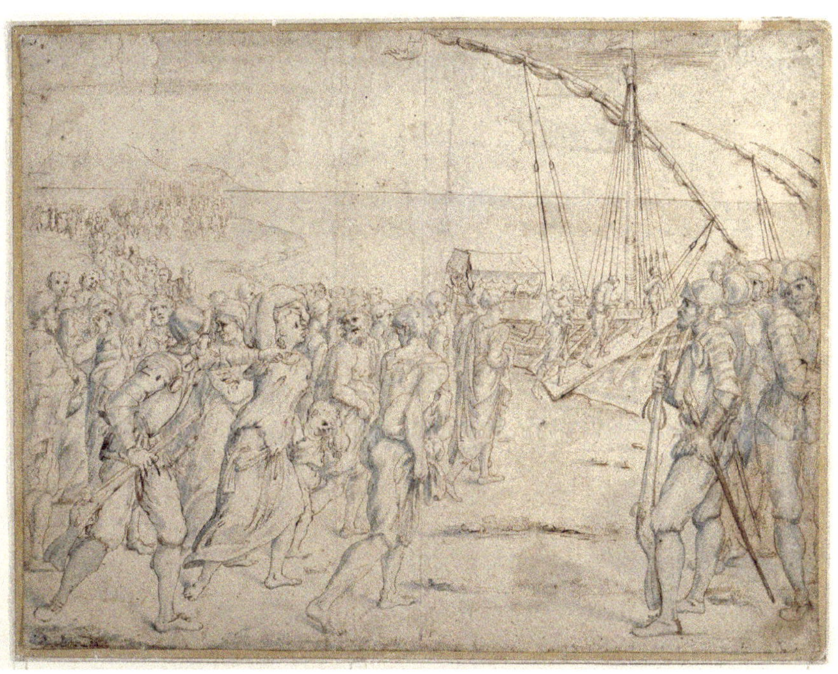

Part II frontispiece: Vicente Carducho, *Expulsion of the Moriscos*, c. 1627. Drawing, Museo del Prado, Madrid. Public domain.

One border between Europe and Africa is the focus of the chapters in this section. They explore human experience more so than geography: the transit of people between these two continents. This experience has more than its share of complexities and contradictions. The route has a deep history, yet it is also actively traversed in the present. Its protagonists have included (and still include) numerous individuals from highly diverse backgrounds: soldiers, priests, peasants, merchants, workers, prophets, and sailors, amid countless others. Their motives have been (and remain) equally diverse, ranging over a long arc of time from political and institutional expansion to more mundane and personal conditions of personal and familial betterment. Examining some of these mobile men and women and the reasons that led them to leave one continent for another is the task – and challenge – that unites these two case studies.

Chapter 2, by James Amelang, opens in the distant past, and centers on a historical experience that constitutes a singular precedent for today's mass mobility from Africa, especially that which takes place from Morocco to southern Spain. Ironically, this precedent moved in the opposite direction from today's flow from south to north. It took place thanks to state-sponsored force, as opposed to the largely voluntary movement in the present. It centers around the expulsion from Spain in 1609–14 of the so-called Moriscos – that is, tens of thousands of individuals of Islamic ancestry who had been baptized as Catholics. This was a much publicized and highly controversial measure whose explicit goal was to purge from the Spanish empire the remaining descendants of the North Africans who had conquered the Iberian peninsula in the distant eighth century and then resided there as Muslims to the early sixteenth century, when they were forcibly converted. The story of the early modern Moriscos, and the reasons why after a long period of coexistence with the "Old Christian" population they were expelled, constitutes one of the most intriguing episodes regarding the presence of Islam in Europe. It also offers much food for thought in the present, for as the Muslim population grows throughout the continent, earlier experiences of coexistence amid religious and cultural difference can serve as references – and warnings – for a continent undergoing rapid demographic as well as cultural transformation.

Chapter 3, by Anna Tybinko, shifts the reader's attention to present-day Spain. It also focuses on the lingering influence of the past, as refracted through the experience and writings of a single individual. These reveal how African immigration, and Moroccan immigration in particular, dredges up Spain's deep history and raises anxieties about its European status. The Moroccan journalist Rachid Nini's now-classic "migrant narrative," *Diario de un ilegal* (*Diary of a Clandestine Migrant*, 1999) offers a stark vision of immigrant life in the coastal area of southeastern Spain. Originally published in Arabic and translated into Castilian with additions by the author in

2002, Nini's *Diary* is a text that was clearly conceived *for* translation for Spanish readers from the start. Taking Nini at his word, his *Diary* clearly provides something more than a warning to fellow Moroccans who, in economic desperation, might turn to a newly European Spain as a nearby land of plenty. Just as Raquel Salvatella de Prada's video installation calls our attention to the struggles of those migrants who attempt to get across the massive fences that separate the Spanish cities of Melilla and Ceuta from Morocco, the European Union's only terrestrial border with Africa, Nini's writing similarly raise awareness about the perils of the sea route. It also draws a parallel with ibn Ziyad's choice to cross the Strait of Gibraltar centuries earlier as a means of legitimizing the movement of people back and forth across the Mediterranean. And this way it debunks the Spanish myth of an "El Dorado" for migrants so frequently used to describe Spain's rapid development following the promulgation of its first immigration law in 1985 and subsequent entry into the European Economic Community in 1986.

J. A.

2

The expulsion of the Moriscos, 1609–14: still more questions than answers

James S. Amelang

Had there been a newspaper in Madrid in 1609, the headline on September 22 would have been a Trumpist's dream come true. It would have read something like "the king decrees that all Muslims are to be expelled from Spain, whether they are true Muslims or not." The article itself would have gone on to explain the decision of the Council of State to exile from Spanish territory virtually all the descendants of the former Muslims of Spain who had converted (or had been converted) to Roman Catholicism, a process which had begun during the later Middle Ages and which had been officially declared "mission accomplished" in 1526. Those who devised the policy and signed the decree that put it in motion would have been pleased to learn what we can see in retrospect: that it was the largest such migration in early modern European history.

As a historian of early modern Europe, that is, the period covering the fifteenth to eighteenth centuries, I have long been interested in the parallel experiences of the two major persecuted minorities of early modern Spain, the converted Jews (Conversos) and Muslims (Moriscos). Like most of my colleagues, I am *not* often called upon to link my work to the present; and the truth is, I very much welcome the opportunity to do so. As a historian who lives in Europe today, the hypothetical headline mentioned above sounds all too familiar, although to be fair, Spain is one of the countries in Europe where one hears *least* about expelling Muslims, and this despite the fact that it has a relatively large Islamic population, in large measure of Moroccan origin. In fact, one of the more encouraging features of politics in Spain now is the relative lack of a right-wing political party or faction calling for anti-Muslim measures, of the sort one finds in virtually the rest of the continent and beyond. Explaining why is a job for a sociologist, political scientist, or perhaps a social psychologist. The task here is a different one: to discuss another very visible differential between Spain and the rest of western Europe. That is the accrual in the Iberian Peninsula beginning in the Middle Ages of a large population of Muslim origin, some of whose

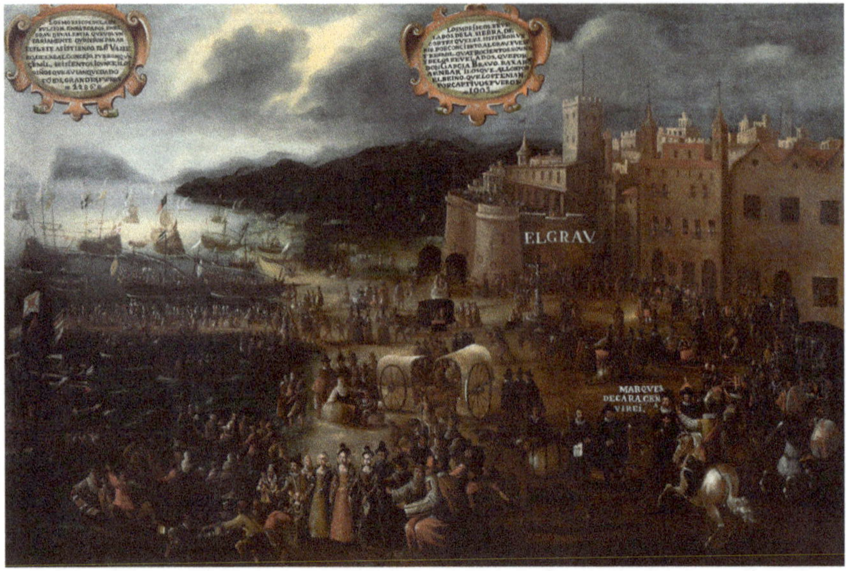

Figure 2.1 Pere Oromig, *Embarque de los moriscos del Grau de Valencia*, 1612. Painting, Valencia, Fundación Bancaja, permanent collection. Public domain.

members genuinely converted to Christianity, while others remained faithful to their ancestral religion. The group as a whole was known as the Moriscos, and are the focus of this chapter.

One way to start discussing the expulsion of the Moriscos is to ask about the relevance for the present day of the expulsion of 1609. As noted above, at first sight the expulsion which began in 1609 seems ready-made for consideration in light of recent events in Spain and elsewhere in Europe (more on this below). After all, it created a strong precedent for mass mobility by migrants between the Iberian Peninsula and North Africa – albeit in the direction opposite to that of today's insistent flow. This is merely one of the similarities between these events that also enshrined very visible differences. The most obvious divergences include the forced, as opposed to voluntary, nature of the two mass movements, along with the direction in which the flow was/is headed. Another telling difference was that at least officially, the expulsion from Spain of the Moriscos was justified not so much as a political measure; instead, the principal rationale for it was religious. Various pragmatic arguments in its favor were offered, and certainly shaped not only the measure but also an important part of popular opinion regarding it. But the crucial justification for the expulsion was the failure on the part of the descendants of former Muslims to shed their ancestors' belief in Islam. It goes without saying that this is a complex issue, which raises complex questions of credibility, the possibility or even desirability of pluralism within a confessional state, contemporary understandings of the relations of this confessionalism with political strength or weakness, and the like. Thus what this chapter does is to outline some of the principal questions raised by the historical experience of Spain's Moriscos. At the same time it will focus on what the recent and quite flourishing historiography regarding the Moriscos and their fate has to suggest (Domínguez Ortiz and Vincent, 1997; Vincent, 2007; Márquez Villanueva, 1998; Harvey 2005; Bernabé Pons, 2009).

The basic facts can be quickly stated by mentioning a few key dates:

- 711: the conquest of Spain by Muslims largely of North African origin;
- 722: the (fairly mythical) beginning of the "Reconquest," or effort by Christians in northern Spain to regain territory by expanding southward;
- 1236: the Christian "recapture" of the Muslim metropolis of Córdoba, followed by Seville in 1248, which left the southern kingdom of Granada as the sole territory under Muslim control;
- 1492: the *Wunderjahr*, which saw not only the final conquest of Granada by Christian armies under king Ferdinand of Aragon and queen Isabella of Castile, but also the expulsion of the Jews and the successful voyage of Christopher Columbus to the western hemisphere;
- 1502: the decision by Ferdinand and Isabella to expel all Muslims from the kingdom of Castile who would not convert to Christianity;
- 1526: the extension of this policy under their successor Charles V to the Crown of Aragon and the rest of Spain;
- 1568–71: a major armed revolt in Granada by Moriscos (former Muslims now converted to Christianity and their descendants), which ended in defeat, widespread destruction, and the dispersal of the survivors of what had been the largest nucleus of Moriscos in Andalusia throughout the rest of Castile;
- 1609: the final solution, i.e. the expulsion of (in theory) all Moriscos – approximately 300,000 in number – from Spanish territories, mostly to Muslim states in North Africa.

The expulsion of the Moriscos from Spain thus comes at the end of a long timeline. It clearly involved a migration, and while some might be put off by the use of that word, given the sheer amount of state-sponsored coercion involved, most social scientists would have no problems with the term. That it was forced did not mean that it was not a migration. In fact, one can properly refer to it as the largest such migration in early modern European history.

It moreover was, or is, an event long encrusted in various mythologies. Some date from the time, and others have a more recent origin. The principal message – and purpose – of the contemporary mythology was apologia,

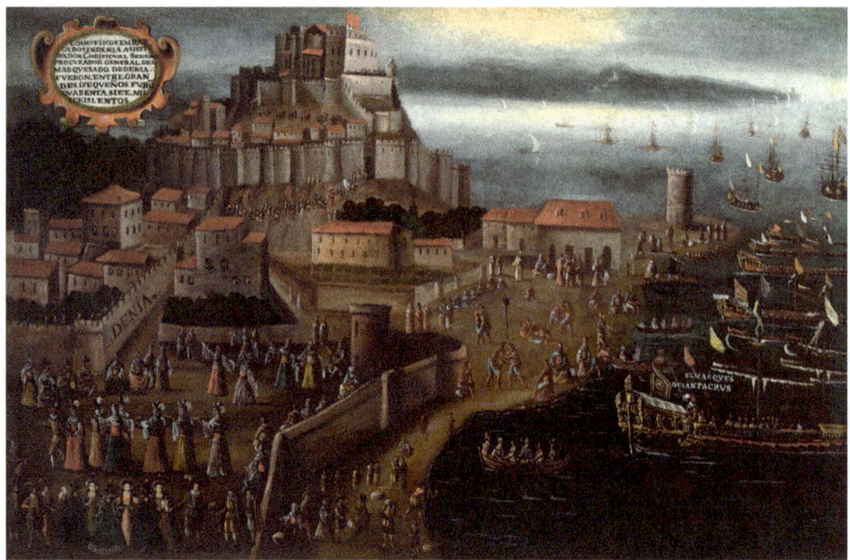

Figure 2.2 Vicent Mestre, *La Expulsiòn en el Puerto de Denia*, 1613. Painting, Valencia, Fundación Bancaja, permanent collection. Public domain.

that is, defense of what turned out to be a highly controversial event. Such efforts focused on both official and unofficial discourse. It is also important to note that only one side of this debate, that of approval, was allowed to be heard in public (Magnier, 2010). The other side, which included criticism of this measure, could reach the public sphere via print or the pulpit only indirectly. One partial result of this skewed situation was that the most vocal contemporary public criticism of the expulsion was voiced by Spain's enemies or rivals in the international arena. And the way many people today read this long-ago event echoes in part this critical discourse. (NB: I emphasize "in part," because these critiques also contained claims and suppositions that virtually all scholars now would not agree with.)

The overriding question today is not so much the simple one of whether the expulsion was a good or bad measure. Historians and others focus on a more complex agenda, one that centers on exactly what happened, why it happened, and what resulted from its happening. Other queries flow from these basic ones. One is whether the expulsion was justified in terms of the factors its partisans adduced as causes. In other words, were the reasons given for the expulsion at the time valid ones in the eyes of contemporaries and subsequent generations of Spaniards who were the beneficiaries or victims of its effects. Another is whether this decision was justified in terms of its effects. This means inquiring whether its impact was successful in the eyes not only of its supporters at the time, but also according to the subsequent judgment of Spaniards and others in the future. Reconstructing the debates among historians over these questions would be a long and arduous task, in part because until recently there has not been a solid enough consensus in this regard. However, historians now benefit from a very lively historiographical moment enriched by ample new research based, in part, upon new sources. Thus the rest of this text will briefly review several major discussions that recent research has produced, and then make some final remarks regarding the directions in which future discussions seem to be heading.

New research and rethinking of the history of the Moriscos has produced various insights. First, we now understand better the political relations between converted Muslims and the Christian majority in early modern Spain. These focus on at least two major themes: the most violent episode in the history of the Spanish Moriscos, the Granada revolt of 1568–71 alluded to above; and above all, what has most attracted new attention, the expulsion itself. Numerous scholars have examined both sets of events in close detail, and with closer attention to precise context. For example, thanks to fine-grained research of the sort found in Rafael Benítez's reconstruction of the trajectory that led to the final decision for expulsion in 1609, we now can see more clearly how much it was the product of a very specific moment, one that saw a weak monarch and his equally beleaguered favorite opting for this move under considerable pressure caused by events and political initiatives elsewhere (Benítez Sánchez-Blanco, 2001; Ehlers, 2006; García-Arenal and Wiegers, 2014). One can also now draw attention to recent revealing work on the international dimensions of the expulsion. One example is a recent issue of the Italian journal *Quaderni Storici* edited by Giovanna Fiume and Stefania Pastore (Fiume and Pastore, 2013). Stressing the mixed reception of the exiled Moriscos in Italy, they document important differences in local responses to this new and rather puzzling category of immigrants. These outsiders met with inconsistent responses even in the parts of the peninsula that were under the direct or indirect control of Spain. This was also true even of independent entities such as Papal Rome, which harbored grave doubts about the practical as well as theological aspects of the expulsion, although it chose not to express them in public.

Recent research has also uncovered and interpreted a great deal of material regarding the social and economic history of the Moriscos. Much of this has focused on the longer term, and continues longstanding and valuable local work in, for example, notarial archives and Inquisition records. The cumulative effect of this new knowledge has been the slow conversion of rumors and stereotypes about Moriscos, often engendered and diffused by their enemies, into better documented social and economic history. Thus, for example, we now have a much finer appreciation of the degree of stratification within Morisco communities. The dominant stereotype in the past was that Morisco settlements were largely undifferentiated, that is, that their members subsisted at the same general level of poverty, and practiced the same economic activities, which were by and large limited to agriculture. We now have a keener appreciation of the existence of greater variation in Morisco economic initiatives, as well as of significant distinctions among Moriscos at the local level, as well as among different types of Morisco communities at a regional level. Predictably, differences among Morisco activities often were more visible at this latter level, and engendered stereotypes that contrasted Castile, for example, with Valencia or Granada, all large areas which housed varied agricultural patterns and social systems (García-Arenal, 1978; Tapia Sánchez, 1991; García Ballester, 1993; Colás Latorre, 1993; Halavais, 2002).

One of the most important developments has been the recent intense focus on Morisco elites, defined in social and economic as well as political terms – which immediately raises the crucial question of the differing degrees of assimilation of these elites into existing power structures. This is, moreover, one of the many questions where one finds it useful to distinguish between the experiences and opportunities of the Moriscos as opposed to the *conversos*, or converts from Judaism, who underwent a parallel experience of largely forced (and similarly incomplete) assimilation into the Christian majority (Stuczynski, 2000; Amelang, 2013; Ingram, 2009). In this regard one of the subjects which has attracted more attention recently is the curious recognition of the existence of a Morisco nobility. That certain descendants of Muslims – especially those related to the royal Nasrid family which ruled Granada at the time of its conquest by Ferdinand and Isabel in 1492 – not only claimed a specific aristocratic status in early modern Spanish society but also were unquestionably recognized as nobles by the authorities and by public opinion is something which decidedly did not happen in the case of the *conversos* (Soria Mesa, 2008; Núñez Muley, 2007).

Much more could be said about this new socio-economic history of the Moriscos. It comes as little surprise to find, for example, greater attention paid to gender differentiation within Morisco communities (Perry, 2005; Martín Casares, 2000; Surtz, 2001). One could easily point to other interesting new work which has similarly revealed much about the forms of distinctiveness and hierarchy in Morisco communities that came into the open thanks to the expulsion itself. The latter obliged the Moriscos to mobilize and convert what resources they had into more mobile forms of capital. The subsequent activation of networks of contacts in order to export this wealth brought to the surface the existence of a cohort of Moriscos with more resources than virtually anyone had suspected. And some of the most interesting information on this question comes from recent research on the clandestine transfer by expelled Moriscos of substantial financial resources across the French border as reported by the Spanish government's wide-ranging espionage networks (Bernabé Pons and Gil Herrera, 2013).

The other major issue being debated in the social history of the Moriscos – and the one that has perhaps done the most to alter traditional views – has been the question of the relations between Moriscos and their "Old Christian" neighbors at the local level. Both the decrees of expulsion and the apologetic literature that appeared in order to justify it constantly asserted, and even took for granted, the existence of profound hostility between the so-called Old versus New Christians. However, the late British scholar Trevor Dadson recently produced an enormous study – almost 1400 pages long – that reconstructs the strenuous efforts, not only by the Moriscos of a small town in La Mancha to defy the expulsion order, but also the equally determined initiatives of their Old Christian neighbors to help them stay in Spain. Dadson's exhaustive documentation and keen eye for reading between the lines of official papers has converted this book into the most innovative (and influential) recent study of the social and economic history of the Moriscos of the past generation. Its principal revelation regards the unquestionable integration of the Moriscos into this rural community, as manifested by the strenuous efforts by both the local inhabitants and their more distant seigneurial lord to retain a large ethnic group whose members were seen as crucially helping to maintain the prosperity of the town during an era of deepening economic decline (Dadson, 2006, 2014; O'Banion, 2017).

All this new work has done much to alter our understanding above all of the impact of the expulsion. As a result, historians are now more inclined to accept the hypothesis that there were both many more Moriscos exempted from exile, as well as many more returnees after having been expelled, than we had previously thought. Given the nature of the documentation, and the obvious need to keep most of this absorption in secrecy, we will never be able to document this dimension of Morisco history with any exactitude. Still, there is no mistaking the tendencies now coming to the fore thanks to this innovative (and strenuous) research.

Finally, great strides have been made recently in the spiritual and intellectual history of the Moriscos. For obvious reasons, this field has largely been in the hands of professional Arabists, who continue to labor on many of the topics of basic philological and religious historical research that began to be addressed in the later nineteenth century. The more visible work in this field includes the preparation and publication of new editions and translations of key texts, including the following examples:

- The first-person account of the so-called "Mancebo" or "young man" of Arévalo, a town in Old Castile (*Tratado*, 2003). This refers to the first-person journal of an anonymous Morisco who at some point in the 1530s was sent by the elders of his community to communicate with other nuclei of crypto-Muslims in central and southern Spain while he studied to become an Islamic spiritual expert. The text provides fascinating accounts of conversations with a wide swath of individuals and groups, most notably a 93-year old illiterate Muslim woman nicknamed the "Mora de Ubeda," famous for her extraordinary oral knowledge of the Qur'an. It also provides an unusually revealing view of the health of crypto-Islam in different regions of the peninsula in the transition from the first to the second generation following the final conversions.

- Various anti-Muslim works, that is, polemics aimed at detaching former Muslim readers and even clerics from their traditions. One of the most revealing and influential among these is a series of dialogues which the Erasmian humanist (and descendant of converted Jews) Bernardo Pérez de Chinchón published in 1535 under the title of the *Anti-Quran* (*Antialcorano*, 2013).

- In my view the most unusual among these primary sources is an auto-biographical text which appeared in the form of a travelogue, by an Andalusian Morisco named Ahmad ibn Qasim Al-Hajari. After starting in Granada, where the author was recruited as a young man to serve on the team of translators of the so-called "lead books" (more on these below), the author escaped to Morocco, where he soon prospered as a political adviser and diplomat. Al-Hajari was then sent as an ambassador to France, and while there traveled widely in Europe before finally returning to North Africa, where he eventually settled in Egypt. The text gives a truly unique glimpse into how a Muslim of Spanish background perceived early modern Europe, and includes reconstructions of his conversations with a wide range of scholars, clerics, government officials, and other interlocutors. It also provides what was perhaps the most succinct summary of the Moriscos' dilemma: their need to practice "the religion of the Christians openly and that of the Muslims in secret" (Ahmad ibn Qasim Al-Hajari, 1997: 64).

But scholars have broken new ground in other ways in addition to editing important texts. One good example of strenuous and innovative work with local sources is Amalia García Pedraza's research in Granada's notarial archives in pursuit of reconstructing attitudes toward death among local Moriscos, especially the more assimilated ones who lived within the city walls (García Pedraza, 2001). And most influential here has been the work of Mercedes García Arenal, an unusually prolific and wide-ranging scholar who has gathered a large circle of colleagues and students to collaborate with her and her frequent co-author Fernando Rodríguez-Mediano in a lengthy series of projects. One useful starting point for following her work – a fair amount of which is available in English – is their joint contribution to a growing body of research and analysis regarding what was easily the most bizarre episode in the entire one-hundred-year history of the Moriscos, the scandal of the *Plomos* (lead seals) of Granada (Barrios Aguilera and García Arenal, 2006; Harris, 2007; García-Arenal and Rodríguez Mediano, 2010; García-Arenal, 2016).

This refers to the "discovery" in Granada beginning in 1588 of a series of objects, mostly lead seals bearing inscriptions in Arabic, that referred directly to the earliest moments of the Christian evangelization of Spain purportedly led by the Apostle James the Greater. Their messages included numerous and frankly shocking revelations, especially the news that the Virgin Mary had been a speaker of Arabic. This surprise was joined by many others, including the existence outside the New Testament of a fifth gospel written in that language, and which reinforced the notion of the existence of an alternative revelation whose geographical center was the city of Granada. Numerous studies of this bizarre episode have been written in the wake of this discovery, which continues to attract the attention not only of Arabists but also of specialists in early modern cultural as well as religious history.

In the aftermath of this new wave of research García-Arenal and Rodríguez-Mediano went on to organize a major European research project known as the CORPI initiative. Its aim was to make further progress in the reconstruction of scholarly familiarity with the fundamental and integral part Islam and the Arabic language played during this pivotal period. The newest development here has been their effort to trace how inter-religious polemic during the sixteenth and seventeenth centuries fostered in southern Europe the development of variants of religious and philosophical skepticism similar to those which emerged in northern Europe in the wake of Western Christianity's splitting into Catholic and Protestant factions (not to mention the older and still ongoing polemics between Christians and Jews that served as another indirect fount of skepticism). Among the first fruits of these excursions into unexplored territory has been a collection of essays from the members of the project, which cover an impressively wide range of topics in Christian and Jewish as well as Muslim history (García-Arenal, 2016; Kimmel, 2015; Pereda, 2017).

If we step back from all this activity and try to get a reading of the scholarly situation now, one senses that the present is marked neither by iron consensus nor by fierce combat among the historians of Moriscos. Instead, what prevails is slow but steady change and updating within the general contours of agreement and disagreement among the specialists, and above all real, visible progress in the forging and dissemination of both specialized and general knowledge regarding a broadly defined collective that has not received the historiographical attention that it deserves. Above all, what has taken place in the last generation has been a significant shift in focus away from the dominant themes of the past, especially the near-exclusive emphasis that assumed that Moriscos were crypto-Muslims, or rather, that assumed that they were *solely* crypto-Muslims. This had of course been the overriding assumption and concern of their persecutors. One crucial result of the broader approach summarized here is that the Moriscos have taken on a more plural and differentiated profile. They now are approached as individual members of communities with specific types of resources and support at their disposal. They moreover mobilized these resources, both material and immaterial, as best as they could as they sought to cope with continuous but far from uniform hostility and mistrust on the part of the Old Christian majority and its leading institutions.

Needless to say, there are many parallels between the general experience of the Moriscos in early modern Spain and the specific case of the recent wanderings Rachid Nini recorded in his diary and which Anna Tybinko analyzes in her companion chapter. (It's almost as if al-Hajari had stayed in southern Spain instead of wandering through northern Europe.) And Raquel Salvatella's project, as outlined in Chapter 10 below, similarly explores a fascinating present-day counterpart to the bygone past of the Moriscos. Seen from these various perspectives the Iberian peninsula stands out in western Europe for the near millenium during which Islam flourished there alongside Christianity and Judaism. The expulsion of the Moriscos in the seventeenth century, which put an end to this lengthy era of mutual accommodation, marked a new period and policy of uniformity and intol-erance that would only gradually be dismantled by the consolidation of modern liberal democracy in the twentieth century. Developments along the way included Spain's acquisition of an empire in northwest Africa, now reduced largely to the two maritime urban enclaves of Ceuta and Melilla. These two cities serve as the friction points – or gateways of opportunity, depending on one's point of view – for numerous sub-Saharan migrants eager to make their way, above all, to France in search of betterment for themselves and their families. That two cities which developed originally as citadels for imperial expansion should now function as conduits for – or conflictive obstacles to – economic migration is a situation rich not only in irony, but also in deep frustration and even collective as well as individual tragedy.

Somewhat by surprise, both the Spanish enclaves in North Africa and Moroccan migration into Spanish territory emerged as international news items just as the final version of this chapter was submitted for publication. In May 2021 a diplomatic crisis erupted between Spain and Morocco as an unspecified number – at least ten thousand, according to media reports – of undocumented migrants crossed unexpectedly from Moroccan territory into the Spanish enclave cities of Ceuta and Melilla. This sudden influx was widely attributed to the suspension of habitual police controls on the Moroccan side of the border, most likely as a form of retaliation against the admission into a Spanish hospital for medical treatment of a prominent leader of the "Polisario Army," a movement strongly opposed by the Moroccan government, which seeks independence for the Western Sahara region. Spanish border police forces were quickly overwhelmed by this surge and military units were dispatched to control this unanticipated demo-diplomatic situation. The crisis has drawn attention to what is widely seen as an anachronistic European presence in African territory, yet one that can also serve as a gateway to higher standards of living and political freedom for the inhabitants of a continent widely acknowledged to house thoroughly corrupt and authoritarian political systems. As such it provides an intriguing contrast – as well as more than a bit of overlap – with the historical experience of the Moriscos, many of whom crossed the same borders (in different directions) in earlier centuries, as they participated in very different conflicts.

References

Ahmad ibn Qasim Al-Hajari (1997) *Kitab Nasir al-din ala 'L'Qawn al-Kafirin* (*The Supporter of Religion Against the Infidel*), eds P. S. Van Koningsveld, Q. Al-Samarrai, and G. A. Wiegers. Madrid: CSIC.

Amelang, James S. (2013) *Parallel Histories: Muslims and Jews in Inquisitorial Spain*. Baton Rouge: Louisiana State University Press.

Antialcorano (2000) *Diálogos christianos, conversión y evangelización de moriscos*, ed. Francisco Pons Fuster. Alicante: Universidad de Alicante.

Barrios Aguilera, Manuel and Mercedes García-Arenal (eds). (2006) *Los Plomos del Sacromonte: Invención y tesoro*. Valencia, Granada, Zaragoza: Universitat de València, Universidad de Granada, Universidad de Zaragoza.

Benítez Sánchez-Blanco, Rafael (2001) *Heroicas decisiones: La Monarquía Católica y los moriscos valencianos*. Valencia: Institució Alfons el Magnànim.

Bernabé Pons, Luis F. (2009) *Los moriscos: Conflicto, expulsión y diáspora*. Madrid: Ediciones de la Catarata.

Bernabé Pons, Luis F. and Jorge Gil Herrera (2013) "Los moriscos fuera de España: Rutas y financiación," in M. García-Arenal and G. Wiegers (eds), *Los moriscos: Expulsión y diáspora*, Valencia, Granada, Zaragoza: Universitat de València, Universidad de Granada, Universidad de Zaragoza, pp. 213–31.

Colás Latorre, Gregorio (1993) "Cristianos y moriscos en Aragón: Una nueva lectura de sus relaciones y comportamientos en el marco de la sociedad rural," *Mélanges de la Casa de Velázquez*, vol. 29, pp. 153–170.

Dadson, Trevor J. (2006) *Los moriscos de Villarrubia de los Ojos (siglos XV–XVIII). Historia de una minoría asimilada, expulsada y reintegrada*. Madrid, Frankfurt: Iberoamericana Vervuert.

— (2014) *Tolerance and Coexistence in Early Modern Spain: Old Christians and Moriscos in the Campo de Calatrava*. Woodbridge Suffolk: Tamesis.

Domínguez Ortiz, Antonio and Bernard Vincent (1997) *Historia de los moriscos: Vida y tragedia de una minoría*. Madrid: Alianza.

Ehlers, Benjamin (2006) *Between Christians and Moriscos: Juan de Ribera and Religious Reform in Valencia, 1568–1614*. Baltimore: Johns Hopkins University Press.

Fiume, Giovanna and Stefania Pastore, eds. (2013) "Diaspora morisca," *Quaderni Storici*, no 144, pp. 663–812.

García-Arenal, Mercedes (1978) *Inquisición y moriscos: Los procesos del tribunal de Cuenca*. Madrid: Siglo XXI.

— (ed.) (2016). *After Conversion: Iberia and the Emergence of Modernity*. Leiden: Brill.

García-Arenal, Mercedes and Fernando Rodríguez Mediano (2010) *Un Oriente español: Los moriscos y el Sacromonte en tiempos de Contrarreforma*. Madrid: Marcial Pons; English version as *The Orient in Spain: Converted Muslims, the Forged Lead Books of Granada, and the Rise of Orientalism*, trans. Consuelo López-Morillas. Leiden: Brill, 2016.

García-Arenal, Mercedes and Gerard Wiegers (eds) (2014) *The Expulsion of the Moriscos from Spain: A Mediterranean Diaspora*. Leiden: Brill.

García-Ballester, Luis (1993) "The Inquisition and minority medical practitioners in Counter-Reformation Spain: Judaizing and Morisco practicioners, 1560–1610," in Ole Peter Grell and Andrew Cunningham (eds), *Medicine and the Reformation*. London: Wellcome Institute Series in the History of Medicine Routledge, pp. 156–191.

García Pedraza, Amalia (2001) *Actitudes ante la muerte en la Granada del siglo XVI. Los moriscos que quisieron salvarse*. Granada: Universidad de Granada, 2 vols.

Halavais, Mary (2002) *Like Wheat to the Miller: Community, Convivencia, and the Construction of Morisco Identity in Sixteenth-Century Aragon*. New York: Columbia University Press.

Harris, A. Katie (2007) *From Muslim to Christian Granada: Inventing a City's Past in Early Modern Spain*. Baltimore: Johns Hopkins University Press.

Harvey, L. P. (2005) *Muslims in Spain, 1500 to 1614*. Chicago: University of Chicago Press.

Ingram, Kevin (ed.) (2009) *The Conversos and Moriscos in Early Modern Spain and Beyond*. Leiden: Brill.

Kimmel, Seth (2015) *Parables of Coercion: Conversion and Knowledge at the End of Islamic Spain*. Chicago: University of Chicago Press.

Magnier, Grace (2010). *Pedro de Valencia and the Catholic Apologists of the Expulsion of the Moriscos: Visions of Christianity and Kingship*. Leiden: Brill.

Márquez Villanueva, Francisco (1998) *El problema morisco (desde otras laderas)*. Madrid: Prodhufi.

Martín Casares, Aurelia (2000) *La esclavitud en la Granada del siglo XVI. Género, raza y religión*, prologue B. Bennassar. Granada: Universidad de Granada.

Núñez Muley, Francisco (2007) *A Memorandum for the President of the Royal Audience and Chancery Court of the City and Kingdom of Granada*, ed. and trans. Vincent Barletta. Chicago: University of Chicago Press.

O'Banion, Patrick (2017) *This Happened in My Presence: Moriscos, Old Christians, and the Spanish Inquisition in the Town of Deza, 1569–1611*. Toronto: University of Toronto Press.

Pereda, Felipe (2017) *Images of Discord: Poetics and Politics of the Sacred Image in 15th-Century Spain*. Turnhout, Harvey Miller.

Perry, Mary Elizabeth (2005) *The Handless Maiden: Moriscos and the Politics of Religion in Early Modern Spain*. Princeton: Princeton University Press.

Soria Mesa, Enrique (2008) *Linajes granadinos*. Granada: Diputación Provincial.

Stuczynski, Claude Bernard (2000) "Two Minorities Facing the Iberian Inquisition: The 'Marranos' and the 'Moriscos'," *Hispania Judaica*, vol. 3, pp. 127–143.

Surtz, Ronald E. (2001) "Morisco Women, Written Texts, and the Valencia Inquisition," *Sixteenth Century Journal*, vol. 32, no 2, pp. 421–433.

de Tapia Sánchez, Serafín (1991) *La comunidad morisca de Avila*. Salamanca: Universidad de Salamanca.

Tratado [Tafsira] del Mancebo de Arévalo (2003) ed. María Teresa Narváez Córdova. Madrid: Trotta.

Vincent, Bernard (2007) *El río morisco*, trans. Antonio Luis Cortés Peña. Valencia, Granada, Zaragoza: Universitat de València, Universidad de Granada, Universidad de Zaragoza.

3

Translating migrant precarity in Rachid Nini's *Diario de un ilegal*

Anna Tybinko

Introduction

Ever since the 1985 *Ley de Extranjería* (LOE) ushered in an unprecedented era of immigration for Spain, Moroccans have represented the single largest group of foreign-born nationals in residence (Aja, 2012: 56). Real numbers are always hard to come by, especially since this law essentially forced migrants into illegality until revisions were introduced in the early 2000s.[1] But civil registries (el Padrón Muncipal) and the Encuesta de la Población Activa (Labor Force Survey) administered by the Instituto Nacional de Estadística (National Statistics Institute or INE) give us a rough idea of this robust and evolving population. The magnitude of migratory flows between Morocco and Spain are not necessarily surprising given their geographic proximity, close historical ties, and Spain's colonial presence in North Africa. However, these same factors make for a complex web of cultural relations, which spans the Strait of Gibraltar, and that is reflected in the interplay of languages and literatures between the two countries.

As discussed in Chapter 2, the expulsion of the so-called Moriscos from Spain, beginning in 1609, can be seen as the closing of one chapter of Spanish history and the beginning of another. James Amelang indicates that, on one hand, the forcible removal of the remaining descendants of the long-standing Muslim population from Peninsular territory and their banishment to North Africa can be seen as the culmination of a longer timeline of events that began the Umayyad conquest of 711. On the other hand, "it created a strong precedent for mass mobility by migrants between the Iberian Peninsula and North Africa – albeit in the direction opposite to that of today's insistent flow" (p. 46, this volume). For example, the enclaves of Ceuta and Melilla – in what would be Morocco – were first occupied by the Spanish Crown in the seventeenth and fifteenth centuries respectively. While they long served as key port cities for a growing empire, their function as military bases saw renewed purpose when Spain sought to extend its influence in the region during the nineteenth and twentieth century.[2] Thus, while Spain's experience as a popular host country may be new, Moroccan immigration reminds Spaniards that despite the division of national territories, the Southern Mediterranean region has been a veritable borderlands throughout the modern era (Pack, 2019). By the mid-1980s, this precedent became worrisome for Spain's newly democratic government as it sought to re-establish a European identity following decades of self-isolation and general stagnation during the authoritarian regime of Francisco Franco (1939–75). Notably, Spain was one of the original 20 member countries to sign the Convention founding the Organisation for Economic Co-Operation and Development (OECD) in 1960 but was only admitted to the European Economic Community in 1986, following the LOE's promulgation due to concerns about its economic stability and the "porousness" of its borders.

With the formation of European Union (EU) in 1993, and the Schengen Area two years later, Ceuta and Melilla became the new European conglomerate's only terrestrial border with Africa practically overnight. As a result, Spain was obliged to engage in a hurried wall-building process and quickly became the veritable face of "Fortress Europe." While this popular turn of phrase references the increased militarization of checks and controls at united Europe's exterior borders, it also recycles terminology coined by Joseph Goebbels during World War II as he sought to convey a sense of security to the beleaguered inhabitants of the Third Reich (Seaton, 1981: 41). This echo of Nazi-era discourse is an eerie reminder that, what former Executive Director of Frontex (the EU's unified border agency), Ilkka Laitinen, calls the EU's "area of Freedom, Security and Justice" (Laitinen, 2007: 128) is similarly predicated on the control and exclusion of racialized bodies.[3] Whether it be from Africa, Latin America, Asia, or the Middle East, most of those "outsiders" who seek their futures in the EU hail from places that experienced the impact of either outright or de facto colonization in the past. In many instances "their forebears contributed to collectively producing the greater part of the material basis for the prosperity of Europe" (De Genova, 2017: 18). However, it is worth noting that while much of Europe experiences these arrivals as the return of the colonized, a North African presence in Spain is perceived not only as a specter of the country's colonial past, but as the return of the fearsome "Moor" (Flesler, 2008). Harkening back to 711 when Tariq ibn Ziyad and his Berber troops crossed the Strait of Gibraltar to establish a series of Muslim dynasties that endured throughout the medieval period, this particular brand of xenophobia recycles the logic of the so-called Christian Reconquest (*Reconquista*) of Iberia to frame the recent influx of workers from Morocco, Algeria, and Tunisia as an "economic invasion."

In line with this volume's mission to shed light on the ways Mediterranean migratory flows, both past and present, have given shape to contemporary Europe, the present chapter will examine how Moroccan journalist Rachid Nini (also spelled Niny) uses multilingual, creative non-fiction to reveal the unsettled nature of Spain's formation as a modern, European nation. As a chronicle of the three years he spent as an itinerant laborer, traveling throughout much of the Spanish Levant (and beyond), the autobiographical *Diario de un ilegal* (*Diary of a Clandestine Migrant*, 2002), offers a fascinating window into a period in which Spain officially took on the polemic role as "gatekeeper" for the European Union. Although the rising tide of immigration in the early 1990s inspired multiple forms of cultural production on either side of the Strait,[4] the *Diario* is unique in both form and content. First of all, Gonzalo Fernández Parilla, the co-translator of the text into Spanish, touts the piece as the first testimonial to be written in Arabic (Morocco's official language) about the experience of Moroccan migrants in Spain (Fernández Parrilla, 2015: 214).[5] However, neither the Arabic version, *Yawmiyyāt muhāyir sirri*, published by the Moroccan Ministry of Culture in 1999, nor its subsequent translation into Spanish published by Ediciones del oriente y del mediterráneo in 2000 are the "original" per se. Given his professional connections, Nini first published the bulk of the *Diario* in feuilleton form in the Moroccan daily, *Al Alam*, and only compiled it after the fact. Nonetheless, when the Spanish version finally hit the bookshelves, Nini averred that he was writing for a Spanish readership all along:

> Allí se sabe todo lo que digo. Aquí no. Aquí, de nosotros, sólo se sabe lo que sale por televisión. Los clichés: la patera, los ahogados, la pesca, el hachís. A las personas no las conocen. Y creo que no quieren saberlo. Hay un bloqueo psicológico histórico. Y los medios y los políticos ayudan a que ese bloqueo no se acabe. (Mora, 2002)

> (There, they know about everything I say. Here, about us, they only know what they see on television. The clichés: pateras,[6] the drowned, fishing, hashish. They don't know actual people. And I believe that they don't want to know. There's psychological, historical blockage. And the media and the politicians make sure this blockage doesn't end.)[7]

In this 2002 *El País* interview with Miguel Mora, Nini not only makes a clear distinction between "here" (Spain) and "there" (Morocco) but also between "us" (Moroccans) and "them" (Spaniards). By inverting the order in which he refers first to place and then people, Nini confirms his position as a Moroccan who writes about the realities of migration from Spain as his locus of enunciation. This curious reversal of "native" languages ironically serves to make the precariousness of the migrant experience legible to a Spanish-speaking audience.

Nini returns to the two countries' historical entanglements time and again, confirming Spanish fears that they are not so different after all. His attempts to underscore the Moroccan's position in Spanish society as the anachronistic "Moor" and inveterate "other" serve to remind Spaniards of their own backwardness. Indeed, as Fernández Parrilla confirms, this view of Spain as both part of and apart from the West is shared by Westerners and Maghrebis (Fernández Parrilla, 2013: 89). Similarly, in analysing Nini's text alongside the work of Tunisian and Algerian authors, Sabrina Brancato argues that "the absence of the common trope of cultural difference is a distinctive and significant element ... of texts by Maghrebi authors in Southern Europe" (Brancato, 2012: 68). To this end, Fernández Parrilla insists that the value of *Diario de un ilegal* resides in this familiarity with, and therefore ability to ironize, the historically embedded nature of Spanish–Moroccan relations and perceptions of one another.[8] Whether "caustic" (Shepherd, 2012: 61), "borderline satire" (Fernández Parrilla, 2015: 216), "sarcastic" or "bombastic" (Lalami, 2011), a penchant for the ironic seems to be Nini's defining trait as a writer. While Nini may be anything but a reliable narrator and is, for many reasons, a problematic public figure, in his irreverent account we find a timely critique of Spain's desperate attempts to Europeanize – often at the cost of its neighbors to the south.

The ideological controversies surrounding the memory of Al-Andalus on either side of the Strait of Gibraltar have long impacted the study, translation, and reception of Arabic literature in Spain (Fernández Parrilla, 2013: 89). In assessing more recent successes and failures to translate Arabic letters into Spanish, Ovidi Carbonell i Cortés lauds Gonzalo Fernández Parilla and Malika Embarek's translation of *Diaro de un ilegal*. According to Carbonell i Cortés, the genius of their work lies in its minimalist approach. The text is presented without footnotes or glossaries, and they avoid resorting to Arabisms in Spanish when direct translation seems otherwise impossible. In this way, the Spanish version avoids "the exoticist solipsism of the Spanish encounter with their Arab/Berber Other" (Carbonell i Cortés, 2003: 148). On the contrary, Arabic terms are occasionally left untranslated, marking them as foreign on a sociolinguistic level. To illustrate this point, Carbonell i Cortés points to a passage towards the end of the *Diario* in which Nini visits Toledo:

> Toledo. Viernes, una y media de la tarde. Me senté en una de las terrazas de Suqadawab. Enfrente está el Arco de la Sangre. No sé de dónde proviene ese nombre brutal, aunque sí sé al menos que en los siglos pasados la plaza de Suqadawab, en uno de cuyos cafés estoy sentado, era el lugar donde se dejaba el ganado antes de entrar a la ciudad. El nombre actual, escrito en el rótulo de mármol blanco, es Zocodover. (Nini, 2002: 175)

(Toledo. Friday, one thirty in the afternoon. I sat at one of the terraces of the Suqadawab. Right across from me was the Arch of Blood. I don't know where that brutal name comes from, although I do at least know that in centuries past the Suqadawab plaza, in one of whose cafés I am sitting was where the livestock were left before entering the city. The current name, written on a marble plaque, is Zocodover.)

Carbonell i Cortés astutely indicates that the normalization of the Arabic *sūq ad-dawāb* (cattle market) functions as a sort of reversed exoticism when aimed at Spanish readers (Carbonell i Cortés, 2003: 148–9), encouraging them to see today's crowded, touristy Zocodover as a bizarre mutation of its former practical self.

While the politics of terminology may seem tangential (at best) for understanding the significance of Nini's work in the Spanish context, the technical prowess of the translation of *Diario de un ilegal* mirrors Nini's own capacity to translate the migrant perspective into terms that are relevant to the average Spaniard. As a shrewd and informed observer of the Spanish political economy, Nini delves into a process that anthropologists (such as Bermant and Suárez-Navaz) have dubbed "refronterización" or re-bordering, wherein Spain's external bordering was replicated internally through the segmentation of labor. By discriminating against migrant workers, Spaniards were able to advance in their own careers and catapult themselves onto the global economic stage. Plenty of valuable scholarship on Nini's *Diario* already exists, much of which builds on the text's chaotic format to highlight the precarious situation of the migrants that cross the Strait of Gibraltar in patera. However, as I will argue in continuation, Nini's tales of the dark underworld of illegal employment that supports Spain's booming tourist industry along the Mediterranean coast communicate the extent to which the precarity of these migrant "Others" is part and parcel of Spain's financial success. Writing in Arabic for a Spanish audience, Nini shows that precarity is borderless – not brought as part of a North African incursion, but inherent in Spain's own self-fashioning as an economically prosperous European nation.

To that end, two intertwined notions of precarity are present in the text. In the Spanish context, this language became more and more popular to describe feelings of displacement and dispossession following the Great Recession. So, on one hand, precarity is an economic term that speaks to the ravages of the 2008 financial crisis and subsequent austerity measures. On the other hand, it describes a state of heightened vulnerability and exposure to violence. The relationship between these two understandings of precarity has been explored at length by Palmar Álvarez-Blanco and Antonio Gómez L-Quiñones in the volume *La imaginación hipotecada: Aportaciones sobre la precariedad del presente*, where they signal that, while the two acceptations have seen divergent trajectories in academic and popular spheres, their connection is possible – if by no means automatic (Álvarez-Blanco and Gómez L-Quiñones, 2016: 10–11). As they see it, precarity is part and parcel of a globalized capitalist economy rather than a state of exception. This is where Judith Butler's ideas about the "differential allocation of precarity" prove particularly useful (Butler, 2009: 3). As Butler advances in *Frames of War: When is Life Greivable?*, the existential (ontological) conception of precariousness – which is ultimately the recognition of human interdependency – is linked to precarity as political concept in that it "also characterizes that politically induced condition of maximized precariousness for populations exposed to arbitrary state violence who often have no other option than to appeal to the very state for protection' (Butler, 2009: 26). I therefore submit that, while David Álvarez reads Nini's *Diario* in relation to the Maghrebi practice of *harraga* (literally, the "burning of borders" through clandestine migration to Europe), Michelle Shepherd interprets the multiple modes of transport present in the diary as metaphor for precarious movement, and Lara Dotson-Renta focuses on the act of transit – or *traslado* (moving [between two places]) – itself (Dotson-Renta, (2008: 437), we must also consider how Nini's act of cultural translation demonstrates that Spain's economic straits are very much predicated on the precariousness of migrant life. In short, that migrant precarity is precarity for all.

A story of Spain

Narrated in the first person, Nini's account of his own exploits abroad also recounts the day-to-day lives of those around him. As he moves from Benidorm to Paris, then Brussels and back to Southeastern Spain, his trajectory gets harder to follow. At times, we find him working in the orange groves in Oliva or as a construction worker in Pego during the low season. Other chapters are dedicated to the laborious hours spent as "pizzero" or tending a bar in Benidorm during peak tourist season. The episodes are typically punctuated by nostalgic reflections about his childhood or university years in Morocco and when nostalgia clearly overpowers him, the later chapters (18–21) fracture into brief log-like entries from various points during his three-year journey, which are always marked by a day of the week and the time, but no specific date. They range from locations like Rabat, where Nini must go every month to pick up his scant pay checks from the newspaper for which he freelances, to Heidelberg, where he finds himself as a tourist. This back and forth, which Shepherd has described as "helter-skelter," is dizzying for the reader (Shepherd, 2012: 59), but effectively conveys Nini's feelings of displacement and precariousness. It all builds up to the conclusion: "Tenía que volver" (Nini, 2002: 197) ("I had to return").

Throughout the narrative, and regardless of his location, Nini gives the reader a sense of the social panorama. In the opening chapters, for example, he describes the cast of characters that accompanies him in Oliva, where he is employed as a *jornalero*, or seasonal worker. Each person is labeled in terms of either ethnic or national identity: there's "Áhmed, el argelino flaco" (Nini, 2002: 12) ("Ahmed, the skinny Algerian"); Miguel, the child of Spanish emigrants who returns after a lifetime in Argentina (Nini, 2002: 10–11), and "Christian, el italiano" (Nini, 2002: 15) ("Christian, the Italian"). The other Moroccans our narrator encounters seem to live an even more itinerant lifestyle than he does: an early example is Jáled, who simply disappears, convinced he's being pursued by the police, and Abdelwahab, who lives out of his car, a Renault Tráfic. Abdelwahab preys on older, single English women, re-selling the trinkets they buy him to fund his drinking habit. The narrator explains that "Para él no existe un país llamado Marruecos. Ni llama a su madre por teléfono. Su padre lo trajo a España antes de la época del visado. Y lo abandonó a su suerte" (Nini, 2002: 29) ("For him, there is no country called Morocco. He doesn't even call his mother. His father brought him to Spain before the visa was instated. And he abandoned him to try his luck"). Abdelwahab's presence seems to remind us that while the constant movement of people and goods between Spain and Morocco has been constitutive of both country's economies (Soto Bermant, 2014), there is no welcoming expat community awaiting Nini abroad. Newly imposed migration controls have made each person's journey a solitary venture, a dance with their own destiny – or a brush with death. Herein lies the power of Nini's testimony – that it manages to convey the impact of the structural forces, such as the brutal imposition of the Schengen Zone (protection of the freedom of some over that of others) on individual lives.

Thanks to Nini's *Diario* we are privy to the internal strife that resulted from northern European fears that Spain would become "la puerta de Africa" ("Africa's front door"). These fears motivated a fence-building process to protect Ceuta and Melilla, quickly converting a formerly porous frontier zone into one of the world's most militarized borders (Brown, 2010). These double-facing steel mesh barriers, or *vallas*, now measure nearly twenty feet and are crowned with razor wire. Thermal cameras and motion sensors scan the generally barren Moroccan landscape, which, along with the Guardia Civil patrolling the Spanish side, lend the mere ten kilometres of perimeter a distinctly prison-like feel. Throughout this volume, we see examples of how various European enclaves serve – and have served throughout history – as important spaces of transit. However, as elucidated by Raquel Salvatella de Prada's installation, *Cornered*, which explores the impassability of Ceuta and

Melilla today, or as Helen Solterer demonstrates vis-à-vis premodern Calais, France, the move to fortify these enclaves leads to both forced enclosures and expulsions. And indeed, in the case of Spain's southernmost territories, the contemporary bordering efforts mentioned above pushed those without the means to arrange for a visa towards the sea route, turning the narrow Strait into a veritable graveyard. What Nini's text demonstrates, therefore, is how the recent collective militarization of Europe's external borders, which culminated in the creation of Frontex (the EU's unified border agency) in 2004, has weaponized the Mediterranean and illegalized the movement of people that characterized the region for centuries.

Rather than his academic prowess or access to publishing outlets somehow distinguishing him from the masses, Nini's participation in harraga seemingly erases his social capital. Numerous scholars warn against taking the work of recognized writers like Nini as a transparent medium for understanding irregular migration,[9] arguing that one's social class overwhelmingly determines the means to migrate and means to publish alike. However, I argue that, despite his public profile, Nini's writing unequivocally conveys the transcendence of the EU border regime. Before leaving home, he tries to solidify his connections with the intellectual class with which he used to associate during university: "Dos días antes de mi partida quedé con algunos amigos para hacerme con direcciones que pudieran ser útiles si algo ocurría o necesitaba una pequeña ayuda económica en algún lugar del viejo continente. Pero la mayoría me dejaron plantado" (Nini, 2002: 54) ("Two days before my departure I made plans with some friends to gather contacts that could be useful if something happened or if I needed a little economic help in the Old Continent. But the majority of them stood me up"). Recalling the sensation of being abandoned by his supposed friends and unable to depend on a reliable network as he faces emigration, Nini remarks bitterly: "Cuando me fui, sólo los ladrones se quedaron a mi lado. En estos tiempos perversos puedes depositar tu confianza en un ladrón, pero no en un intelectual" (Nini, 2002: 54) ("When I left, only the thieves stayed by my side. In these perverse times you can deposit your confidence in a thief, but not an intellectual"). United by their juridical standing – or lack thereof – Nini finds companionship in those who share his extra-legal status.

Nini regularly confirms this experience with affirmations like: "En España, al llegar, la mayoría de mis amigos eran ladrones" (Nini, 2002: 52) ("In Spain, upon arriving, the majority of my friends were thieves"). But while this example is phrased in the past tense, others bring us closer to the present: "Hasta ahora no me he encontrado más que con ladrones. No he conocido ni a un solo escritor o periodista. Tal vez sea mejor así" (Nini, 2002: 53) ("Until now I haven't connected with anyone other than thieves. I haven't met a single writer or journalist. Maybe it's better this way"). Of course, as is the case throughout much of the text, it is nearly impossible to tell how much time has passed between his arrival and the "now" of his present-tense claim. Days, months, and years all blend together in a style that Álvarez calls "narrative vagrancy" (Álvarez, 2013: 158).

During a brief stint north of the Pyrenees, Nini is hosted by one of the thieves, Mustafa. Despite his complaints that in Spain everyone treats him strangely when he tries to communicate in French (Nini, 2002: 73–4), Nini never seems comfortable in Paris. All of his opinions about France are framed in opposition to his friend's: "Mustafa cree que Europa es una tierra de botín para los argelinos. Especialmente Francia. Dice que aunque se pasara toda su vida robando no compensaría lo que Francia robó durante los año que estuvo en Argelia" (Nini, 2002: 55) ("Mustafa thinks that Europe is a land of bounty for Algerians. Especially France. He says that even if one spends one's whole life stealing it would never make up for what France stole the years it was in Algeria"). This anecdote points to the historical valences of harraga – for as sociologist Amade M'charek explains: "Folded into harraga is a story of colonial and postcolonial relations. For a long time after official independence it was easy to travel from the Maghreb countries to the former colonizer" (M'charek, 2020: 419). But given that this more fluid movement between former colony and metropole has been stymied by European unification, Nini seems to be inserting a question mark here: is the possible "bounty" of Europe worth the life-threatening journey or the constant exposure to violence needed to access it?

The incredulity with which Nini greets Mustafa's comments is further underscored when he considers the misadventures of other Algerian friends in Spain, almost all of whom have been stopped by the police and several of whom have even received deportation orders demanding that they repatriate within ten days. However, Nini adds: "ninguno abandona esta tierra. Es como si se hubiera convertido en su propia tierra. Donde están sus verdaderas raíces. La policía también sabe que ellos no regresarán. Por eso, la primera vez que los detienen registran su nombre y ya no vuelven a molestarlos" (Nini, 2002: 63) ("none of them abandon this country. It's as if they've turned it into their own country. Where their true roots are. The police also know that they won't go back. That's why the first time they detain them they take down their names and don't bother them again"). Once in Europe, the mechanisms of surveillance and harassment force these migrants into an autonomous state, a land of their own.

Nini, too, suffers from this association with illegality. Referring to himself and his fellow Moroccans he returns disgustedly to the stereotypical image of migration presented by the Spanish media: "La televisión ofrece de nosotros la imagen de un país que no es más que una flota incesante de pateras" (Nini, 2002: 73) ("The television offers of us the image of a country that is nothing more than an incessant fleet of pateras"). The damaging effects of this association go beyond stereotypes: midnight raids, internment in a detention center and deportation are all real risks. Thus, Nini admits to living in constant fear. It is only in the presence of Macarena, his Spanish girlfriend (about whom we learn little more than her name), that he says he feels comfortable even looking at a police car: "A veces lo hago en venganza por todos los momentos en los que estaba solo. Y probablemente alerta" (Nini, 2002: 28) ("Sometimes I do it out of revenge for all the times I was alone. And probably on edge"). It's as if even meeting the gaze of this inanimate object is an act of defiance: one that he is incapable of when the officers stop him on the street or initiate a body cavity search without warning, under the suspicion that he might be hiding hash somewhere obscene. This dynamic eventually becomes far too taxing and as he leaves Spain, Nini attests:

> Me he cansado de estar siempre alerta. Quiero salir de casa sin tener esa sensación. Caminar en compañía de alguien sin que el coche de policía se detenga detrás de mí, sin tener que dar explicaciones ni pedir permiso. Me he cansado de esconderme siempre como un imbécil. Y de correr cuando había que salir huyendo. Quiero mirar a mi alrededor y ver a mis semejantes. Que mi aspecto no le produzca extrañeza a nadie. (Nini, 2002: 197)

> (I have gotten tired of always being alert. I want leave home without this sensation. To walk in the company of someone without a police car pulling up behind me, without having to give explanations or ask permission. I have gotten tired of always hiding like an idiot. And running when it's time to flee. I want to look around and see people that look like me. And that my appearance doesn't astonish anyone.)

In the above passage Nini responds to the way his juridical invisibility has also made him a highly visible Other in Spain. His rationale reads as excuses, perhaps directed at a Spanish audience, for why his clandestine mode of existence is no longer viable – or why Spain is not worth the sacrifice of suffering these harrowing experiences on a daily basis. What he ultimately detests is the precarity of the migrant situation in Spain or, to use Butler's definition, "their exposure to violence, their socially induced transience and dispensability" (Butler, 2009: xvii). Following Shepherd, Álvarez, and Dotson-Renta, I concur that the same conditions that render migrant lives precarious in the dangerous journey across the Strait are to be found throughout *Diario de un ilegal*, even on tierra firme. However, I also insist that, in burning Europe's borders, Nini finds himself amongst the *precariato* that Butler has described as inhabiting the "limits of the frame," wherein their violent subjugation becomes the "presupposed background of everyday life" (Butler, 2009: xvi).

In defining precarity, Butler clarifies that it is not necessarily synonymous with *bare life* or the extra-juridical status of Europe's perpetual outsiders, because "to be protected from violence by the nation-state is to be exposed to the violence wielded by the nation-state, so to rely on the nation-state for protection from violence is precisely to exchange one potential violence for another"' (Butler, 2009: 26). In this particular case, migrants may be suffering from the violence of the national, but it is Spain that should be wary of the supposed protections supra-national conglomerations like the EU have to offer. This is what Nini is getting at with ironic statements like:

> En la actualidad, España es el país de Europa menos racista, lo he leído hoy en el periódico. Han publicado un estudio sobre cómo perciben los españoles a los extranjeros y a los gitanos. En algunos de esos pueblos remotos a cuyos campos fuimos a trabajar, la gente apenas sabía nada de los marroquíes. Todo lo que sabían se remontaba a antiguas leyendas sobre los moros que habían ocupado a su tierra. Y a los que habían expulsado de mala manera. (Nini, 2002: 74)

> (Currently, Spain is the least racist country in Europe. I read it today in the newspaper. They published a study about Spaniards' perceptions of foreigners and gypsies. In some of the remote villages in whose fields we went to work, people barely knew anything about Moroccans. Everything they knew was based on ancient legends about the Moors who had occupied their lands. And that they had been expulsed in an ugly way.)

These newspaper claims ring false in the face of everything else Nini has told us, not to mention that the pairing of the first statement and his description of the treatment he receives in the Spanish countryside reads as almost oxymoronic. As someone who is writing these words to be published in a Moroccan newspaper and who has since built his career around supposed truth telling through journalism, the fact that Nini is the one questioning this report feels, once again, almost meta-ironic. Yet while Nini seems generally oblivious to this larger irony, he deftly illustrates how Spain's multifarious attempts to join the ranks of "post-racial" Europe constitute acts of violence in and of themselves. Firstly, in an oft-cited poll taken only a few years later, Spaniards would cite immigration as one of their greatest concerns, thus challenging the earlier charade of acceptance.[10] Secondly, and perhaps more importantly for a country with an ongoing colonial presence in North Africa, and one that fought wars in Morocco in both the nineteenth and twentieth centuries, only being able to recognize present-day Moroccans in terms of medieval taxonomies is delusional at best.

Questions of cultural superiority and inferiority, and false lines drawn between "global North" and "global South," continue to haunt Nini throughout his journey. Looking for housing in Pego, he finds an advertisement in the local paper for a room in a shared apartment. His housemates are a retiree that Nini refers to as "La señora Carmen" and a middle-aged Andalusian man named Juan. Juan turns out to be an alcoholic – whose own children have taken him to court for his abusive tendencies – as well as a Franco sympathizer (Nini, 2002: 129). Having unwittingly agreed to share space with an ultra-nationalist, Nini succinctly sums up the situation in his curt way: "Juan lleva cincuenta años sin quedarse mucho tiempo en un trabajo. Cree que los trabajos estables y cómodos los hacen los inmigrantes y los extranjeros" (Nini, 2002: 124) ("Juan has spent fifty years without spending much time in any one job. He thinks the stable, comfortable jobs are all taken by immigrants and foreigners"). And later: "Hay un tipo de hombres que echar al mundo la culpa de todo. Creo que Juan es uno de esos" (Nini, 2002: 128) ("There is a type of guy that blames the whole world for everything. I think Juan is one them"). Juan thus becomes a stand-in for those who espouse xenophobic attitudes to cover up their own personal failings and Nini's more polished demeanour seems to confound him:

> Quería saber por qué había venido a esta ciudad, de qué vivía y cómo me permitía tres platos distintos en una sola comida. Por qué no me parecía a los otros moros que salían regularmente en televisión bajándose de las pateras y subiendo, en el mejor de los casos, a los coches de policía y, en el peor, entregados a las olas que acunan sus cadáveres rumbo al Paraíso. La señora Carmen le dice que soy una persona con estudios y que, precisamente por eso, le caigo bien. Pero Juan quiere saber más. (Nini, 2002: 127)

> (He wants to know why I have come to this city, what I live on and how I can afford eating three different dishes in one single meal. Why I didn't look like the other Moors that appear regularly on television stepping out of pateras and climbing, in the best of cases, into police cars and, in the worst, delivered to the waves that cradle their cadavers on the way to Paradise. Señora Carmen tells him that I'm an educated person, and precisely for that reason, she likes me. But Juan wants to know more.)

This is a prime example of the moments in which Nini's supposed first-person account somehow morphs into the third-person narration of the thoughts and observations of those around him. By eliding direct or reported speech attributes, it is as if Juan is speaking through him as Nini replays his housemate's inquiries over and over in his head. Mediated by the shadow of detention or death represented by the pateras, Juan's xenophobically driven interrogation reads as particularly absurd. Nini may not have come by patera and his educational level might far surpass that of Juan, but they move constantly between the same type of odd jobs to make ends meet. It speaks to the extent to which the border acts as a regulator of human capital leaving Juan nothing to fear.

Through the figure of Juan, Nini additionally demonstrates that racism is not just "an autonomous force, an additional factor shaping late capitalist forces toward class segmentation" (Suárez-Navaz, 2004: 6). Instead, as Liliana Suárez-Návaz has suggested, it emerges from constant relational processes of negotiation between individual in the social sphere (Nini, 2002: 54). Juan, like the many other Spaniards Nini profiles briefly, is complicit in manipulating the limits of representation. Of course, Juan's befuddled belief that immigrants occupy the comfortable jobs in some ways is the least egregious. There's Alberto, the contractor in Pego, who, after a great deal of back and forth with his personal lawyer, forces Nini and the other undocumented workers to come to the construction site during siesta hours when he's certain no agents from the Ministerio de Trabajo will make a surprise visit (Nini, 2002: 136). It's also the many individual police officers perpetuating the climate of fear cited earlier. At the very end of his *Diario*, Nini claims that precisely because young Spaniards do not want to be employed in agriculture or other physical labor:

> si te piden los papeles, basta con abrir la palma de la mano delante de la policía, para que sepan que te ganas el sustento en el campo y te dejen seguir tu camino. En esta península los dedos agrietados les sirven a los inmigrantes árabes les sirven de carné de identidad mejor que esos otros azules casi imposibles de conseguir. (Nini, 2002: 127)

> (If they ask for your papers, it's enough to open the palm of your hand in front of the police so that they know you earn your living in the fields and let you keep going.[11] On this peninsula rough fingers serve as an identification card for Arab immigrants, better than those other blue ones that are almost impossible to obtain.)

With respect to these same lines, Shepherd insists that "the reader is painfully aware that this sort of physical currency carries no weight with the authorities and the undocumented have one option, to flee, when faced with such an interrogation" (Shepherd, 2012: 61). Yet, for once, I am not so sure Nini is being ironic, such was the demand for migrant fieldhands during this era of economic boom. I do, however, agree with Shepherd that "this comment resonates with the notion of embodied labor" (Nini, 2002: 61), in that, whether this type of interaction is real or fabricated, it conveys the extent to which migrant illegality is the necessary foil that confirms Spain's legality within the EU system – in the company of the very member states that once took advantage of undocumented Spanish labor within their now non-existent borders.

Conclusions

There is mutual agreement amongst scholars that Nini's narrative, like other "migrant narratives," pokes holes in the prevailing myth of an economically sound Europe – one in which migrants (the bulk of them ex-subjects from Europe's former colonies) will *finally* be able to access the stores of colonial wealth merely by stepping foot on European soil (Brancato, 2012: 72–3; Shepherd, 2012: 61–2; Álvarez, 2013: 160–4). Typically, this dream of a "land of plenty" is belied by emphasizing its inaccessibility through the counter-vision of a Fortress Europe – the brutal set of border regimes established precisely to curtail migrant mobility while preserving and protecting white privilege (in both an economic and territorial sense). However, as I have addressed here, *Diario de un ilegal* takes a slightly different approach. Nini certainly reveals the extent to which this privilege is perennially inaccessible to the racialized North African "Other," but he also seems to suggest that Spain's reliance on migrant labor to "move up in the world" (and again, I am playing with a possible double entendre here and thinking of a movement upwards in terms of both social mobility in addition to geopolitical North–South location) is a sign of its fragility, its vulnerability on the "fringes of Europe" (Zea, 1970), rather than its European prowess.

Nini ultimately expresses his frustration with the lack of compassion he encounters on the part of many Spaniards for, as he explains it:

> Los españoles no saben gran cosa de los inmigrantes. Al menos las nuevas generaciones. Las generaciones anteriores vivieron la emigración durante la Guerra civil y durante el régimen del general Francisco. Y por eso conocen el infierno que es emigrar. Se fueron a México, Argentina, Francia y no sé qué otros lugares. Y ahora no se avergüenzan de sí mismos cuando, al ver una persona de rasgos árabes dicen: "Uuuh, ya han vuelto esos moros!" (Nini, 2002: 83).[12]

> (Spaniards do not know much about immigrants. At least the younger generations. The earlier generation lived through the years of emigration during the Civil War and under the Franco regime. That's why they know how hellish it is to emigrate. They went to Mexico, Argentina, France, and Germany and I don't know where else. And now they are not even embarrassed of themselves when, upon seeing a person with Arab features, they say: "Ugh, those Moors are back already!")

Given that he is talking about "Spaniards" as a whole in the third person, it would seem that Nini's target audience for this particular rant is in fact the *Diario's* initial readership back in Morocco. He is railing against what Raquel Vega-Durán has called Spain's "historical amnesia about its own past as a land of emigrants – emigrants who themselves knew what it was like to be an immigrant in another country" (Vega-Durán, xiv). Yet in doing so, he reveals the desire to somehow break down this barrier. He is urging these oblivious "new generations" to reckon with what the encounter between citizen and non-citizen feels like from the migrant, or outsider, perspective.

It is also a warning in some ways. Because, despite the paranoia of people like Juan, migrant labor has been consistently channeled into niches abandoned by native workers (Cornelius, 2004: 400). Spain went from the country with Europe's highest official unemployment rate (around 23%) in the early 1990s, to one of the fastest growing economies by 1996 with unemployment down to about 13% at the turn of the millennium (Cornelius, 2004: 400, 422). All of this while the country saw its largest influx yet of Moroccan migrants.[13] The promulgation of the 1985 LOE and Spain's subsequent accession to the European Economic Community in 1986 ended "fifty years of international ostracism" which in turn "produced a strong rhetoric about a 'European ethos' based on common citizenship" (Suárez-Navaz, 2004: 3). Within this new schema, the illegalized African worker – and the "Moor" in particular – was necessarily positioned as antagonistic to the Spanish population, devoid of the new rights and liberties these Spaniards could claim as EU members. However, as Nini seems to insinuate, the differentiation between the native and foreign populations in Spain is largely driven by the promise of European privilege and not necessarily by concrete material differences. *Diario de un ilegal* thus offers an important rendering of the years building up to the 2008 financial crisis for the many Spaniards still reeling from the fallout. Although Spain's economy did expand exponentially during the 1990s and early 2000s, Nini's testimonial begs the question: how much of that financial success relied on not-so-glamourous practices of workplace discrimination and labor market segmentation? By targeting a Spanish audience, and particularly by doing so in Arabic, he brings the migrant experience to bear on Spain's past and future.

Notes

1 This first version of the Ley de Extranjería, La Ley Orgánica 5/1985, sobre derechos y libertades de los extranjeros en España, has been strongly criticized for focusing exclusively on migratory controls rather than the "rights and liberties of foreigners in Spain" as claimed. It made no provisions for asylum or family reunification, and those wishing to travel on a work visa had to obtain a work contract from Spain ahead of time and back in their country of origin. This particular requirement was a near impossibility in a pre-internet age, meaning that the law essentially only allowed for illegal entry or a brief stay on a tourist visa (Cachón Rodríguez, 2006: 21). By the early 1990s the situation was so acute that the government implemented emergency "regularization" campaigns every year between 1993 and 1999 in an attempt to legalize the precarious working conditions of tens of thousands of people (Cachón Rodríguez, 2006: 24). See the Introduction for a detailed description of how this legislation has evolved over time.

2 This includes various incursions against Riffian tribes such as the Spanish–
   Moroccan War (1859–60) and the Battle of Annual (1921), as well as the Spanish
   occupation of the Western Sahara (1884–1976), and the Spanish Protectorate
   in Morocco (1912–56), which led to much of the friction in the Rif.

3 This description of the Schengen Zone comes verbatim from an essay written
   by Brigadier General, Ilkka Laitinen, former Executive Director of Frontex.
   Frontex stands for "the European Agency for the Management of Operational
   Cooperation at the External Borders of the Members States of the EU," and
   the abbreviation likely comes from the French "frontiers exterieuers" (Laitinen,
   2007: 128). This type of concerted policing effort, intended to enhance mobility
   within Europe, was promised by the Treaty of Rome (1957), the common
   market's founding document, and established by the EC Council Regulation
   2004/2007.

4 See Flesler (2008) for an analysis of the Spanish cultural production that emerged
   during this era and Ricci (2014) for the incredible depth and breadth of Castilian
   and Catalan writing in Morocco from the same period – much of which focuses
   on migration.

5 According to Fernández Parrilla, Nini's testimonial builds on a much longer
   tradition of emigration literature in Arabic, where *rihla* or travel literature has
   been one of the most important prose genres. Cristián Ricci explains that much
   like *Diario de un ilegal*, the first literary works addressing the modern migration
   of North African citizens to Europe during the 1970s were written in Arabic,
   and points to Abdallah Laroui's 1971 *al-Gurba* (translated in English as *The
   Exile* or *The Loneliness*) and Mohamed Zafzaf's 1970 *al-Mar'a wa-l-warda* (*The
   Woman and the Rose*) (Ricci, 2017: 584). This was followed by a large amount
   of Francophone literature on the topic published in both Morocco and France.
   As Fernández Parrilla indicates, Spain did not become a popular destination until
   the 1990s. Since then, *harraga* literature has become a true subgenre on both
   sides of the Strait of Gibraltar (Fernández Parrilla, 2015: 212). Spanish-language
   publications include Mohamed Azirar's 1988 *Kaddour "el fantasioso"* (*Kaddour
   "The Fantasy,"* published as a feuilleton in the daily francophone Moroccan
   daily, *L'Opinion*), Abdelkader Uariachi's 1990 *El despertar de los leones* (*The
   Awakening of the Lions*), Mohamed Sibari's 1993 *El caballo* (*The Horse*, first
   published as feuilleton in *L'Opinion* in 1990), and finally, *El diablo de Yudis*
   (*The Devil of Yudis*, 1994), which received significant critical attention as the first
   novel by a Moroccan author to have been written in Spanish and published in
   Spain (Campoy-Cubillo, 2012: 129; Fernández Parrilla, 2015: 213; Ricci, 2017:
   584). We could also point to collaborations between Spanish and Moroccan
   authors such as Pasqual Moreno Torregrosa and Mohamed El Gheryb's *Dormir
   al raso* (*Sleeping Unsheltered*, 1994). However, I am intrigued by the uniqueness
   of *Diario de un ilegal* as an original Arabic publication seemingly aimed at a
   Moroccan audience that is then translated fairly quickly into Spanish – due, we
   can assume, to Nini's dedication to depicting migrant life in Spain rather than
   the trials and tribulations of the migratory process, or even frustrated migration
   attempts, as seen in these earlier publications.

6 Patera is one of many names for the various types of small boats used to try and access Spain by sea. Migrants choose this mode of transport in order to avoid the physical border controls in Ceuta and Melilla, or when taking the ferry across the Mediterranean between Morocco and Spain. While a mere 14 kilometers of water separate the two countries, pateras are ill-equipped for such a journey and, since the fortification of Ceuta and Melilla in 1993, have led to thousands of deaths per year. The *Missing Migrants Project* collects data on numerous migration routes worldwide. It offers the ability to focus on Mediterranean routes with a breakdown between the Eastern, Central, and Western. The Eastern route is primarily composed of boats departing Moroccan points for Spain.

7 All translations into English are my own unless otherwise indicated.

8 "Mas allá del testimonio, único y de gran interés, el valor de la obra radica en el tono irónico, incluso satírico en ocasiones, que Nini mantiene a lo largo del libro, como cuando, con conocimiento de la historia compartida, aborda cuestiones del discurso popular y xenófobo, como la de que estamos siendo de nuevo invadidos por los marroquíes y por los musulmanes en general" (Fernández Parrilla, 2015: 216) (Beyond the testimony it offers, one that is unique and of great interest, the value of the work [*Diario de un ilegal*] resides in the ironic tone, even satirical sometimes, that Nini maintains throughout the book. Like when, with knowledge of the shared history [of Spain and Morocco], he addresses issues of popular, xenophobic discourse, like that we are again being invaded by Moroccans and by Muslims in general).

9 See Flesler (2008: 194) and Álvarez (2013: 154).

10 Raquel Vega-Durán explains that by the end of the 1990s "this diverse and now visible economic migration was so remarkable that by 2000 Spaniards listed it on official surveys as their third most pressing concern, behind terrorism and unemployment" (Vega-Durán, 2016: 3). Referring to an INE (Instituto Nacional de Estadística) survey, Vega-Durán is referring to a shift in public opinion that can be seen as directly linked to the violent attacks on North African migrant groups in Terrassa, Barcelona in July 1999, and in El Ejido, Almería, in February 2000. For more on these brutal race riots see Flesler (2008: 2–3), Cornelius (2004: 418–19), and the SOS Racismo publication *El Ejido*.

11 In the Spanish version, Nini uses the word *sustento*, or sustenance, which I think is very appropriate here in terms of referring to basic survival or subsistence, but it does not translate well.

12 I have translated *generaciones nuevas* as "younger generations" rather than "new generations" for the coherence of the entire quote. However, I cite the turn-of-phrase, "new generations," in my analysis because it gets at the idea of the freshness – and subsequent obliviousness – of those who have only ever known democracy rather than those who grew up during the Franco dictatorship in Spain (1939–75) or the Moroccan monarchy of Hassan II (1961–99) followed by that of his son, Mohammed VI (1999–present).

13 In 2001, the INE reported that 247, 872 Moroccans were living (*empadronado*) in Spain, representing 15.8% of the total number of registered foreign residents – and the single largest group by country of origin. These numbers, of course,

only represent those who registered themselves in their municipality which many undocumented migrants are afraid to do.

References

Aja, E. (2012) *Inmigración y democracia*. Madrid: Alianza Editorial.

Álvarez, D. E. (2013) "Recording Daily Life in the Margins of History and of the Nation: Rachid Nini's Diary of a Clandestine Migrant," *Biography: An Interdisciplinary Quarterly*, 36(1), pp. 148–78. doi:10.1353/bio.2013.0002.

Álvarez-Blanco, P. and Gómez L-Quiñones, A. (eds) (2016) *La imaginación hipotecada: aportaciones al debate sobre la precariedad del presente*. Madrid: Libros en Acción.

Brancato, S. (2012) "Burning Heaven: Southern Europe in Maghrebi Migration Narratives," *Expressions Maghrebines*, 11(2), pp. 63–73.

Brown, W. (2010) *Walled States, Waning Sovereignty*. New York: Zone Books; Distributed by the MIT Press.

Butler, J. (2009) *Frames of War: When is Life Grievable?* London; New York: Verso.

Cachón Rodríguez, L. (2006) "Los inmigrantes en el mercado de trabajo en España," in Aja, E. and Arango, J. (eds) *Veinte años de inmigración en España: perspectivas jurídica y sociológica (1985–2004)*. Barcelona: Fundació CIDOB, pp. 175–201.

Campoy-Cubillo, A. (2012) *Memories of the Maghreb: Transnational Identities in Spanish Cultural Production*. New York: Palgrave Macmillan.

Carbonell i Cortés, O. (2003) "Semiotic Alteration in Translation: Othering, Stereotyping and Hybridization in Contemporary Translations from Arabic into Spanish and Catalan," *Linguistica Antverpiensia, New Series – Themes in Translation Studies*, 0(2), pp. 145–59.

Cornelius, W. A. (2004) "Spain: The Uneasy Transition from Labor Exporter to Labor Importer," in Cornelius, W. A. et al. (eds) *Controlling Immigration: A Global Perspective*. 2nd edition. Stanford, CA: Stanford University Press.

De Genova, N. (2017) "The Borders of 'Europe' and the European Question," in De Genova, N. (ed.) *The Borders of "Europe": Autonomy of Migration, Tactics of Bordering*. Durham, NC: Duke University Press, pp. 1–35.

Dotson-Renta, L. N. (2008) Translated Identities: Writing between Morocco and Spain," *The Journal of North African Studies*, 13(4), pp. 429–39. doi:10.1080/13629380801918905.

Fernández Parrilla, G. (2013) "Translating Modern Arabic Literature into Spanish," *Middle Eastern Literatures*, 16(1), pp. 88–101.

— (2015) "Emigración y literatura árabe: tránsitos identitarios," in *Emigracion y literatura: historias, experiencias, sentimientos*. Santiago de Compostela: Universidad de Santiago de Compostela, Servizo de Publicacións e Intercambio Científico (Actas del Coloquio Internacional Santiago de Compostela, 13–14 de noviembre de 2014, Catedra UNESCO 226 sobre Migracións), pp. 203–26.

Flesler, D. (2008) *The Return of the Moor: Spanish Responses to Contemporary Moroccan Immigration*. West Lafayette, Ind.: Purdue University Press.

Laitinen, I. (2007) "Frontex and African Illegal Migration to Europe," in Gebrewold-Tochalo, B. (ed.) *Africa and Fortress Europe: Threats and Opportunities.* Aldershot; Burlington, VT: Ashgate, pp. 127–38.

Lalami, L. (2011) "Journalist Rachid Nini Jailed in Morocco," *Newsweek*, June 26, www.newsweek.com/journalist-rachid-nini-jailed-morocco-67985 (Accessed July 8, 2020).

M'charek, A. (2020) "Harraga: Burning Borders, Navigating Colonialism," *The Sociological Review*, 68(2), pp. 418–34. doi:10.1177/0038026120905491.

Mora, M. (2002) "Un repaso a la España clandestine: el poeta marroquí Rachid Nini publica 'Diario de un ilegal'," *El País*, June 14, https://elpais.com/diario/2002/06/14/cultura/1024005609_850215.html (Accessed July 17, 2018).

Nini, R. (2002) *Diario de un ilegal.* Translated by G. Fernández Parrilla and M. Embarek López. Guadarrama (Madrid): ediciones del oriente y del mediterráneo.

Pack, S. D. (2019) *The Deepest Border: The Strait of Gibraltar and the Making of the Modern Hispano-African Borderland.* Stanford, CA: Stanford University Press.

Ricci, C. H. (2014) *¡Hay moros en la costa! Literatura marroquí fronteriza en castellano y catalán.* Madrid: Iberoamericana.

Ricci, C. H. (2017) "A Transmodern Approach to Afro-Iberian Literature," in Delgado, M., Lonsdale, L., and Muñoz-Basols, J. (eds) *The Routledge Companion to Iberian Studies.* London; New York: Routledge, pp. 583–95.

Seaton, A. (1981) *The Fall of Fortress Europe 1943–1945.* New York: Holmes & Meier Publishers, Inc.

Shepherd, N. M. (2012) "Migration and Mobility in Rachid Nini's *Diario de un ilegal*," *Vanderbilt e-Journal of Luso-Hispanic Studies*, 8, pp. 55–64.

Soto Bermant, L. (2014) "Consuming Europe: The Moral Significance of Mobility and Exchange at the Spanish–Moroccan Border of Melilla," The Journal of North African Studies, 19(1), pp. 110–129. doi:10.1080/13629387.2013.862776.

Suárez-Navaz, L. (2004) *Rebordering the Mediterranean: Boundaries and Citizenship in Southern Europe.* New York: Berghahn Books.

Vega-Durán, R. (2016) *Emigrant Dreams, Immigrant Borders: Migrants, Transnational Encounters, and Identity in Spain.* Lewisburg: Bucknell University Press.

Zea, L. (1970) *América en la historia.* Madrid: Editorial de la Revista de Occidente.

PART III

Migrating in Italian

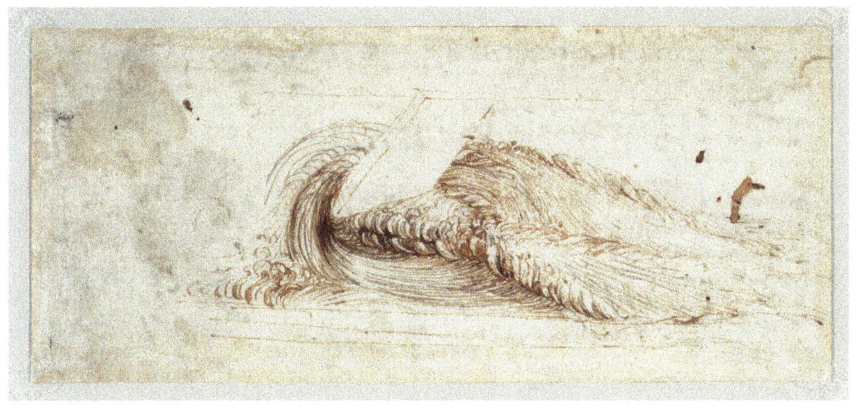

Part III frontispiece: Leonardo da Vinci, "A deluge," c. 1517–18. Black chalk, pen and ink, wash. 16.2 × 20.3 cm. Public Domain: Google Art Project, inv. no. 912380.

The peninsula and nearby islands now called Italy – what is a border and gateway between Europe and Africa – are the focus of these chapters. Their work reveals how this constructed political barrier is often problematized or undone in art and literature. In Chapter 4, Akash Kumar analyzes Sicily in the poetry of Ibn Hamdîs and Morocco in Dante's *Divine Comedy*, in part to decolonize the way that these medieval authors are too often separated and interpreted via the lens of nationalism and nineteenth-century disciplinary formations. Kumar examines the placement of Ibn Hamdîs' Arab poetry in Italian anthologies in terms of the complex relationship between linguistic and national identity. In Chapter 5, through comparison with more studied English-language migration literature anthologies, Saskia Elizabeth Ziolkowski focuses on a 2018 Italian collection of stories, *Anche Superman era un rifugiato: Storie vere di coraggio per un mondo migliore* (*Superman Was a Refugee Too: True Stories of Courage for a Better World*) to highlight how Italy's literary history, including the idea of Dante as a refugee, suggests the possibilities of multilingual world-making that offers a vision of inclusion beyond national boundaries, in which literature plays a central role. Ziolkowski foregrounds Italy's contemporary struggles to confront the colonialism, racism, and antisemitism of its past and present as it navigates its political and cultural position between Europe and Africa. In Chapter 6, Tenley Bick examines the Italian artist Mimmo Paladino's 2008 work, *Porta di Lampedusa, porta d'Europa* (Gateway to Lampedusa, Gateway to Europe), located on the Italian island of Lampedusa, which is closer to Tunisia than Sicily. Bick reveals how the artwork's placement, materials, and modifications, including interventions by other artists, reveal not only the complex, varied, and often conflicting reactions of Italians today to migration from Africa, but also the connections of these varied reactions in terms of Italian colonization and decolonization. Bick argues that Paladino's work should be understood in the framework of entropic monumentality; she shows the artwork's fluid, decolonizing power in contrast with monuments that exert power. All three authors discuss works – the poetry of Ibn Hamdîs and Dante, the collection *Anche Superman era un rifugiato*, and Paladino's *Porta di Lampedusa, porta d'Europa* – in terms of openness. They interpret Italy as a space that has always been a crossroads and created art that represents its hybridity.

S. Z.

4

"The world is my homeland": exile and migration, from Ibn Hamdîs to Dante

Akash Kumar

When 'Abd al-Jabbar ibn Hamdîs left Sicily as a young man in 1078, one wonders if he knew that he would never return. Indeed, Sicily figures in his poetry for the rest of his days as a homeland, a paradise taken from him by Norman infidels. His travel across the Mediterranean world, from his native Noto in southeastern Sicily to al-Mahdiyya in present-day Tunisia to Seville and back to North Africa again, trace a telling pattern of interconnectedness, as well as the difficulties of making one's way through the regional political turmoil of the eleventh and twelfth centuries.

It is by no means difficult to forge a connection across linguistic, cultural, and religious boundaries between Ibn Hamdîs and the poet of the *Commedia*. These were individuals forced from their homes who sought recourse in poetry, both as an expression of nostalgia and as a means to express their political vitriol in the hopes of changing their world. And the stakes of making this connection, far from being oriented to the long history of scholarship on Dante and Islam that sought to argue for or against the influence of the Islamic visionary tradition upon the writing of the *Divine Comedy*, instead rest on nuancing our view of the late Middle Ages in Italy in order to privilege the experience of migration and cultural alterity as lying at the heart of vernacular literary production.

The *dīwān* (anthology) of Ibn Hamdîs is vast, amounting to some 370 poetic compositions that range widely in genre. And it has not lacked for critical intervention and commentary, from the nineteenth-century historian Michele Amari, to modern scholars oriented to both its Sicilian character and its context in the wider span of neoclassical Arabic poetry.[1] But there remains work to be done in integrating the poetry of Ibn Hamdîs more fully into the tradition, both scholarly and pedagogical, of medieval Italian culture.

There are *qasidas* (odes) that directly evoke the memory of Sicily, which have become known as the *Siqilliyat*, but they are by no means uniform in their evocation of the land. Sometimes they are in the vein of a lament for the lost homeland, a celebration of its beauty, and the flowering of Arab culture before the Norman conquest; other times they are a bitter indictment of the Norman conquerors of the land and even of those Muslims who did not leave and perhaps did not resist enough for the poet's liking.

In a tender ode that celebrates the time of youth from the perspective of a more sober old age, the poet regales his audience with descriptions of beautiful young men and women, free-flowing wine, and the sensory delights of spices, jewels, and music. Only in the last lines does he finally reveal that he is not only beyond the halcyon days of youth but that he has been thrust out of his beloved homeland of *Siqiliyya*. "*Dakartu Siqiliyya wa al-ās yahayyaj lil-nafs tadakāraha*" "Sicilia mia. Disperato dolore / si rinova per te nella memoria" ("I remember Sicily, and pain is kindled in my soul at the memory of her") (Corrao, 2002: 161). I am citing the Arabic line alongside an Italian poetic translation and my own, more literal English translation of the Arabic original. I do so in order to adequately represent the multilingual nature of the sort of criticism that I seek to engage in, and hope that such an act might urge us to nuance our historical perspective. In order to emphasize a more recent form of reception, both scholarly and artistic, I am citing from the version of this *qasida* presented in Francesca Maria Corrao's *Poeti arabi di Sicilia*, an anthology that the noted Italian Arabist first assembled in 1987 and published with Mondadori.[2] Corrao provided a number of well-known Italian poets with her own translations of selected medieval Arabic poetry of Sicily by different poets and asked them to make their own poetic versions of them. The result is an important one, a way of emphasizing the historical presence of a different language and culture and inscribing it into the canon of Italian letters by means of employing well-known contemporary poets and artistic figures. This particular ode, for example, was poetically translated by Toti Scialoja, a poet of some note but a very well-known Roman painter and an established presence at the Academy of Fine Arts. We might thus think of a migration of poetry, inflected by translation yet transforming the notion of Italian identity.

Such attention to the multilingual strands of the Italian poetic tradition resonates with Valerio Magrelli's 2015 anthology *Millennium poetry: viaggio sentimentale nella poesia italiana*, in which the scholar and poet gathers the poetry that is most dear to him from across the centuries. After beginning with the anonymous ninth-century composition known as the *Indovinello veronese*, Magrelli inserts this very same poem by Ibn Hamdîs in the Scialoja translation that he borrows from Corrao's anthology. His justification underscores both the poet's liminal status as well as the importance of including him in such an anthology. Magrelli writes, "Ebbene, sia pure nella consapevolezza di compiere un arbitrio, ritengo che la decisione sia giustificata dal fatto che i versi di Ibn Hamdîs, oltre ad essere stati vergati in una parte di ciò che oggi chiamiamo Italia, proprio della sua perdita si parlano" ("And yet, even with the awareness of making an arbitrary call, I hold that the decision is justified by the fact that the verses of Ibn Hamdîs, beyond having been written in a part of that which we today call Italy, in fact speak of its very loss") (Magrelli 2015: 22).[3] Magrelli makes an important distinction between what was and what is, that which "oggi chiamiamo Italia" was by no means a unified and uniform political entity at the time of this poetic composition. He might overreach in speaking of all of this poet's verses as having been written *in* the part of present-day Italy that is the island of Sicily – perhaps some were in the poet's youth, others were certainly written in other places across the Mediterranean – but rightly shifts the focus to the status of Sicily as an island containing many Mediterranean identities that do not all fit so neatly into the narrative of one Italy.

Magrelli is keenly interested in this sort of complicating of national identity, and he makes this clear in the introduction to his anthology. He draws upon the work of the scholar Furio Brugnolo on foreign writers who have written in Italian through the centuries and his own experience as editor of a multilingual series of books, "Scrittori tradotti da scrittori" ("writers translated by writers"), in order to transform the moniker "poeti italiani" into something more capacious and "dare spazio alla poliglossia e al multiculturalismo" ("give space to multilingualism and multiculturalism") (Magrelli, 2015: 8). This leads him to not only include the ode of Ibn Hamdîs but also to anthologize Poliziano's Greek verse, Milton writing in Italian, and the like. In an especially significant move, Magrelli chooses to include a passage from Dante's *Commedia* not in Italian but in Occitan. He draws from the *Purgatorio* 26, where the Occitan poet Arnaut Daniel closes the canto by speaking in his own poetic language and thus continues in Dante's radical vernacular experiments of combining languages and cultures.

But before moving forward to Dante, I would like to return to Ibn Hamdîs and to the nature of his poetic engagement with the homeland that he left behind. There is perhaps a risk in emphasizing only the softer side of his nostalgia, one that feeds into the romantic and overly abstracted figure of the poet in exile. William Granara has focused attention on the later panegyrics and elegies of the corpus of Ibn Hamdîs in order to consider his "poetics of jihad," which he reads not as a theologically reductive stance of Islam against the world but rather as a means of motivating his audience to retake his homeland: "Ibn Hamdis's 'jihad' was not universal eternal, absolute or theological; it was a custom-made poetics to fit the particular history and geography of Sicily as extended metaphor for all that was transcendent to Islamic history and Arabic literature" (Granara, 2019: 118). This perspective is a salutary one. It prevents us from falling prey to the enervating charm of poetic nostalgia. Granara (2019: 131) posits that the poet's move from Seville to Ifriqiya around 1091, which coincided with the completion of the Norman conquest of Sicily (finally including Noto, his native city) meant that Ibn Hamdîs was in direct proximity with thousands of Muslim Sicilian refugees and thus turned his poetry in a more explicitly political direction.

And yet, we might also think about those that remained in Norman Sicily, indeed even those that were drawn to the court of Roger II. Abu 'Abdallah Muhammad al-Idrīsī, the cartographer born in Ceuta around 1100, is one such individual. His travels in Spain and North Africa mirror those of Ibn Hamdîs (though his journeys also extend to England, France, and Asia Minor), but far from feeling unwelcome or excluded from Palermo, he accepts the invitation of Roger II around 1138 to come to his court. His crowning achievement, in collaboration with other scholars of the court, was a geographical compendium and world map that came to be known as the Tabula rogeriana, or Book of Roger. It is marked by an elaborate introduction that lavishes praise on the Norman ruler, going so far as to call him one "who crafts so many positions of power and erects summits of high-mindedness that reach the stars."[4] I will return to the issue of title in a moment, but it is worth highlighting the contrast between Ibn Hamdîs and al-Idrīsī: one feels he must leave, never to return, and the other is invited and flourishes; one rails against the occupiers, the other lauds his patron as an exemplary ruler and intellectual.

And so, the poet might represent cultures in opposition, and the cartographer might celebrate the multicultural production of knowledge. Ibn Hamdîs longs for the Siqilliyya that was, al-Idrīsī praises Roger for the Sicily that is. The "truth" is undoubtedly somewhere in between. For Ibn Hamdîs, those who stayed and did not resist were traitors. But collaboration has its benefits, and might be said to feature more strongly in Roger II's court than in the subsequent Hohenstaufen rule of Frederick II. Much as we might point out certain multicultural aspects of the Federician court and uphold his epithet "stupor mundi" ("wonder of the world") to a degree, we must also see and acknowledge the expulsion of Muslims from the island of Sicily to the Pugliese town of Lucera from 1224 to 1239.[5]

And perhaps this is the benefit of a map such as that of al-Idrīsī: it takes us out from a focus on prominent individuals with whom it remains possible to make abstract and ambiguous the ideas of exile, migration, and cultural belonging and instead asks us to move our attention outward to a connected world in a form that might be unfamiliar to our eyes. The image of this particular map is the oldest surviving example, from a manuscript housed at the Bibliothèque nationale de France, but even this dates to circa 1300. This is a substantial remove from the original composition of the work in 1154. There is reference in the introduction to the work to a map that was inscribed in silver, but it has not survived. The map and the extensive work from which it springs serve an important role in complicating narratives of the backward nature of medieval cartography.

This map of the world is, to Western eyes, a map turned upside down. South is up, Mediterranean connectivity is privileged, and we must adjust our perspective accordingly. This is not atypical in the Islamic cartographic tradition that informs al-Idrīsī's work, but it nonetheless serves to defamiliarize and recontextualize the shape and orientation of the world. As Ahmad points out, there is evidence that al-Idrīsī uses a combination of Islamic and Western sources in his work, certainly for the various descriptions of the regions that rely on the observations of travelers, but even to the point of using different sets of measures, ones current in Arabic and others in Sicily at the time.[6] This is a move that might speak to a multiplicity of audiences, a combination of the local and the global. Such cultural fusion abounds in Arab-Norman architecture of the period, from pleasure palaces in Palermo, such as the Zisa, to the Palatine chapel that demonstrates Norman, Byzantine, and Arab influence.

But even from the standpoint of the title, the work of al-Idrīsī stands out with regard to pointing out the difficulty, the violence, the audacity of travel: *Nuzhat al-mushtāq fi'khtirāq al-afāq*, an entertainment for those who desire to cross the horizon. That word for crossing, *ikhtirāq*, might be rendered more viscerally and violently as a breaking. It is a telling combination of elements: pleasure, desire, and travel as a violent crossing of boundaries. Such an ambiguity resonates with the cross-cultural experience of migration and exile that I'd like to carry over to a reading of Dante.

In reading the trauma and difficulty of exile in Dante's poetry, I am doing the very opposite of something new. This has been a commonplace for centuries and is apparent even in the most superficial reading of the *Commedia*. But therein, perhaps, lies the problem. As Edward Said tellingly observed, "Exile is strangely compelling to think about but terrible to experience" (Said, 2000: 173). There is a disconnect between the abstract and the experience of trauma, and as much as we might romanticize the poet or writer in exile, we do an injustice to the reality of their suffering. In that well-known essay, "Reflections on Exile," he goes on to ask a pointed question:

> Is it not true that the views of exile in literature and, moreover, in religion obscure what is truly horrendous: that exile is irremediably secular and unbearably historical; that it is produced by human beings for other human beings; and that, like death but without death's ultimate mercy, it has torn millions of people from the nourishment of tradition, family, geography? (Said, 2000: 174)

It is certainly no coincidence that the cover of the volume in which this essay was collected, *Reflections on Exile and Other Essays*, is adorned with

Domenico Peterlin's 1865 painting, "Dante in Exile," and indeed Dante comes up later in this essay as an emblem of just how unpleasant and vindictive exiles can be ("Who but an exile like Dante, banished from Florence, would use eternity as a place for settling old scores?" (Said 2000: 182)). But Said's observation of the confluence of views on exile in literature and religion is a telling one; in both cases, there is a distancing to either privilege the art that is produced or the afterlife that might be obtained. In this regard, I wonder if it might be preferable to shift to the term migration. What might it mean to term Dante not as a poet in exile but as a migrant poet, or a poet of migration? For that matter, how might our attention to the cross-cultural affinities forged in the *Commedia* with regard to the suffering and value of others, those countless individuals torn "from the nourishment of tradition, family, geography" (Said, 2000: 174), be encouraged by such a shift?

In 1929, Erich Auerbach came out with his first academic book, *Dante: Poet of the Secular World* (though it was not until 1961 that this book was translated into English). It is a work that sets the stage for his magisterial *Mimesis* and it does so by holding, seemingly against the grain of reading him as a wholly religious poet, that Dante was a great realist author. In summing up the poem, he writes,

> Thus in truth the *Comedy* is a picture of earthly life. The human world in all its breadth and depth is gathered into the structure of the hereafter and there it stands: complete, unfalsified, yet encompassed in an eternal order; the confusion of earthly affairs is not concealed or attenuated or immaterialized, but preserved in full evidence and grounded in a plan which embraces it and raises it above all contingency. (Auerbach 2007: 133)

This emphasis on the real, on the stuff of history, means encouraging a reading of the poem that is not limited to theology alone. By that same token, as Auerbach calls Dante poet of the secular world, I would, in turn, call him poet of the decolonized world.

In this, I draw from the approach of Teodolinda Barolini who seeks to detheologize Dante in the interest of reading the poem narratologically. In her groundbreaking study of the poem, *The Undivine Comedy* (1992), Barolini writes, "detheologizing is a way of reading that attempts to break out of the hermeneutic guidelines that Dante has structured into his poem, hermeneutic guidelines that result in theologized readings whose outcome has been overdetermined by the author. Detheologizing, in other words, signifies releasing our reading of the *Commedia* from the author's grip, finding a way out of Dante's hall of mirrors" (Barolini, 1992: 17). In similar fashion, I hold that decolonizing Dante means releasing our reading from the thrall of nationalism that holds the poet of the *Commedia* to be the father of language, culture, and nation. As Saskia Ziolkowski points out in Chapter 5 (this volume), literature is vitally implicated in Italy's concept of itself, and the dark side of this link is perhaps most clear in the example that she provides of every issue of the Fascist magazine *La difesa della razza* (*The Defense of Race*) having a citation from Dante's *Commedia* on its cover.

Decolonizing Dante means opening our reading of the poem to global and cross-cultural currents. We might consider affinities with world authors, not in the vein of source study but with an expanded approach to the era in which Dante lived. Though a couple of centuries removed, Ibn Hamdîs functions marvelously in this respect. So, too, might the almost contemporary Indian poet Amīr Khusrō, whom I have been reading of late in concert with Dante.[7] We might interrogate more fully the presence of the medieval Mediterranean in hybrid language, references to trade routes and peoples across the globe, and consider tensions between local rootedness and the cultivation of an unmoored global self throughout Dante's corpus.

Such a global turn is one that Auerbach himself anticipated. In his 1952 essay "Philology and *Weltliteratur*," the German scholar turns to the medieval in his stirring conclusion, which promotes a philology that is not bound by nation alone. He writes, "In any event, our philological home is the earth: it can no longer be the nation' (Auerbach, 1969: 17). He goes on to assert that this is a return "in admittedly altered circumstances, to the knowledge that prenational medieval culture already possessed: the knowledge that the spirit [Geist] is not national" (Auerbach, 1969: 17). After naming medieval names that would support such separation on ideological grounds such as spiritual poverty and holding the material world to be alien, Auerbach then cites from Hugh of St. Victor's *Didascalion* the compelling lines, "Delicatus ille est adhuc cui patria dulcis est, fortis autem cui omne solum patria est, perfectus vero cui mundus totus exilium est" ("He for whom the homeland is sweet is delicate, he for whom every soil is homeland is stronger, but he for whom the whole world is exile is perfect") (Auerbach, 1969: 17).[8] Within this spiritual tradition, the ideal of exile and alienation is promoted with the perspective of the transitory nature of earthly things. Auerbach, however, has very different purposes. With the final lines of his essay, he turns this citation instead to the dismantling of wholly nationalist philology in favor of a more global embrace: "Hugo intended these lines for one whose aim is to free himself from a love of the world. But it is a good way also for one who wishes to earn a proper love of the world" (Auerbach, 1969: 17). This move implicates a link between the nationalist and the theological; it also reveals how these impulses might be subverted to more grounded and cosmopolitan purposes.

It is no coincidence that Said would use the very same lines from Hugh of St. Victor in his essay on exile some decades later. In fact, I cite from

Edward and Maire Said's translation of the Auerbach essay that was published in a 1969 issue of the journal *The Centennial Review*. Said acknowledges Auerbach as his source of this citation, and writes:

> Erich Auerbach, the great twentieth-century literary scholar who spent the war years as an exile in Turkey, has cited this passage as a model for anyone wishing to transcend national or provincial limits. Only by embracing this attitude can a historian begin to grasp human experience and its written records in their diversity and particularity; otherwise he or she will remain committed more to the exclusions and reactions of prejudice than to the freedom that accompanies knowledge. (Said, 2000: 184)[9]

Said elaborates on what Auerbach alluded to: that adopting this globally nuanced perspective is vital for us as scholars to be able to truly and freely read that which we study.

And with that I would like to turn to such a globally oriented reading of Dante as poet of migration. It was quite telling to me that Theresa May in an October 2016 speech at the height of Brexit debates proclaimed, "But if you believe you are a citizen of the world, you are a citizen of nowhere. You don't understand what citizenship means." May seemed to be calling out the "elite," but her remarks of course implicate the thrall of nationalism. Such a stance flies in the face of Dante's expanded notion of citizenship, one that holds it up as a virtue but shifts the paradigm of *civitas* to encompass a more diversified composition. In his treatise on vernacular eloquence, *De vulgari eloquentia* (1.6.3), Dante notably writes, "Nos autem, cui mundus est patria velut piscibus equor" ("To me, however, the whole world is homeland, as the ocean is to fish") (Alighieri, 1996: 13). Dante makes clear that he holds the world to be his homeland, even though he loves his native city of Florence so much that he suffers unjust exile for it. In making this move within the grounded context of his thoughts on language, he opposes his worldly conception and emphasis on reason to the provincial belief of those who reside in the village of Pietramala who think so much of their own language that they believe it to be the universal mother tongue that Adam himself spoke.

The philosopher Kwame Anthony Appiah, in response to May, writes, "Real cosmopolitanism is not a privilege; it is an obligation. It does not belong to the rarefied circles of some frequent flyer upper class. It belongs to anyone who cares about global justice, about the environment, about the alleviation of strife and carnage beyond our immediate national borders" (Appiah, 2016).[10] In this regard, when Dante sees home as Morocco at the end of *Purgatorio* 4, when Beatrice tells him that he will be "cive / di quella Roma onde Cristo è romano" ("citizen of that Rome where Christ is a Roman") in *Purgatorio* 32.101–2, when he speaks to Charles Martel about global citizenship in *Paradiso* 8, he is embodying Appiah's sense of cosmopolitanism.[11]

In closing, I'd like to turn to a reading of Morocco across *Inferno* 26, which recounts the last voyage of Ulysses, and *Purgatorio* 4, a canto of difficult climbing, a playful yet bittersweet reunion with an old friend, and astronomical reckoning. These two moments of the poem are the only times that the word "Morocco" comes up. Both of these canti also celebrate and temper desire as a quintessential Dantean theme. From Ulysses' "folle volo" ("mad flight," *Inferno* 26.125) across the sea, to Dante-character's arduous flight up the mountain of Purgatory ("ma qui convien che l'om voli" ("here, a man must fly") *Purgatorio* 4.27), there is a Mediterranean bond that stretches across cultures and centuries to link these journeys that endeavor to go beyond prescribed limits.

From the very first moment of Ulysses' recounting of his final voyage, one that goes beyond the limits of the epic tradition before Dante, we have a sense of Mediterranean history pulsing in the names and places evoked. The voice that comes forth from the flame lays out the voyage home that will not last, saying, "Quando / mi diparti' da Circe che sottrasse / me più d'un anno là presso a Gaeta / prima che sì Enëa la nomasse" ("When / I sailed away from Circe, who'd beguiled me / to stay more than a year there, near Gaeta – / before Aeneas gave that place its name") (*Inferno* 26.90–3). In the intersecting epic voyages of Ulysses and Aeneas, we see an awareness of names and the cultural weight they carry. That place where Ulysses was kept existed before Aeneas named it after his nursemaid, as told by Virgil's *Aeneid*. And so, indeed, we have an awareness of the cultural mixing poetically narrated by these epics, as Greek gives way to Trojan and then Roman.

When Ulysses lays out the geographical parameters of his final voyage beyond the western limit of the world, we find a way of connecting across multiple shores of the Mediterranean. He recounts, "L'un lito e l'altro vidi infin la Spagna, / fin nel Morrocco, e l'isola d'i Sardi, / e l'altre che quel mare intorno bagna" ("I saw as far as Spain, far as Morocco, / along both shores; I saw Sardinia / and saw the other islands that the sea bathes") (*Inferno* 26.103–5). Ulysses sees one shore and the other, and we find still more specificity in the verses that follow as he recounts that he passed the columns of Hercules and left behind sight of both Seville and Ceuta.

These places named – Spain and Morocco, Seville and Ceuta – of course take us back to the movements of Ibn Hamdîs and al-Idrīsī across their Mediterranean worlds. Within this volume, we have the stunning artistic work *Cornered* by Raquel Salvatella de Prada that represents the status of Ceuta, in particular, as a place marked by the history of migration. The installation poignantly captures the struggles and frustrations of contemporary migrants, but it also urges us to consider the long history of such acts of crossing over, as we might see evoked in Dante's Ulysses.

The scholar Maria Corti, some decades ago, argued that we might consider this moment of *Inferno* 26 through the perspective of what she termed "interdiscorsività," a way of reading common tropes across a cultural heritage that is not predicated upon the argument that there is a direct source of transmission to be found. This is an important distinction: Corti claims that the shared prohibition of passing beyond the Strait of Gibraltar points to "the striking relationship between the Christian and Arab worlds at the outset" – not that the presence of a statue in Morocco warning travelers to go no further in the work of Arab geographers served as a source for Dante, but rather that attention to this shared cultural interest in defining the limits of the world merits attention and calls out the connective tissue of Islamic, Christian, and Greco-Roman thought (Corti, 2007: 59).[12] Al-Idrīsī's map provides an interesting perspective in this regard: on the western edge, we see some islands that are likely the Canary Islands. Indeed, in the *Nuzhat al-mushtāq*, with that suggestive title implicating the violence of the going beyond the limits that is inherent in the experience of travel, we have a story of travelers going to those islands and making a successful return.

Such an archipelagic focus might also bring us to the work of Édouard Glissant. In the grand anthology of poetry he assembled very close to the end of his life, *La terre, le feu, l'eau, et les vents: une anthologie de la poésie du tout-monde*, Glissant includes part of *Inferno* 26 as somehow important and emblematic of his poetic and philosophical notion of "tout-monde" that urges us to rethink categories of cultural identity.[13] This act of anthologizing creates what Alexandre Leupin calls a "Glissant canon," and might be considered alongside Valerio Magrelli's act of anthologizing, which includes Ibn Hamdîs as an Italian poet and chooses to emphasize Dante's linguistic experimentalism instead of his Tuscan verse (Leupin, 2021: 131).

I turn now to the second and final mention of "Morrocco" in Dante's *Commedia*. *Purgatorio* 4 is a canto filled to the brim: there is the difficult climb in which we feel the physical presence of the mountain, the erudite conversation on issues of astronomy, time, and celestial positioning, and the playful reunion with an old friend. Though the canto opens with a universalizing simile of human experience wherein great delight or great pain will cause us to neglect all else in our view, it quickly moves to characterize the arduous ascent up a steep mountain path by grounding it in intensely local experience and topography:

> Vassi in Sanleo e discendesi in Noli,
>   montasi su in Bismantova e 'n Cacume

con esso i piè; ma qui convien ch' om voli;
dico con l'ale snelle e con le piume
del gran disio, di retro a quel condotto
che speranza mi dava e facea lume. (*Purgatorio* 4.25–30)

(San Leo can be climbed, one can descend / from Noli, and ascend Bismantova
/ and Cacume with feet alone, but here / I had to fly: I mean with rapid wings
/ and pinions of immense desire, behind / the guide who gave me hope and
was my light)

By focusing on the steep paths to get to hill towns such as San Leo near
Rimini or Noli (near Savona), Dante seeks to actualize his otherworldly
travel experience for a carefully chosen vernacular audience. But even in
these two choices, he is ranging geographically in the north from eastern
Italy to the northwest of the Riviera. From hill towns he moves to geological
features: Bismantova is a rock formation in the Apennines of Reggio Emilia
(due west of Bologna) and Cacume represents a move decidedly south to a
peak in the province of Lazio (between Rome and Naples). With its clear
tie back to Ulysses in the language of flight and longing, those rapid wings
and feathers of great desire, the statement by Dante that he must fly up the
steep mountain path is given local relevance across the length and breadth
of the Italian peninsula.

In this regard, there is a contrast between this first part of the canto and
the great astronomical theme that dominates much of the rest of it, which
enforces a planetary perspective in considering the position of the sun and
seasons in the southern hemisphere. When Dante, exhausted from such a
grueling climb, pauses to look back, he realizes that the sun is not where
he expects it to be in the sky. Virgil explains to him that he must think
globally, putting Jerusalem at one antipode and the mountain that they are
climbing on the other. In the same way that Ulysses' mad flight through
the Mediterranean vacillated between one shore and the other ("l'un lito
e l'altro" in *Inferno* 26.103), so too does Virgil's explanation rely on a
formal equivalency that has the path of the sun pass by Jerusalem on the
south and the mountain of Purgatory on the north. As shores relate, so do
hemispheres.

We might look at this alternation between intensely local references to
Italian geography and the planetary, celestial perspective that emerges in
this astronomical consideration through the lens of world literature. Neil
Lazarus argues for a "local cosmopolitanism" that sets upon readers the
task of situating themselves in context (Lazarus, 2011: 119). Jahan Ramazani
asks whether poetry might complicate assumptions about localities, and
sets the task of reconfiguring before us: "It may be time to explore such
questions from the perspective of a polytemporal, polyspatial poetics and

consider a different way of understanding poetry's relation to place, particularly as the transnational turn in the humanities reconfigures our understanding of how localities are enmeshed within the global" (Ramazani, 2020: 55).

I believe we can read the end of *Purgatorio* 4 in light of this critical perspective, and indeed that it is vital to apply such reading practices beyond the confines of the modern and postcolonial. On the one hand, this canto has the intensely local and personal flair of a reunion with Dante's Florentine friend Belacqua, a maker of musical instruments who is defined by his endearing laziness. On the other hand, at the very end of the canto, is Virgil's reminder that the climb must go on in the form of a time check: it is noon here and night is falling on Morocco.

In the reunion with Belacqua, there is sweetness and playful banter: he calls Dante out for his exhaustion at the climb, Dante calls him out for his laziness. And Belacqua hits the nail on the head in jabbing at Dante's insatiable curiosity to know how things work. Belacqua's was a young death and this reunion, like those with other friends in *Purgatorio* such as Casella in *Purgatorio* 2 and Forese Donati in *Purgatorio* 23, is a way for Dante to go home to the Florence that he has lost through exile. The way that such purgatorial reunions are received and adapted, as Ziolkowski brings to our attention in Paolo di Paolo's story in *Anche Superman era rifugiato*, work to enhance our reading of Dante as migrant and refugee.

But the shift to a planetary perspective at the end of the canto is a telling one. It is a return to the language of Ulysses' travel, our second and final mention of Morocco in the *Commedia*:

> E già il poeta innanzi mi saliva,
> e dicea: "Vienne omai; vedi ch'è tocco
> meridïan dal sole e a la riva
> cuopre la notte già col piè Morrocco". (Purgatorio 4.136–9)

> (And now the poet climbed ahead, before me, / and said: "It's time; see the meridian / touched by the sun; elsewhere along the Ocean, / night has now set foot on Morocco.")

Being on the other side of the world has a curious effect. We have to account for jet lag, calculate time relative to our present position and the home that we've left behind. But that home is not named Florence or any of the Italian toponyms that we have encountered earlier in the canto. Instead, it is a place on the other side of the Mediterranean. In the embrace of travel and the necessary breaking of his cultural horizons, perhaps Dante has found a new home in Morocco and the sea that bathes it.

Dante's global perspective that enables him to see Morocco as home connects not just to his expanded planetary awareness in cartographic terms, but also to his radical stances of sympathy for the cultural other. In *Paradiso* 19, we have three groups named that might be traditionally excluded from a Christian idea of virtue that might merit salvation: Indians, Ethiopians, and Persians. The searing question posed about the justice in condemning a virtuous man born on the banks of the Indus river based solely on his lack of knowledge of Christianity finds a radical response in the statement that an Ethiopian might be saved while the Christians going around saying "Christ, Christ," might not be (*Paradiso* 19.109–14). We then find a shift to the idea that Persians might put Christian rulers to shame, and a catalog of the misdeeds of European rulers that extends for a full 36 verses (*Paradiso* 19.112–48), forming the acrostic L-U-E (a Latinate word for plague) and so indicting political misrule as a plague upon the people. The end of the canto is thus an important recentering of these issues of cultural difference and merit in a grounded sociopolitcal reality.

This, I hold, is what Dante asks us to do in mapping the metaphysical and the empirical together, and it is not divorced from the poem's primary ethical concerns but rather related to what Theodore Cachey calls the "cartographic impulse."[14] We might see the results of this practice in the 1544 treatise by Pierfrancesco Giambullari, *Del sito, fórma, & misúre*

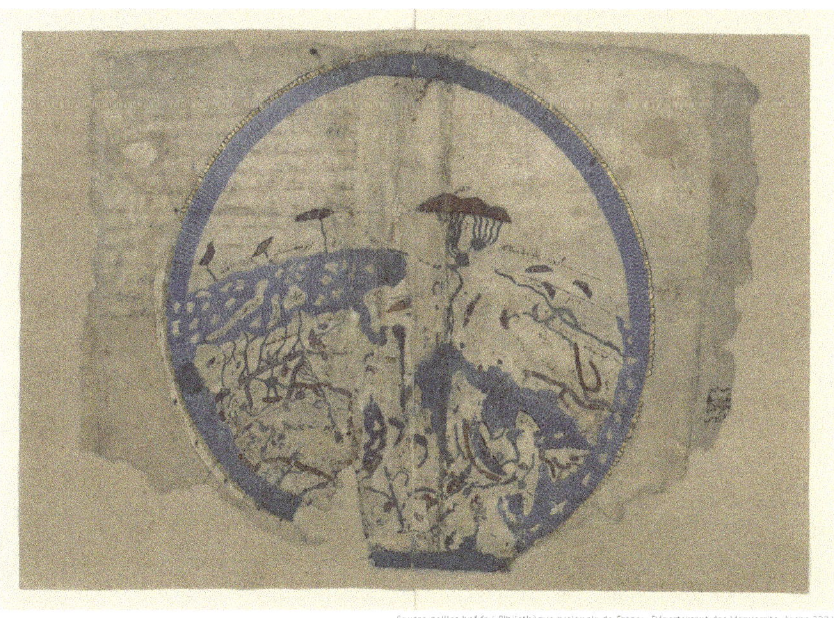

Figure 4.1 al-Idrīsī's world map, BNF MS Arabe 2221, fol. 3v-4r. Courtesy of gallica.bnf.fr.

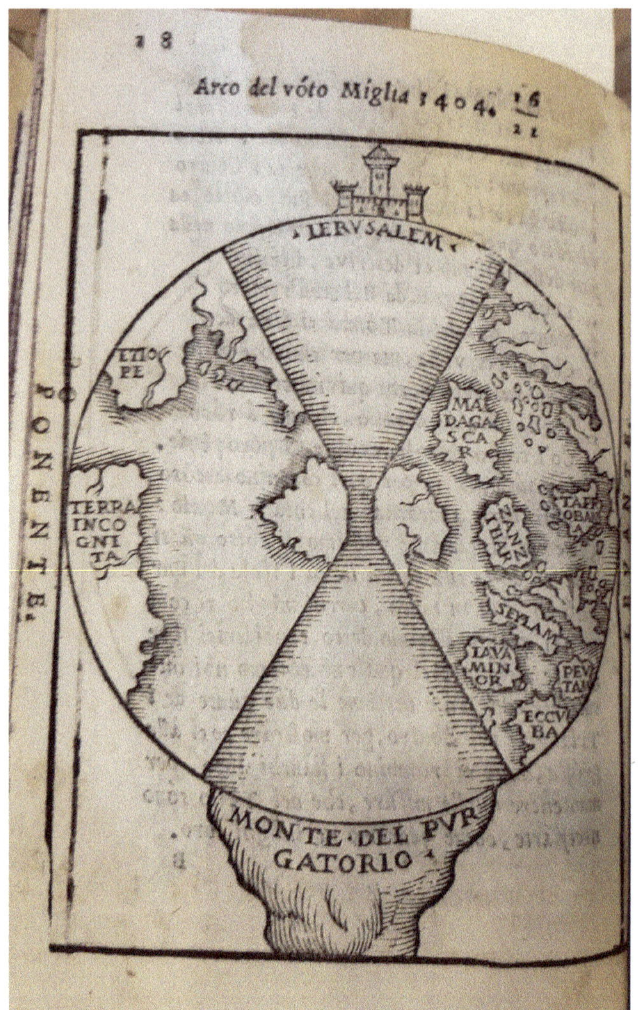

Figure 4.2 Pierfrancesco Giambullari's world map with Inferno and Purgatorio. *Del sito, fórma, & misúre déllo Inférno di Dante* (Florence, 1544). Image courtesy of Lilly Library, Indiana University, Bloomington.

déllo Inférno di Dante (*On the site, form and measurements of Dante's Inferno*). On page 18 of this treatise, we find a map of the globe that seeks to superimpose Dante's poetic geography on to the real world so that, in addition to the landmasses, we have a view inside to the pit of hell and we have the mountain of Purgatory rising upward in the southern hemisphere. While there was much Renaissance interest in mapping and measuring Dante's afterlife, this map is atypical, standing apart from many others that seek to depict the structures themselves without a thought to the globe on which they poetically reside. In the Lilly Library catalog, which is where I had occasion to examine this volume some time ago, there is an annotation that cites collector Henry Harrisse's 1866 *Bibliotheca americana vetustissima*, where he writes that it should be placed among books relating to America because of this map.[15] Indeed, to the left, we find Ethiopia and Terra Incognita, a suggestive grouping that asks us to consider how cultural difference and pushing beyond the limits of the known world are linked in the poem and occasion those moments of radical affinity, global perspective, and cultural syncretism. Giambullari's map, in other words, urges us to see the connected world as Dante did, to consider its limits and embrace its migrations.

Notes

1 For an overview of Ibn Hamdîs in modern scholarship, see Granara (2019), especially pp. 99–104. Granara's book is an invaluable and incisive study of Muslim Sicily as seen by poets, chroniclers, jurists, and beyond.

2 I am citing, however, from the more recent reissue of this anthology, Corrao (2002: 161). This anthology is notable for its insistence not only on the Italian poetic translations assembled but also for including the original Arabic text on the facing page.

3 Translation is mine.

4 See Granara (2019: 143–4) for the translation of this portion of the introduction. See also Mallette (2005: 146–8) for another portion of the introduction that focuses attention on the intellectually sound methodology apparently used by Roger to make the work happen. Mallette's work in considering Sicily through its transition from Arab to Norman to Hohenstaufen rule and the multilingual traditions that are manifest remains a valuable antidote to monolingual approaches of reading late medieval Italy.

5 On the complexities of this process and the ambivalence of Frederick's relation to Muslims, see Metcalf (2009: 275–94).

6 See Ahmad (1992: 160).

7 For my work on this subject, see Kumar (2021).

8 Auerbach is citing specifically from *Didascalion* 3.20. Translation is mine.

9 For more on Auerbach's Turkish period and the writing of *Mimesis*, see Konuk (2010).

10 Cosmopolitanism has of course long been on Appiah's mind. See Appiah (2006) and (2019).

11 All citations of the Italian text of the *Commedia* follow Petrocchi 1994. English translations are from Allen Mandelbaum's 1982–86 text (New York: Bantam),

available at Digital Dante: https://digitaldante.columbia.edu/. Accessed February 16, 2022.

12 I cite from the English translation of Corti's essay (Corti, 2007). This particular work on Ulysses and the Pillars of Hercules extends back to her 1993 *Percorsi dell'invenzione*.

13 My thanks to Helen Solterer (Duke) for this reference. There is much to be gained in considering Dante through the perspective of Glissant's various formulations of language and world philosophy, from "'creolisation' to 'Relation' to 'tout-monde.'"

14 See Cachey (2010: 325). Cachey makes a key point in emphasizing Dante's own cartographic leanings, as opposed to the position that mapping Dante's afterlife was a later Renaissance interest.

15 I am grateful to the Lilly Library (IU Bloomington) for being able to examine this early print book and for their permission to reproduce the image here.

References

Ahmad, S. Maqbul (1992) "Cartography of al-Sharīf al-Idrīsī" in J. B. Harley and David Woodward, eds. *The History of Cartography*, vol. 2, book 1, pp. 156–72. Chicago, IL: University of Chicago Press.

Alighieri, Dante (1994) *La Comedia secondo l'antica vulgata*, 2nd edition. Giorgio Petrocchi, ed. Milan: Mondadori.

— (1996) *Dante: De vulgari eloquentia*. Steven Botterill, ed. and trans. Cambridge: Cambridge University Press.

Appiah, Kwame Anthony (2006) *Cosmopolitanism: Ethics in a World of Strangers*. New York: W. W. Norton.

— (2016) "'Mrs May, we are all citizens of the world,' says philosopher." BBC News, October 29, www.bbc.com/news/uk-politics-37788717. Accessed July 1, 2021.

— (2019) *The Lies that Bind: Rethinking Identity*. New York: Liveright.

Auerbach, Erich (1969) "Philology and 'Weltliteratur'," Maire and Edward Said, trans. *The Centennial Review* 13.1.

Auerbach, Erich (2007) *Dante, Poet of the Secular World*. Ralph Manheim, trans. New York: New York Review of Books.

Barolini, Teodolinda (1992) *The Undivine Comedy: Detheologizing Dante*. Princeton, NJ: Princeton University Press.

Cachey, Jr., Theodore J. (2010) "Cartographic Dante." *Italica*, 87, pp. 325–54.

Corrao, Francesca Maria, ed. (2002) *Poeti arabi di Sicilia*. Messina: Mesogea.

Corti, Maria (2007) "Dante and Islamic Culture." Kyle M. Hall, trans. *Dante Studies*, 125, pp. 57–75.

Glissant, Édouard (2010) *La Terre, le feu, l'eau, et les vents: une anthologie de la poésie du tout-monde*. Paris: Galaade.

Granara, William (2019) *Narrating Muslim Sicily: War and Peace in the Medieval Mediterranean World*. London: I. B. Tauris.

Konuk, Kader (2010) *East West Mimesis: Auerbach in Turkey*. Palo Alto, CA: Stanford University Press.

Kumar, Akash (2021) "Vernacular Hybridity Beyond Borders: Dante, Amīr Khusrō, Sandow Birk" in Nick Havely, Jonathan Katz, and Richard Cooper, eds. *Dante Beyond Borders: Contexts and Reception*. Cambridge: Legenda.

Lazarus, Neil (2011) "Cosmopolitanism and the Specificity of the Local in World Literature," *The Journal of Commonwealth Literature*, 46.1, pp. 119–37.

Leupin, Alexandre (2021) *Édouard Glissant, Philosopher: Heraclitus and Hegel in the Whole-World*. New York: SUNY Press.

Magrelli, Valerio, ed. (2015) *Millennium poetry: viaggio sentimentale nella poesia italiana*. Bologna: Il Mulino.

Mallette, Karla (2005) *The Kingdom of Sicily, 1100–1250: A Literary History*. Philadelphia, PA: University of Pennsylvania Press.

Metcalf, Alex (2009) *The Muslims of Medieval Italy*. Edinburgh: Edinburgh University Press, 2009.

Petrocchi, Giorgio ed. (1994) *La Comedia secondo l'antica vulgata*, 2nd edition. Milan: Mondadori.

Ramazani, Jahan (2020) *Poetry in a Global Age*. Chicago, IL: University of Chicago Press.

Said, Edward (2000) *Reflections on Exile and Other Essays*. Cambridge, MA: Harvard University Press.

5

Superman in Italy: the power of refugee artists

Saskia Elizabeth Ziolkowski

This chapter examines an Italian collection of refugee stories from 2018, *Anche Superman era un rifugiato: Storie vere di coraggio per un mondo migliore* (*Superman Was a Refugee Too: True Stories of Courage for a Better World*) to analyze key elements that Italian literature brings to discourses about migration literature. With the increase of migration to Italy, and the harsh Bossi-Fini immigration laws of 2002, a growing number of scholars have examined migration in Italian literary and cultural studies, but English-language anthologies and criticism still often overlook Italian work. Restricting analyses of literature in Italian to just Italian studies contributes to an international power imbalance, which is reflected not only in migratory movements, but also literary studies as a field. Arguing for the importance of including untranslated works in debates about migration literature, I put *Anche Superman era un rifugiato* in conversation with two well-known collections, *The Displaced: Refugee Writers on Refugee Lives* (2018) and *The Penguin Book of Migration Literature: Departures, Arrivals, Generations, Returns* (2019), in order to trace how Italy is positioned in these three migration literature anthologies and to show how Italy decenters ideas of one-directional migratory movement.

The English-language collections share various qualities with *Anche Superman era un rifugiato* that underscore shared investments in challenging concepts of migration but also shed light on the Italian collection's unique configuration. *The Displaced* is a collection of contemporary essays edited by Viet Thanh Nguyen, the award-winning author of *The Sympathizer* (2015) and *The Committed* (2021). *Anche Superman era un rifugiato* is a collection of stories co-edited by Igiaba Scego, the award-winning author of *Oltre Babilonia* (2008), *Adua* (2015), and *La linea del colore* (2020). Nguyen and Scego's collections emphasize refugees as artists and authors, *The Displaced* in its choice of contributors and *Anche Superman era un rifugiato* with the subjects of its stories. Nguyen and Scego's own novels also bear important thematic relationships to their edited volumes: both authors' fictional and non-fictional work have been central for motivating public conversations about racism and migration, primarily in the United States for Nguyen and in Italy for Scego. The Italian writer has also characterized her last three novels as a "trilogia della violenza coloniale" (Scego, 2020: 360) (trilogy about colonial violence). Scego aims to decolonize the space of Italian literature, not only with her own writing but also with her edited volumes (Ferracuti, 2020: 49): *Italiani per vocazione* (2005, with works by authors who moved to Italy), *Future: Il domani narrato dalle voci di oggi* (2019, a collection by Afro-Italian women authors), and *Africana: Raccontare il Continente al di là degli stereotipi* (2021, works representing Africa's contemporary diversity), as well as *Anche Superman era un rifugiato*, which she co-edited with the UNHCR (UN Refugee Agency, the office of the United Nations High Commissioner for Refugees).

Anche Superman era un rifugiato and *The Penguin Book of Migration Literature* emphasize the long history of migration in literature. *The Penguin Book of Migration Literature* represents a selection of migration literature from the eighteenth to the twenty-first century, while *Anche Superman era un rifugiato* portrays the journeys of refugees from antiquity to today. The two collections call attention to space as well as time, since their works purposefully map multiple movements of people from around the world. These volumes' global structures underscore migration literature's transnational nature. While constructing a vision of what migration literature means, these anthologies raise questions about what the literary can and cannot accomplish, especially in terms of understanding migrant experiences in order to change the treatment of people who cross borders.

Italy is often described as a country that changed from being one of emigrants, with Italians moving to America or northern Europe to find better economic prospects in the nineteenth and early twentieth centuries, to one of immigrants, where an estimated 8% of the population today is foreign born.[1] From the 1870s onward, about twenty-six million people left Italy (Fiore, 2017: 4; Gabaccia, 2003: 1).[2] Providing the exact numbers for Italian migration is difficult, not only because of the challenges of precisely counting human movement but also because many emigrants returned to Italy or emigrated multiple times. Teresa Fiore's *Pre-Occupied Spaces: Remapping Italy's Transnational Migrations and Colonial Legacies* examines the challenges of characterizing Italy and migration: she notes that in 2014 there were about the same number of Italians living abroad as the number of foreigners living in Italy (Fiore, 2017: 3), which undermines narratives that frame Italy as simply transitioning from a country of emigrants to one of immigrants in the 1970s and 1980s.

Before the citizenship laws of 1992 and the Bossi-Fini migration laws a decade later, Italy's history of emigration provided a reason to expect that

Italy would be more welcoming than other European countries to immigrants.[3] In the introduction to his 2001 collection, *ItaliAfrica: Bridging Continents and Cultures*, Sante Matteo directly links African immigrants in Italy to Italian immigrants in the United States, surmising that Africans in the peninsula, like Italian Americans, would lose their minority status over time: "The status of African immigrants in Italy is more akin to that of Italian immigrants in America at the turn of the last century than to that of previous Africans who left their homes as slaves or ex-colonials" (Matteo, 2001: 6). Italy's history, geography, and politics highlight the complexity of describing migratory movement, and the issues with assuming all countries follow similar models in terms of migration.

In part because of Italy's proximity to Africa, the co-editor of *Anche Superman era un rifugiato* Scego has argued that the country has a fear of being Black.[4] Scego's statement can be approached from a variety of angles, including racism, politics, or geography. Jennifer Gugliemo and Salvatore Salerno's *Are Italians White? How Race is Made in America* explores how Italians are situated in racial constructions and exposes the contradictions involved in establishing racial differences. Camilla Hawthorne examines the racism of Italy's debated citizenship policies, which prioritize bloodlines (*ius sanguinis*) and the children of older Italians (even if they have never been to Italy), rather than those born in Italy (*ius soli*).[5] Melissa Coburn has succinctly brought together many of the specificities of Italy and discrimination: "Italians have all, at some point, been the target of racializing discrimination. As an example of such discrimination, consider the prejudicial saying that 'Africa begins at the Alps.' The imagined border with Africa shifts from one interlocutor to the next: 'Africa begins at Rome' or 'Africa begins at Naples' are equally commonplace expressions that may still be heard today" (Coburn, 2013: 13).[6] Calling attention to Italy's long history as a place of transition, Scego argues that Italy must confront its racism in order to move forward: "In its heart, as a Mediterranean state, Italy knows itself to be a country with strong links to Africa. It could be the perfect pivot between continents, between Europe and Africa, yet it persists in denying its mixed-race identity as a country made of diversity. Everyone has passed through here: Arabs, Austrians, Africans, the French, the Spanish. This is Italy, a mixture of different blood and skins. When it finally accepts this identity, it will once again be the *Bel Paese* we all love" (Scego, 2018c). *Anche Superman era un rifugiato* contributes to understanding Italy as a pivot between countries and continents.

In the first section of this chapter, "The paratexts of migration anthologies: locating Italy," I compare *Anche Superman era un rifugiato* with the more discussed English-language works to show the importance of considering migration from Italy's position, instead of, for instance, that of the United

States or United Kingdom. In the second section, "Migrant, refugee, and in exile: a long literary history," I consider the uses of the terms "migrant," "refugee," and "in exile" in these anthologies, noting how the development of national identities and literary histories influence critical understandings of these terms. The importance of Italy's pre-national medieval literature continues to shape both how more recent migrant writers engage Italy's literary traditions and also how Italian literature is incorporated in anthologies. Focusing on the contrasts between *Anche Superman era un rifugiato* and the English-language anthologies, I will also analyze differing concepts of authorial identity. In the third section, "From Superman to 1938: literary collections as dialogues," I discuss how *Anche Superman era un rifugiato* reveals the connections between colonialism, migration, racism, and anti-semitism in Italian history and criticism. Like other chapters in this volume, the analysis of *Anche Superman era un rifugiato* focuses on the significance of including a broad historical view of migration, the possibilities of Romance-language spaces to offer alternative perspectives to those grounded in Anglophone ones, and the potentialities of art and literature in critical conceptions of migration.

The paratexts of migration anthologies: locating Italy

Literary anthologies make arguments through their organization and selections. They may make visible a previously ignored connection between authors' works, propose a canon, or formulate a new field. In the early twentieth century, English poetry collections helped define modernist verse.[7] In part as a response to the framing of migration as a series of crises and the dehumanization of refugees in the media, numerous recent anthologies offer different ideas of migration through literature.[8] Even limiting the selection to just anthologies in Italian or English from 2018 and 2019 generates a lengthy list beyond *Anche Superman era un rifugiato*, *The Displaced*, and *The Penguin Book of Migration Literature*.[9] These anthologies vary in terms of who is included in the categories "migrant," "refugee," or "in exile," as well as what migration literature itself encompasses. Often framed as a point of transition rather than a destination, the descriptions of Italy in these works reveal connections between the places in a migrant's journey and between the journeys of migrants from different periods, from Aeneas to Dante to today, raising the question of who is included in this category and why.

With its layered construction, *Anche Superman era un rifugiato* underscores connections between migrants over time. Each story combines the narrative of a recent refugee with that of an internationally known one from the past.

These famous refugees' stories predate this century and include fictional figures, such as Aeneas, Hercule Poirot, and Superman, as well as non-fictional ones, such as Dante, Marc Chagall, and Hannah Arendt. The Italian authors of the stories spoke to the contemporary refugees, whose words are often directly cited in the works. The authors of *Anche Superman era un rifugiato* take a variety of approaches to combining the stories from the past with those of the present, as well as how they incorporate their conversations with the twenty-first-century refugees. The recent refugee's phrases may be woven into the story or italicized to differentiate them from the author's narration. The refugee from the past may be a figure of inspiration, may communicate in a dream, may appear as the author of a book, may transform into a bird, or the story may be told in parallel to the twenty-first century refugee's story. The variety of ways that the past – fictional and non-fictional – is incorporated into the stories emphasizes how literature inspires, changes, or speaks to the present and future, in terms of an individual and collectively. With their pairs of refugee characters, the collection is purposefully constructed around literature's ability to serve as a bridge between people from different time periods and places.

The recent refugees of *Anche Superman era un rifugiato*, like the more famous ones, are subjects, not only because of their difficult journeys, but also because of what they have created. The famous characters are, in order of appearance, Rudolf Nureyev, Dante Alighieri, Marlene Dietrich, Nadia Comăneci, Miriam Makeba, Joseph Conrad, Marc Chagall, Hannah Arendt, Freddie Mercury, Aeneas, Chico Buarque, Superman, and Hercule Poirot. Most of the twenty-first-century refugees are also artists, dancers, singers, and poets. The more recent refugees are Ahmad Joudeh, Alaa Arsheed, Mohamed Keita, Rose Lokonyen, Emi Mahmoud, Mercy Akuot, Abdalla Al Omari, Abdullahi Ahmed, Amani Zreba, individuals in the group "Diamo rifugio ai talenti," Dagmawi Yimer, Tareke Brhane, and Alidad Shiri. These refugees are also often internationally known and have become more so since the publication of *Anche Superman era un rifugiato*.

Each story is accompanied by a related illustration by various artists. For the most part, a single image depicts the two refugees together in a way that relates to how the story has brought them together. Laura Riccioli portrays a dancing Ahmad Joudeh looking up at the ballet dancer Rudolf Nureyev and a swallow, a central party of the collection's first story (Figure 5.1). Mariachiara di Giorgio portrays Abdullahi Ahmed and Hannah Arendt, in the company of other figures, both staring out at the viewers (Figure 5.2). The artists' and authors' works, within the collection and outside of it, underscore the varied ways art and literature are in conversation with each other. Some of the artists and authors had worked together on previous projects, while other artist-author pairs collaborated together for the first

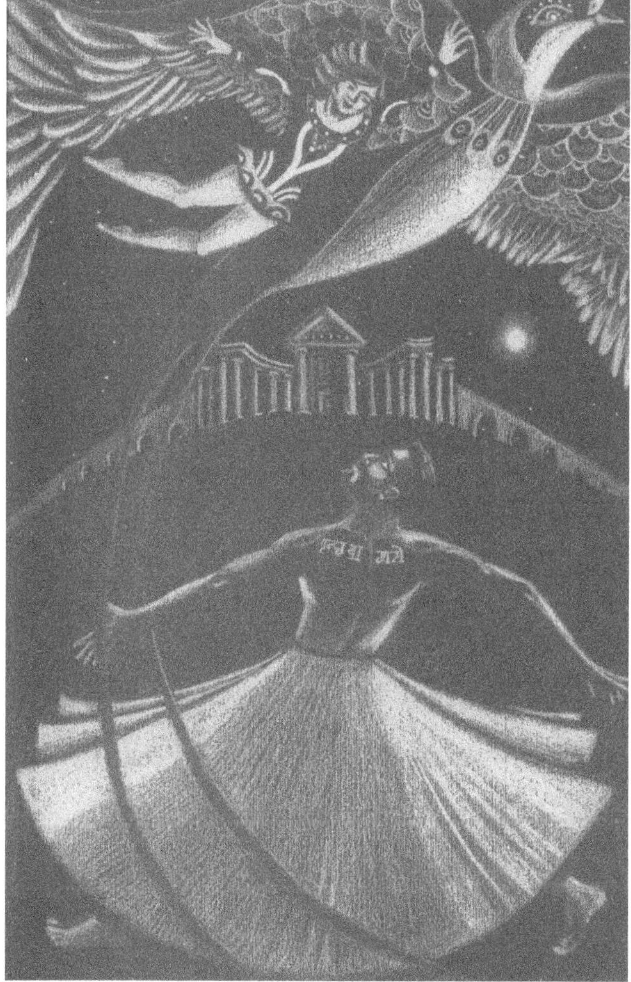

Figure 5.1 Laura Riccioli, "Gli uomini rondine." © Laura Riccioli. Courtesy of the artist.

time for the volume.[10] The illustrations vary stylistically, but most of them highlight the connections between the two refugee figures of the story while also accentuating their individual abilities.

The volume's illustrations of refugees dancing, painting, playing the violin, and helping others make the works more appealing for a younger audience, while also challenging common media representations of refugees. In the early twenty-first century, the largest number of migrants to Italy have come from (in order): Romania, Albania, Morocco, China, and Ukraine,

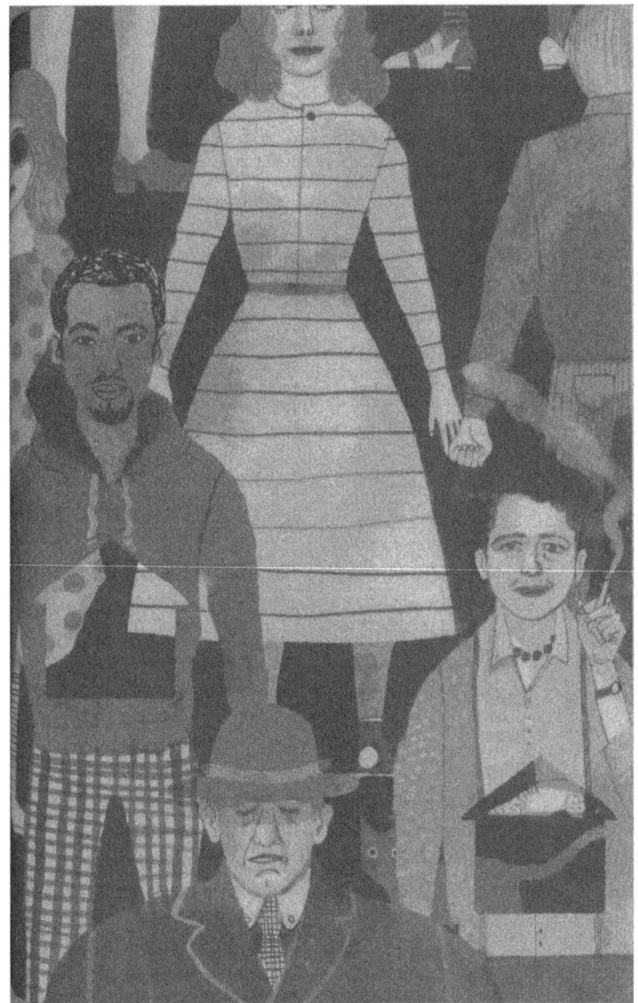

Figure 5.2 Mariachiara di Giorgio, "I posti che siamo." © Mariachiara di Giorgio. Courtesy of the artist.

but the most common representations of immigration to Italy are ones of crowded boats of Black African refugees trying to reach Lampedusa, an Italian island closer to Tunisia than Sicily. This disjunction suggests the vital importance of portrayals in shaping how migration is understood. Photojournalist Darrin Zammit Lupi's photographs for Reuters have, for instance, been used by multiple articles across media. Highlighting the danger required to reach Italy, many of Zammit Lupi's photos feature crowds of Black people in boats (Figure 5.3) or in the water, almost drowning. These

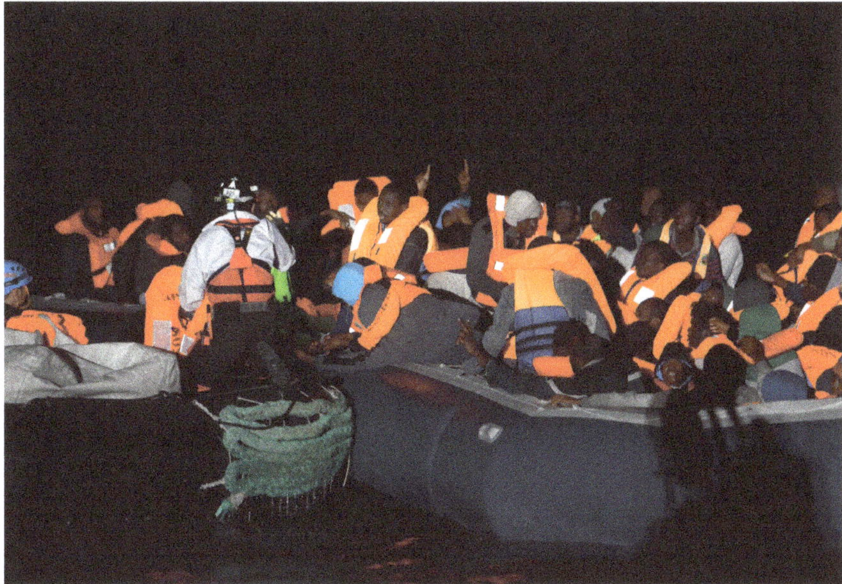

Figure 5.3 Darrin Zammit Lupi, "Rescue at Sea 2" from the series *On Board the Aquarius, December 2017*. Courtesy of the Rubenstein Library, Duke University.

powerful images of dehumanization can prompt a viewer to sympathize with or pity the migrants' situation, but the photo also frames them in a fixed, dehumanized shot.

Federica Mazzara's *Reframing Migration: Lampedusa, Border Spectacle and Aesthetics of Subversion* argues that images can problematically fix the loss of life around Lampedusa as "border spectacle," but that art can subvert views of migrants in and around Lampedusa. In chapter 6 below, Tenley Bick analyzes art located on Lampedusa itself, especially the Italian artist Mimmo Paladino's 2008 work, *Porta di Lampedusa, porta d'Europa* (Gateway to Lampedusa, Gateway to Europe) in terms of its decolonial fluidity and in contrast with monuments as exertions of power. The illustrations of the stories in *Anche Superman era un rifugiato*, as the refugees themselves, also disrupt mainstream images of migration. For instance, Abdalla Al Omari, paired with Marc Chagall in Michela Monferrini's story, is famous for painting world leaders as refugees (Figure 5.4). In order to shift the Eurocentric idea of what an African migrant or traveler includes and the concept of what a migrant is, artists and authors of *Anche Superman era un rifugiato* counteract a widespread view of Africans as exemplifying migrants.[11] American media, for instance, often ignores migrations within Africa or to Turkey, in contrast to the focus on the smaller number of migrants to Lampedusa.

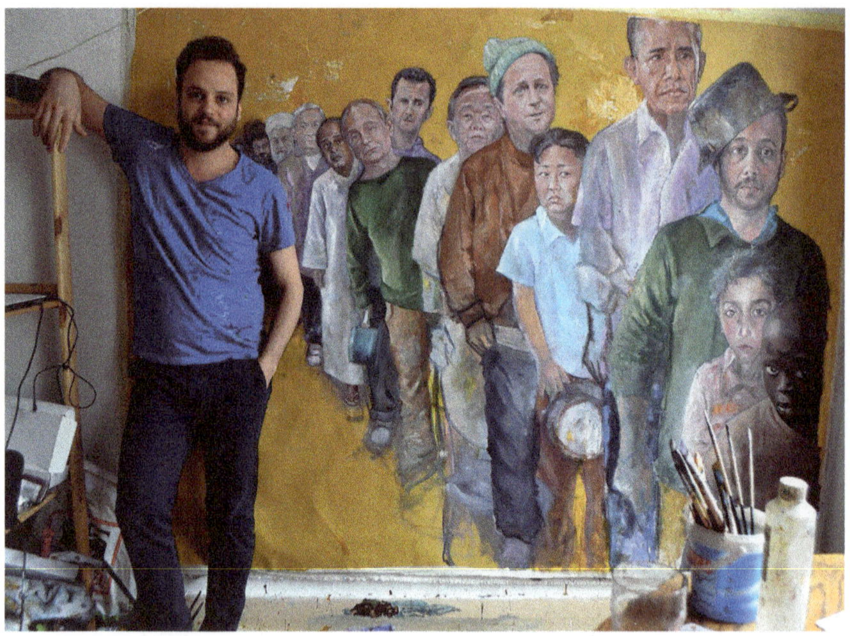

Figure 5.4 Abdalla Al Omari, "The Queue" from *The Vulnerability Series* (2017). © Abdalla Al Omari. Courtesy of the artist.

Even when the Italian collection's stories include Lampedusa, the refugees' narratives always continue beyond this moment of peril to focus on their lives and later actions.

Whereas most of the short stories in *Anche Superman era un rifugiato* have an initial illustration followed by the text, the titular tale is a graphic story, written and illustrated by the same person, Giuseppe Palumbo. Each line of text in "Anche Superman era un rifugiato" is accompanied by two images: the one above the text depicts Superman's journey from his home planet to earth and the one below shows the refugee Tareke Brhane's journey from Eritrea to Italy. Both show the transitions the men undergo, first fleeing for their lives (Figure 5.5), then adjusting to life in a new place, and then working to help others (Figure 5.6), Superman as Superman and Taneke Brhane as the president of the Comitato 3 ottobre, which pushed for a day of remembrance for migrants who perished off the coast of Lampedusa on October 3, 2013, as well as for recognition of the plight of migrants more generally. Palumbo's pictures draw on widespread images of Superman but also of refugees in the media. The work calls attention to how many refugees' narratives follow the pattern of a well-known superhero, including a need to leave, facing incomprehension in a new place, and then helping others.

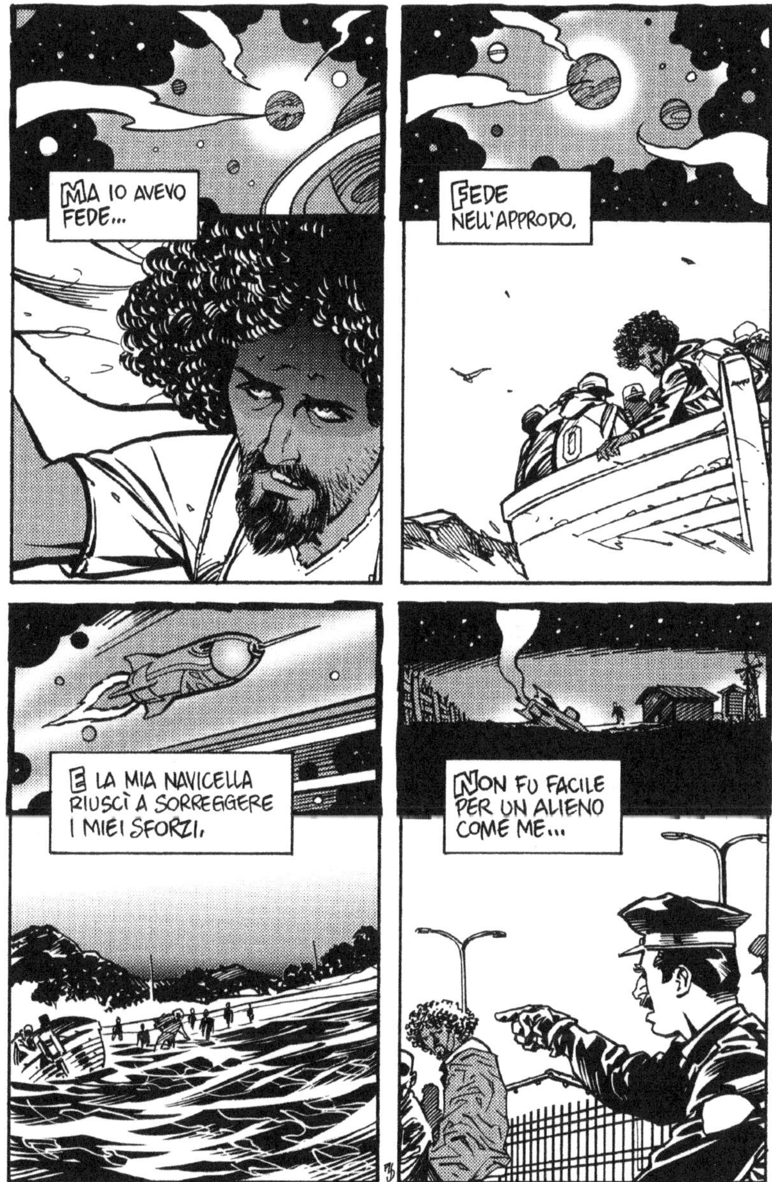

Figures 5.5 and 5.6 Giuseppe Palumbo, pages from "Anche Superman era un rifugiato." © Giuseppe Palumbo. Courtesy of the artist.

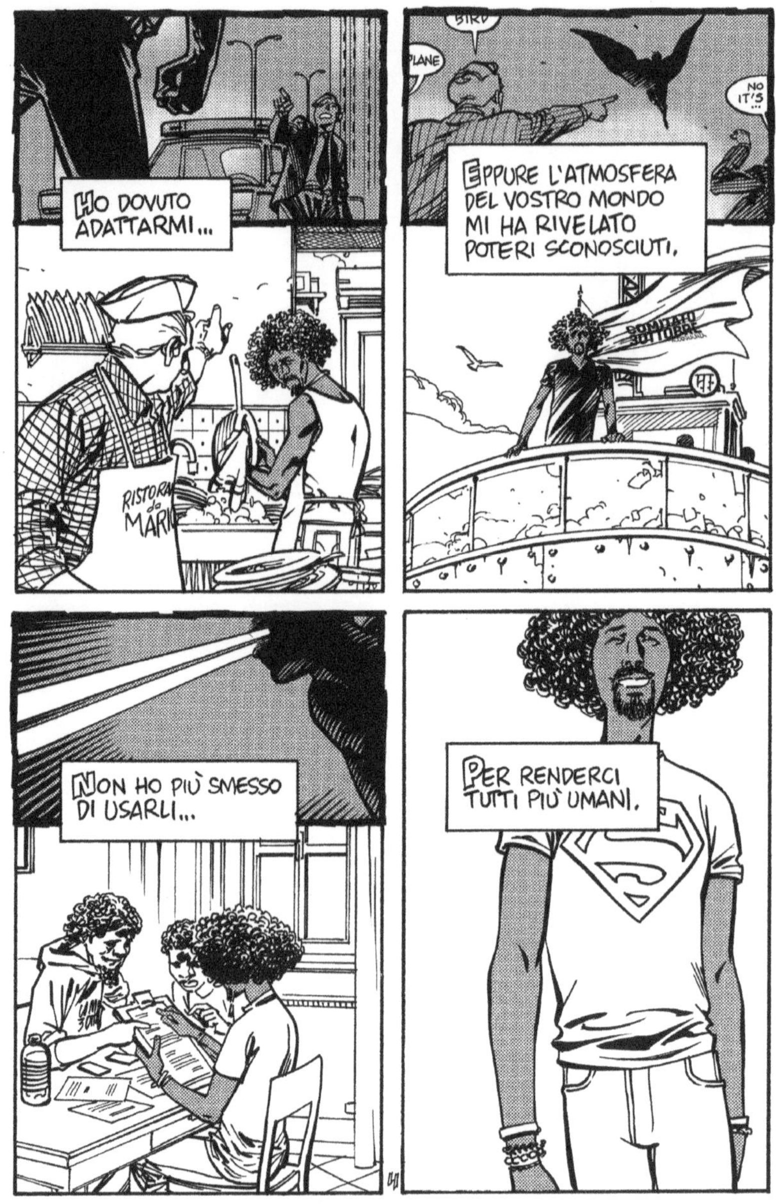

Figures 5.5 and 5.6 (Continued)

Subverting dehumanizing portrayals of migrants as border spectacle, the parallels between the journeys of Brhane and of Superman show how numerous refugee tales could be rewritten following the format of Superman's story and how this popular American superhero figures as a refugee.

Despite Italy's important role in migration, both to and within Europe, the country is not as central as the United States, England, Germany, or France in discussions of migration or migration literature.[12] Although the introduction to *The Penguin Book of Migration Literature* emphasizes its global nature, 28 out of its 32 pieces were written in English. The few languages from which the works are translated are French, German, and Arabic. This focus on English-speaking countries as the assumed physical destinations, and English as the linguistic one, indicates how English-language globality can degenerate into provincialism.[13] Many of the authors who write in English in *The Penguin Book of Migration Literature* and also *The Displaced*, which is composed of untranslated works in English, were not born speaking the language. At times, the dominance of English emphasizes immigration (the destination) and occludes linguistic emigration. This perspective also centers migration to English-speaking countries as paradigmatic, often ignoring the cases of migration to and from French, Italian, or Spanish speaking countries, among others.

In *Immigrant Fictions: Contemporary Literature in an Age of Globalization*, Rebecca L. Walkowitz argues that migration literature challenges views of English fiction as homogenous and monolingual. Caryl Phillip's anthology *Extravagant Strangers: A Literature of Belonging* (1997) shows how English fiction can challenge what is considered British: "For many British people, to accept the idea that their country has a long and complex history of immigration would be to undermine their basic understanding of what British fiction means" (Phillips, 1997: xii). *The Penguin Book of Migration Literature*, meanwhile, points out that, "While one can find origin-specific anthologies (e.g. African, Caribbean, or South Asian diasporas) and destination specific ones (e.g. Canadian, British, or US immigrant literature), this is the first collection to offer a global, comparative scope" (Ahmad, 2019: xv). Despite its claim, migration literature anthologies, such as *The Penguin Book of Migration Literature*, are often debated, and perhaps even constructed, as if their goals were akin to Phillip's anthology: to shift the concept of English fiction. While this challenge is a critical one, it potentially overshadows more global (not Anglo-global) questions and issues. A focus on migration literature in English underscores the issues of English colonization and decolonization, minimizing the differing cases of French, Italian, or Spanish colonization, among others.

The frequent assumption that authors write in English potentially recreates the power dynamics these works may aim to contest, with the migrant as viewed (or object) and the English speaker as viewer (or subject). In her important analysis of the development of refugee anthologies as a genre, Emma Bond suggests how anthologies potentially limit what one considers part of a genre or even of history:

> Yet on the macro-level, the anthology is also subject to the ulterior practices of intentional selection on the part of the editors and publishers that might risk allowing one particular history to emerge instead of another. It thus also runs the risk of fixing history into that one image that it has decided to communicate, and in so doing, might unintentionally end up "fixing" cultural differences as well. (Bond, 2019: 161)

The migrant may write or be described, but the English-speaking non-migrant is assumed to be the audience, the one enacted upon and transformed by the work.

Migration literature anthologies present not only different potential world maps (what spaces are included) but also a sense of time (what periods of migration are included). Anglophone criticism of migration literature and anthologies often overlook Italian works in which connections across time, especially between the medieval period and today, tend to play a vital role. Focusing on English-language works prioritizes modern migration literature, again reflecting how the study of migration literature has developed in English. Phillips' introduction to *Extravagant Strangers* persuasively argues: "To my way of thinking, English literature has, for at least 200 years, been shaped and influenced by outsiders" (Phillips, 1997: x). What "outsider" or "stranger" would mean in the Italian context is more fluid, since Italy was not a country two-hundred years ago. Many authors, such as Dante, have been in exile or made to migrate within the peninsula itself. The idea of exile or migration between different parts of Italy continued long after the nation's unification in the nineteenth century. Mussolini forced many Italians he considered dangerous to Fascism into *confino*, "internal exile." This policy was important in terms of development of the "Southern Question," since primarily northern Italians were sent to southern Italy where they experienced the great differences between the North and South of their country. Discussions of migration and Italy in the 1950s and 1960s often focus on the move many southern Italians made to the more economically prosperous North of Italy. The prejudice southern Italians faced has shifted somewhat onto non-Italian migrants as the number of migrants in Italy has increased. This exile within a country, an important feature of Italian history, is less frequently covered in migration studies, which tends to emphasize big moves and assume that it entails crossing at least one national boundary.

Collections' paratexts, the words and images around the stories that mediate a readers' understanding of them – from book covers, to subheadings, to chapter titles – often reveal the different directions that a reader could be pulled in terms of time, space, and genre when approaching anthologies of migration literature. Under each selection in *The Penguin Book of Migration Literature* is a place with an arrow to somewhere else: for instance, Julie Otsuka, "Come, Japanese!" Japan → USA; Francisco Jiménez, "Under the Wire," Mexico → USA; Eva Hoffman, from *Lost in Translation*, Poland → Canada. Although the potential complexities of assuming that a character (or author) finds a final destination are suggested in the two examples where the space after the arrow is left blank, the labelling itself sets up a teleological structure of spatial, one-directional movement, based primarily on nations.[14] The boundaries of migration literature, as framed by *The Penguin Book of Migration Literature*, reflect how globalism, literary markets, and issues of migration are intertwined. English-speaking destinations, linguistic and physical, dominate. In contrast to the United States' eight or the UK's ten, Italy appears only once in these directional lists.

Dinaw Mengestu's "An Honest Exit," Ethiopia → Sudan → Italy → UK → USA, is the only story to list five countries underneath it. Italy is significantly in a spot with multiple arrows, marking transitional places before the final destination of the United States. "An Honest Exit" reflects on the country's in-between status at several points: "In Italy he was given asylum and set free. From there he works his way north and then west across Europe" (Mengestu, 2019: 88). As much as an entry point to one nation, Italy represents a door to Europe.[15] While the story describes some migrants as always having planned to leave Italy, others readjusted once there: "Rome is not what I thought it would be. France will surely be better" (Mengestu, 2019: 88). Occupying a spot between Ethiopia and the United States, between Sudan and the United Kingdom, Italy presents a different focal point from which to consider migration, one which frequently reveals how interconnected places are and that migration almost always involves more than a point A of departure and a point B of arrival.

In the collection *The Displaced*, authors such as David Bezmozgis, Fatima Bhutto, Joseph Kertes, Maaza Mengiste, and Dina Nayeri reflect on what being a refugee means. Italy again appears as a transitional space, for Jews leaving Hungary in the 1950s or the Soviet Union in the 1980s and people leaving Eritrea and Ethiopia today. On the way from Riga in the Soviet Union to Toronto in Canada (after thinking they would end up in Los Angeles, Atlanta, Melbourne, and Israel), David Bezmozgis describes his family's temporary period in Vienna and Rome (Bezmozgis, 2018: 36). When moving from Iran to the United States, Dina Nayeri's "The Ungrateful Refugee" describes "spending two years in refugee hostels in Dubai and Rome" (Nayeri, 2018: 138). Considering migration from the perspective of Italy highlights the unexpected connections between places, like Rome and Dubai or Vienna, with journeys over and over again reflecting the potential randomness of home and nationality. Examining Italy's role in migration literature challenges any concept of destinations as destined. "Second Country" by Joseph Kertes elucidates the links between places and chance involved in finding a homeland: "The West must have felt guilty, so they opened their doors to us. At the grand bus station in Vienna, Hungarians got free tickets to anywhere they wanted to go in Europe. Each bus was labeled with a different capital – take your choice: Paris, Rome, Bonn, Madrid, Amsterdam, Brussels, Lisbon, and beyond – London, Stockholm, Copenhagen" (Kertes, 2018: 108). Rome repeatedly comes up as a city people consider making their home, but which ultimately ends up being just a stop on their travels. Focusing on Italy reveals the difficulties of knowing what spaces are transitory or destinations in an individual's journey.

In other essays in *The Displaced*, Italy's museums and cafés (or rather caffès) make an appearance, contrasting the routes tourists and refugees follow to and through the country. In "Flesh and Sand," Fatima Bhutto discusses going to the Fondazione Prada in Milan to see Alejandro G. Inarritu's virtual reality installation of the experience of walking through to desert to enter Arizona. In Maaza Mengiste's "This is What the Journey Does," the author observes a refugee from a coffee shop: "I know there is nothing really special about him, not in Florence, Italy. He is just one of the many refugees or migrants who have made their way here from East Africa, a physical embodiment of those now-familiar reports and photographs of migration" (Mengiste, 2018: 129). The author suggests the significance, not only of her own observation, but also of that of the refugee's: "If he looks at me, then our lives will unfold and in front of us will be the many roads we have taken to get to this intersection in Florence and we will reveal ourselves for what we are: immigrant, migrant, refugee, African, East African, Black, foreigner, stranger, a body rendered disobedient by the very nature of what we are" (Mengiste, 2018: 132). Mengiste suggests the power of recognition as she contemplates the potential connections between her past and that of someone who has ultimately ended up in a very different situation. Mengiste emphasizes the transformations the journey entails for a migrant and the difficulty of finding a place even when one has found a home. Italy's role in these works also suggests the problem of considering Europe purely through representations from its members with the greatest political strength.

While Italy is primarily a transitional space in *The Penguin Book of Migration Literature* and *The Displaced*, the language of *Anche Superman era un rifugiato* could suggest that Italy would play a central role in the work. One could expect the language of a volume, English or Italian, to drive the configuration of the work itself, particularly in terms of which nations are included. While this is true of *The Penguin Book of Migration Literature*, Italy does not dominate as a destination in *Anche Superman era un rifugiato*, though it plays a somewhat larger role than in the English-language anthologies. As the title itself suggests with "Superman," an American hero referenced in English rather than as *superuomo*, Italian scholars and authors are more likely to put their country in a comparative perspective than those from countries who more obviously impact global discourses. Since there are multiple moves in each story, with numerous transitional spaces, a paratext with arrows identifying directional moves between nations as in *The Penguin Book of Migration Literature* would be extremely complicated, if not impossible. The paratexts of *Anche Superman era un rifugiato* instead identify the author and the two primary characters of each story. The table of contents lists the titles of the stories and the authors, while each story's page header provides the name of the author and then the subjects of the story: a famous refugee of the past, from Aeneas to Freddie Mercury, and a twenty-first century refugee, preceded by a title page with the name of the story, the name of the illustrator, and the image inspired by the work.

Although it does not declare itself as such, the volume is, in some ways, more global than *The Penguin Book of Migration Literature*, but the concept of "global" often implies a larger (English-speaking) audience. The fact that the stories of *Anche Superman era un rifugiato* are written in a language that is not always considered global, again raises the question of how linguistic and geopolitical movement are framed from the vantage point of countries that consider themselves destinations and the defining forces of globality. These power structures can be reified by the limited number of translations into English from other languages and the publishing practices that consider discussions of works not in English to be niche. Apparent marginality (like Italy's) becomes a place of experimentation, where ideas are brought into contact in a way that they are not necessarily in centralized discourses. This space of experimentation promotes considering migration across space, time, and languages. For *Anche Superman era un rifugiato* these concepts are forged through art, not only by the stories themselves, but also due to the artists described in the works.

In Paolo Di Paolo's "Una nuvola di note" ("A cloud of notes"), Dante's *Divine Comedy* provides a model for the unification of two friends (one of whom turns out not to exist), offers a reference point in terms of artistic collaboration, and is also discussed within the story itself. The story begins "Una delle cose più belle che possano capitarti nella vita è ritrovare un amico che avevi perso di vista" (Di Paolo, 2018: 26) ("One of the most beautiful things that can happen to you in life is to see again a friend that you have not seen for a while"). Alaa Arsheed, a violinist, is in an Italian city and runs into his friend Moosa. They reminisce about the artistic circle they had in Afghanistan, which they have both fled because of the war. Alaa plays music to accompany Moosa's description of Dante. It turns out Moosa never made it to Italy. Like Dante in purgatory when he sees Casella, who set his poetry to music, these friends are unable to embrace: "perché Casella era una specie di fantasma, o comunque un ricordo, un'immagine senza corpo. Come Moosa, di cui si sono perse completamente le tracce, e con lui di tanti altri, nella terra da cui Alaa è venuto via" (Di Paolo, 2018: 31) ("because Casella was a kind of ghost, or in any case a memory, an image without a body. Like Moosa, whom he had completely lost the traces of, and along with him many others, from the land that Alaa had left"). Music and literature reunite these pairs of friends when they are no longer able to meet in reality. The Italy where Alaa and Moosa appear to meet is paralleled to purgatory, where Dante meets Casella in the *Divine Comedy*. While Dante, like all subjects of the volume, is included partially because of his experience as a refugee, at the same time, much of the story dwells on Dante's poetry, its models of friendship, its descriptions of loss, and the journey from hell to paradise.

Flora Farina's story "Gli uomini rondine ("The swallow men") opens the collection (Figure 5.1) and reflects on the ability of dance and narrative to bring together people with different backgrounds. The narrative starts with Rudolf Nureyev's point of view as a dancer, who dreams of a swallow, a migratory bird. In the next section, the swallow speaks to Ahmad Joudeh (both men are referred to using their first names). Moving between the two perspectives, the story reveals how the two men are linked by more than their incredible dancing abilities. Rudolf was born on a trans-Siberian train, in motion. Born in a Palestinian refugee camp in Syria, Ahmad is without a stable home because of the bombing. Their fathers condemned them for dancing. Rudolf decides to leave the Soviet Union and asks for political asylum in Paris. Ahmad leaves Syria for Amsterdam. The swallow inspires bravery in them both and connects their stories. The freedom of the bird's movements points to the lack of freedom Nureyev has in the Soviet Union and Joudeh in Syria, but also symbolizes the freedom they find in dance, suggesting connections between the movements of migration and dance itself. The bird seems to go where it is needed and at the end appears ready to narrate Joudeh's story to Nureyev: "Sei tu? Sei tornata rondinella! Racconta allora, su racconta" (Farina, 2018: 22) ("Is that you? You've returned, dear swallow! Tell us then, come on tell us"). The movement of the bird through time suggests connections between all people who need to leave their homelands, no matter what prompts their departures. In reality, Nureyev died not long after Joudeh was born.

Joudeh became known internationally because of his dancing. The subject of a Dutch documentary, he moved from Syria to the Netherlands in 2016. In Syria he danced in the Palmyra theater, used by ISIS for executions and then partially destroyed. When Joudeh was threatened for his dancing, his reaction was to have "Dance or Die" tattooed in Sanskrit on his neck, the place where the blade would touch were he beheaded. The same motto, in Italian, provides the title of his autobiography *Danza o muori*. In the acknowledgements to his autobiography, Joudeh credits the Italian dancer Roberto Bolle (who writes the preface to the book) with having made his dreams a reality.[16] Joudeh's story shows both the power of art to connect and its dangers, since death threats directly related to his pursuits as a dancer. In part because of the important role Bolle played in his development as a dancer and for his international status, Joudeh's autobiography is originally in Italian, written for an Italian audience, although Joudeh does not live full-time in Italy. Joudeh's memoir highlights how the international nature of art does not necessarily follow the movement of people.

The fact that the subjects of the works in *Anche Superman era un rifugiato* are often better known internationally than the authors disrupts the power dynamics of many migration tales that follow a similar format of authors narrating stories told to them by refugees. Especially because of the parallels established in the pairings, several of the stories potentially contradict expectations of who a refugee is. Nureyev's departure from Soviet Union, for instance, is usually described as a "defection" and he is not often referred to as a "refugee." The UNHCR spokesperson for southern Europe, Carlotta Sami, introduces *Anche Superman era un rifugiato* with an observation about the potentially distancing effects of the word "refugee": "Mia nonna è stata una rifugiata. Ma io l'ho capito solo pochi anni fa"' (Sami, 2018: 5) ("My grandmother was a refugee. But I only realized this a few years ago"). She is surprised to find a refugee so close, within her family. *Anche Superman era un rifugiato* similarly aims to push the reader's understanding of who is a refugee to be more inclusive.

Migrant, refugee, and in exile: a long literary history

Viet Thanh Nguyen's introduction to *The Displaced* also starts with a consideration of the negative connotations of the word "refugee": "I was once a refugee, although no one would mistake me for being a refugee now. Because of this, I insist on being called a refugee, since the temptation to pretend that I am not a refugee is strong" (Nguyen, 2018: 11). Nguyen highlights how the term refugee is controversial, demanding, and threatening. He builds on a tradition of refugee, transnational, and migrant authors reflecting on what they should be called. Hannah Arendt's "We Refugees" (originally published in 1943) also begins with the problems of the term:

> In the first place, we don't like to be called "refugees." We ourselves call each other "new comers" or "immigrants." Our newspapers are papers for "Americans of German language"; and, as far as I know, there is not and never was any club founded by Hitler-persecuted people whose name indicated that its members were refugees. (Arendt, 1994: 110)

"Refugee" authors repeatedly confront a description they would not necessarily choose for themselves.

As Nguyen makes clear in his introduction, the term "refugee" does not neutrally describe a person who has fled from their homeland, but also often connotes a negative judgment that the descriptions "migrant" or "in exile" do not necessarily. The terms "refugee" and "migrants" began to be used more than "in exile" in the 1930s. Exile, described by Julio Cortázar as "a universal theme, at least since the laments of an Ovid or a Dante"' (Cortázar, 1994: 171), often suggests a longer tradition and greater status than "refugee" or "migrant." "In exile" potentially indicates that the person has found a new place to be (in exile), as opposed to a "refugee:" again in Nguyen's words, "These displaced persons are mostly unwanted where they fled from; unwanted where they are, in refugee camps; and unwanted where they want to go" (Nguyen, 2018: 17). A modern author in exile points to the individual's experience and often characterizes a writer who wrote before leaving their home, whereas a refugee writer tends to suggest that the writer is part of, or even represents, a group of people who left their country.

Briefly considering *The Heart of a Stranger: An Anthology of Exile Literature* (2020) in terms of *The Penguin Book of Migration Literature* and *Anche Superman era un rifugiato* highlights the complicated relationship between the way exile, migration, and refugee are used when discussing literature. *The Heart of a Stranger*, edited by André Naffis-Sahely, an Italian-Iranian who grew up in Abu Dhabi and now lives in Los Angeles, and *The Penguin Book of Migration Literature*, edited by Dohra Ahmad, both include works by Olaudah Equiano (born in the 1740s) and Phillis Wheatley (born in the 1750s). Due to the view that writers in exile are part of an extensive literary history, Equiano is preceded chronologically by a range of writers in *The Heart of a Stranger*, in contrast to *The Penguin Book of Migration Literature* where he is the earliest author. Like *The Oxford Book of Exile*, the 2020 collection starts with biblical selections that show the longevity of this literary tradition (Simpson, 1995). Exile literature underscores how humans reflecting on being forced to find new homes is a central element of literary history. With selections from authors such as Homer, Sappho, Xenophanes, Plutarch, Du Fu, and Abd al-Rahman I, *The Heart of the*

Stranger includes translations not only from Latin, Greek, Hebrew, Chinese, and Arabic, but also a sizable list of other languages from around the world.[17] The collection's numerous translations from the Italian range from Dante's encounter with Cacciaguida in the *Divine Comedy* to Ribka Sibhatu's twenty-first-century poem "In Lampedusa." Dante appears again in *The Heart of the Stranger* as the focus of Giacomo Leopardi's "On the Monument to Dante Being Erected in Florence," which dwells on the need for a monument honouring Dante in the city from which he had been exiled.

While Dante's placement in collections of exile literature is part of a long tradition, Aeneas and Dante's roles in *Anche Superman era un rifugiato* prompted several far-right journalists to react with vehement denial of the appropriateness of the term "refugee," since they viewed the term as a disparagement. In *Il Primato Nazionale*, a publication connected with the far-right group CasaPound, Marco Scarsini questions, "in che modo Enea può essere definito un rifugiato in Italia se il fondatore della sua stirpe vi era nato?" (Scarsini, 2018) ("in what way can Aeneas be defined a refugee in Italy if the founder of his race (*stirpe*) was born there?"). This tortured attempt to claim that the fictional character Aeneas was not a refugee because of his bloodlines reveals not only the negative connotations of "refugee" for certain readers, but also the significance of Aeneas as a founding figure for Italy.

It is hard to imagine a similar critical debate in the United States over categorizing American authors or characters as refugees, because of literature's insignificance for the country's national identity. From Aeneas, to Dante, to contemporary fiction, literature plays an especially large role in Italy's concept of itself, which relates in part to the country's literary history and later unification. Italy as a literary concept long predates its existence as a nation. In response to Klemens von Metternich's jab at the Congress of Vienna that Italy was merely a "geographical expression," Giosuè Carducci claimed that it was instead "un'espressione letteraria, una tradizione poetica" (a literary expression, a poetic tradition).[18] The sense that Italy and her literature were one and the same continued well after the Risorgimento and Italy's unification. Every issue of the Fascist magazine *La difesa della razza* (*The Defence of Race*, 1938–43) has a Dante quote on the front cover. The Fascists who put together the journal found Dante as significant as statistics, history, or racist science for persuading the public that Jewish and Black people should be excluded from Italian society. In 1960, Carlo Levi again highlighted the important relationship between Italy and her literature: "Tutti i suoi artisti e i suoi poeti l'hanno, descrivendola, determinata" (Levi, 1960: viii) ("All of her artists and poets have, in describing the country, determined it"). In Italy the literary plays an important role for members of diverse political parties and perspectives.[19]

Critics have observed that Italian migration literature does not always fit well into the model provided by earlier discussions of migration literature, in part because of how quickly migrant writers engaged the Italian canon, again revealing the importance of literature to being Italian.[20] This suggests both the difference of the Italian situation and the need for models of migration literature to consider multiple cases since literature varies in its relationship to nationhood and identity. Anglophone criticism and works have increasingly been invested in authors primarily representing their own experiences, which could suggest the collaborative stories of *Anche Superman era un rifugiato* are problematic, as the Italian writers incorporate tales from the past and also stories from refugees that the authors themselves obviously did not experience. Most of the authors contributing to *Anche Superman era un rifugiato* were born in Italy. This lack of direct connection between the authors' backgrounds and their subject matter distinguishes it from many English-language collections.

The penultimate piece in *Anche Superman era un rifugiato* is, however, non-fiction by a refugee author. Alidad Shiri describes his experiences while making his way from Afghanistan to Pakistan, Iran, Turkey, Greece, and eventually Italy: "Il viaggio di un migrante spesso dura anni, è una lotta continua tra la vita e la morte" (Shiri, 2018: 181) ("A migrant's journey often lasts years, it is a continual struggle between life and death"). While several of the ideas in this work relate to ones found in the fictional stories, he addresses a refugee's travails and the reader more directly: "Vorrei invitare voi lettori, grandi o piccoli, a fare leva sulla vostra sensibilità e umanità: non c'è nessun motivo, nessuna giustificazione, per trattare male chi è arrivato o arriva, rispendendolo al mittente come fosse un pacco indesiderato" (Shiri, 2018: 182–3) ("I would like to invite you, readers young and old, to employ your sensitivity and humanity: there is no motive or justification to treat poorly those who have arrived or arrive, returning them to their senders as if they were an undesired package"). Shiri ends by saying that his request is not a political manifesto, but "un semplice invito all'umanità" (Shiri, 2018: 183) ("a simple invitation to humanity").

His non-fictional contribution, entitled "Un semplice invito all'umanità," suggests one way all of the collection's stories could be understood, but part of the power of literature is that it does not have to be interpreted in just one way. This simplistic statement may seem unnecessary, but with migration literature there has been an increase in approaches that assume a strong correlation between biography and literature, which flattens the potentialities of literature. Especially when a work partly asks the reader to reconsider identities or the relationship between writing and history, recent English-language criticism has tended to focus on authors whose biographies inspired their characters. Many of the authors selected for *The*

Penguin Book of Migration Literature share similar backgrounds (if not the same) to those of their characters and several of the works are also categorized as memoirs. The collection includes powerful works by a variety of important authors, but the selection process set certain limits to what "migration literature" can be and, therefore, suggests limits to how much authors can imagine beyond their own experiences and what fiction means when it comes to crossing borders.

"Migrant literature" now often refers to people who migrated to Europe or America from somewhere else in recent decades and who write about migration, with an assumption that biography should reflect literary content or literary content biography. The shift from a discussion of "authors in exile," which tended to emphasize writers who had intellectual status before migration, to "migrant literature" aimed to draw attention to migrant voices that had been ignored. Carine M. Mardorossian has called attention to how "while the shift from exile to migrant literature helped challenge an unproblematical reliance on the category of experience as the basis of explanation in literary criticism, the same kind of undertheorized relation to experience seems to have resurfaced in critical approaches to the new migrant aesthetics" (Mardorossian, 2003: 18). This trend of identifying experience with literature has only grown in more recent critical discourses. *Writing Across Worlds: Literature and Migration* (1995) analyzes Cesare Pavese's *La luna e i falò* (*The Moon and the Bonfires*, 1950) (White, 1995: 7–8). Today, authors like Pavese, who never saw the America described in his novel, are frequently excluded when it comes to "migration literature."

Considering *The Penguin Book of Migration Literature* and *Anche Superman era un rifugiato* together raises the question of what migration literature can encompass and how important an author's background is for the label. In "Fascinated to Presume: In Defense of Fiction," Zadie Smith argues against the collapse of authorial identity and literary perspective:

> Full disclosure: what insults my soul is the idea – popular in the culture just now, and presented in widely variant degrees of complexity – that we can and should write only about people who are fundamentally "like" us: racially, sexually, genetically, nationally, politically, personally. That only an intimate authorial autobiographical connection with a character can be the rightful basis of a fiction. I do not believe that. I could not have written a single one of my books if I did. (Smith 2019)

She points to how limiting what an author can describe would restrict literature in terms of production, content, and form:

> Fiction was suspicious of any theory of the self that appeared to be largely founded on what can be seen with the human eye, that is, those parts of our selves that are material, manifest, and clearly visible in a crowd. Fiction – at

least the kind that was any good – was full of doubt, self-doubt above all. It had grave doubts about the nature of the self. (Smith 2019)

Smith's persuasive argument for the power of literature in part takes aim against the – as she describes it – popular belief that identity determines perspective, including in literature. The contrasts between *Anche Superman era un rifugiato* and *The Penguin Book of Migration Literature* indicate how culturally determined this belief might be. The structure of *Anche Superman era un rifugiato* fits the concept of literature as a conversation, one that takes place between different people from across time periods and that leads authors as well as readers beyond themselves.

From Superman to 1938: literary collections as dialogues

The long lists of authors, past refugees, recent refugees, illustrators, and editors (Scego and the UNHCR) highlight the amount of collective work that went into *Anche Superman era un rifugiato* – with collaborations between the artists who provide the images for each story with their authors, as well as collaborations between the authors and the artist refugees, who narrated their experiences before the authors composed their stories.[21] Three of the authors of *Anche Superman era un rifugiato* also contributed to *1938: Storia, racconto, memoria* (*1938: History, Story, Memory*), a volume of works reflecting on the 1938 Racial Laws that marked the beginning of official Fascist antisemitic policies. The overlap of authors contributing to *1938* and *Anche Superman era un rifugiato* indicates perhaps a stronger belief in the power of literature to express the doubts Zadie Smith describes, because the authors' backgrounds did not determine their inclusion in the collections. The authors who contributed to both *1938* and *Anche Superman era un rifugiato* – Igiaba Scego, Carlo Greppi, and Helena Janeczek – are, respectively, a Roman author whose parents left Somalia for Italy, a historian and author from Turin, and an author who grew up in Germany and whose Polish mother was a concentration camp survivor.

Scego, Greppi, and Janeczek's stories reveal the connections between migration, racism, antisemitism, and colonialism in Italy. As migration to Italy has increased, Italian writers and critics have paid more attention to Italy's role as a colonizer and the country's history of racism. Migration raises questions about a country's colonialism, even if most of the immigrants did not arrive from formerly colonized countries. Italy's over sixty years as a colonizer in places now known as Libya, Somalia, Ethiopia, Eritrea, the Dodecanese Islands, and Albania, contributed to destabilizing these countries. People are escaping wars and poverty partially resulting from the earlier

Italian presence, and Italy's membership in Frontex (the EU's unified border agency) reveals the continuities of Italy's involvement in these areas. In the past, critics often left Italy out of examinations of colonialism, racism, and antisemitism. Italian scholars and authors redress this gap, offering critiques of what has been ignored in Italy, but also of the problem of ignoring Italy.[22] A wide range of Italianists have revealed Italy's particular position as a country of emigrants and immigrants, invaded and invading, in terms of dealing with its colonial legacy.[23] The titles of their works, such as Teresa Fiore's *Pre-Occupied Spaces: Remapping Italy's Transnational Migrations and Colonial Legacies*, Stephanie Malia Hom's *Empire's Mobius Strip: Historical Echoes in Italy's Crisis of Migration and Detention*, and Pamela Ballinger's *The World Refugees Made: Decolonization and the Foundation of Postwar Italy*, indicate the dynamic relationship between Italy's colonial past and its present day, especially in terms of migration.

In *Paradoxes of Postcolonial Culture: Contemporary Women Writers of the Indian and Afro-Italian Diaspora*, Sandra Ponzanesi explores Italy's perception of itself as colonized: "despite its aggressive past, Italy still perceives itself more as a colonized country than as a colonizer. Its internal divisions are in fact due to a long history of invasion. Foreigners were always on its territory, including the Greeks, Arabs, Spanish, French, Austrians, and Germans"' (Ponzanesi, 2004: 105). Issues of colonization, migration, racism, and antisemitism were long ignored in Italy, but are topics of increasing analysis. The Italian phrase *Italiani brava gente* ("Italians, good people") sums up the wilful ignorance of Italians' role in violent acts of the twentieth century. By offering a particular myth of Italy, the phrase portrays Italians as incapable of any great wrongdoing, especially in contrast to Nazi Germans or imperialist Brits and French. But in exploring how Italians did, in fact, play a role in twentieth-century atrocities, scholars today have identified *Italiani brava gente* as a sign of Italy's refusal to entirely confront its past (Fogu, 2006; Del Boca, 2005; Levis Sullam, 2018: 143). This is a past that includes, among other tragedies, the devastating violence of Italy's more than half a century as a colonizer and the persecution of Jews in the 1930s and 1940s.[24]

By weaving together scenes from the Fascist period with life in the twenty-first century, Scego, Greppi, and Janeczek make explicit connections that were accentuated under Fascism and often ignored after Fascism. They emphasize that colonialism, racism, and antisemitism were not products of Fascism, but that Fascism showed the way they intersect and reinforce each other. The discourses about postcolonialism, the legacy of the Shoah, racism, migration, and sexism have sharply increased in Italian studies and are therefore more interconnected than in some places where the fields are more established, and have become at times not just separate, but also contentious.

While many scholars have explored the connections between racism, colonialism, and migration in Italian literature, I want to highlight how Italian authors who focus on these topics also often incorporate Jewishness and antisemitism into their works, adding another layer to these debates.

"La chat'" ("Chat"), Scego's contribution to *1938*, connects what is happening in Italy today to the Fascist period in Italy, not directly equating them, but showing the dangers of considering Italian racism and antisemitism under Fascism as a period of exceptionalism, rather than elements of society that need to be constantly confronted. In present-day Italy, the narrator considers a chat group composed of mothers. Her son lets her know that certain mothers, the parents of Eritrean immigrants, have been excluded from the group. The narrator confronts the other mothers, who respond with disparaging comments about Africans and Black people, which causes the narrator to consider her Jewish grandmother's experiences of hiding to avoid persecution during World War II. Though there is no resolution to the mothers' racism, the narrator continues to speak up for the Eritrean refugees, reflecting that her grandmother would be proud of her for taking a stand. Italy's histories of antisemitism, colonial racism, and present-day racism are linked in the story. While there are relatively few Eritreans in Italy today, their inclusion in this story points to Italy's history of colonialism, since Italians were present as colonizers in Eritrea from 1882 to 1941. Under Fascism, prejudices were encouraged to foster antisemitism and colonization. The journal dedicated to promulgating racist thought, *La difesa della razza* (*The Defence of Race,* 1938–43), contains side-by-side articles on rejecting Jews from Italian society and the need to colonize Africa because of proposed Italian superiority.

Similar to Scego's "La chat," Greppi's story in *Anche Superman era un rifugiato* points out parallels between experiences of Jewish Europeans during World War II and those of African refugees today. In Greppi's "I posti che siamo" ("The places we are"), the narrator addresses Abdullahi Ahmed, a refugee from Somalia, in part to highlight the correspondences between his story and Hannah Arendt's: "In Europa in quegli anni c'era la Guerra, nel periodo in cui Hannah attraversava le frontiere di nascosto, dico, esattamente come in Somalia quando sei dovuto scappare tu" (Greppi, 2018: 121) ("In Europe in those years there was the War, in the period in which Hannah crossed the borders hidden, I mean, exactly as in Somalia when you had to escape"). The narrator calls attention to how the nationalism of the 1940s contributed to the problems refugees face today: "Molti dei problemi che la Somalia ha avuto negli anni successivi sono dovuti a questo: al fatto che gli italiani hanno rapinato il paese a lungo, proprio nel periodo in cui Hannah cercava di scappare dal nazzismo"' (Greppi, 2018: 120) ("Many of the problems that Somalia had in subsequent years are because of this:

the fact that Italians ransacked the country for a long time, in the period in which Hannah was trying to escape from Nazism"). Greppi highlights Italy's role as colonizer in Somalia and how many current international issues can still be traced back to national aggression before and during World War II.

Janeczek's "Il viaggio più lungo è diventare chi sei" (The longest journey is to become who you are) in *Anche Superman era un rifugiato* and "Trieste in Love" in *1938* both highlight the ways private experience and history intersect and how invisible background can be. "Il viaggio più lungo è diventare chi sei" weaves together the life of Freddie Mercury and Amani Zreba, starting with Queen's participation in the Live Aid concert: "Però nessuno di quelli che seguono l'esibizione legendaria ha la più pallida idea che anche Freddie Mercury sia arrivato dall'Africa"' (Janeczek, 2018: 127) ("However none of those following the legendary show had the faintest idea that Freddie Mercury had also arrived from Africa"). This story emphasizes how a person's "refugee" identity is not necessarily visible. In "Trieste in Love," characters also have multiple identities and names that do not always reveal how they are part of political change or what they have experienced in their own journeys.

In an article about Janeczek winning the prestigious Strega prize in 2018, Scego considers how the award is notable both because a woman had not won it in 15 years and because it was the first time an author not born and raised Italy had received the prize:

> Ed è questa migrazione linguistica che fa della sua vittoria allo Strega una vittoria storica non solo per lei, ma per il paese. È la prima volta che la letteratura italiana è così dichiaratamente multiculturale. Lo è sempre stata, ma non si è mai raccontata in questo modo. Pensiamo solo al padre dell'italiano, Alessandro Manzoni. Anche lui in fondo ha scritto il suo capolavoro, *I promessi sposi*, in una lingua non sua. (Scego, 2018c)

> (And it is this linguistic migration that makes her Strega victory not only a historic victory for her, but also for the country. It is the first time that Italian literature is this overtly multicultural. It has always been, but is has not ever described itself in this way. We need only think of the father of Italian, Alessandro Manzoni. Even he after all wrote his masterpiece *The Betrothed* in a language that wasn't his).

As Scego's comment suggests, Italy and its literature have always been in a dynamic process of development. Who are the real Italians, or what real Italy is, has been a debate since before Italy's unification in the nineteenth century or it becoming a republic in the twentieth century.

While the challenge of responding to immigration is a newer one for Italy, the country's regional differences and late unification in the 1860s mean that Italy has continually interrogated what being Italian means, from before its founding to today.[25] Roberto Dainotto calls attention to how the diversity of Europe is often ignored in formulations of European identity: "*Europe (in Theory)* questions Eurocentrism not from the outside but from the marginal inside of Europe itself" (Dainotto, 2007: 4). His work ends with an analysis of how the Muslim history of Sicily has been overlooked in constructions of European identity and historical narratives. In Chapter 4 above, Akash Kumar examines how the writing of Ibn Hamdîs both should and has been included in explorations of Italian literature.

The concept of a homogenous Italy, anachronistic in any time, also entails ignoring its vast regional diversity, like that of Sicily's, which was developed in part by the regions' varied relationship with other kingdoms, empires, and nations. Showing how people have always been in movement and crossing the boundaries we have created, *Anche Superman era un rifugiato* emphasizes how refugees create art and change the world with it. The volume includes not only new voices, like those of Joudeh and Brhane, in the Italian cultural landscape but also other figures, like Aeneas and Dante, who have long been part of the Italian imaginary. The volume confronts potentially negative stereotypes of refugees with historical, fictional, and present-day examples. In its incorporation of historical and literary figures, the volume suggests the power of drawing not only on the past, but also what has been imagined in the past.

In the Anglophone world, critics have increasingly focused on how literature draws, or perhaps even should draw, on reality and have given a decreasing amount of attention to its potential power to act upon the world. *Anche Superman era un rifugiato* and *The Displaced* share a number of similar goals, including narrating the experience of refugees, changing the perception of who a refugee is, and highlighting the significance of art for understanding displacement. Both also make a material donation to refugee causes. One Euro for every copy of *Anche Superman era un rifugiato* goes to the UNHCR and 10% of the proceeds from *The Displaced* goes to the International Rescue Committee. In the introduction to his collection, Nguyen argues, "Readers and writers should not deceive themselves that literature changes the world" (Nguyen 2018: 20). He urges readers to close the volume, go out, and do something. The subtitle of *Anche Superman era un rifugiato* – *Storie vere di coraggio per un mondo migliore* (*True Stories of Courage for a Better World*) – indicates a conviction that stories can change the world. *Anche Superman era un rifugiato* is brought into schools for students to read, demonstrating a belief in how the collection's stories can accomplish something and that literature shapes our reality.

An Italian anthology of migration literature from 2010 also bears a subtitle that suggests literature influences the world: *Rondini e ronde: Scritti migranti per volare alto sul razzismo* (*Swallows and patrols: Migrant writing in order to fly above racism*). The introduction of this collection ends: "Nello spazio della frontiera tutto può accadere e il catalizzatore di questo avvenimento possibile è la letteratura" (Tuadi, 2010: 10) ("In the frontier space anything can happen and the catalyst for this possible happening is literature"). Literature is framed as a catalyst, as something that causes change. Discussing Italy, where literature plays a more visible role in the country's national awareness also points out the significance of paying attention to the transitory places of migration, politically and culturally, since they offer different ideas of place and the canon.

As evidenced by the title of *Rondini e ronde* (*Swallows and patrols*), *rondini*, "swallows," are consistent images in discussions and representations of migration in Italian work. They appear in the title of the first story of *Anche Superman era un rifugiato* and in the title of Helena Janeczek's powerful novel *Le rondini di Montecassino* (*The Swallows of Monte Cassino*). In Farina's story "Gli uomini rondine" ("The swallow men") – which focused on Joudeh, Nureyev, and swallows – and in Janeczek's novel, the *rondini* are both actual birds and symbols for the movement of people in their works. Free and beautiful, migratory birds move back and forth and belong to multiple places. This image of migration contests the metaphors often used in journalism to discuss migration. Refugees, for instance, "flood" into a country, or the numbers of refugees "surge." In "Migration, Metaphor and Myth," Liudmila Arcimaviciene and Sercan Hamza Baglama argue that the English-language metaphors commonly used to discuss refugees create "a feeling of insecurity and panic that people generally experience in the face of natural disasters" (Arcimaviciene and Baglama, 2018: 9). Metaphors are determined in part by a language, its culture, and its literature.

Both *Anche Superman era un rifugiato* and *Rondini e ronde* forcefully portray the aesthetic position that Sam Durrant and Catherine M. Lord argue for in their introduction to *Essays in Migratory Aesthetics*: "Rather than being a representation of the world, art is an act of world making that alters, however subtly, the fabric of cultures in which we live" (Durrant and Lord, 2007: 13). Migration literature, in contrast to visual art, exists in a language. Migrant authors often make a choice about the language they will use. In her discussion of migratory aesthetics, Mieke Bal highlights the site-specificity of art making: "Since art making is a material practice, there is no such thing as site-unspecific art" (Bal, 2007: 25). The questions of materiality and the book are more complicated and abstract than with many other art forms. A longer literary work can, in fact, be produced in multiple places – and exile, migrant, or transnational literature often is. The end of *Ulysses*, whose author Ezra Pound called "a refugee from Trieste" (Ellmann, 1966: 358), locates the places where James Joyce wrote his masterpiece: "Trieste-Zurich-Paris, 1914–1921." The question of a text's location in terms of its production relates to the more discussed and broader issue of where a finished work of literature exists, as F. W. Bateson asked, "If the Mona Lisa is in the Louvre, where are *Hamlet* and *Lycidas*?" (Bateson, 1972: 9–10).

In part because the location of literary works is open and fluid, language and literature are framed as homelands for writers who have left or had to leave their countries.[26] Theodor Adorno claims, "For a man who no longer has a homeland, writing becomes a place to live" (Adorno, 2005: 87). Émile Cioran states, "One does not inhabit a country; one inhabits a language. That is our country, our fatherland – and no other" (Cioran, 2012: 12). Czeslow Milosz is often quoted as having said "Language is the only homeland."[27] Ignoring non-English works creates an image of the world that is primarily Anglophone and potentially erases these homelands, where migration and the nation have distinct histories. Not only are language and literature sometimes described as a homeland for migrants, but also migration leads to literature in terms of experience and the need to narrate. André Naffis-Sahely argues, "Civilization begets exile; in fact, being banished from one's home lies at the root of our earliest stories, whether human or divine" (Naffis-Sahely, 2020: 1). While Naffis-Sahely points out the long history of the relationship between migration and literature, Aleksandar Hemon suggests its power today to lead to narrative: "Migration generates narratives; each displacement is a tale; each tale unlike any other" (Hemon, 2018: 92). How these tales intersect with each other and build on those of the past is for-mulated through both the construction of anthologies and critical work. The multiple migration narratives in Italian draw on a somewhat different literary tradition, intellectual landscape, and metaphors for refugees, migration, and exile. Considering the construction of not just English-language antholo-gies but also others, like Italy's, suggest the possibilities of multilingual world making. *Anche Superman era un rifugiato: Storie vere di coraggio per un mondo migliore* (*Superman Was a Refugee Too: True Stories of Courage for a Better World*) offers a vision of hope in which literature plays a central role, serving as a potential example, not just for Italians, but also more broadly.

Notes

1 Fiore's *Pre-Occupied Spaces* (Fiore, 2017) examines the complexities of Italy in terms of migration, pointing out how it is much more complicated than a change from emigration to immigration, since emigration did not end and there were earlier examples of immigration.

2 Gabaccia notes that this is when Italy, as a country, began to keep track of the movements of its citizens; before then they would not have been Italians emigrating but categorized by their regional identities.

3 *The Black Mediterranean* discusses the racism on the part of the politicians who proposed these laws: "consciously instrumentalized the trope of African invasion to push through exceptional political measures, which dangerously infringe on basic human rights (amongst others by directly financing Libyan border guards who notoriously abuse migrant's fate) and which have dramatically reduced the possibilities of political asylum across Mediterranean waters" (Danewid et al., 2021: 11).

4 Discussed during the July 14, 2020 virtual conference "Razzismo strutturale: Scambi di prospettive tra Italia e Germania / Struktureller Rassismus: Italienische und Deutsche Perspektiven im Austausch".

5 See Hawthorne (2019a; 2019b). For more on Italy's citizenship laws see also Tuckett (2018).

6 "While all Italians have at times been racialized by such concepts, not all Italian populations have been targeted equivalently by racist ideology. The north of Italy has historically been protected from many of the racializing distinctions that disadvantaged Italians of the south and the islands. Italian race discourse also held a prominent role in Italian attempts to establish colonies in northern Africa. Jews, the Roma and Sinti peoples, and minorities of non-European origins within Italy have also endured particular disadvantages" (Coburn, 2013: 13).

7 See for instance Nichols (2006).

8 The anthologies vary in their modes of composition, from ones that comprise works written specifically for the collection to ones that offer a selection of already published works that span different historical periods and locations. Bond (2019) analyzes the development of the genre of the refugee anthology. She focuses in particular on *The Displaced* and *Banthology*.

9 See for instance: *Parole oltre le frontiere: Dieci storie migranti* (*Words beyond Borders: Ten Migrant Stories*, 2018); *Banthology: Stories from Banned Nations* (2018); *A Country to Call Home: An Anthology on the Experiences of Young Refugees and Asylum Speakers* (2018); *Noi e gli altri: tredici ragazzi raccontano i migranti* (*We and the Others: Thirteen Youths Talk About Migrants* (2018); *Refugee Tales III* (2019); *Ink Knows No Borders: Poems of the Immigrant and Refugee Experience* (2019).

10 For instance the artist Laura Riccioli and Flora Farina, author of the story about Joudeh and Nureyev, published a children's book together in 2017, *Lina e il canto del mare*.

11 "This projected image [of an African women who demands respect from a European country] is in stark contrast with the daily images of the clandestine emigrants who risk their lives in the boats of fortune that have sadly transformed the Mediterranean into a giant cemetery for African migrants" (Sarr, 2019: 65).

12 For a discussion that engages Italy, past and present, see Wallace (2015–16).

13 For a scholarly treatment that makes Italy central to the understanding of migrant literature, see Gnisci (2006).

14 See M. NourbeSe Philip's "Zong! #5" and Edwidge Danticat's "Children of the Sea" for the works that have blank spaces.

15 For a discussion of refugees, Italy, Europe, and borders see Sredanovic (2019).

16 In 2018 Joudeh danced with Bolle on his program "Danza con me" ("Dance with me") to "Inshallah" sung by Sting at Bolle's request.

17 The languages include Russian, German, Burmese, Armenian, Persian, Kurdish, Irish Gaelic, French, Spanish, and Italian.

18 Quoted in Jossa (2006: 20). Stefano Jossa's *L'Italia letteraria* explores how Italy's late founding and literary history gave its literature a large role in the country's perception of itself.

19 While the UNHCR websites in English, French, Spanish, Slovene, Dutch, Chinese, Portuguese, Japanese, Indonesian, Hungarian, Bulgarian, and Russian contained similar content in 2019, the Italian one highlighted *Anche Superman era un rifugiato*. The significant cultural and intellectual role authors play in Italy is also demonstrated by the number of them who are also journalists and academics.

20 See Lausten (2010: 99).

21 The authors of the pieces are: Flora Farina, Paolo Di Paolo, Patrizia Rinaldi, Alessandro Raveggi, Lilith Moscon, Davide Morosinotto, Michela Monferrini, Carlo Greppi, Helena Janeczek, Franesco D'Adamo, Igiaba Scego, Giuseppe Palumbo, and Alidad Shiri. The illustrators are: Laura Riccioli, Fabio Visintin, Tiziana Romanin, Marco Paschetta, Francesco Chiacchio, Marino Neri, Laura Scarpa, Mariachiara di Giorgio, Rita Petruccioli, Marco Brancato, Fabio Santomauro, Giuseppe Palumbo, and Giovanni Scarduelli.

22 There were exceptions to the general neglect of Italian colonialism. Angelo De Boca's extensive work (*Gli italiani in Africa orientale* – three volumes, 1976, 1979, 1982) marks an important moment in the study of Italian colonization and is often pointed to as the beginning of its study. He has also produced a huge amount since then, including *Italiani, brava gente?*

23 See the work of, for instance, Fiore, Parati, Ben-Ghiat, Fuller, Lombardi-Diop, Ponzanesi, Ballinger, Hom, and Duncan. As Parati has stated: "Past and present narratives on internal and external otherness propose Italy as a crossroads where difference and the recognition of sameness meet and invade cultural and linguistic territories" (Parati, 2005: 37).

24 For foundational examples of the wide-ranging work on Italian colonialism that exists in English see Andall and Duncan (2005); Ben-Ghiat and Fuller (2005); and Lombardi-Diop and Romeo (2012).

25 "Never before has Italian culture faced the challenge of welcoming and allowing different cultures to grow and flourish on its own soil, in its own language, through its own publishing and film industries" (Bond et al., 2015: 2). This edited volume, *Destination Italy*, offers a productive and varied overview of Italy, migration, and artistic representation.

26 In "We Refugees," Hannah Arendt meanwhile talks about losing language as a refugee: "We lost our home, which means the familiarity of daily life. We lost our occupation, which means the confidence that we are of some use in this world. We lost our language, which means the naturalness of reactions, the simplicity of gestures, the unaffected expression of feelings" (Arendt, 1994: 110).

27   This quote appears in many places without further bibliographic details. I have
quoted it from the *The Tribe of Dina: A Jewish Women's Anthology* (Klepfisz,
1990: 160).

References

Adorno, T. (2005). *Minima moralia: Reflections from a Damaged Life*. E. F. N.
Jephcott, trans. New York: Verso.

Ahmad, D. (2019). "Introduction" in Ahmad, D. (ed.), *The Penguin Book of Migration
Literature*. New York: Penguin, pp. xv–xxix.

Andall, J. and Duncan, D. (eds). (2005). *Italian Colonialism: Legacy and Memory*.
New York: Peter Lang.

Arcimaviciene, L. and Hamza Baglama, S. (eds). (2018). "Migration, Metaphor
and Myth in Media Representations: The Ideological Dichotomy of 'Them' and
'Us'," *SAGE Open* 8(2), April 1, pp. 1–13.

Arendt, H. (1994). "We Refugees" in Robinson, M. (ed.), *Altogether Elsewhere:
Writers on Exile*. San Diego: A Harvest book, pp. 110–19.

Bal, M. (2007). "Lost in Space, Lost in the Library" in Durrant, S. and Lord, C.
M. (eds), *Essays in Migratory Aesthetics: Cultural Practices Between Migration
and Art-Making*. New York: Rodopi, pp. 23–36.

Bateson, F. W. (1972). *Essays in Critical Dissent*. London: Longman.

Ben-Ghiat, R. and Fuller, M. (eds). (2005). *Italian Colonialism*. New York: Palgrave
Macmillan.

Bezmozgis, D. (2018). "Common Story" in Nguyen, V. T. (ed.), *The Displaced:
Refugee Writers on Refugee Lives*. New York: Abrams Press, pp. 35–42.

Bond, E. (2019). "Assembling the Refugee Anthology," *Journal for Cultural Research*
23(2), pp. 156–72.

Bond, E., Bonsaver, G., and Faloppa, F. (2015). "Introduction" in Bond, E., Bonsaver, G., and Faloppa, F. (eds), *Destination Italy: Representing Migration in
Contemporary Media and Narrative*. Oxford: Peter Lang, pp. 1–28.

Cioran, E. M. (2012). *Anathemas and Admirations*. Richard Howard, trans. New
York: Arcade.

Coburn, M. (2013). *Race and Narrative in Italian Women's Writing since Unification*.
Madison, NJ: Fairleigh Dickinson University Press.

Cortázar, J. (1994). "The Fellowship of Exile" in Robinson, M. (ed.), *Altogether
Elsewhere: Writers on Exile*. San Diego: A Harvest Book, pp. 171–8.

Dainotto, R. M. (2007). *Europe (in Theory)*. Durham, NC: Duke University Press.

Danewid, I., Proglio, G., Pesarini, A., Hawthorne, C., Raeymaekers, T., Saucier,
P. K., Grechi, G., and Gerrand, V. (eds). (2021). "Introduction" in The Black
Mediterranean Collective (eds), *The Black Mediterranean: Bodies, Borders and
Citizenship*. Cham, Switzerland: Palgrave Macmillan, pp. 9–28.

Del Boca, A. (2005). *Italiani, brava gente?* Vicenza: Neri Pozza.

Di Paolo, P. (2018). "Una novola di note" in Scego, I. and UNHCR (eds), *Anche
Superman era un rifugiato: Storie vere di coraggio per un mondo migliore*. Milan:
Mondadori, pp. 24–31.

Durrant, S. and Lord, C. M. (2007). "Introduction" in *Essays in Migratory Aesthetics: Cultural Practices Between Migration and Art-Making*. New York: Rodopi, pp. 11–20.

Ellmann, R. (ed.). (1966). *Letters of James Joyce*. New York: Viking Press.

Farina, F. (2018). "Gli uomini rondine" in Scego, I. and UNHCR (eds), *Anche Superman era un rifugiato: Storie vere di coraggio per un mondo migliore*. Milan: Mondadori, pp. 8–24.

Ferracuti, A. (2020). "Igiaba Scego: Scrivo per decolonizzare la letteratura italiana," Interview, *Left* 21 (May 22–28), pp. 48–51.

Fiore, T. (2017). *Pre-Occupied Spaces: Remapping Italy's Transnational Migrations and Colonial Legacies*. New York: Fordham University Press.

Fogu, C. (2006). "*Italiani brava gente*: The Legacy of Fascist Historical Culture on Italian Politics of Memory" in Lebow, R. N., Kansteiner, W., and Fogu, C. (eds), *Politics of Memory in Postwar Europe*. Durham, NC: Duke University Press, pp. 147–76.

Gabaccia, D. R. (2003). *Italy's Many Diasporas*. London: Routledge.

Gnisci, A. (ed.) (2006). *Nuovo Planetario Italiano: Geografia e antologia della letteratura della migrazione in Italia e in Europa*. Troina: Città aperta.

Greppi, C. (2018). "I posti che siamo" in Scego, I. and UNHCR (eds), *Anche Superman era un rifugiato: Storie vere di coraggio per un mondo migliore*. Milan: Mondadori, pp. 112–23.

Guglielmo, J. and Salerno, S. (eds). (2003). *Are Italians White? How Race is Made in America*. New York: Routledge.

Hawthorne, C. (2019a). "Making Italy: Afro-Italian Entrepreneurs and the Racial Boundaries of Citizenship," *Social and Cultural Geography* (March 28), pp. 704–24.

Hawthorne, C. (2019b). "Black matters are Spatial Matters: Black Geographies for the Twenty-First Century," *Geography Compass* 13(11), pp. 1–13.

Hemon, A. (2018). "God's Fate" in Nguyen, V. T. (ed.), *The Displaced: Refugee Writers on Refugee Lives*. New York: Abrams Press, pp. 91–104.

Janeczek, H. (2018). "Il viaggio più lungo è diventare chi sei" in Scego, I. and UNHCR (eds), *Anche Superman era un rifugiato: Storie vere di coraggio per un mondo migliore*. Milan: Mondadori, pp. 124–39.

Jossa, S. (2006). *L'Italia letteraria*. Bologna: Il Mulino.

Joudeh, A. (2018). *Danza o muori*. Milan: DeA Planeta Libri.

Klepfisz, I. (1990). "Fradel Schtok," in Kaye-Kantrowitz, M., Klepfisz, I., and Hyneman, E. F. (eds), *The Tribe of Dina: A Jewish Women's Anthology*. Boston: Beacon Press.

Kertes, J. (2018). "Second Country" in Nguyen, V.T. (ed.), *The Displaced: Refugee Writers on Refugee Lives*. New York: Abrams Press, pp. 105–12.

Lausten, P. S. (2010). "Living in a Language: Italian Migration Literature" in Gebauer, M. and Lausten, P. S. (eds), *Migration and Literature in Contemporary Europe*. Munich: Martin Meidenbauer, pp. 93–111.

Levi, C. (1960). *Un volto che ci somiglia: Ritratto dell'Italia. Fotografia di János Reismann*. Turin: Einaudi.

Levis Sullam, S. (2018). *The Italian Executioners: The Genocide of the Jews of Italy*. O. Smyth and C. Patane, trans. Princeton: Princeton University Press.

Lombardi-Diop, C. and Romeo, C. (eds). (2012). *Postcolonial Italy: Challenging National Homogeneity*. New York: Palgrave Macmillan.

Mardorossian, C. M. (2003). "From Literature of Exile to Migrant Literature," *Modern Language Studies* 32(2) (November), pp. 15–33.

Matteo, S. (2001). "Introduction: African Italy, Bridging Continents and Cultures" in Matteo, S. (ed.), *ItaliAfrica: Bridging Continents and Cultures*. New York: Forum Italicum, pp. 1–22.

Mazzara, F. (2019). *Reframing Migration: Lampedusa, Border Spectacle and the Aesthetics of Subversion*. Oxford: Peter Lang.

Mengiste, M. (2018). "This is What the Journey Does" in Nguyen, V. T. (ed.), *The Displaced: Refugee Writers on Refugee Lives*. New York: Abrams Press, pp. 129–36.

Mengestu, D. (2019). "An Honest Exit" in Ahmad, D. (ed.), *The Penguin Book of Migration Literature*. New York: Penguin, pp. 69–89.

Naffis-Sahely, A. (ed.). (2020). *The Heart of a Stranger: An Anthology of Exile Literature*. London: Pushkin Press.

Nayeri, D. (2018). "The Ungrateful Refugee," in Nguyen, V. T. (ed.), *The Displaced: Refugee Writers on Refugee Lives*. New York: Abrams Press, pp. 137–50.

Nguyen, V. T. (ed.). (2018). *The Displaced: Refugee Writers on Refugee Lives*. New York: Abrams Press.

Nichols, J. G. (2006). "Ezra Pound's Poetic Anthologies and the Architecture of Reading," *PMLA* 121(1) (January), pp. 170–85.

Palumbo, G. (2018). "Anche Superman era un rifugiato" in Scego, I. and UNHCR (eds), *Anche Superman era un rifugiato: Storie vere di coraggio per un mondo migliore*. Milan: Mondadori, pp. 168–74.

Parati, G. (2005). *Migration Italy: The Art of Talking Back in a Destination Culture*. Toronto: University of Toronto Press.

Phillips, C. (1997). "Preface" in Phillips, C. (ed.), *Extravagant Strangers: A Literature of Belonging*. London: Faber and Faber, pp. x–xi.

Ponzanesi, S. (2004). *Paradoxes of Postcolonial Culture: Contemporary Women Writers of the Indian and Afro-Italian Diaspora*. New York: SUNY.

Sami, C. (2018). "Introduzione" in Scego, I. and UNHCR (eds), *Anche Superman era un rifugiato: Storie vere di coraggio per un mondo migliore*. Milan: Mondadori, pp. 5–7.

Sarr, F. (2019). *Afrotopia*. S. Burk, S. Drew, and S. Jones-Boardman, trans. Minneapolis: University of Minnesota Press.

Scarsini, M. (2018). "Enea è un rifugiato? Il suo avo Dardano ci risponde con un categorico 'No'," *Il Primato Nazionale* (November 24). www.ilprimatonazionale.it/approfondimenti/enea-rifugiato-dardano-risponde-categorico-no-97219/ (Accessed October 20, 2021).

Scego, I. (2018a). "La chat" in Levis Sullam, S. (ed.), *1938: Storia, racconto, memoria*, Florence: Giuntina, pp. 99–112.

Scego, I. (2018b). "Italy is My Country – But it Must Face its Racist History," *The Guardian* (September 16) www.theguardian.com/world/2018/sep/16/italy-must-face-racist-history (Accessed October 20, 2021).

Scego, I. (2018c). "La vittoria di Helena Janeczek allo Strega va oltre la letteratura," *Internazionale* (July). www.internazionale.it/opinione/igiaba-scego/2018/07/06/ helena-janeczek-premio-strega (Accessed October 20, 2021).

Scego, I. (ed.). (2019). *Future: Il domani narrato dalle voci di oggi*. Florence: effequ.

Scego, I. (2020). *La linea del colore*. Milan: Bompiani.

Scego, I. (ed.). (2021). *Africana: Raccontare il Continente al di là degli stereotipi*. Milan: Feltrinelli.

Scego, I. and UNHCR (eds). (2018). *Anche Superman era un rifugiato: Storie vere di coraggio per un mondo migliore*. Milan: Mondadori.

Shiri, A. (2018). "Un semplice invito all'umanità," in Scego, I. and UNHCR (eds), *Anche Superman era un rifugiato: Storie vere di coraggio per un mondo migliore*. Milan: Mondadori, pp. 175–83.

Simpson, J. (ed.). (1995). *The Oxford Book of Exile*. Oxford: Oxford University Press.

Smith, Z. (2019). "Fascinated to Presume: In Defense of Fiction," *The New York Review* (October 24). www.nybooks.com/articles/2019/10/24/zadie-smith-in-defense-of-fiction/ (Accessed October 20, 2021).

Sredanovic, D. (2019). "Defining Borders on Land and Sea: Italy, the European Union and Mediterranean Refugees, 2011–2015" in Linhard, T. and Parsons, T. H. (eds), *Mapping Migration, Identity, and Space*. Cham, Switzerland: Palgrave Macmillan, pp. 233–56.

Tuadi, J. (2010). "Prefazione" in De Marchi, S. (ed.), *Rondini e ronde: Scritti migranti per volare alto sul razzismo*. Milan: Magrovie Edizioni, pp. 5–10.

Tuckett, A. (2018). *Rules, Paper, Status: Migrants and Precarious Bureaucracy in Contemporary Italy*. Stanford: Stanford University Press.

Walkowitz, R. L. (2006). "The Location of Literature: The Transnational Book and the Migrant Writer" in *Immigrant Fictions: Contemporary Literature in an Age of Globalization*. Madison: University of Wisconsin Press, pp. 527–45.

Wallace, D. (2015–16). "Itinerari europei medievali e moderni," *Scritture Migranti* 9–10, pp. 199–227.

White, P. (1995). "Geography, Literature, and Migration" in King, R., Connell, J., and White, P. (eds), *Writing Across Worlds: Literature and Migration*. New York: Routledge, pp. 1–19.

6

Porta di Lampedusa, porta d'Europa: contemporary monumentality, entropy, and migration at the gateway to Europe

Tenley Bick

Risposi non faccio monumenti. (Mimmo Paladino, 2019)[1]

(I replied, I don't make monuments.)

On June 28, 2008, a work of art by contemporary Italian artist Mimmo Paladino (b. 1948, Paduli) was permanently installed on the southern-most point of Lampedusa, the tiny Italian island (and southern-most point of Italy) located in the southern Mediterranean, 120 miles south of Sicily and 70 miles east of the North African Tunisian coast (Figure 6.1). Entitled *Porta di Lampedusa, porta d'Europa*, meaning Gateway to Lampedusa, Gateway to Europe (in reference to Lampedusa's nickname), the terracotta-and-iron open portal functions as a symbol of Italian and European hospitality for migrants from North and East Africa who frequently arrive on the island (or are brought to it) during attempts to cross the Mediterranean. Despite the portal's message of unconditional invitation (it lacks a door, the other meaning of the Italian noun *porta*, and therefore cannot be closed), the work also functions as a memorial to migrants who will never reach Lampedusa, who can never be welcomed. Promoted and commissioned by Amani, a non-governmental aid organization that serves African youth in Kenya, Zambia, and Sudan, as well as publishing house Arnoldo Mosca Mondadori (owned at the time by then Prime Minister Silvio Berlusconi's media corporation, Mediaset), the *Porta* was made in dedication to the memory of the many migrants and refugees who lost their lives during cross-Mediterranean passage in the two decades prior to the work's realization.

Eight years later, amidst Italian and EU shifts to non-assistance practices for migrants in the Mediterranean, *Porta di Lampedusa, porta d'Europa* became the site of a little-known artistic intervention. On October 5, 2016, two days after the third annual *Giornata della Memoria e dell'Accoglienza*

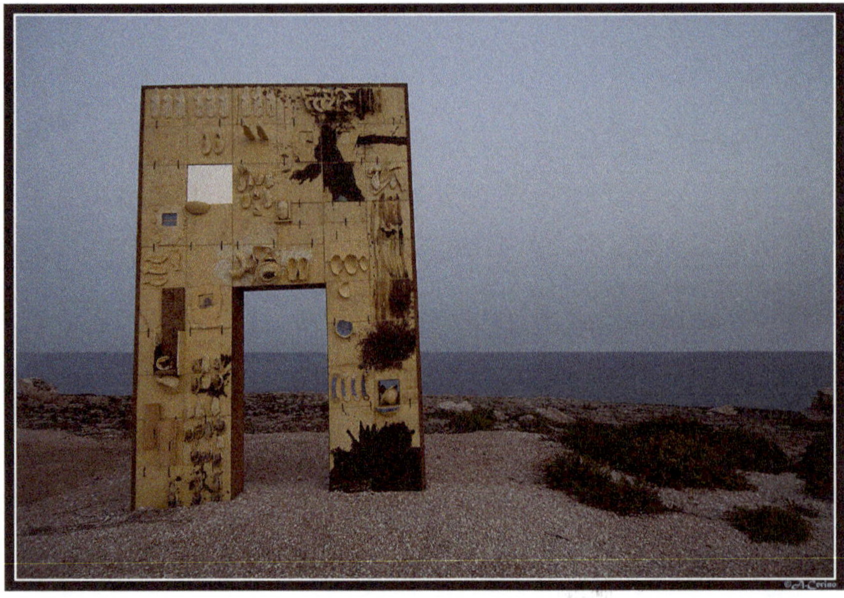

Figure 6.1a Mimmo Paladino, *Porta di Lampedusa, porta d'Europa* (Gateway to Lampedusa, Gateway to Europe), 2008. View from Lampedusa (facing shore). Photo: Alessandro Cerino. © Mimmo Paladino. Courtesy of the artist.

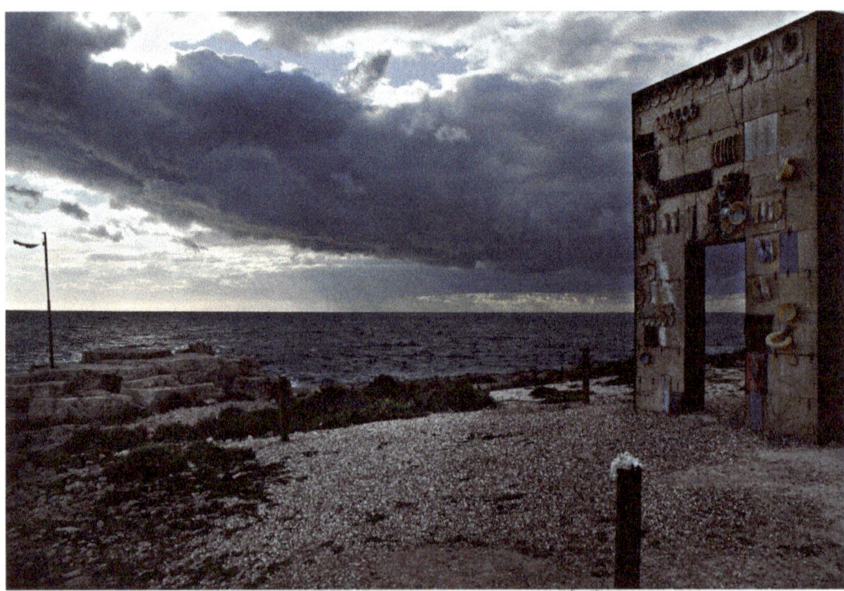

Figure 6.1b Mimmo Paladino, *Porta di Lampedusa, porta d'Europa* (Gateway to Lampedusa, Gateway to Europe), 2008. View from shore (facing Lampedusa, to the right). Photo: Franco Guardascione. © Mimmo Paladino. Courtesy of the artist. Reproduced with photographer's permission.

(Italy's National Day of Remembrance and Hospitality), which commemorates the tragic 2013 shipwreck off the coast of Lampedusa that resulted in the death of 368 migrants, Italian artist Arabella Pio (b. 1980, Milan) sealed the gateway with cement bricks, walling off the gateway's open portal.[2] Designed by Pio and then made by a local fabricator for the work's installation on site, the bricks were modeled after headstones found in Lampedusa's cemetery, specifically those used to mark the graves of anonymous migrants, many of whom are interred on Lampedusa. Each of Pio's bricks was inscribed with the following words: "migrante non identificato qui riposa": here lies an unidentified migrant (Pio, 2016). They were stacked inside a structural frame, also made by the fabricator, placed inside the gateway. As the artist began stacking the bricks, locals inquired about the intervention, and then lent a hand. The resulting work, entitled *Porta d'Europa*, was in place for only a few hours (Figure 6.2). It was installed by the artist temporarily after requests for municipal permits were declined. It was the only time the work was ever assembled (Pio, 2019).

In the short decade framed by Paladino's and Pio's works, Lampedusa was at the center of intense debates in Europe around renewed migration from the Middle East and Africa. While Paladino's work has been celebrated as a somber artistic work and popular symbol of *accoglienza* (hospitality) or Italian State empathy for migrants and immigrants, a point the artist wanted the work's opening to symbolise (Paladino, 2019), Pio's intervention received little attention. The intervention and its surrounding circumstances led to a crisis of practice for Pio, who became disillusioned with institutions (including municipalities, in her case, as a public artist). She thereafter increasingly distanced herself from her work. Its components now reside in the artist's garage in Milan (Pio, 2019) – stored simultaneously ready-at-hand, like surplus building materials, and out-of-sight, like something precious or occasional, for which there's no room or need in the day-to-day.

Building upon recent scholarship in Italian studies, which has addressed histories of Lampedusa's role in Italy's mobility regimes past and present, and supported by interviews with the artists, this chapter examines Paladino's and Pio's works within the contexts of cross-Mediterranean migration from Africa to Italy, the related colonial histories of this space, and contemporary debates on monumentality and migration within postcolonial discourse in Italy. Using formal and social art historical analysis, with special attention to the position of the *Porta* within the context of Paladino's practice, as well as these works' divergent framings of monumentality, memorialization, and Italian-African relations, the chapter examines the inattention to Pio's intervention and argues that these works index shifting contemporary responses in Italy to shifts in migration policy. At the same time, as a study of contemporary Italian artistic responses to migration, it situates both

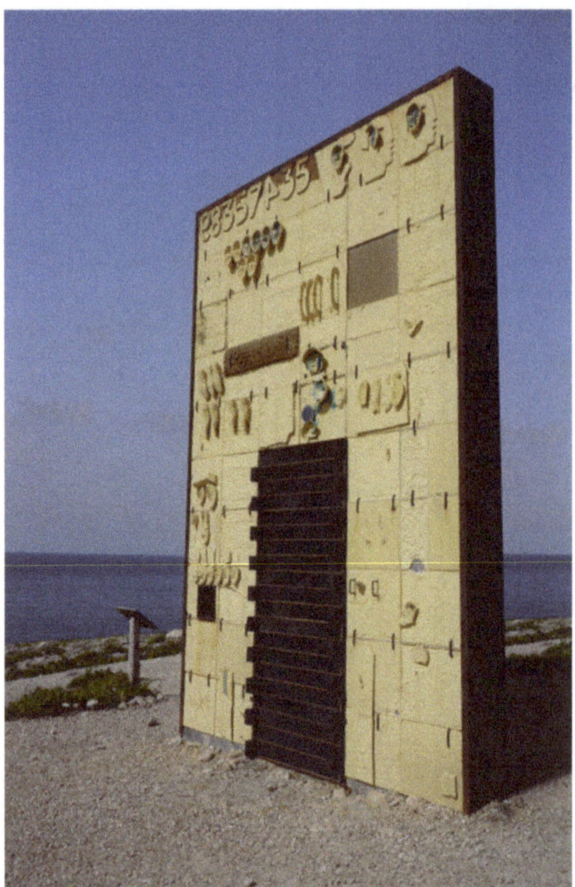

Figure 6.2 Arabella Pio, *Porta d'Europa*, 2016. Artistic intervention in Mimmo Paladino's *Porta di Lampedusa, porta d'Europa* (2008), October 5, 2016. Photo: Arabella Pio. © Arabella Pio. Courtesy of the artist.

works in relation to their art historical precedents. It argues that these works model what we might call an entropic monumentality: a condition and articulation of temporary historical memorialization which, in this case, in contemporary Italian culture, is distinguished by its inclination to undermine coloniality that undergirds monuments and their function as exertions of power. In the context of Lampedusa, these works position the territorialized Italian Mediterranean as a site of failed empathy, in Paladino's case, and as a site of Italian colonial and neo-colonial violence and popular apathy in Pio's. The chapter concludes with a discussion of related explorations of monumentality by artists responding to Italian narratives of postcolonial reparation, including one work made contemporaneously to Paladino's by

British-Ethiopian artist Theo Eshetu, on Italy's repatriation of the damaged Axumite fourth-century Stele of Axum to Ethiopia.

A sea change: contemporary counter-migration and Italy's former fourth shore

Oriented toward Zuwara, Libya (instead of the nearer Tunisia), a key point of cross-Mediterranean departure for North and East African migrants, Paladino's gateway and its siting frames the Mediterranean between Europe and Africa as a geography in crisis, yet still a Eurocentric one. The work's title and position underscore the point that control of cross-Mediterranean mobility falls under the dominion of European territory. Its title also means "Gateway *of* Lampedusa – Gateway *of* Europe" – as in "Lampedusa's Gateway, Europe's Gateway." Access to Europe and the ability to move across borders, the work suggests, is a proprietary form of agency that belongs to Europe. The monument frames, pictorially and architecturally, a view of waters where thousands of people continue to lose their lives only a very short distance away, as in the disaster of October 3, 2013, when 368 migrants died in a shipwreck less than a half mile off the shores of Lampedusa, so close to the gateway to Europe, so close to Europe's gateway to itself.[3]

In an interview in late 2019 with the author, Paladino looked back on the work and described the site as a marginal place in both geography and topography: "l'idea era di fare un'opera direttamente su uno scoglio estremamente distante, e quindi diciamo forse un luogo più estremo dell'Europa" ("the idea was to do a work directly on an extremely distant cliff, and therefore perhaps on the outermost place in Europe"). The work's siting on a double precipice – on a cliff, on the so-called edge of Europe – and orientation toward Libya call to mind histories of Italian empire and colonization, which expanded this boundary and reframed the Mediterranean, North African coast, and large parcels of North and East Africa as Italian territory. In ancient Rome, North African territories were consolidated into Roman provinces including *Africa Proconsularis*, spanning from northeastern Algeria to Tripoli (Bullo, 2002: 1–3); in the early twentieth century, in liberal and Fascist Italy, North and East African colonies were formalized in the Italian colonial states of *Africa Settentrionale Italiana* (1911–41) and *Africa Orientale Italiana* (1936–41).[4]

The Porta's design as an architectural form associated with passage and dwelling – post-and-lintel archaic architecture was a key reference for Paladino – is complicated by its "open-door" invitation. At the very site of geographical and historical confinement, that is, on a former carceral island, we find the work as a symbol for welcoming that is nevertheless haunted by violent histories of state geographical constructions across this borderland. This borderland also serves as a center for migrant detention in the present, in a folding over of past into present that Stephanie Hom has called "empire's Mobius strip" (Hom, 2019; Deleuze and Guattari, 1983: 139–46).[5] Indeed, under Mussolini, Libya was famously dubbed Italy's *quarta sponda*, Italy's "fourth shore." Italy's Mediterranean colonies under Fascism were to be populated by Italian workers; mass population projects in the 1920s and Italy's agricultural colonization of Libya culminated in the presence of 30,000 Italian colonists by the late 1930s, tasked with farming Italian land in Libya (Cresti, 2005: 74, 80; Locatelli, 2016: 135). This expansion was driven by a form of internal colonialism in Italy, which sought to maintain northern wealth in the country by channelling southern peasants into emigrant colonial communities in Africa, luring (and expelling them from mainland Italy) with the promise of work (Srivastava, 2018: 2–3).[6] This expansion was also imagined in mass culture of the period, as David Forgacs (2014: 78) has demonstrated; Italy's Mediterranean colonies were positioned through photography and mass media as both an extension of the metropole and margin thereof.

In Paladino's work, less than a century later, the relationship between Lampedusa and Italy's former fourth shore is reversed. The *Porta* underscores Lampedusa as the European (and European-controlled) site of migrant entry, even though migrants, as historians of contemporary Italy have noted (O'Healy, 2016: 152; Foot, 2018: 406), more often arrive by other means. The work repositions a rocky outcropping on a tiny island, far flung from Italy and Europe, as the gateway to an expansive but unified European state – a point that would be underscored by later historical discussions of Lampedusa's position, "where Europe began, and ended" (Foot, 2018: 404). The work also positions the Mediterranean between North Africa and Europe as one of unidirectional transit. In turn, it marks Libya in the contemporary moment as a non-European site despite its function as a European borderland, as underscored by its policing by Frontex (the EU's unified border agency). It also positions Libya as a synecdoche for a unified but fragmenting Africa, whose peoples long to emigrate.

Events that were contemporaneous with the realization of the *Porta* also called to mind Italy's historical conquest of Africa, and Libya in particular. The work was commissioned and made during the same year as Italy's apology and accord with Libya (signed August 30, 2008 by Libya's then president, Muammar Gaddafi, and Berlusconi) for atrocities committed during its colonial occupation and rule of the country from 1911 to 1943. On August 31, 2008, Berlusconi apologised to Gaddafi for Italy's colonial occupation of Libya from 1911 to 1943 (Hassan, 2013: 53). Under Italian colonial conquest and rule, 100,000 Libyans – then approximately 1/8th of Libya's population – were killed by chemical warfare, concentration camps, and other means by liberal and Fascist Italian forces following victory in the Italian–Turkish war of the early 1910s through the dissolution of Italy's colonies (Del Boca, 2003: 25–7). The *Trattato Italia–Libia di amicizia, partenariato e cooperazione* (Italy–Libya Treaty of Friendship, Partnership and Cooperation) of 2008 granted reparations in the amount of five billion dollars to Libya as well as repatriation of the so-called *Venere di Cirene* (Venus of Cyrene), a classical Roman marble copy of a Hellenistic original sculpture, uncovered by Italian soldiers in 1913, which was shipped to Italy in 1915, where it had since remained (Sarrar, 2008). The 2008 apology was the first ever from the Italian State for its colonial history, the glaring absence of which was remarked upon just years prior in 2005 by Italian historian Angelo Del Boca (2005:195–202). Repatriation of the statue and a formal state apology veiled a key goal for Italy: the solidification of new counter-migration and maritime agreements between Italy and Libya, which sought to have Libya police migrants seeking to reach Italy and to instead return them to Libya. Indeed, restitution of the statue had been promised in 2002 – both by decree from the minister of the *Ministero per i beni e le attività culturali e per il turismo*, Giuliano Urbani, and by Berlusconi during a State visit to Libya.[7] The fact that the promise of restitution had been made six years prior to its eventual 2008 return suggests that the timing of actual restitution on Italy's part was closely connected to state desire for new counter-migration policy with Libya – a desire perhaps veiled itself by the dedication of Paladino's *Porta* to the memory of deceased migrants on the eve of Berlusconi's apology. After all, the *Porta* was an indirectly government-funded work of art; we recall that its corporate sponsor, publishing house Arnoldo Mosca Mondadori, was owned at the time by Mediaset, Berlusconi's media corporation.

The fraught relationship between Italy's contemporaneous address of Mediterranean anti-migration policy with Libya on the one hand, and its colonial history with that same state, on the other, is prudent to discussions of artistic discourse in Italy on the migration crisis, especially given Italy and the EU's continued work to have Libya police migration and force asylum seekers back to Libya.[8] It is in this context that migration and histories of colonialism were first linked in contemporary Italy in mainstream media and culture.

Flanked by World-War-II era bunkers for the Italian army, located not far from Lampedusa's military port where rescued migrants are brought, but well away from the inland immigrant detention center on the island, as architect and researcher Chiara Dorbolò (2018) has noted, the monument seems to stand at odds with the assertions of what Dorbolò has called an "invisible border" in Lampedusa and across the Pelagian islands to which it belongs. As a door, however, as Dorbolò asserts, it is a kind of sign for an "invisible wall," a wall between Italy and Africa that we cannot see.

This narrative becomes more complicated when we consider the title of the monument, which underscores broader European control of migration that has emerged in recent years. This reading aligns with what Sandro Mezzadra has called the "new European migratory regime," as opposed to historical "management of mobility" bound up with the creation of national territories (Mezzadra, 2012: 40, 44). By contrast, the new European migratory regime, as Mezzadra argues, is characterized by the EU's *post-national* work with organizations such as Frontex to police the "external frontiers" and borders of the EU.

Other scholarship on Italian histories of mobility control necessitate both a national and post-national approach to this problem. In her important study of the connections between Italian colonialism in the past and migration-related "crises" in the present, Stephanie Hom has examined Lampedusa's detention centers in relation to the island's historical function from the mid-nineteenth to early twentieth centuries as one of Italy's many carceral islands for members of the Libyan resistance and other political dissidents (actual or accused) (2019: 16–17). The violence of Italian transport and incarceration of members of the Libyan resistance is little known, as are many of the atrocities committed by Italy in Libya.[9] In Italy's contemporary spaces of "mobility control" and an extension of the country's historical space of empire, Hom has similarly argued that migrant detention in Lampedusa offers a shift away from the free flow of a globalized world. She writes: "What is happening on Lampedusa, then, can be seen as a renewed Manichean division of the world into those who move by choice and those who are moved by force ... a rigidity that takes shape among the flows and liquidity said to characterise our global age" (2019: 23).

Paladino's *Porta d'Europa* has been upheld by Lampedusa's local government and by the Italian State as a poignant monument and icon of Italian hospitality. Despite contemporaneous expansions of anti-migration policy, it has been used as a political tool to articulate Italian State empathy for refugees, as evidenced by President Sergio Mattarella's visit on June 3, 2016. It has also figured prominently in popular culture. In late 2016, the *Porta* appeared in a music video (directed by Stefano Carena) for rapper Willie Peyote's (Guglielmo Bruno) 2015 song, "Io non sono razzista ma..." ("I'm not racist but..."). In the video, which was sponsored by the municipality of Lampedusa and Linosa, Peyote performs on various sites around the two Pelagian islands, including the famous graveyard of migrant boats on Lampedusa, as well as broader Italy, emphasizing long histories of migration that were formative to "Italian" culture. Peyote is joined through montage by multi-ethnic community members who dance and lip sync at major sites associated with migration and immigration in Peyote's native Turin in the northwestern province of Piedmont; the open-air market of Porta Palazzo and the city's neo-Moorish synagogue figure prominently throughout the video (Figure 6.3a–c). Peyote repeatedly performs in front of Paladino's *Porta*, singing about widespread racism and xenophobia in Italy, highlighting domestic fears of unemployment despite public discourse on Italian *accoglienza* and *integrazione* of migrants. For the discerning viewer, the *Porta d'Europa* in Lampedusa is juxtaposed with the *porte* (doors and gateway spaces) of the synagogue (which features distinctive Arab-influenced horseshoe arches) and Porta Palazzo in Turin – a place that is frequently racialized and discussed among white *torinesi* as dangerous, due to the high presence of multi-ethnic vendors. This juxtaposition serves to underscore a national need for the welcoming of immigrants around Italy and the influences of histories of migration on Italian culture. In the video, Peyote also points to widespread Italian perceptions that recent waves of migration are a new phenomenon, citing recent histories of Italian emigration: "L'immigrazione è la prima emergenza in televisione, che poi non è tutta 'sta novità, pensa a tuo nonno arrivato in Argentina col barcone" ("Immigration is the first emergency on television, that in the end isn't all new, think of your grandfather who arrived in Argentina by large boat"). The *Porta* here functions as a symbol of anti-racism.

These concerns with the politicized mediation of spaces associated with migration align with existing concerns regarding the biased depictions of migrants. More specifically, they draw our attention to specific representations of Lampedusa – a site which major art exhibitions, namely *La Terra Inquieta* (curated by Massimiliano Gioni, La Triennale di Milano, 2017), have problematically positioned, vis-à-vis the mayor of Lampedusa's own words about the island, as a site of dignity for migrants. Italian maritime and immigration policy became even more restrictive in 2015, when the Italian navy began refusing to assist migrant ships in need of rescue, as documented in recent works by American and Italian artistic duo Lorenzo Pezzani and Charles Heller in their project, Forensic Oceanography (est. 2011): a "sub-domain" of the pair's Forensic Architecture agency. Through an intensively research-focused creative practice, Forensic Oceanography documents this shift towards non-responsiveness and sea closure that led to the deaths of thousands of people, while forcing (and criminalizing) rescue efforts by non-governmental organizations and private companies; their works, *Death by Rescue* (2016) and *Mare Clausum* (2018), both of which were also featured in *Liquid Violence* (2018), use data visualizations and installations to inform viewers of specific operations that have led to the unnecessary death of migrants at sea.[10] Changes that Forensic Oceanography has traced were expanded by the 2018 elections of interior minister and Lega leader Matteo Salvini and the Lega-Cinque-Stelle Coalition government. Prior to the elections, the *Porta* had been slated to appear on

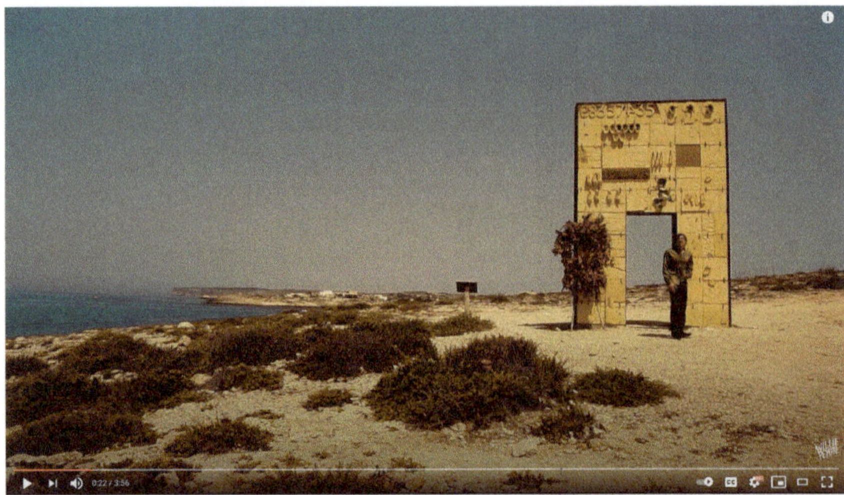

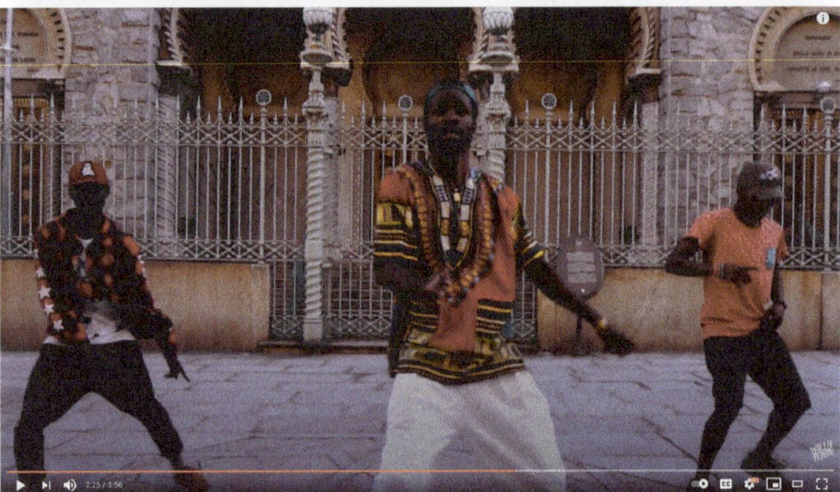

Figure 6.3a–c Screenshots of Willie Peyote, "Io non sono razzista ma…" ("I'm not racist but…"), music video, 2016. Colour, 3:56. Directed by Stefano Carena. From top to bottom, left to right, the sites are Porta d'Europa (Lampedusa), the synagogue of Turin, and Porta Palazzo (Turin).

a commemorative Italian postage stamp; the stamp, planned for a series on civic duty, was subsequently canceled in September of 2018 ("Migranti," *La Repubblica*, 2018).

The work's opening seems to align with Paladino's broader reflections on islands not as sites of confinement, as they have been historically used (as under Fascism), but perhaps of great opening:

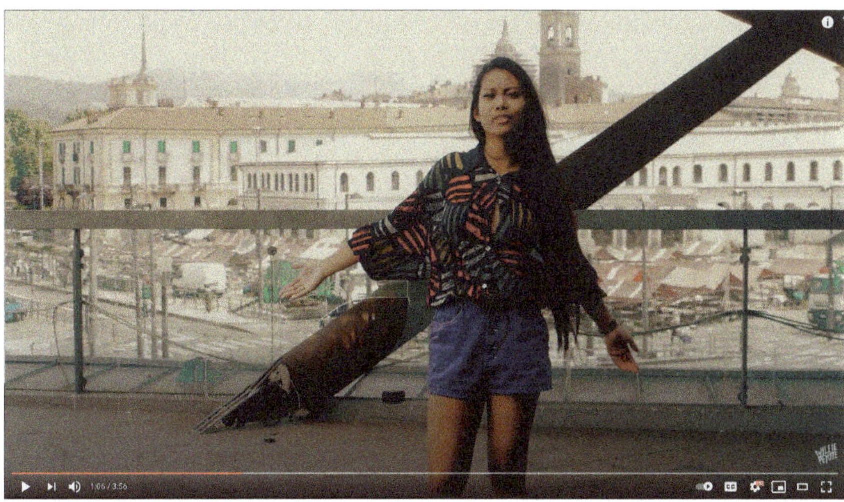

Figures 6.3a–c (Continued)

Però è sempre come dire un'apertura – ma, insomma, cosa c'è di più ampio e libero di un'isola in mezzo al mare. Cioè non hanno confini naturalmente, se non il mare, insomma. … C'è il mare. … Quindi è qualcosa di appparentemente è costrittiva, ma poeticamente o concettualmente la cosa più ampia e aperta che ci può essere, penso lì. La forma più ampia di libertà probabilmente, no? Però un'isola non si può scappare facilmente. Quella è anche vera, insomma, come non si può arrivare facilmente, perché c'è il mare. Quindi c'è la doppia possibilità: di grande apertura sull'infinito ampio che è il mare inversa anche una difficoltà di scardinare e di andare via (Paladino, 2019)

(But it's always, you know, an opening – but, really, what is there that's wider and freer than an island in the middle of the sea. They don't have borders, naturally, if not [that of] the sea, in other words. … There's the sea. … So it's something that at first glance is constrictive, but poetically or conceptually [it's] the most wide open thing there can be, I think. Probably the widest form of liberty, no? But you can't escape an island easily. That's also true, in the end, just as you can't get there easily, because there's the sea. Therefore, there is the double possibility: of a great opening onto the vast infinity that is the sea, countered by the difficulty of scattering and of leaving.)

The rhetoric of opening has long histories in migration and empire for Italy. Paladino's words in this case are haunted by spectres of Italian Fascist imperialism. On May 9, 1936, following Italy's conquest of Ethiopia, Mussolini proclaimed the establishment of Italy's Empire. In his "Discorso di proclamazione dell'Impero," Mussolini outlined two new laws, declaring Italy's rule over Ethiopia's Empire and its peoples, while proclaiming the king of Italy now emperor of Ethiopia. For this discussion, of key importance to the proclamation is Mussolini's framing of the establishment of empire by way of an analogy of great opening: "Ecco la legge, o italiani, che chiude un periodo della nostra storia e ne apre un altro come un immense varco aperto su tutte le possibilità del futuro" ("Here is the law, oh Italians, that closes a period of our history and therein opens another, like an immense gap that is open to all the possibilities of the future"), reads the lead-in to the new laws. The establishment of the Italian Empire (and the territorial expansion that came with it) was imagined as a great opening to the future, to a new future history. With this semiotic history of empire in mind, this opening in Paladino's *Porta* indexes a clear shift in its symbolism: from a colonial symbol of imperial expansion (and persecution of peoples) to a postcolonial symbol of hospitality for migrants in the present who, as in Italy's colonized subjects in Libya and other parts of Africa, were also persecuted, only this time by non-assistance.

Entropic monumentality: an operation of small destruction, of telluric agitation

Existing scholarship – predominantly in cultural studies – has framed the *Porta* as a "colossal monolith" (Hom, 2019: 61) and as a "monument" among other "symbolic acts of remembrance" on the island (Ritaine, 2015: 135), emphasizing an impressive scale and monumentality for the work even as they have acknowledged its subsequent erosion. Closer art historical study of the work, however – in addition to the artist's own assertion that he does not make monuments – reveals qualities that challenge these readings. The work's relatively earthen materials and structure (purposely used by the artist), seen best in the two terracotta facades, as well as its exposure to the elements, human scale, and slim profile (from which view it is, notably, rarely photographed), underscore its potential frangibility (Figure 6.4). It is a rather slight slip of a structure. None of these are characteristics of a colossal monument.

In my interview with Paladino, he recounted that he was asked to make a monument dedicated to the memory of migrants who died during their attempts to cross the Mediterranean. His response to the request was "non faccio monumenti" ("I don't make monuments"; Paladino, 2019). Indeed, contrary to its function as a public memorial and permanent work of art, the *Porta* was not necessarily conceived to last. Paladino envisioned turning the work, made of natural materials, over to the environment:

> Diciamo che simboleggiando anche che doveva forse diventare un problema drammatico ma limitato nel tempo, e quindi come questo problema poteva

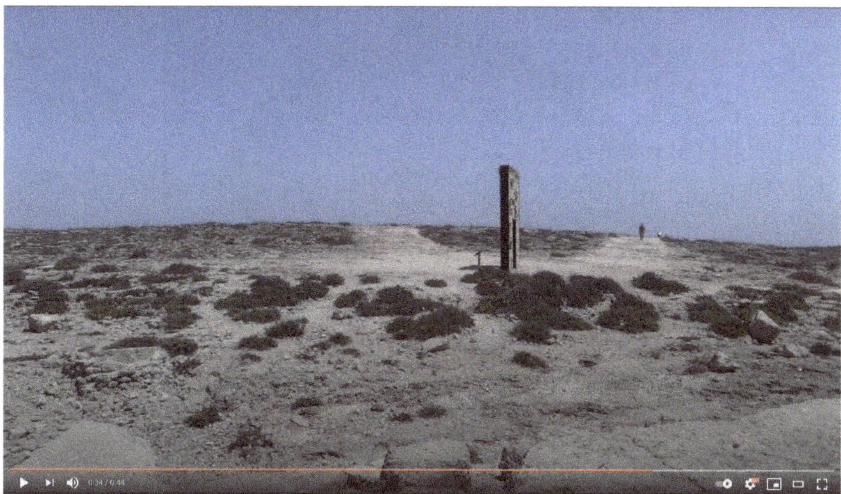

Figure 6.4 Mimmo Paladino, *Porta di Lampedusa, porta d'Europa*, 2008. Side view. Screenshot from video posted to YouTube by Luca Urbinati, "Porta d'Europa e bandiera della Pace – Lampedusa," May 22, 2017: www.youtube. com/watch?v=c7JeRTgXstM (accessed February 16, 2022).

come dire esaurirsi, questo sbarco di immigranti, così la porta non ha più senso di esistere insomma. E diciamo che poi alla fine questo era la mia idea molto poetica ... sto facendo un'operazione di piccola distruzione, ma non distruzione, per consuma, l'eroda, e per cui, questa terra comincia di essere corrosa dal mare (Paladino, 2019).

(We can say it's also symbolizing that perhaps [migration] had become a problem that was dramatic but limited in time, and so this problem could, you know, have expired, this landing of immigrants, in which case the gateway would no longer have any reason to exist. And let's say that in the end this was my very poetic idea ... I'm executing an operation of small destruction but [also] not destruction, rather to eat away and erode it, and because of that, this earth begins to be corroded by the sea.)

For Paladino, the idea was that the work's natural material repertoire would lend itself to adaptation by nature itself.

The terracotta slabs were made in the historic ceramic-arts center of Faenza, located in the north-central province of Ravenna. The *Porta* was then assembled in the artist's native Paduli in southern Italy, ninety minutes inland from Napoli, in the province of Campania, after which it was transported to Lampedusa for installation. The potential fragility and archaic nature of the artist's material repertoire underscores his interest in making a non-monumental work. The *Porta* has faded and eroded over the years.

The glazes have faded, some of the terracotta slabs have been replaced, and ceramic objects have detached and broken off of its surface. The work has deteriorated so much that in the summer of 2020, Italian corporations launched campaigns to "save the Porta d'Europa" as a "symbol of the solidarity of Lampedusa" through matched donations for its restoration.[11]

A regular grid of ceramic square slabs comprises the facades of the *Porta*, each measuring ten squares in height by six squares across, held together with iron rivets. The rivet process is a historical method of ceramic repair that pre-dates the development of synthetic adhesive in the mid-twentieth century (Albert, 2012: S1–S2). The resulting effect is an aesthetic of joining and of historical repair. Upon closer inspection, however, we find that some rivets appear in the middle of an uncompromised slab, in the absence of a join. The rivets are present to create an *aesthetic* of reconnection rather than reconnection in actual fact. The decorative rivets undermine the constructivist aesthetic of the rivets elsewhere on the work. The suggestion is a disruption of an aesthetic of structural logic. Rivets are used to repair; in this case, however, repair (and reparation) is superficial. It is an empty gesture.

Underscoring this point are the everyday items that appear in partial or unpaired form, with jagged edges (seen on ceramic bowls) and in piecemeal compositions. Forms that read at first like pairs are revealed to be uncoupled singles; the modeled feet at upper left are both right feet, and the shoes are both left. The not-a-pair of un-paired shoes resonates with the iconography of migrant death that has consolidated on Lampedusa; un-paired shoes that wash ashore are shown in an exhibition space in town (at the associazione Askavusa) alongside recovered prayer books, Qur'ans, and other possessions (Turrisi, 2011). The objects are, for Paladino, the most "umani e poveri" ("human and impoverished"), the simplest – whatever people who are migrating can carry (Paladino, 2019).

The work is partially glazed with a matte black, ink-colored wash-like glaze, smeared upwards, poured, splattered. One blot, on the right post if facing the ocean, includes a figure whose arms are stretched upward. Incised into the clay in *sgraffito*, the figure's corporeal form is rendered by the removal of material – that is, its presence is articulated through material absence. In another area of the *Porta*, one square seems to have been removed. It is covered with a mirror panel that reflects the sky. Another cut-out still was made into a pass-through shelf, further underscoring the work as one that frames passage. A pair of heads, one facing right, one left, also indicate a dialogical encounter.

The monument is constructed of two iron portals framed by facades of ceramic slabs, held together with iron brackets as described above. Sculptural elements decorate the surface in low and high relief. We see modeled shoes at lower-left, a group of bowls, a line of nine right hands in the upper-left, adapted hamsa, perhaps, a few fish, and a number of hats, including one, now broken, in a cutaway on the right-hand side that looks out onto the sea. The *Porta*'s iconography includes objects that are familiar but without owners. The objects seem abandoned. Their groupings suggest the many who have lost their lives. Other signs, like the hamsa, might be signs of protection for those still to come. A few heads in profile stand out in low relief, painted with images of the sea, as if to say the sea is on their mind. A trio of hats is also present; one appears to have been swept up, another sits horizontally, brim to the tile, while another is turned over entirely on the shelf, topsy-turvy. The sculptural imagery found on the *Porta* includes iconography that is commonly found in Paladino's works. The head, numbers, and geometric sequences have long appeared in his work, as have references to travel and nomadism, frequently made through the use of boats, airplanes, and geographical forms as motifs in his work.

Paladino is best known as an artist associated with the Italian neo-expressionist movement of the late 1970s and 1980s known as the Trans-vanguardia, whose artists were theorized by the Italian art critic Achille Bonito Oliva as "nomads." Unlike the model of nomadism that modeled an "internationalistic utopia of art," which Bonito Oliva found in Arte Povera – the movement that preceded the Transavanguardia – the Transa-vanguardia's nomadism would be "both diverse and diversifying" between individual works. Paladino has been celebrated in Italian art criticism and in certain discourses of contemporary art history as a postmodern nomad, for his pastiche of signs and symbols, suggestive iconographies, and, in Bonito Oliva's view, ability to render painting "a meeting and expansion place," with "the range of vision of cultural motives" (1979: 20). For Paladino, a southern Italian artist, the Transavanguardia was appropriately a southern phenomenon, as opposed to the northern Italian orientation of Arte Povera. The artist has frequently discussed the qualities of "l'artista meridionale" ("the southern [Italian] artist"). In 1984, Paladino reflected on the energy and vitality of the south of Italy, as a southern Italian artist, in association with the Biennale Sud:

> Mediterranean artists wish to communicate in a linguistic form bound up with their homeland but without any sacrifice of an international vocation. Decen-tralization stimulates a different form of creative intelligence. I say this as an artist who was born in the south, left the south and returned to the south. Here there is the art of centuries, there are signs of thousands of invasions and thousands of cultural interferences that come from the Byzantines, to the Normans, to the French ... But landscape is certainly one of the elements of telluric agitation [irrequietezza tellurica] that characterize the southern artist.[12]

Paladino often refers to this telluric agitation – an unease, or restlessness, of the soil and earth as planet – alongside references to the subterranean.

The connection to geologic time held specific potency in the turbulent socio-political context of the late 1970s and early 1980s in Italy, that is, toward the end of years of unrest in the country.

Indeed, the Transavanguardia was also an implicit if not willed response, as Paladino put it, to the horrible historical period in Italy known as the "anni di piombo" or "years of lead," in which Italy experienced paramilitary domestic terrorism and widespread socio-political unrest. If the political years of the 1960s had transformed into terrorism, as Paladino sees it, then artists felt an imperative to bring formal liberty back to their work, to tell history in a different way (Paladino, 2019). Bonito Oliva would call the work of the Transavanguardia an affirmative practice, characterized by flows and an expansive "fluid penetration" (1979: 20). Of importance to this discussion is that Bonito Oliva's expansionist rhetoric often positioned the work of art as one that acquires land: "The work becomes a microcosm which grants and establishes the opulent capacity of art to repossess, to return to being a land-owner" (1979: 20). Indeed, many of Paladino's works of the period referred to faraway places and people, relative to the artist.

Alongside his exploration of nomadism through iconography, Paladino explored this theme through quasi-cartographic strategies and topographical mark-making, beginning in the early 1970s. His *Geografie mentali* (*Mental Geographies*) and *Costellazione* (*Constellation*) drawings conjure imaginary places of the mind, in visual language that looks scientific (Celant and Borromeo, 2017: 61). In an untitled work from 1971, Paladino included textual elements that referenced "territorio ignoto" ("unknown territory") and a "confine naturale" ("natural border"): imaginary geographies and refusals of cartographic logic (and state borders).

If the *Porta d'Europa* extends a much longer current of imaginary and conceptual geographies in the artist's practice, it also includes more concrete references to the realities of the one it frames. On both sides of the *Porta*, a series of numbers borders the top edge of the gateway. When facing Lampedusa – that is, when facing Europe – the numbers are, for the most part, neatly ordered and spaced; two of the integers appear in reverse or mirror script, resulting in an aesthetic of two perspectives encountering one another on a typographical surface positioned between the two. When facing the sea – that is, when facing Africa – the numbers appear in a less logical jumble. Nearly all appearing in mirror script, they are also crowded together and rotated around a vertical axis. The numbers are illegible. Adjacent to the numbers is a splatter of black glaze that extends to the numbers' surfaces; the numbers appear to have been scrambled as a result of a violent action. Theirs is a condition of aftermath.

Supporting this point is the artist's own reflection on the semiotics of reportage surrounding migration in relation to this work. As he put it to me: "We never hear where [migrants] are from. We only hear the numbers:

100 Arabs, 100 Africans" (Paladino, 2019). The numerical forms on the *Porta*, for Paladino, nod to this depersonalized, arguably dehumanizing rhetoric that circulates around migration of non-European peoples. As John Foot has described the coverage of *sbarchi* (landings) on Lampedusa in his history of Italy since 1945: "The stories were rarely human ones, but largely transmitted through faceless numbers" (2018: 404).

Two gateway structures precede the Lampedusa *Porta* within the artist's practice: *Porta selvaggio-selvatico* (Savage-Wild Gateway) from 1979 and *Sud* (South), a cast bronze work from 1984 (Figure 6.5 a–b). In *Sud* we encounter a partially open portal that measures nearly twenty feet in height.

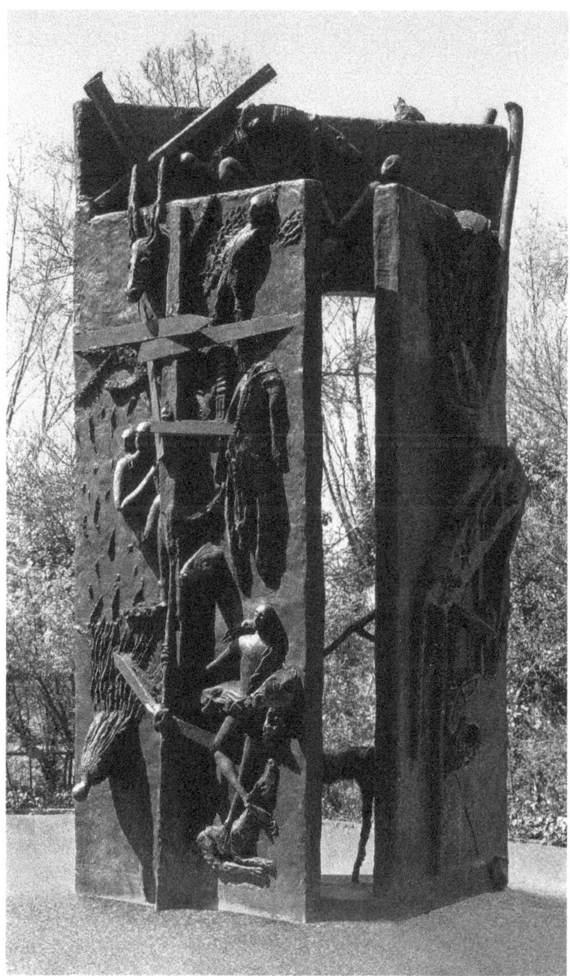

Figure 6.5a Mimmo Paladino, *Sud* (South), 1984. Collection: Sherry and Joel Mallin, New York. Photo: Unknown. © Mimmo Paladino. Courtesy of the artist.

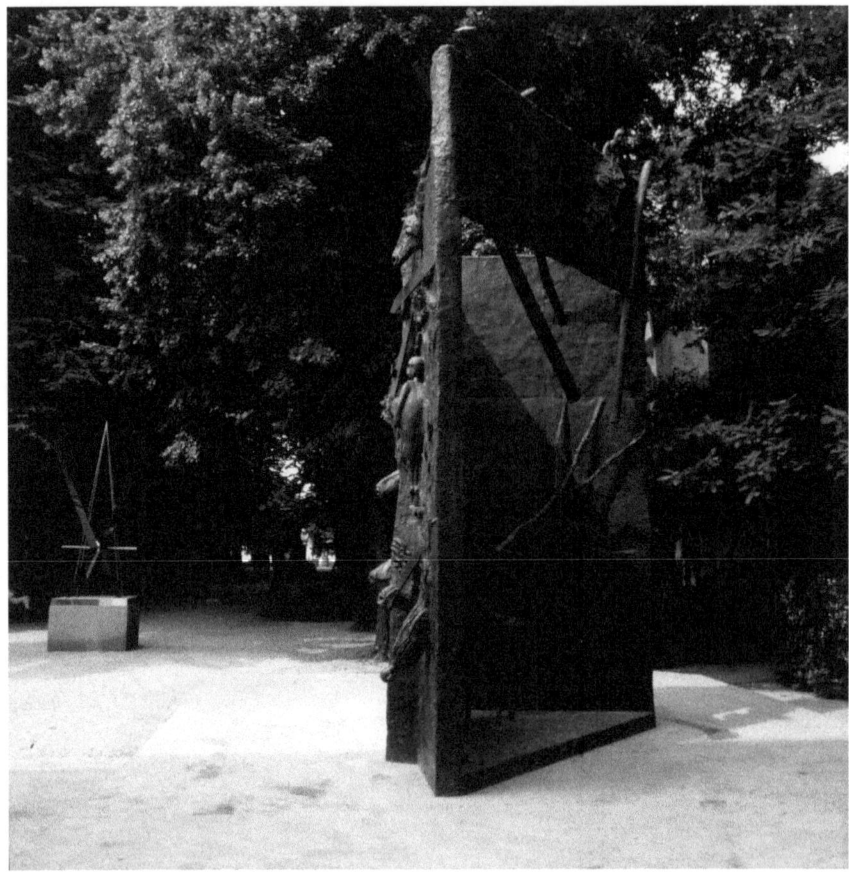

Figure 6.5b Mimmo Paladino, *Sud* (South), 1984. Collection: Sherry and Joel Mallin, New York. Photo: Unknown. © Mimmo Paladino. Courtesy of the artist.

Its doors feature wild animals and figures emerging out of the metal panels in low relief. Reflecting on the work, which Paladino regards as more closely aligned with architecture than sculpture, the artist recounted: "And so it is like a gateway, a gate left half-open onto something, onto an imaginary edifice, like ancient medieval gates" (Paladino, 1984).[13] Alongside these sculptural works, Paladino also made a series of painted *Porte* in the late 1970s and early 1980s, in the form of large shaped canvases, each seven to eight feet in height, which lean against walls. These works include *Porta* (1980) but also *Tropico* (Tropic; 1979).

Of particular relevance among these precedents is Paladino's *Menelik* (1978; Figure 6.6). The work bears the name of the Ethiopian emperor (Menelik II, 1844–1913, generally referred to as Menelik), who famously

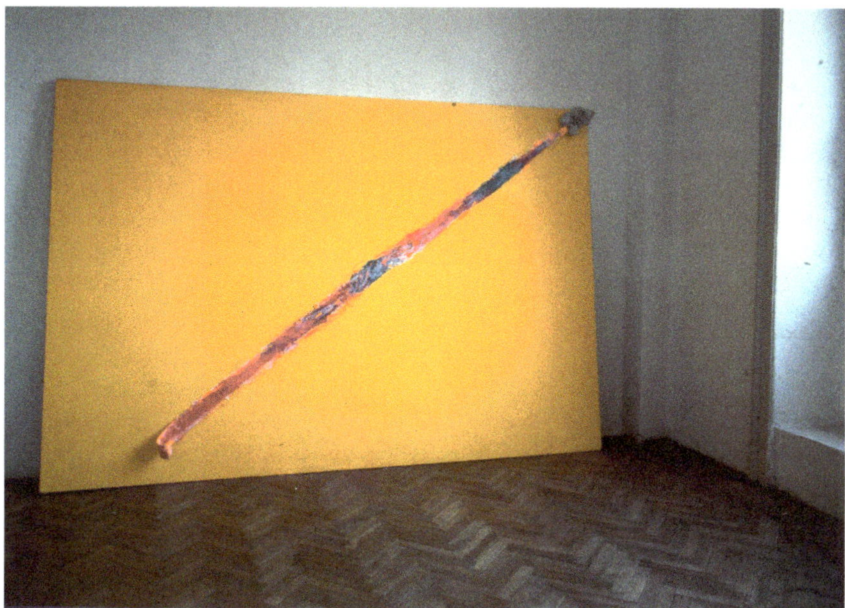

Figure 6.6 Mimmo Paladino, *Menelik*, 1978. Installation at the Galleria Franco Toselli, Milan. Photo: Salvatore Licitra. © Mimmo Paladino. Courtesy of the artist.

defeated Italy at the Battle of Adwa in 1896, and thereby ended Italy's first attempted colonization of Ethiopia. In the artistic context of the late 1970s in Italy, these works were received as modelling an expansion of interiority. Jean-Christophe Ammann (1979: 99) described Paladino's works as having "il prolungamento *per eccesso* … di una condizione tutta interiore" ("the extension *to the extreme* … of an entirely interior condition", emphasis in original). Notably, in his review of Paladino's exhibition at Franco Toselli in Milan, where *Menelik* was shown, Ammann omitted the title of the work even though an installation photograph of it was published in the review. Without the title, Ammann's description of the immensely long tongue that diagonally spans the canvas is decontextualized. In Italy, Menelik's "linguistic cunning," as some Italian artists have described it, which protected Ethiopian sovereignty in international policy, is well known; paper party horns in Italian are sometimes referred to as "lingue di menelicche" (tongues of Menelik) (Bick, 2021).[14] Might these works have been bound up with an interest in envisioning histories of anti-colonialism, specifically in relation to Italian colonial conquest of Africa?

Unlike these precedents, Paladino distinguished the *Porta di Lampedusa* as having a wide-open gateway: "Quindi era proprio una volta doveva essere aperta, logicamente simboleggiava l'accoglienza" (Paladino, 2019) (It was therefore really a time where it had to be open, logically symbolizing hospitality). We might also see the work as being simultaneously aligned with these precedents; Paladino's works of the 1970s seem to suggest a colonial gaze or nostalgia, as well as a neo-Orientalism and primitivism found in many areas of Italy's avant-gardes in the 1970s. At the time, these works reflected the impact of the post-World War II formation of *terzomondismo* or "Italian Third-Worldism" in the Italian Left. Neelam Srivastava (2018: 197) has discussed *terzomondismo* as a form of internationalism in postwar Italy, which had roots in anti-colonial and anti-Fascist movements in Italian culture. *Terzomondismo* was the site of an anti-imperial imaginary, in which the Italian Left found "new forms of solidarity with Marxist and anti-imperialist decolonization movements outside Europe". But Paladino's frequent references to the South (writ large), to tropics, and to historical anti-colonial figures like Menelik, championed by liberal Italy's first anti-colonial movements in the late nineteenth century, suggest not only a form of international "Third-Worldist" solidarity but an appreciation of and identification with both Italian and global Southernness that would be highlighted in the critical framework that distinguished the Transavanguardia.[15] This identification with Southernness goes beyond existing readings of *meridionalismo* (Southern Italian-ness) in Paladino's work of the 1980s, as Arthur Danto has argued. For Danto, the "spirito del Sud" the "spirito del *Meridionalismo* [sic]" is registered in Paladino's interest in "manufatti – gli utensili, le armi, gli animali – che appartenevano alla cultura greca, etrusca, troiana e gotica" ("artifacts – utensils, weapons, animals – that belonged to Greek, Etruscan, Trojan and gothic culture") and use of "frammenti amalgamati" ("amalgamated fragments"), as found in southern Italian architecture (Danto, 2014). Some decades later, looking through the lens of Paladino's *Porta* on Lampedusa – a gateway that opens onto a specific history of Paladino's practice and "Southern" Italian avant-gardism in the Transavanguardia – we can perhaps see that this Southernness in Paladino's work may have been aligned with broader anti-colonial and anti-imperial thought in Third-Worldism and the global South.

Indeed, the Transavanguardia often called for a return to the self, for a reinvestment in cultural roots, and reflected an appreciation of southern Italian culture and Southernness associated with agriculture and archaism. Southern Italy has often been understood as a different Italy than the north, often qualified in racialized terms as theorized by Antonio Gramsci ([1926] 1978) in "the southern question."[16] Paladino's works often referred to a generalized South, suggesting his exploration of areas and places distant from those that were familiar to him nevertheless reflected an affinity (however problematic) with Southernness, in terms of a connection with the earth and with nature.

To that end, while the memorial was a thing done, for Paladino, qualified by a need in a specific moment, it was also something that the artist imagined might be given over to nature itself. "Per me," Paladino (2019) recounted, "la *Porta* è lì. Se un giorno resterà niente, va ben. C'è un altro significato. Non è fatta di qualcosa che volutamente sparisce. È che è fatta con qualcosa che forse sparisce. … una materia fragile, e comunque immaginavo che la stessa natura potrebbe essere modificarla" ("For me, the *Porta* is there. If one day nothing remains, that's fine. There's another meaning. It isn't made of something that deliberately disappears. It's that it's made with something that might disappear.

What I propose is that we might understand Paladino's work as one that models an entropic monumentality, which might be found in other locales and geographies. This proposal is distinct from Hom's reading that the work's erosion, understood as accidental, models a temporary permanence that aligns with the island's model of detention under the terms of *permanenza temporanea* (temporary permanence/residency). Recent debates surrounding monuments in various contexts have provided occasion for new conceptualizations of the function of monuments that align with this model. In 2018, South African scholar Sarah Nuttall wrote: "I think that monuments ought to be built now with an inbuilt understanding that they are interventions of sorts, temporary exhibits of a kind, that stand or fall on what they have to communicate and that must face the possibility of their demise, replaced by a better set of occasions for public thought" (2018: 111). While Nuttall's argument for a monumentality to be intervened in aligns with contemporary debates surrounding monuments to colonists around the world, earlier discussions of such monuments might be traced to artistic debates of the 1960s.

Discussion of entropy and monumentality dates to 1966, when American artist Robert Smithson famously framed experiments in new anti-Classical, anti-illusionistic, geometric sculptural practices associated with Minimalism as characterized by an "entropic mood" and "sub-monumentality." For Smithson, the works of Donald Judd, Sol LeWitt, and other American artists of the period were not works that encouraged historical reflection. Rather, these works were characterized by a new kind of monumentality, tailored "to or against entropy" (1966: 26–7). In "Entropy and the New Monuments," published in *Artforum* in the summer of 1966, Smithson wrote: "In a rather round-about way, many of the artists have provided a visible analogue for the Second Law of Thermodynamics, which extrapolates the range of entropy by telling us energy is more easily lost than obtained, and that in the ultimate future the whole universe will burn out and be transformed into an all-encompassing sameness" (1966: 27). Associated with cultural theory around new technology, Smithson's framework envisions that the work of these artists "neutralize the myth of progress" (as he wrote of American artist Sol LeWitt's works). Smithson's ideas were followed by discussions in the critical discourse surrounding Minimalism, most specifically by Gregory Battcock (1968) who suggested that Minimal artists were interested in a monumentality that would be characterized by temporariness (as opposed to permanence). For Battcock, Minimal artists wanted to make monuments that would give way to new directions in the future, as opposed to the historicity associated with (permanent) monuments that, in his view, served as an impediment to future innovation (1968: 20). It is important to note that the Transavanguardia and earlier Italian avant-gardes of the 1960s were keenly aware of Minimalism, whose perceived commercial aesthetic for some Italian critics reflected a dangerous trajectory in artistic practice.[17] They were also keenly aware of Smithson, who, in collaboration with Fabio Sargentini's Galleria l'Attico in Rome, completed his first earthwork outside of Rome: *Asphalt Rundown* (1969) (Sullivan, 2021) – a work that, along with Smithson's Post-Minimalist work of the period, is associated with catalysing the turn toward entropy in sculpture of the period. Smithson's work, realized by pouring "several tons of asphalt" down the edge of an out-of-use quarry, has been described as a massive but temporary intervention. The "expressed monumentality" (as opposed to de facto monumentality) of Smithson's "Italian intervention," as Marin R. Sullivan (2021: 236) has deftly written, is characterized by an impermanence and industrial engagement that offered a "new monumentality for the postwar transatlantic world."[18]

Similar issues to Smithson's would be navigated in the critical discourse of the late 1970s and early 1980s surrounding the Transavanguardia. Writing in *Domus* in 1981, Tommaso Trini described Paladino's work as "facendo errare un'opera *smemorata*" ("causing an *absent-minded* work to wander". Emphasis in original) – notably using the Italian *smemorata* to describe the work of art as forgetful, with a word form that signals a removal of memory. Trini would connect this anti-mnemonic operation to broader shifts in the configuration of time in the space of memory in the present; for Trini, "il futuribile coincide con il prestorico" ("futurity coincides with the prehistoric") in new memories, even as he hopes for the growth of "l'arte della smemoratezza" (Trini, 1981: 124) (the absent-minded art).[19]

Forgetting has also been recently addressed in scholarship on Smithson. Art historian James Meyer has narrated the renewed interest in entropy and monuments in contemporary art as "the Smithson return": part of a broader return of artistic strategies of the 1960s in art of the present that, in this case, focuses on an exploration of "entropy as monument" (2019: 151). Meyer adeptly situates Smithson's works of the late 1960s and early 1970s – which explored entropy in informalist ephemeral sculptures made of piled and poured organic materials, as well as earthworks and architectural interventions – within the "dialectic of the transitory and monumental" (2019: 253) explored in Post-Minimalism (as well as late nineteenth-century Baudelairean modernism). Writing on Smithson's *Partially Buried Woodshed* (1970) – one of the artist's best-known works, realized through the dumping of dirt on top of a woodshed at Kent State University until the central beam cracked – Meyer traces the other lives of the work – as a symbol of the Kent State massacre that followed, for example. He finds in Smithson's entropic work an "anti-monument that countered the Ozymandian fantasy of eternal memory through its slow erasure" (2019: 254).

With these earlier discussions in both primary and secondary scholarship in mind, what differentiates the contemporary entropic monumentality I want to get to here is its clear imbrication with (undoing) coloniality associated with monuments in Italy as exertions of power. This form of entropic monumentality is inclined to decolonial fluidity (as opposed to imperial "openings") and flows of shared terrain (Mignolo, 2018: 135–42).[20] Monuments in the contemporary Italian context, and specifically surrounding the commission of this work, are bound up with the widespread theft of artworks and monuments in North and East Africa that accompanied liberal and Fascist colonialism, not to mention longer histories of monuments as war spoils dating to ancient Rome. They are also bound up with articulations of empire. Brian McLaren has recently discussed Mussolini's privileging of ancient sites and monuments in Rome to model contemporary Rome as a racial and imperial urban landscape. During Hitler's 1938 visit to Rome, he was paraded by ancient Roman monuments and sites (the Colosseum, the Via dell'Impero, the Arch of Constantine), as well as the Stele of Axum, on Viale Africa. This route, as McLaren has adeptly demonstrated, was a "curatorial effort" through which Rome's ancient monuments and sites would be "fused with Fascist and Nazi-inspired expressions of power" (2021: 23–4). Ann Thomas Wilkins (2005: 61–2) has also discussed the function of the Obelisk of Axum in Fascist Italy, specifically as a symbol of Roman victory over an African nation. In 1937, a photograph of the stele was juxtaposed with a photo of the Augustan Circus Maximus obelisk (as well as the also-stolen Lion of Judah) in the Mostra Augustea della Romanità: "Mussolini, like Augustus, appropriated a monument symbolic of its place of origin – a nation that had fallen to his troops – and reerected it in Rome. … the obelisks exalted Augustus and Mussolini, the individuals responsible for the Roman victories over two African nations' (2005: 62). With this history of the imperial (and racial) function of monuments in Italian space in mind, what Paladino's work seems to suggest is that the logic and form of this memorialization is not monumental – cannot be monumental – because monumentality in Italy is undergirded by coloniality – that is, following Walter Mignolo, exertions and acquisitions of power.

This point is further supported by the timing of Paladino's work. The *Porta* was made in the early moments of a (short) wave of repatriation. The fourth-century Stele of Axum was repatriated to Ethiopia in 2005, after nearly seven decades of display in Rome following its theft by Fascist colonial forces in 1936. It was brought to Rome in 1937 (Thomas Wilkins, 2005: 61). It was only returned after it was damaged by lightning in 2002, leading the Italian State to store it for years before returning it to Ethiopia. The Venus of Cyrene was repatriated to Libya in 2008. Alongside the repatriation of these monuments came the *respingimenti* (turnings-back or push-backs) of asylum seekers (Foot, 2018: 405).

A monumental intervention, ignored

As detailed above, it is in the context of these changes – shifts to Italian and EU non-assistance practices, and the worsening crisis in 2015–16 – that *Porta di Lampedusa, porta d'Europa* became a site of intervention for another Italian artist: Arabella Pio (Figure 6.2). Citing a frustration with the use of the *Porta* to create an image of Italian welcoming, Pio, on October 5, 2016, having been denied permission by the city to execute her work two days earlier, on the third anniversary of the 2013 shipwreck off the island's coast, closed the gateway with re-creations of headstones found in Lampedusa's cemetery, where there are many dedicated to anonymous migrants.

Pio's interventionist work aimed to critique the socio-political and distinctly moral image that had been constructed around Lampedusa by 2016. What I mean by interventionist art, as I've written elsewhere, is creative practice that intervenes in or alters an existing form. In this definition, form should be understood expansively: it includes material, site, and place. An intervention calls attention to and disrupts that original form and its significations. Through strategies of adaptation and revision, interventionist practice interrupts and recodes their sites. Interventionist art has both a formal and operational logic then: these are works that *make* and *do* things. At the same time, they also unmake and undo seemingly naturalized orders of signification and worldviews. However temporary, interventionist art can destabilize entrenched systems of meaning.

Through this mode of practice, Pio's intervention destabilized the moral image of Lampedusa that had been upheld despite the disasters of migrant deaths that resulted from Italian and EU non-assistance. At the time of Pio's intervention, Lampedusa had helped many migrants, but the withdrawal of support from Italy and Europe more broadly had strained the island and ran counter to the singular narrative of hospitality that had been constructed around the island at the center of debates around migration policy and controls (Pio, 2019). As she put it in 2019:

> Lampedusa adesso è meno al centro nel dibattito politico, ma qualche anno fa lo era ancora molto, e, intorno all'isola si è creato una sorta di narrativa di come questa isola fosse un esempio morale nel Mediterraneo di accoglienza … c'era una spinta io credo in Italia, generalmente di accoglienza, adesso sicuramente non tutti ma prevale anche una grossa spinta di chiusura.

> (Lampedusa now is less at the center of political debates, but a few years ago it was still very much so. Around the island a sort of narrative was created of how this island would be a moral example of hospitality in the Mediterranean … there was a push I believe in Italy, generally for hospitality, certainly not from everyone now, but a big push for closure also prevails.)

I want to highlight that Pio's intervention walled off the gateway from the shores facing in. Each brick reads: "migrante non identificato qui riposa" ("here lies an unidentified migrant"; Figure 6.7). The words span three lines of text, one above the other, recapitulating the stacked form of the wall; the lettering, however, is slightly irregular in kerning and alignment, which suggests an urgency in production. Lasting only a few hours, the intervention,

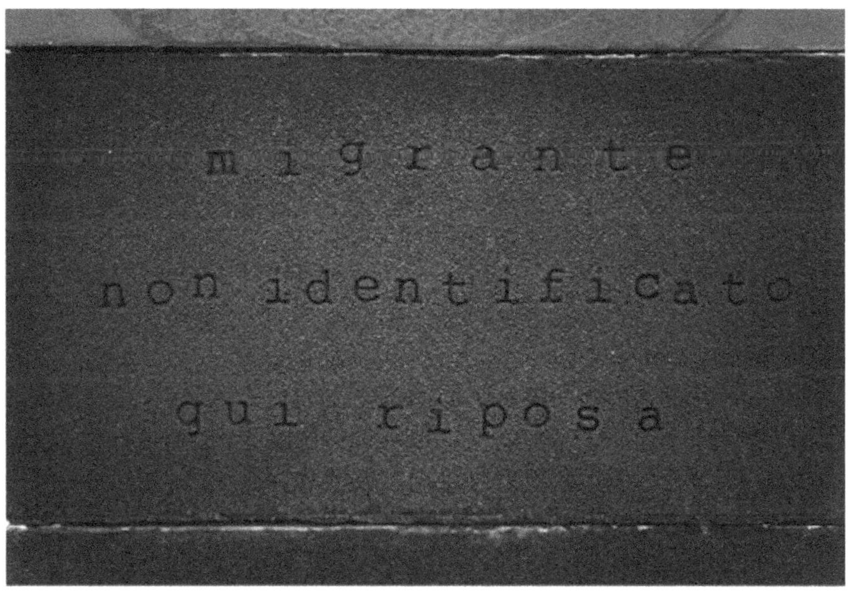

Figure 6.7 Arabella Pio, detail of *Porta d'Europa*, intervention in Mimmo Paladino's *Porta di Lampedusa, porta d'Europa* (2008), October 5, 2016. The text reads: "Here lies an unidentified migrant." Photo: Arabella Pio. © Arabella Pio. Courtesy of the artist.

entitled *Porta d'Europa*, was and remains documented on Pio's website but has gained little to no attention. Her intervention not only registered shifts in Italian (and EU) migration policy in artistic form, but connected the many who died at sea, whom we think about as we look through Paladino's gateway, to the contemporaneous delay, and at times refusal, of the Italian government and the EU to respond to shipwrecks in which migrants are losing their lives, especially at the peak of the so-called "crisis" of renewed Mediterranean migration in 2016. If rescues were conducted, and more resources were deployed, Pio's works suggests, fewer people would tragically lose their lives so close to Lampedusa. Fewer would be interred in the Lampedusa cemetery. What her work positions at the gateway to Europe, at Europe's gateway to itself, is a site of indirect genocide.

Pio's own reflections on her family history offers one potential reason for widespread Italian inattention to her work and general disregard for the State's non-response to migrant deaths in the Mediterranean. Her grandparents lived in Somalia for many years, as did her mother, when it was an Italian colony; her grandfather worked for an Italian company near the American military base. Her family has fond memories of the period, and of vacations on which they would return to Somalia thereafter. While for Pio and her family, colonialism provided economic opportunity and beautiful memories, these experiences point to the complexity of historical events and the necessity to deal with issues in collective memory. As she put it:

> dall'altra parte ha creato una serie di situazioni con cui noi oggi tutti facciamo i conti … L'idea credo di queste due realtà, di come un evento storico possa avere queste due facce – c'è la mia, quella della mia famiglia, e quella di altre persone. Come si incontrano, e come interagiscono tra di loro, ha in qualche modo sempre fatto parte della mia vita.

> (on the other hand, it created a series of situations that we're all dealing with … The idea, I believe, of these two realities, of how a historical event can have these two faces – there's mine, that of my family, and that of other people. How they meet, and how they interact with each other, has always in some way been a part of my life.)

Pio's practice is therefore aligned with two key directions in post-war and contemporary art. First, we are reminded of work by artists in post-Fascist contexts who have explored problematic family histories – as in German artist Gerhard Richter's *Onkel Rudi* (Uncle Rudi, 1965) (Curley, 2013: 136–7), and in Italy, recent work by Alessandra Ferrini (see *My Heritage?* 2020). Second, Pio's work is aligned with interventionist public practice – especially work that is unsanctioned. Contemporary street art in southern Italy has proliferated in response to Italian non-assistance of migrants, calling attention to the high numbers of migrant deaths that continue even today. Consider two works of street art in Palermo in 2018: both by an artist who signs their work "VIA," these works call for passers-by to pay attention to migrant deaths in the Mediterranean and to speak out against racism (Figure 6.8a–b). Allowed to remain in place for longer than Pio's work, they remind people of the crisis in real time – not in the poetic form of entropic monumentality, but as urgently explicit reminders of the human lives at stake. These are calls to action in the space of the everyday.

The inattention to Pio's intervention is additionally remarkable given that the *Porta* has recently been the site of another intervention that by contrast received some news coverage. In June of 2020, the *Porta* was shrouded in fabric, mostly colored black, and bound with circles and circles of brown packaging tape. The result was a wrapped structural form that recalled the works of French artists Christo and Jeanne Claude. Indeed,

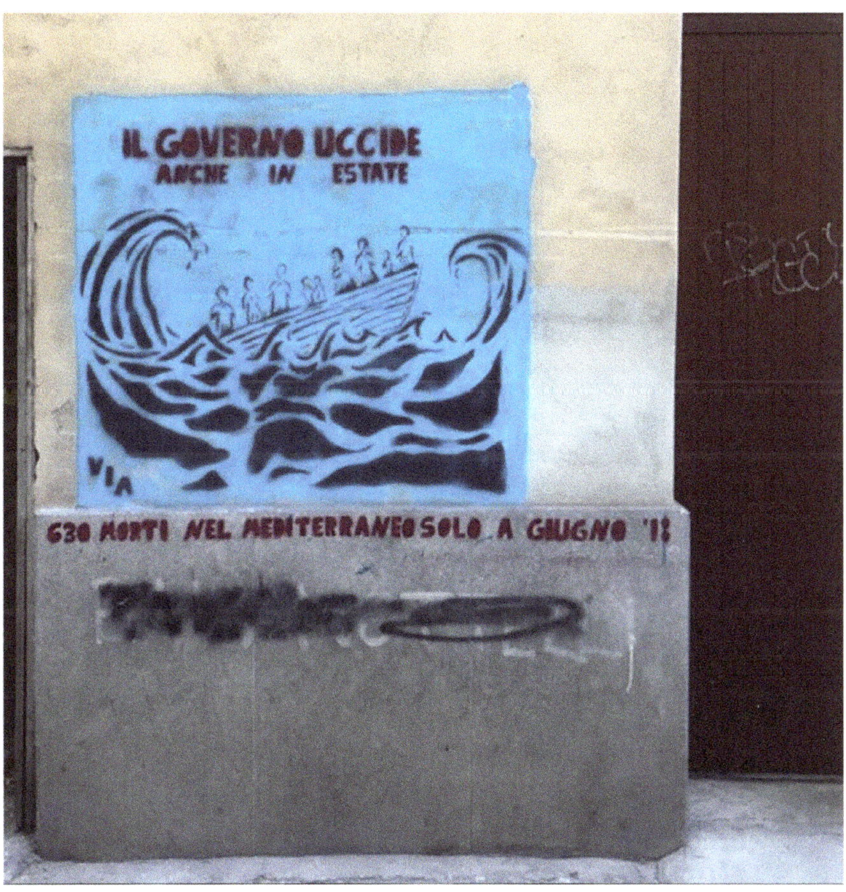

Figure 6.8a Street art by VIA, Palermo, July 2018. The text reads: "The government kills in the summer too. 630 dead in the Mediterranean in June '18 alone." Photo: Tenley Bick.

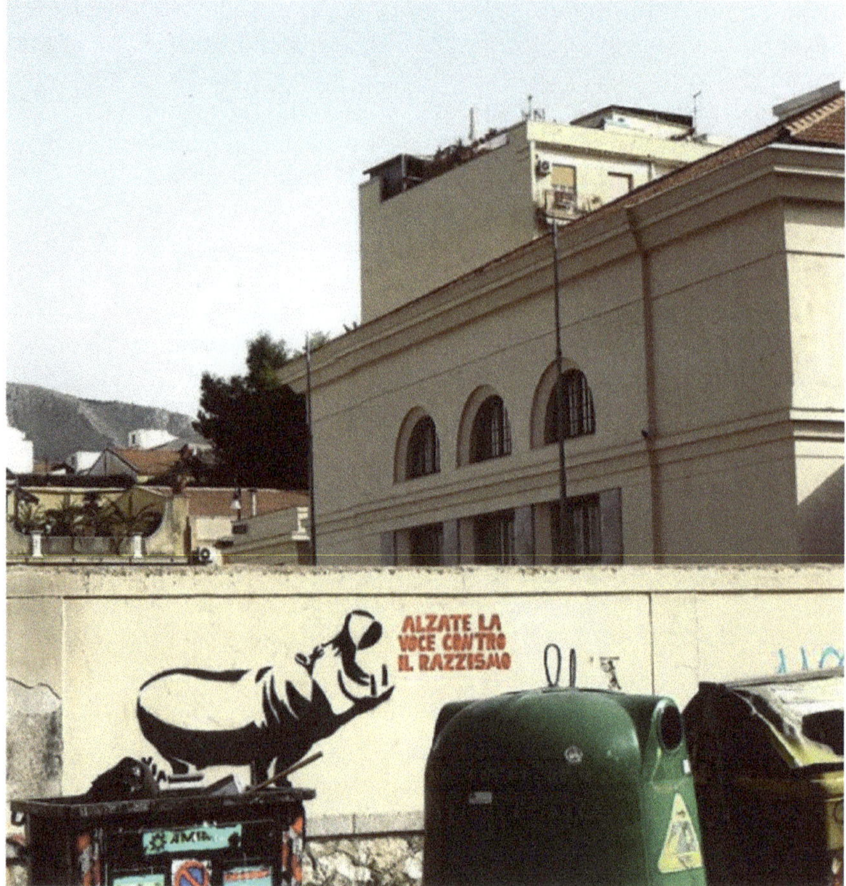

Figure 6.8b Street art by VIA, Palermo, July 2018. The text reads: "Speak out against racism!" Photo: Tenley Bick.

media coverage reported that Paladino noted the action took place a few days after Christo's death (Cadolini, 2020). The mayor of Lampedusa, Totò Martello, denounced the 2020 intervention. Major national newspaper *La Repubblica* quoted Martello at length in its reporting on the event for its Palermo edition:

> It is a petty action that hurts the image of Lampedusa … and above all hurts Lampedusians … The State has to reaffirm its presence on the island and also has to do it through concrete actions Eof support for a community that continues to "hold open" this gateway in the name of human rights, notwithstanding enormous sacrifices and notwithstanding someone's intention to close it. (Reale, *La Repubblica*, 2020)[21]

Of note is that Martello emphasized the need to keep the *Porta* open rather than Lampedusa, Italy, or Europe, as places of asylum.

Conclusion: the work of art as decolonial gateway

Alongside these works, contemporary Italian artists of African descent, and other African artists, have made works that address repatriation of monuments by Italy to African countries – much of which has been aligned with the shifting discourse on Italian colonialism. Italian author Igiaba Scego, who is of Somali heritage, has written extensively on monuments and urban space in Italy in relation to Italian colonialism, racism, and popular amnesia around its histories. In *Roma negata: Percorsi postcoloniali nella città* (2004), Scego poignantly narrates a visit to Rome's Piazza di Porta Capena, where the stolen Obelisk of Axum had been displayed since its theft by Fascist forces in 1936. The site is now home to a memorial dedicated to the victims of September 11. The absence of monuments dedicated to the memory of the hundreds of thousands of victims of Italian colonialism, as Scego writes, is an act of erasure, driven by a collective will to forget (Scego, 2014: 16–9; Bick, 2021: 65–6).

Other artists in Italy of African descent have since made works that seek to visualize the Stele of Axum (Tigrinya: ሐወልቲ አኽሱም), which is also known as the Obelisk of Axum, perhaps as a sign of mnemonic insistence: that is, of an insistence to remember these histories. Contemporaneously with Paladino's work on Lampedusa (and with the repatriation of the Venus of Cyrene to Libya), British-Ethiopian artist Theo Eshetu (b. 1958), who moved to Rome with his family at age ten, has also considered the historical and mnemonic resonances of the Ethiopian stele in his work, *The Return of the Axum Obelisk* (2009). Eshetu's fifteen-monitor video installation screens footage of the disassembly, storage, and eventual transport and reinstallation of the stele in its original site in Tigray in northern Ethiopia, the historic site of the ancient civilization of Axum. The stone column histori-cally had many functions, first as a symbol of power in the Axumite Empire (Axis Gallery) and as a funerary stele. Eshetu's work undermines the long assertions of colonial power that had been associated with the display of the Stele of Axum in Rome, where it was originally displayed in front of the *Ministero delle colonie* (Ministry of Colonies) (Axis Gallery) – even after the formal end of Italian Fascist colonialism. Interspersed with footage of the Stele's return to Ethiopia, Eshetu includes the story of the Queen of Sheba and her son by King Solomon, a narrative of great importance for modern Ethiopian history; born in Ethiopia, her son would later rule as King Menelik I (Axis Gallery).

At the beginning of the COVID-19 lockdown in Italy, Jem Perucchini (b. 1995), a Milan-based Italian artist of Ethiopian heritage, began painting the Stele of Axum based on a photograph of the monument from Wikipedia; the result, shown to me over video chat during lockdown, was a painstakingly crafted oil painting that depicts the monolith in situ (Perucchini, 2020; Bick, 2020; Figure 6.9). Unlike the photograph, Perucchini's depiction of the Stele casts a single stark shadow, unconventionally rendered as a beam of light. This work recalls the telluric agitation that Paladino described decades prior. At the moment of confinement, in his adopted homeland, Perucchini turned to a monument whose famed repatriation, some fifteen years prior, in his work seems to signify postcolonial resilience, thereby modelling a narrative of the inevitability of return and telluric diasporic connectivity. Perucchini also *détourned* landscape itself. By removing other structures on the grounds around the stele and erasing the dirt path in front of it, where we now find ochre soil, Perucchini created new logics of earth and light. Recasting shadow as illumination, he also transformed the blue, earth-bound sky in the photograph, opening it up, with a break in his now stormy clouds, into a celestial swirling galactic cosmos, stippled with interplanetary dust. In *Axum*, both content and work of art serve as decolonial gateways onto different histories and futures, as well as geospatial orders. Telluric agitation here has given way to expansive belonging and cosmic thinking.

Acknowledgments

I am indebted to Mimmo Paladino, Arabella Pio, and Jem Perucchini for generously discussing their work with me and for providing image permissions for this chapter, as did photographer Franco Guardascione. I am also grateful to Helen Solterer and Vincent Joos for their editorial stewardship of this volume. Research and writing of this chapter was facilitated by the support of a scholar-in-residence position at Magazzino Italian Art Foundation (Cold Spring, NY), and by Florida State University. My sincere thanks to Nancy Olnick, Giorgio Spanu, and Vittorio Calabrese at Magazzino. Additional thanks to the Galerie Christian Stein, Silvia Valisa, Kristin Dowell, Victoria DeBlassie, and especially Stephanie Hom for conversations about this work.

Notes

1　Author's note: all translations in this chapter are by the author unless otherwise noted. Published English translations have been used when possible. Artist interviews by the author were conducted in Italian.

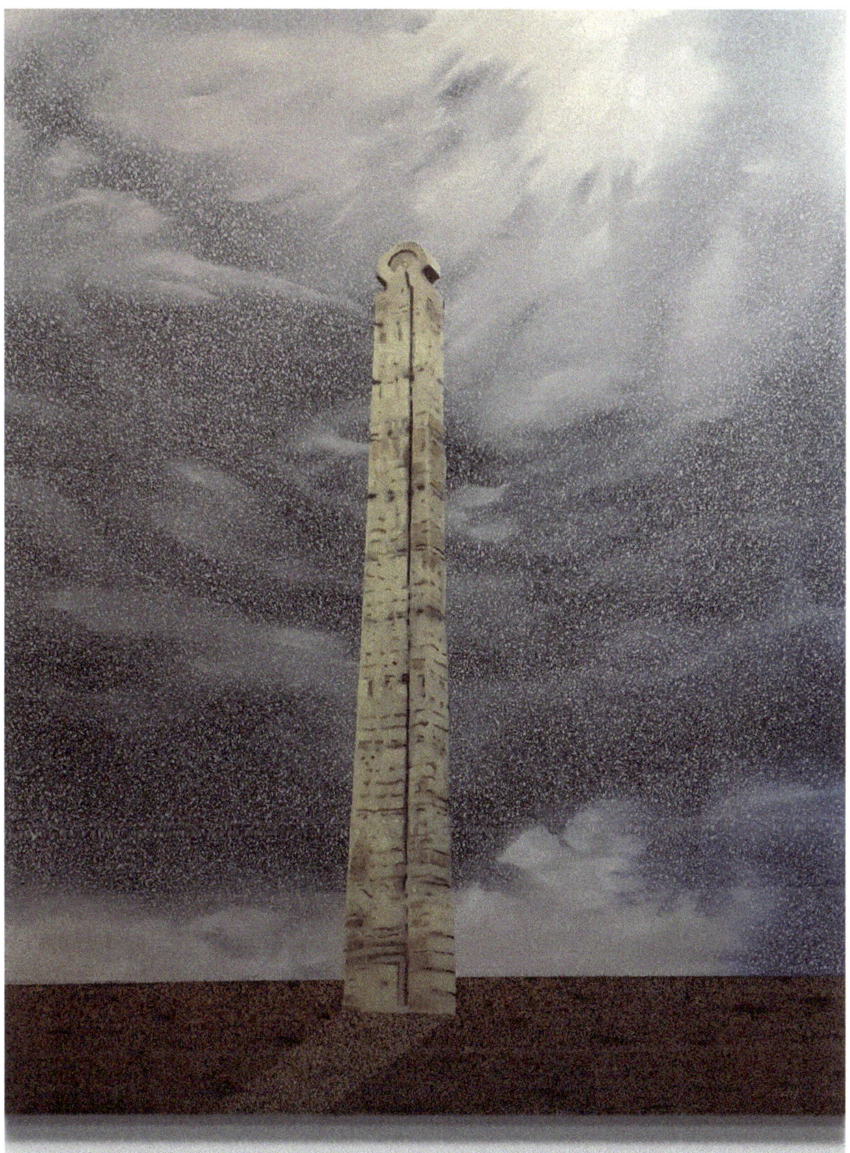

Figure 6.9 Jem Perucchini, *Axum*, 2020. Collection: Daniele and Karen Rigamonti. © Jem Perucchini. Courtesy of the artist.

2 Pio confirmed with the author that she alerted Paladino to her plans to stage an intervention in his work. He responded, per Pio, in full agreement, citing the appropriateness of the moment for such a work, and viewing his own work as a kind of "appoggio," or support, for Pio's intervention, as Pio put it. Paladino did not recall the request, in conversation with the author, but was undisturbed to learn of the intervention.

3 Reports of the recorded deaths for the 2013 shipwreck vary, with some numbering in the 380s. This number comes from UNHCR Italia: www.unhcr.org/it/cosa-facciamo/la-nostra-voce/3-ottobre/ (accessed February 20, 2019).

4 Bullo's study opens with a discussion of waterways as means of internal communication within *Africa Proconsularis* and the Tripolitan coast as, by contrast, "the way out to sea" for the main routes that pass through the "desert hinterlands" of the province. The Libyan coast has, from Italy's imperial history from the ancient world to the modern period, functioned as a colonized point of maritime departure.

5 This passage draws upon Deleuze and Guattari's discussion of deterritorialization and the primitive territorial machine, in which earth is unified, even if people are divided. Also see Hom's excellent chapter, "The Island" on Lampedusa's carceral history and present as a detention center.

6 Srivastava draws upon Mark I. Choate's theorization of emigrant colonialism in Italy. See his *Emigrant Nation: The Making of Italy Abroad* (Cambridge, MA: Harvard University Press, 2008).

7 Italian newspaper reports highlighted these earlier promises of restitution as well as initial discussions dating to 1989. See "La Venere di Cirene torna in Libia restituita la statua della discordia," *La Repubblica* (August 30, 2008).

8 We might think here of Matteo Salvini's work in Libya as Deputy Minister of the Interior. Salvini's anti-immigration policy aligned with the far-right nationalist party, the Lega, of which he is a key figure in Italian politics.

9 Hisham Matar has written of the atrocities incurred by Libyans under Italian occupation, and the condition of being Libyan today as living with unanswerable questions about what transpired during this period, for which little documentation remains. See Hisham Matar, *The Return: Fathers, Sons and the Land in Between* (New York: Random House, 2016), pp. 126–40.

10 See, for example, Forensic Oceanography, *Mare Clausum: The Sea Watch vs Libyan Coast Guard Case* (2018): https://forensic-architecture.org/investigation/seawatch-vs-the-libyan-coastguard (accessed February 20, 2019).

11 See Unicoop Firenze, "La Porta di Lampedusa" (July 31, 2020): www.youtube.com/watch?v=XvrRIuF9G2w (accessed October 17, 2021).

12 Paladino, "Abbiamo resistito ai tempi bui: Ora l'energia è tellurica," *Corriere della Sera* (September 13, 2004): n.p. [Corriere Eventi]. The majority of this passage was published in an English translation in Celant, *Paladino*, 2017: 624. I have translated the passage regarding "the art of centuries".

13 Partially reproduced in English translation, which I quote here, in Celant and Borromeo (2017: 251).

14 The artists I refer to here are Luca Cinquemani, Andrea Di Gangi, and Roberto Romano of the collective Fare Ala, based in Palermo.

15   More recent work in contemporary Italian art has highlighted the history of Italian anti-colonial movements that championed Menelik in their rallying cry, "Viva Menilicchi!" ("Long Live Menelik!"). See Fare Ala and Wu Ming 2's 2018 project, entitled *Viva Menilicchi!* for Manifesta 12, and the chapter on the project in Bick (2021).

16   Also see Stephanie Hom on the southern question in relation to Lampedusa's history (Hom, 2019: 36–7).

17   The most notable example is Germano Celant's theorization of Arte Povera. See Celant (1967).

18   See Sullivan (2021): my sincere thanks to the author for sharing the manuscript of this essay with me in advance of its publication. Also see chapter 3, "Slow Dissolves: Robert Smithson in Rome," in Sullivan (2017).

19   Translations of "il futuribile …' through "l'arte della smemoratezza" are by the author. Other cited passages are quotations from the abridged English translation that was published in *Domus* alongside the original Italian.

20   This theorization is informed by Walter Mignolo's discussion of coloniality as the hidden space of modernity, and of fluidity as anathema to foundational ideas of Western civilization.

21   The intervention recalled Christo and Jeanne Claude's trademark sculptural and architectural interventions, in which the artists wrapped fabric around major museums, structures, and sculptural monuments. From the late 1960s to early 1970s, Christo wrapped a number of monuments in Italy, including the monument to Vittorio Emanuele II in the Piazza del Duomo in Milan (1970) and a large section of the Aurelian walls in Rome (1974). These followed his "Temporary Monuments" of 1968, in which he had proposed to wrap the National Gallery of Modern Art in Rome. See Lippard and Jon Chandler (1968), and Marson (2014): https://lagallerianazionale.com/blog/wrap-museum-il-progetto-di-christo-per-la-galleria-nazionale. Accessed 1 September, 2021.

References

Albert, Kasi (2012). "Ceramic Rivet Repair: History, Technology, and Conservation Approaches," *Studies in Conservation* 57, supplement 1, 24th Biennial IIC Congress: The Decorative: Conservation and the Applied Arts, S1–S8. www.tandfonline.com/doi/abs/10.1179/2047058412Y.0000000022. Accessed June 25, 2021.

Ammann, Jean-Christophe (1979). "Espansivo eccessivo: Osservazioni sulla giovane arte italiana." *Domus*, 593 (April), 98–9. Domus Archive (online). Accessed June 28, 2021.

Axis Gallery. (n. d., after 2009). "Theo Eshetu: The Return of the Axum Obelisk." https://axis.gallery/theo-eshetu-the-return-of-the-axum-obelisk/. Accessed April 1, 2021.

Battcock, Gregory (1968). "Introduction." In *Minimal Art: An Anthology*, edited by Gregory Battcock, 19–36. New York: Dutton.

Bick, Tenley (2020). "'My World Now is Black in Color': Pandemic-Era Programming, Anti-Racist Activism, and Contemporary Art in Italy." *CAA News* (August 11).

www.collegeart.org/news/2020/08/11/international-news-my-world-now-is-black-in-color-tenley-bick/. Accessed February 28, 2022.

Bick, Tenley (2021). "Ghosts for the Present: Countercultural Aesthetics and Post-Coloniality for Contemporary Italy. The Work of Fare Ala and Wu Ming 2." In *Global Revolutionary Aesthetics and Politics after Paris '68*, edited by Martin Munro, William J. Cloonan, Barry J. Faulk, and Christian P. Weber, 45–77. Lanham, MD: Lexington Books.

Bonito Oliva, Achille (1979). "The Italian trans-avant-garde." Translated by Michael Moore. *Flash Art*, 92–3 (October–November), 17–20.

Bullo, Silvia (2002). *Provincia Africa: Le città e il territorio dalla caduta di Cartagine a Nerone*. Rome: L'Erma di Bretschneider.

Cadolini, Maria Cristina. (2020). "A Lampedusa la Porta d'Europa di Mimmo Paladino," *Metropolitan Magazine* (June 20). https://metropolitanmagazine.it/porta-europa-paladino/. Accessed June 25, 2021.

Celant, Germano (1967). "Arte Povera: Appunti per una guerriglia," *Flash Art*, 5 (November/December), 3–4.

Celant, Germano (ed.) (2017). *Mimmo Paladino*. Milan: Skira.

Celant, Germano and Diletta Borromeo (2017). "Chronology: 1984." In *Mimmo Paladino*, edited by Germano Celant. Milan: Skira.

Cresti, Federico (2005). "Colonization of Cyrenaica." In *Italian Colonialism*, edited by Ruth Ben-Ghiat and Mia Fuller, 73–82. New York: Palgrave Macmillan.

Curley, John J. (2013). "Paranoid Styles: Warhol's and Richter's Conspiracy Theories of Painting". In *A Conspiracy of Images: Andy Warhol, Gerhard Richter, and the Art of the Cold War*, edited by John J. Curley, 117–59. New Haven and London: Yale University Press.

Danto, Arthur C. (2014). "Mimmo Paladino: Dalla transavanguardia al meridionalismo," *Rivista di estetica* [Online], special issue, supplement to n. 55. https://doi.org/10.4000/estetica.2335, http://journals.openedition.org/estetica/2335. Accessed October 17, 2021. Originally printed in 2014 in *Rivista di estetica*, 55, pp. 41–9.

Del Boca, Angelo (2003). "The Myths, Suppressions, Denials, and Defaults of Italian Colonialism". In *A Place in the Sun: Africa in Italian Colonial Culture from Post-Unification to the Present*, edited by Patrizia Palumbo, 17–36. Berkeley: University of California Press.

Del Boca, Angelo (2005). "Obligations of Italy to Libya". In *Italian Colonialism*, edited by Ruth Ben-Ghiat and Mia Fuller, 195–202. New York: Palgrave Macmillan.

Deleuze, Gilles and Félix Guattari (1983). *Anti-Oedipus: Capitalism and Schizophrenia*. Translated by Robert Hurley, Mark Seem, and Helen R. Lane. Minneapolis: University of Minnesota Press.

Dorbolò, Chiara (2018). "The Invisible Wall of Lampedusa: Landscaping Europe's Outer Frontiers", *Failed Architecture*. https://failedarchitecture.com/the-invisible-wall-of-lampedusa-landscaping-europes-outer-frontier/. Accessed February 20, 2019.

Foot, John (2018). *The Archipelago: Italy Since 1945*. London: Bloomsbury.

Forgacs, David (2014). *Italy's Margins: Social Exclusions and Nation Formation since 1861*. Cambridge: Cambridge University Press.

Gramsci, Antonio ([1926] 1978). "Some Aspects of the Southern Question" (October). In Gramsci, *Selections From Political Writings (1921–1926)*. Translated and edited by Quintin Hoare, 441–62. London: Lawrence and Wishart.

Hassan, Salah M. (2013). "Africa in Venice: Visibility is Not the Question'. In *Alfredo Jaar: Venezia, Venezia*, edited by Adriana Valdés, 53–5. New York: Actar Publishers.

Hom, Stephanie Malia (2019). *Empire's Mobius Strip: Historical Echoes in Italy's Crisis of Migration and Detention*. Ithaca and London: Cornell University Press.

Locatelli, Francesca (2016). "Migrating to the Colonies and Building the Myth of 'Italiani brava gente': the rise, demise, and legacy of Italian settler colonialism'. In *Italian Mobilities*, edited by Ruth Ben-Ghiat and Stephanie Malia Hom, 133–51. Oxfordshire and New York: Routledge.

Lippard, Lucy and John Chandler (1968). "The Dematerialization of Art," *Art international* 12:2 (February), 31–6.

Marson, Stefano (2014). "Wrap Museum: Il progetto di Christo per la Galleria Nazionale," *La Galleria Nazionale Blog*. https://lagallerianazionale.com/blog/wrap-museum-il-progetto-di-christo-per-la-galleria-nazionale. Accessed September 1, 2021.

Matar, Hisham (2016). *The Return: Fathers, Sons and the Land in Between*. New York: Random House.

McLaren, Brian L. (2021). *Modern Architecture, Empire, and Race in Fascist Italy*. Leiden: Brill.

Meyer, James (2019). *The Art of Return: The Sixties & Contemporary Culture*. Chicago and London: University of Chicago Press.

Mezzadra, Sandro (2012). "The New European Migratory Regime". In *Postcolonial Italy: Challenging National Homogeneity*, edited by Cristina Lombardi-Diop and Caterina Romeo, 37–50. London: Palgrave.

Mignolo, Walter D. (2018). "The Conceptual Triad: Modernity/Coloniality/Decoloniality." In Walter D. Mignolo and Catherine E. Walsh, *On Decoloniality: Concepts, Analytics, Praxis*, 135–42. Durham, NC: Duke University Press, 2018.

"Migranti, cancellato il francobollo ideato per celebrare Lampedusa 'porta d'Europa'." *La Repubblica* (September 13, 2018). www.repubblica.it/cronaca/2018/09/13/news/cancellato_il_francobollo_per_celebrare_la_porta_d_europa_di_lampedusa-206345919/. Accessed February 28, 2019.

Nuttall, Sarah [and Achille Mbembe] (2018). Untitled response to "A Questionnaire on Monuments," edited by Leah Dickerma, Hal Foster, David Joselit, and Carrie Lambert-Beatty. *October*, 165 (Summer), 111–14.

O'Healy, Áine (2016). "Imagining Lampedusa." In *Italian Mobilities*, edited by Ruth Ben-Ghiat and Stephanie Malia Hom, 152–74. London and New York: Routledge.

Paladino, Mimmo in Mario Carbone (1984). *Artisti allo specchio. Mimmo Paladino*, color, 27:34, Rai Tre television programme.

Paladino, Mimmo (2019). Skype video interview by Tenley Bick, 45:00, Cold Spring (NY) and Milan (November 8), unpublished.

Perucchini, Jem (2020). Zoom video interview by Tenley Bick, 45:00, Cold Spring (NY) and Milan (July 17), unpublished.

Pio, Arabella (2016). "Porta d'Europa." Artist's statement: www.arabellapio.it/porta-deuropa/. Accessed February 28, 2022.

Pio, Arabella (2019). Skype video interview by Tenley Bick, 1:04:38, Cold Spring (NY) and Milan (October 31), unpublished.

Reale, Claudio (2020). "Lampedusa, la Porta d'Europa impacchettata e sigillata," *La Repubblica* (June 3). https://palermo.repubblica.it/cronaca/2020/06/03/news/lampedusa_la_porta_d_europa_impacchettata_e_sigillata-258342606/. Accessed September 1, 2021.

Ritaine, Évelyne (2015). "Quand les morts de Lampedusa entrent en politique: *damnation memoriæ*." *Cultures et conflits*, 99–100, Effets-Frontières en Méditerranée: Contrôles et violences (Fall/Winter), 117–42.

Sarrar, Salah (2008). "Gaddafi and Berlusconi Sign Accord Worth Billions," *Reuters* (October 30). www.reuters.com/article/uk-libya-italy-idUKLU1618820080830. Accessed February 20, 2019.

Scego, I. with photographs by Rino Bianchi. (2014). *Roma negata: Percorsi post-coloniali nella città*. Rome: Ediesse.

Smithson, Robert (1966). "Entropy and the New Monuments," *Artforum*, 4:10 (June), 26–31.

Srivastava, Neelam (2018). *Italian Colonialism and Resistances to Empire, 1930–1970*, Cambridge Imperial and Post-Colonial Studies Series. London: Palgrave Macmillan.

Sullivan, Marin R. (2017). "Slow Dissolves: Robert Smithson in Rome." In *Sculptural Materiality in the Age of Conceptualism: International Experiments in Italy, 1966–1972*, edited by Marin R. Sullivan, 90–125. New York: Routledge.

Sullivan, Marin R. (2021). "Sculpture in the (Ancient) City: Calder, Smith, and Smithson in Italy". In *Republics and Empires: Italian and American Art in Transnational Perspective, 1840–1970*, edited by Melissa Dabakis and Paul Kaplan, 223–39. Manchester: Manchester University Press.

Thomas Wilkins, Ann (2005). "Augustus, Mussolini, and the Parallel Imagery of Empire." In *Donatello Among the Blackshirts: History and Modernity in the Visual Culture of Fascist* Italy, edited by Claudia Lazzaro and Roger J. Crum, 53–66. Ithaca and London: Cornell University Press.

Trini, Tommaso (1981). "Mimmo Paladino. La lingua Mozart." *Domus*, 615 (March), 124–5.

Turrisi, Alessandra (2011). "A Lampedusa i custodi dei ricordi perduti in mare," *Avvenire.it* (April 14). www.avvenire.it/attualita/pagine/foto-sbiadite-lettere-scarpe-spaiate-a-lampedusa-i-custodi-dei-ricordi-pe_201104140756178170000. Accessed June 25, 2021.

PART IV

Migrating in French

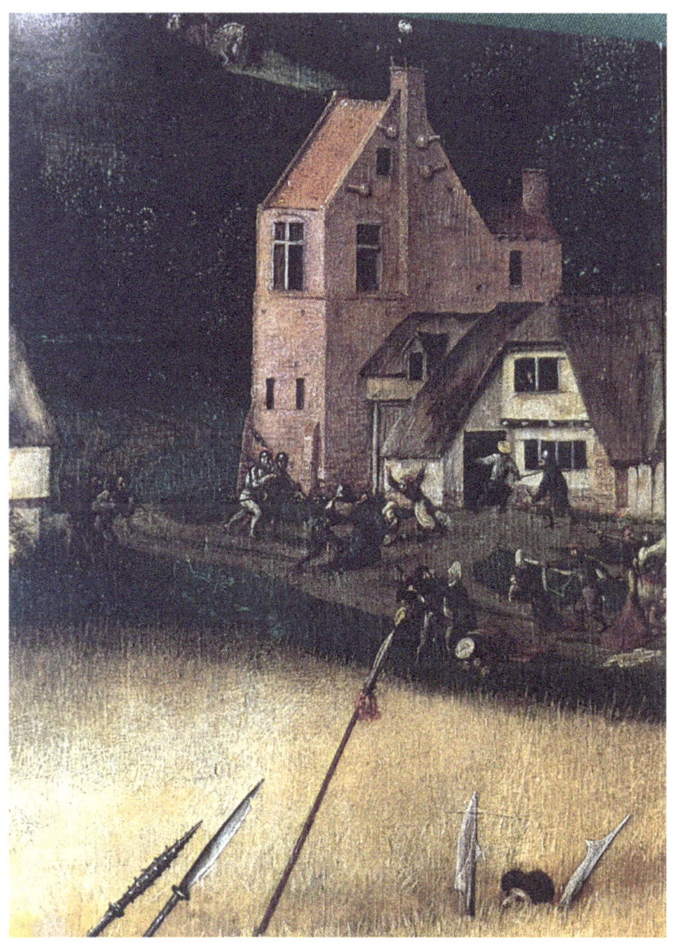

Part IV frontispiece: Joachim Patinir, *Rest during Flight to Egypt*, 1518–20. Painting. Madrid, Museo del Prado, detail. Public Domain.

Calais, France, is the focus of the chapters in this section. Currently, this city makes headlines as one hotspot of the so-called immigration crisis in Europe. Once local authorities began to evict immigrants squatting in empty buildings and factories within city limits in 2015, immigrants had no choice but to build a large tent camp on bogland close to the port. The Camp of La Lande, also called the "Jungle," was a busy hub where migrants lived and fought, with the help of their activist allies, for the right to move freely and work in Europe. Journalists and tabloid writers alike often contrasted the "Jungle" with the city of Calais, conceived as a closed area belonging to "locals" who felt invaded. The French police supervised the demolition of this camp in October 2016.

The two chapters in this section offer a much more complex portrait of Calais. Their interpretative work presents a city and region constantly reshaped by flows of people, goods, and ideas, across royal boundaries in its early history, and transnationally. Helen Solterer, in Chapter 7, examines Calais as an enclave, both a state and an imaginative space. She turns to writers to consider how Calais provides a paradigm for recognizing premodern migrants, their need for safe haven, and their search for safe passage. For chroniclers and poets writing about the fourteenth-century English siege of Calais, the port city never was an impenetrable fortress, but it was nonetheless constructed in stone and in words as a shelter from invading and oppressive forces. Bridging premodern fiction of a besieged city with narrative and poetry about the current state of the city and immigration, Solterer argues for the influential role of creative writers in witnessing today's Calais as an enclave where migrants continue to be trapped, and continue to respond to the impasse creatively. While separated by centuries, migrants' struggle for freedom of mobility is comparable to the plights of people who lived in premodern Calais.

Both during the premodern period and during the past hundred years, Calais has remained a place of international tensions and collaborations, a place that both welcomes and evicts people. Vincent Joos, in Chapter 8, explores the continuity between the management of hundreds of thousands of colonial and indentured workers at the end of World War I and today's anti-immigration policies and practices imposed by the French and British states. Focusing on the case of Chinese indentured laborers, he shows how the French state created an immigration system meant to exclude non-Europeans and nonwhite people from settling in France in the early 1920s. The migrants who are presently trying to cross the French–English border face similar racial discriminations and the same extreme – and even fatal

– danger involved in attempting to settle in western Europe. Both chapters situate Calais as a cultural, linguistic, and geopolitical crossroads built and unbuilt through struggles between dominant factions and people from all walks of life who are trying to open horizons of freedom.

V. J.

7

Calais-enclave: fictions for locking in and opening up, 2018–1346

Helen Solterer

"A base of military operations … a commercial dépôt, a fortress … the last city England would abandon."[1] Is this post Brexit Calais today, acting as security guard for the British?[2] Or post 2018, when the Sandhurst treaty fixed the French-British border there, on the European continent? (Guérin, 2018)

This is, in fact, Calais in 1396: a portrait of the port city after a brutal siege, drawn by writers. They speak of Calais at a time when an early treaty in the long line of Franco-English agreements was negotiated, when it first became a part of England. These chroniclers signal the quandary facing inhabitants blocked in the city and environs.

This premodern Calais epitomizes the situation many recognize in 2021: a town walled up and heavily defended, with several groups locked in a struggle for autonomy and freedom of movement. Over the centuries, the technology of defense has developed in sophisticated ways. The struggle has grown larger in scale, and the people are migrating from a wider world; Kurds, Eritreans, Sudanese in Calais today, en route to Britain, make up a greater mix than the Flemish, Genoese, and Turks who converged on the premodern city.[3] Yet Calais' quandary looks stubbornly consistent through time: the town exists as an *enclave* – a site enclosed and transformed legally into a singular state.

Calais is constructed again and again as such a place locking people in, and keeping others out. With the influx of women with children and men identified as migrants over the last decade, the enclave is being configured once more. This is the latest chapter in a lengthy, tumultuous history, one much longer than the present-day and twentieth-century account that anthropologists are pursuing (Agier, 2018: 8). It is one that began during the so-called Hundred Years' War of premodern times, when Calais was trapped between forces allied with the French kingdom and those with the English – to devastating effect for thousands of people, known and unknown.[4] Through this first siege, as numerous images such as Figure 7.1 depicts it, the city became an enclave.

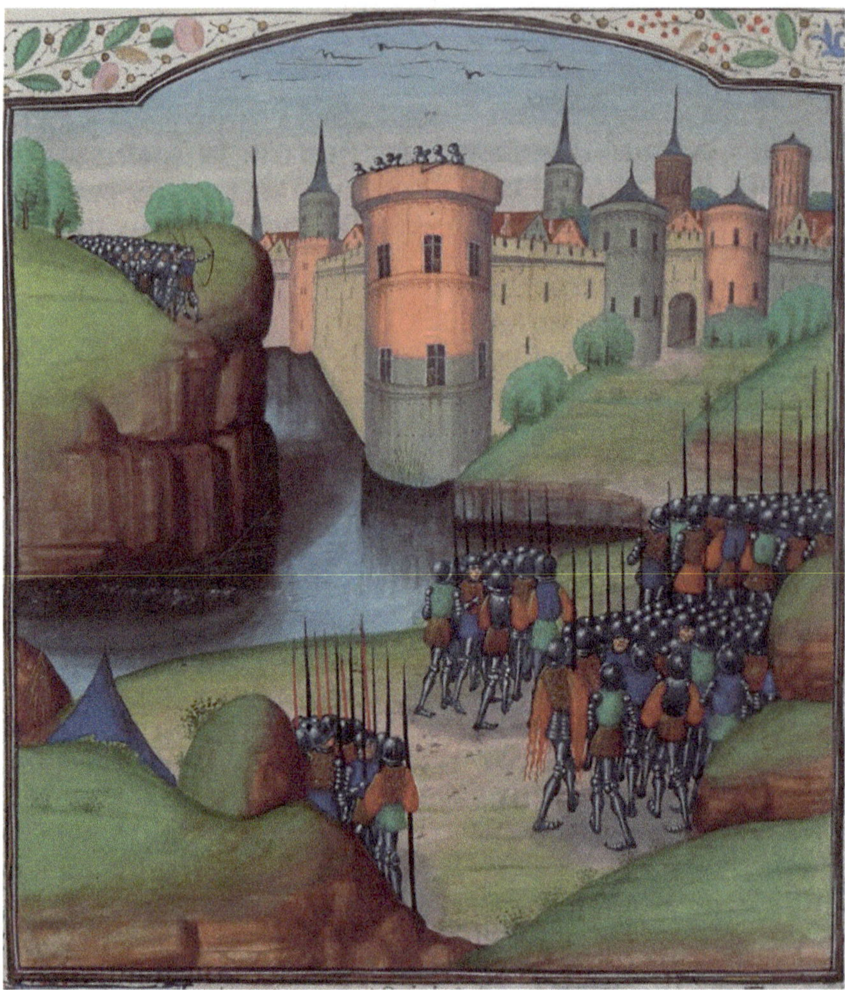

Figure 7.1 Jean de Wavrin, *Anciennes Chroniques d'Angleterre*, fifteenth-century manuscript. Paris, BNF f.fr. 76, 168v, detail. Courtesy of gallica.bnf.fr.

This chapter investigates Calais-enclave in its geographical, politico-legal and – above all – cultural sense. The idea of enclave is crucial for our subject of migration, and its history around Europe, because it responds to people's fundamental search for a place of their own. It came out of those exceptional, protracted situations when people were surrounded by dominant political forces controlling their movements. Developed to address their need to defend their place under threat, it was also put to the test by others forced to flee, in search of a safe haven. Calais is a paradigmatic enclave: at many times recurring in the city's life, it held numerous people within its walls, and kept countless others outside. The first major episode of such a lockdown, in the 1340s, will be the focus of this chapter. Examining this premodern Calais-enclave will establish deeper ground for understanding the predicament of all those stuck in repressive circumstances around Calais today. Furthermore, it will introduce another conception and evidence of so-called migrants in the city. The figures of men, women, and children in premodern Calais are not called migrants, yet its enclave, with its drama of forced enclosure and expulsion makes clear how their situation corresponds to that of the thousands of people trapped in the city today. I join historians Claudine Billot and Sharon Farmer in viewing the thousands expulsed and enmired in fourteenth-century Calais as migrants.[5]

Fiction represents a major way into Calais. Take the example of Maylis de Kerangal, in 2015, when migrants were falsely identified as a crisis for a world-wide public. Her remarkable essay, *At this Stage of the Night*, triggered by news of the deaths of thousands of migrants, suggests how writers felt called to action (de Kerangal, 2015). This proved as true when the fortified city was first besieged in 1346, as in 2015. Premodern writers were among the first responders to the enclave under siege. Their writing offers immediate witness to the peoples of Calais. It represents them in literal detail, and with symbolic force. This chapter looks to the chroniclers and poets who configure and narrate Calais. These writers are of particular interest because of the ways they recount its peoples and invent new expressive languages for them. Both types of writer realize fiction's promise to make something true. What does chronicler Froissart bring into focus through his day-to-day observations of fourteenth-century Calais under siege? What does poet Eustache Deschamps make audible through personal expressions of distress and outrage in the enclave? These are also questions that engage contemporary writers responding to Calais today.

Emmanuel Carrère chronicles what happens to those caught within the high security walls, as those outside whom photographer Eric Leleu has been documenting since 2017 (Figure 7.2). Patrick Chamoiseau creates a poetic voice of protest with them. The work of all four writers together, I argue, reveals fiction's power to recognize the migrants of Calais-enclave. Bringing Froissart and Deschamps together with Carrère and Chamoiseau begins to compose their full cultural history. Furthermore, it shows how their writing creates an alternative space for Calais' migrants. The premodern poets, as much as the contemporary, exploit the resources of fiction, not only to represent migrants, but to mark out an imaginary realm for them that is a provocation to others.

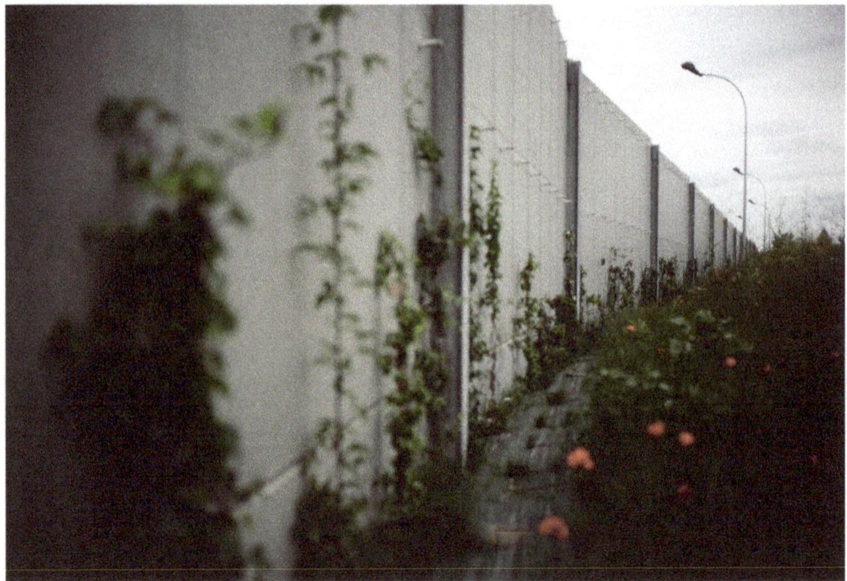

Figure 7.2 Great Wall securing road to British customs in the port, Calais, October 2017. Photo: Eric Leleu.

Geography, law, culture

First, the geography of enclave: at ground level, the site encloses land within another larger and dominant territory. Early cases are found in Europe where mountain ranges or the sea shapes an enclosure of sorts (Farran, 1955: 296–8; Catudal, 1979: 4–5). Melilla and Ceuta in Morocco are examples, Spanish enclaves implanted on the southern Mediterranean coast during the first Crusades. In Laia Soto Bermant's current-day ethnography, they are places still riven by uneasy lines that mean Muslim and Christian inhabitants living "together" are kept apart (Soto Bermant, 2015, 2017). In Raquel Salvatella de Prada's installation, *Cornered*, these two enclaves are also passageways; migrants from West Africa converging there, over recent years, attempting to cross over into Spain. Calais is another such enclave. Located at the narrowest stretch of the Channel, it faces England, twenty miles across the water, as we find in one of the earliest, geographically accurate maps (Figure 7.3). Now, even on a cloudy night, it's easy to see how one domain can extend over into the other; Sandgate, the small port on one side of the Channel, facing Sangatte, with its own history of refugees, on the other.

It was people acting, of course, who transformed Calais' geographic site into a political enclave. When the English monarch Edward III's soldiers

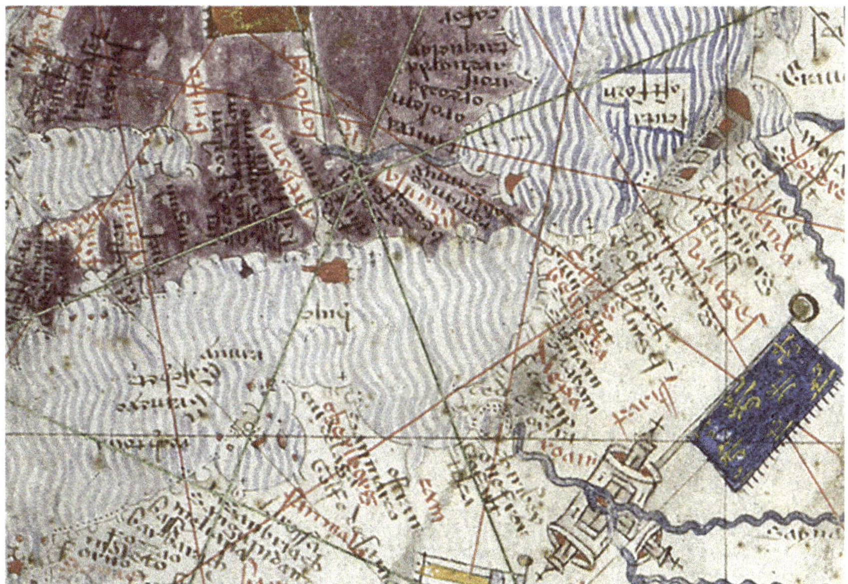

Figure 7.3 Abraham Cresques, *Atlas Catalan*, c. 1375. Paris, BNF, f.esp. 30, fol. 3, detail. Courtesy of gallica.bnf.fr.

invaded the continent, the townspeople had to secure the area around them. The term, *enclave,* begins to appear during this time of dynastic land-grab. It is forged in conquest and colonization that played out during the first year-long English siege of Calais. The term occurs increasingly in a cluster of expressions in royal letters and customary law from the region. "At the far end of France"; "at the limits of Picardy and Flanders" are phrases referring to enclaves as frontiers, what we call "borders."[6] These first occurrences of the term in French confirm its political sense. Through such language of a feudal system, a sovereign lord lays claim to the land delineated. The enclave is invested with his authority, and this in relation to claims of rival lords controlling the larger adjacent properties. This process of carving out an autonomous enclave engages the municipality as well. As another political group in search of its own independent ground, the town also emerged as a crucial force supporting its people.

It will take violent upheavals over two centuries to solidify Calais-enclave. Many early modern maps such as Braun & Hogenburg's trace the enclosure that French forces wrested from the English, for what would seem like one last time, in 1558 (Figure 7.4). The ongoing social struggle would reinforce it again on multiple occasions right up to our own day. The highly contested

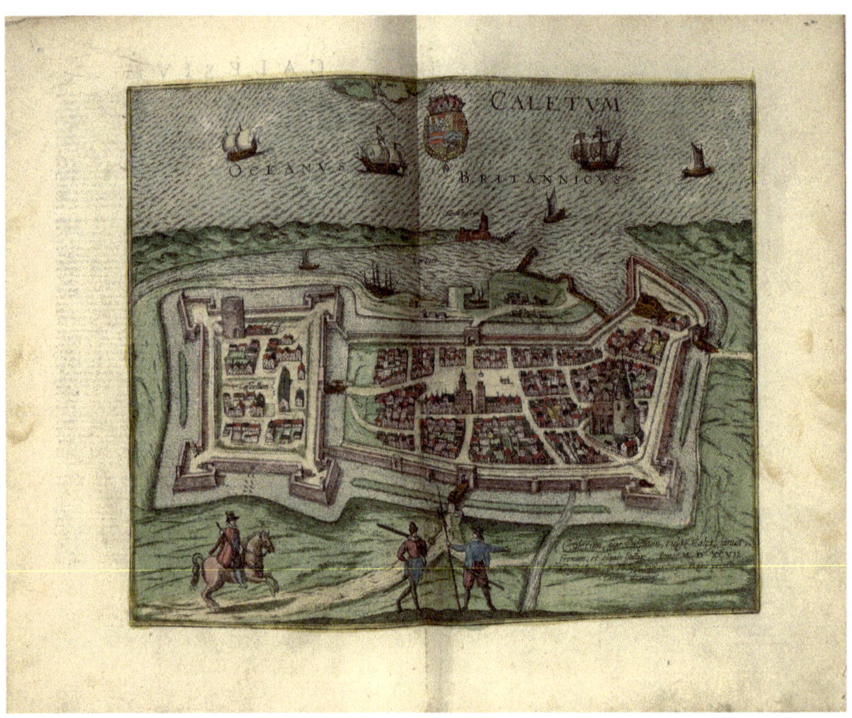

Figure 7.4 Georg Braun et al., *Civitates Orbis Terrarvm*, Cologne, 1612–18. Washington, DC, Library of Congress. www.loc.gov/item/2008627031/ (accessed February 16, 2022).

terrain and coastline that is the North of France, Flanders, and the Low Countries, would prove the crucial locale for this political process.

The second, legal sense of the enclave developed in this region as well. It was here that Hugo Grotius, a Dutch jurist, conceived of the related notion in international law.[7] Extraterritoriality designates a legal right to exercise authority in a limited space, within territory belonging to the dominant political power. It establishes a zone, no matter how small, in which an alternate jurisdiction operates, one intended to balance power relations between vying political states. Grotius's own experience is telling. He fled his homeland of Holland because of religious oppression, and crossed over into France. His flight suggests the link between the necessary, special legal status of such an extraterritorial zone and the refuge it offers. Grotius is a migrant *avant la lettre*, and he draws on what he went through to devise an idea crucial to all forced to flee. According to his notion of extraterritoriality, a place that represents an enclave gains legal sovereignty. This closed-off space becomes a safe, autonomous one for people in need. Against all the odds – restricted room and invasive political power – Grotius' enclave creates an extra territory that offers to a protected minority space along a border, or within a larger domain.

Today this idea in international law prevails; and it characterizes even those circumscribed zones lodged at the heart of dominant nation-states. These "pockets," or "territorial enclaves," as legal scholars analyze them, provide the testing ground for the legal rights of stateless migrants (Aumond, 2015). At the moment, Calais presents such an enclave, one in double jeopardy. It is a place where the rights of those who are held up there can be acknowledged legally, as local associations in Calais support. It is also a place where such rights of migrants are far from being defended consistently by the municipality, or respected by the police, as an inquiry commissioned by the French government under pressure makes clear (Nadot and Krimi, 2021; Aumond, 2015: 1816).

This legal and geographical understanding of the enclave feeds its culture. In premodern northern France, Flanders, and the Low Countries, it is enriched by fictions that represent people being locked in, and others that open up an imaginative space for them. The word establishes this. Enclave: to "key in." Its meaning confirms a sense of enclosure and secured containment. The term emerged in both French and English, when the lock and key mechanism was an important technology of defense.

Figure 7.5 shows the lock on the gate securing the capital of the French-speaking Walloon region, and seat of the wife of the first English king to besiege Calais. The lock's function of closing and opening the city is duplicated in the artistic metalwork, in a scene of a woman on guard, controlling the movement of all who approach.

Writers were quick to invent with the image of the lock and key, and the idea of enclave. They personify the device, and give it a voice (Figure 7.6). In a fable well known in premodern Europe, they use it to promote the value of social cohesion: the lock and key, fitting well with one other, "teach us how to live with our neighbor in peace and accord ("*qui nous enseigne que paysiblement et d'ung accord debvons vivre avec nostre prochain*").[8] Writers also transpose the image into a powerful metaphor for intimate, precious human feelings about ourselves and belonging (Ainsworth, 1990: 103). The heart becomes the most personal enclave, as the *Romance of the Rose* famously depicts it; the lover's heart holding all emotion in a place not to be divided.[9] According to legend, Mary, Queen of Scots, spoke of her passionate attachment to Calais in this way several centuries later. After her kingdom lost the city to France in another struggle over the enclave, she is imagined saying: "When I am dead and cut open, they will find Calais inscribed on my heart."[10]

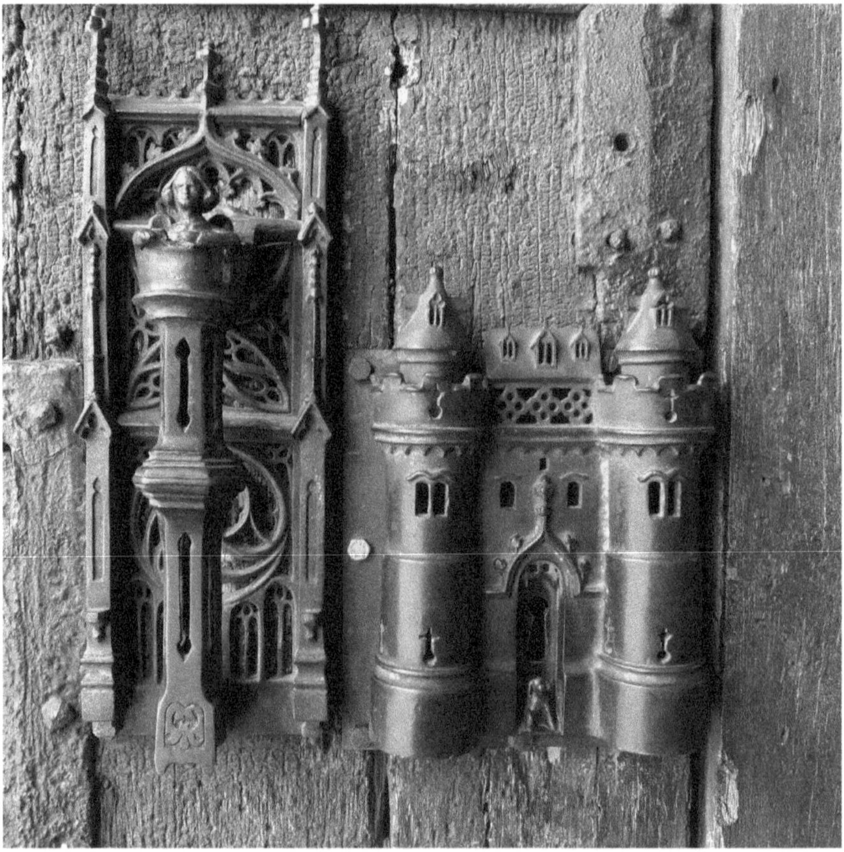

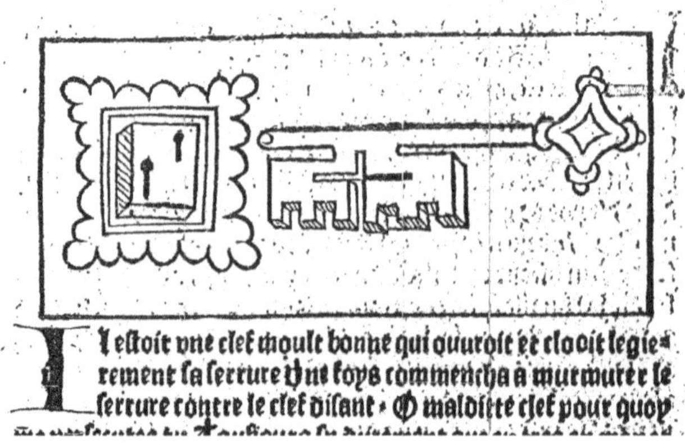

Figure 7.5 Copy of fifteenth-century lock on City Hall Front Gate, Mons, Hainaut county, Belgium. Wikimedia Commons image. Photo: Ad Meskens.

Figure 7.6 Colard Mansion, *De la Clef et de la serrure*, 1482, Paris, BNF Rés. Gr-Yc-32, p. 23, detail. Courtesy of gallica.bnf.fr.

Insiders/outsiders, a city in suspense/in motion

The enclave in all these senses brings us to considering several defining ways writers represent Calais. They use two dialectical relations to characterize the place and its people. When the space of an enclave is enclosed, it hinges on an "inside" and an "outside." The human tension intensifies between those held within and those without: between defenders holding tight, and those on the move; between city people within, and those seeking new ground from without. Outsiders are often given a name in the multilingual writing typical of premodern territories in France and England. They are called in the administrative language of the day, in Alain Chartier's Latin, the "Have-nothing," the *nihil habentes*.[11] "Insiders," we can call, by contrast, the "Have-plenty." Premodern fictions such as the chronicle, build this dialectical relation between these two groups into the enclave. It has an architecture, a fortified one with crenelated walls, turrets, and elaborately built gates. In Calais, which endured decades of war during the fourteenth century, the "insiders" were the city's burghers, merchants and laborers, none of whom were called to war by the ordained system of social role in premodern Europe (Jehel, 1994: 59–69). The urban poor were caught within the stronghold as well. So were sea-faring Calaisians, disparaged routinely as pirates. Outside were the adventurers, not only the international mercenaries supporting French and English royalty, but the poor as well. Rural workers and vagabonds were also trapped, in as precarious a position as city-dwellers.

When we look at this dialectical relation between those people "inside" and "out" in its contemporary rendition, we find that it does not correspond neatly with what premodern writers represent. Dynastic wars had turned this northern area into a further field for exploiting newly occupied lands and peoples. So did the early modern Habsburgs in the Spanish Netherlands, the *Países Bajos Españoles*. The struggles over free-er human relations during modern times have changed the body politics. Yet the inequalities dividing groups remain plain: those recognized as belonging locally, and those not; those declared citizens, and those not. The dialectic between "insiders" and "outsiders" is tenaciously consistent. Today in Calais, the roughly 72,000 insiders also cut across social class and origin; and the outsiders, the "Siberians," in the local lingo for migrants around town and the area, the roughly 1000 counted this year, are internationally diverse.[12] The line separating those "inside" and "out" is more than a boundary, more than a political fault-line between native and foreign. It is a socio-economic barricade dividing those French and European residents having plenty from those on the move seeking a better life. In Spain's borderlands, as Anna Tybinko analyzes them, in the Italian archipelago that public artists shape, as Tenley Bick shows, this inside/out division is also starkly in evidence.

In a series of maps over the last decade, geographer Philippe Rekacewicz outlines this fortress Europe, with Calais on its ramparts, bracing against the pressures of young Maghrebi, sub-Saharan Africans and those from the Levant outside its doors.[13]

When this "inside"/"outside" tension polarizes the main groups of people, a second dialectics appears: one of stasis and movement. Calais-enclave and its peoples under siege typifies this. During the first of numerous early modern sieges, Calais was subjected to a full year's conflict with antagonists inside and outside the city wall, hunkered down. Froissart, among several writers recounting the stand-off in 1346, accentuates the distress of the immobilized.[14] Despite hundreds of inhabitants released to move out safely, chroniclers represent a grim picture: famine forces the besieged to eat the remaining rats; heat exhaustion slays hundreds of those making war against Calais. In the grip of siege, the city appears static – time held in suspense. The only choice seems to be to break the inside/outside stand-off and open the vulnerable town up for negotiation. We have the celebrated scenario of six burghers sacrificing themselves to save the famished city.[15] All accounts of the siege culminate in these men exiting the city, stripped of their city clothes, relinquishing the city keys to Edward III. Calais' stasis is broken by tragic surrender (Figure 7.7).

Writers representing this premodern enclave at a breaking point reveal a paradox. No matter how effective the military operation of besieging, the stasis that resulted was never absolute. Despite the fortifications bolstering the frontier of Calais, the lines drawn were never impenetrable. Froissart's chronicles of Calais under siege teem with episodes of men, women, and children in motion.[16] The right to safe passage authorized frail city dwellers to quit the city, as well as the noble cohort negotiating with the English. Military men also came and went throughout the year, including Calais' French allies on the seas, who could sail in with supplies, or disrupt passage of the English back across the Channel.

Another kind of movement picks up when burghers and merchants mobilized: an economic one. The enclave is energized by their trading, and with the so-called "Have-nothing" as well. Those in Calais attempt to keep something of a livelihood going; outside, the English camp set up weekly markets. At the height of the siege, basic commercial activity continues. This bartering is such a signature trait of Calais that Froissart devotes an entire, lesser-known episode to it:

> Comment le capitaine de Calais vendit Calais au capitaine de Saint Omer et comment le roy d'Angleterre le seust avant qil la peust delivrer. (Toulouse, Bibliothèque municipale mss. 511, fol. 157–159)

> (How the Captain of Calais sold Calais to the Captain of Saint Omer, and how the king of England found out about it before he could deliver on it.)

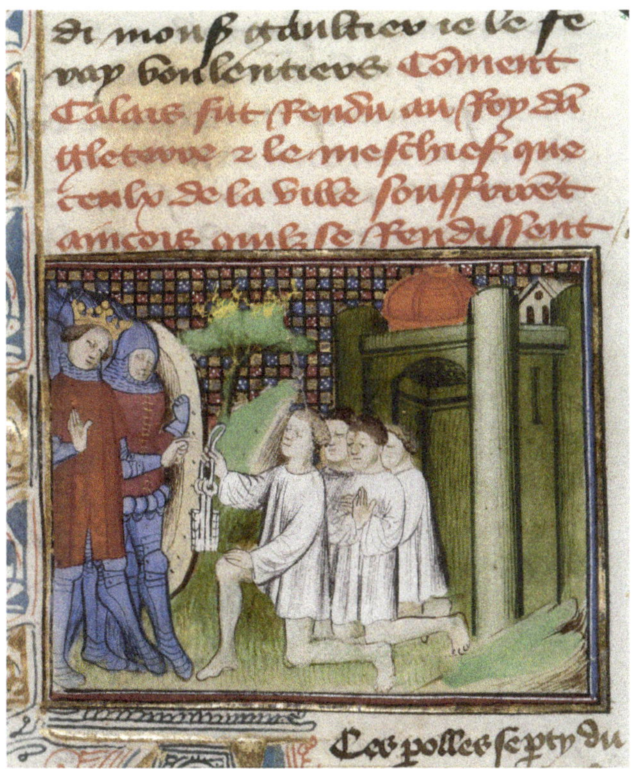

Figure 7.7 Jean Froissart, *Chroniques*, c. 1415, Paris, BNF f.fr. 2663, fol. 164v. Courtesy of gallica.bnf.fr.

After the English take possession of Calais and, in turn, are locked in by their adversaries, one of their men barters with the French. The Lombard Aymeri de Pavia purchases the beloved port city the French could not regain in battle at that stage. This treacherous "selling out" is the flipside of the burghers' sacrifice for Calais. Commodifying the city breaks its stasis a second time. Instead of people standing still on principle, in this alternate plot, they move money around. Economic activity saves the situation; Italian bank loans make it possible. This pragmatic plot is never configured in heroic terms, yet it proves just as integral a part of the besieged enclave as the tragic, sacrificial one.

Chronicle and ballad

From the earliest years when writers witnessed Calais-enclave emerging, they focused their work on its people. In both French and English-speaking circuits, they acted on their behalf, representing those both "inside" and "outside," their need to move unimpeded, their search for their own safe place. Chronicle writers stand out first because their reports on the chain of events narrate people's experience in lucid prose (Spiegel, 1997: 193). Their "literature of fact," as the form is defined, can continue indefinitely to give an overview of the actions of men, women, and children. Poets are equally telling in other ways. Their work relays individual voices speaking out. Ballads, in particular, are outbursts, expressing emotions made clear and memorable through rhymed refrains (Roubaud, 1997: 16). Writers practicing both these genres contribute decisively to building Calais-enclave.

First, Froissart and his renowned *Chronicles*. This writer was not personally implicated in the conflict over Calais. Neither a spokesman on the French nor English side, he was more allied with the French-speaking Queen of England, Philippa, a compatriot from Hainaut. His narration of the day-to-day events of the 1346 siege navigates between the opposing royal camps.

Figure 7.8, depicting the four different sovereigns he addressed, includes the French Philip VI, the English Edward III, but also Alfonso III, king of Leon and Castile, and William III of Flanders.[17] This double diptych identifies them all as peers in warfare, just as Froissart does at the outset of his *Chronicles*, adding the kingdoms of Scotland and Brittany as well. It also shows how misleading it is to nationalize the premodern conflict, to make it a French affair. Not only does such a configuration diminish the many parties involved, it also makes slight of the ongoing communication between them (an "English" letter delivered to the French king in upper left image).

Froissart's first *Chronicle* entries about preparations for the siege detail this political picture too.

> Car le roy de France avoit establi si bonnes gens d'armes par les forteresces qui estoient en cest temps autour de Calais, et tant de Genevois et de Normens mariniers sur mer, que les Anglois qui vouloient aler fourrer ou aventurer ne l'avoient pas davantage, mais trouvoient souvent des rancontres durs et fors. (Besançon, Bibliothèque municipale, mss. 864, fol. 147v)

> (The king of France had brought in such good military men to the fortresses that were all around Calais, and so many Genoese and Norman sailors on the sea that if the English attempted any engagement or ventured anything, they were often met with tough, strong resistance.)

A French Calais introduces diverse groups. Far from a homogeneous community, it is made up not only of those from the region, but from a maritime network that connected seamen of the Channel and the Atlantic with Mediterranean ones. Some four hundred years before the political regime of nation-states took hold, we discover the enclave creating a body politic that is neither national nor international – in a political sense. We can call

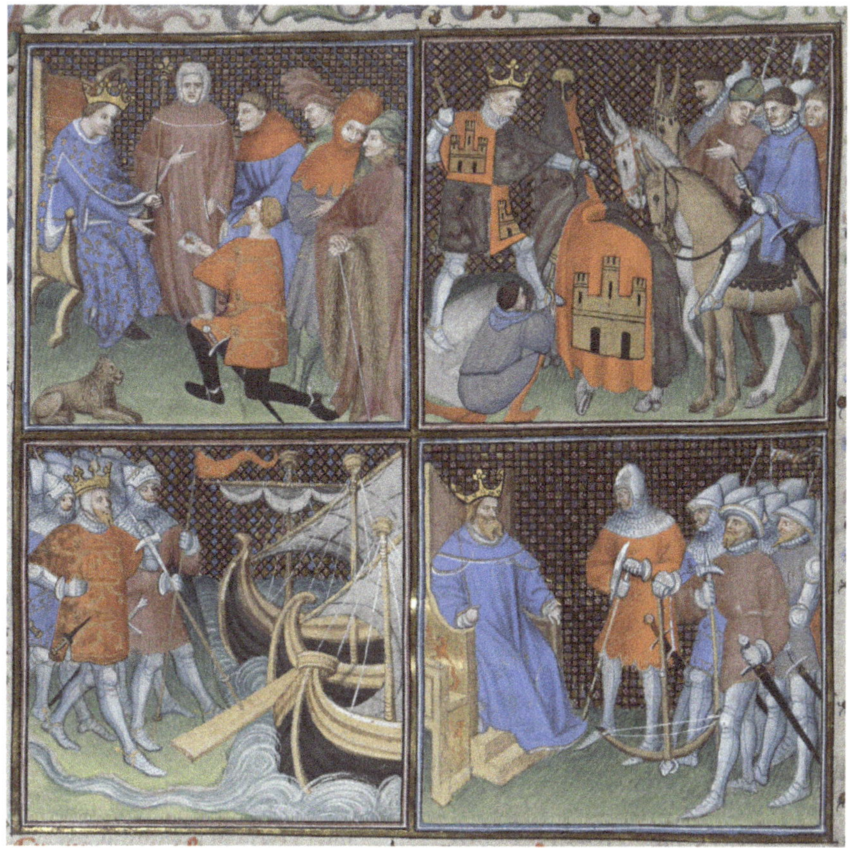

Figure 7.8 Jean Froissart, *Chroniques*, c. 1400, the Hague, KB, ms. 72. A 25, fol. 1. Courtesy of Koninklijke Bibliotheek.

it, more accurately, multi-cultural – the character of Calais, in fact, before the siege began.

This is the profile, too, of every large premodern military force of seigneurial lords operating in this northern region; akin to the foreign mercenaries of modern times depicted so precisely by Jacques Callot in his engravings, *Miseries of War* (*Grandes misères de la guerre*) (1633).[18] Froissart's *Chronicles* records their decisive involvement. It signals the wide range of relations between various groups across Europe. It reminds us that the claims of a French people besieged by an English one rests on the backs of a heterogeneous, polyglot multitude. This is fundamentally at odds with any national construction of the enclave, then, and again, now. Its general social make-up during the fourteenth century corresponds in a significant degree to contemporary Calais, whose residents today include a notable percentage of Maghrebi, Levantine, and eastern European background. The city around 2020 also appears a socio-cultural mosaic.

When Froissart takes us into Calais, how does he represent those populating the besieged city and environs? He does not focus on the noble, military class alone, nor on the burghers who exemplify the city's independence. He narrates the besieged city's struggle with the English across social groups. Two scenes exemplify a style that presents the widespread suffering of people on equal terms.[19] A laborer's boy is seen enduring just as much as everyone else. So are a priest and two guardians of the laws and customs of the city, all left behind during the final stages of the siege. The chronicler zeroes in, then, on the last survivors. This trio embodies a final lifeline of communication, transmitting what Calais is, and what it can signify to the next generations.

Froissart witnesses a range of people in the besieged enclave whose political allegiances are finally less significant than their socio-economic ranks. By highlighting their common efforts for the civic good, he fosters solidarity. He is first and foremost a social chronicler. His narrative makes this clear: no single individual is developed fully into a character. Froissart depicts instead the collective life of Calais-enclave that is richer than its well-known bourgeois one.

Why does this writer commit to chronicling a diverse society across its ranks? Froissart is pursuing what is dubbed today, shuttle diplomacy. Not only does he introduce the multiple parties, he is working to represent as many of the vying vantage points on this conflicted society as possible. The writing creates this multiple outlook. In subsequent chapters, narrating the ongoing tension between English Calais and the surrounding sovereign states, Froissart underscores all the rival parties involved (1991: 207). When the English king descends on Calais in 1359: "Germans, Flemish, Burgundians, Habsburg, Brabant: an entire assembly all together" ("*Allemants, Flamens, Bourguignons, Hasbegnons, Braibenchons et tous ensemble*"). Froissart characterizes Calais-enclave, on the contested frontline of struggles, as engaging far more people and extending beyond the French–English face-off. Calais, in his view, *is* the frontier, marking the border for the first time in French. To acknowledge the many parties involved means, for this writer, assuming the pivotal role of mediating between them all.

Today, a fellow chronicler of Calais, Emmanuel Carrère, takes a leaf from Froissart's book. His reporting, combined with reflection, investigate a spectrum of people. His *Letter to a Calaisian Woman* came out in 2016, at the height of the so-called migrant crisis (Carrère, 2016a).[20] It appeared almost simultaneously in the British press, quickly followed by Spanish and Italian versions. What Carrère represents brings us into the city, *intra muros*. In his style of creative writing devoted to subjects rarely in the limelight, and other unsavory ones, he directs his narrative to city residents responding to the migrants who began squatting downtown in abandoned warehouses.

> La dentelle qui avant la guerre employait quelque vingt mille personnes, et encore cinq mille il y a vingt ans, n'en emploie plus que quatre cents. De la centaine d'usines, il ne reste que quatre. Les bâtiments des autres ne sont plus que d'énormes carcasses de brick desossées et noircies, aux cours envahies de rouille et de mauvaises herbes, idéales pour des squats: c'est là que s'abritaient les migrants jusqu'à ce que la mairie les en expulse, l'an dernier, pour les entasser dans la jungle où ils dérangeraient moins, penseait-on, les Calaisiens. Pour qu'ils ne soient pas tentés de revenir, on a muré toutes les portes et fenêtres. (Carrère, 2016a: 36)

> (The lace industry used to employ some 20,000 before the war; and even 20 years ago, 5,000. Today, they employ no more than 400. Of the hundred factories, only 4 remain. The other buildings are nothing more than huge brick carcasses, dirty and decaying, their courtyards rusty and taken over by weeds. A perfect squat. That's where migrants took refuge up until the Town Hall expelled them, last year, to throw them all together in the Jungle, where they cause less of a problem, so they thought. To prevent them from coming back, all the doors and windows were walled up.)

This cityscape is a field of combat, turned now into an ironic double of the besieged stronghold it once was. In it, Carrère portrays individuals, some named, some not: Kader Haddouche, high school teacher, first generation Calaisien of Algerian background; Ghizlane Mahtab, housewife whose wifi coverage attracts migrants to her street; the parish priest in Fort Nieulay, a working-class neighborhood and site of an early modern siege; a militant member of the neo-nazi association enraged over lack of security; and the anonymous letter writer of the title who warns him about selling Calais out again.

Carrère's character studies place the city's "insiders" and "outsiders" on a par, facing a comparable dilemma. They are all caught between sovereign English territory in city center port, and the Wall built around the Tunnel connecting France and Britain; between unresponsive governments on both sides of the Channel, and the so-called Jungle. They are all enmired in tough living and working conditions; squalid for some, alienating for others. Carrère juxtaposes these people to humanize the enclave's full, conflicted social life. The men and women in the city, as in the Jungle, may share more in their everyday than the nationalist discourses dividing them. His portraits, much like Froissart's narrations, represent them trapped together in a painful situation, in "this landscape now transformed into a giant moat" (Carrère, 2016a: 35).

"There's always a new language to come"

Now to the poets. The premodern balladeers, who practiced a form beloved for its rounds of personal expression, gathered around Calais. In the first person, they give witness; their poetry construct the place anew. Deschamps, for one, composed ballads that declare who he is, and voice his visceral involvement in the conflict:

> Je suis né de la terre autrefois vertueuse Mais Dieux merci, toute plaine de blé Ont les Anglais le feu bouté dedans. Deux mille frans m'aleur guerre couté. Je serai desormais Brulé Deschamps. (Deschamps, 1893: Ballade 835)[21]

> (I was born of land that once was fortunate. But God help us, the English torched the plains of wheat everywhere. War has cost me two thousand francs in revenue. From now on, I'll be Burnt in his fields.)

The poet takes a name that places him and identifies him with wanton destruction. He is writing from terrain far less recognized than the city-enclave but no less under siege. The ballad's refrain declares his identification with farmland devastated by the scorched earth warfare that English forces inflicted on territory surrounding Calais and other towns.

> Las! Ma terre est destruite et ruyneuse, Je suis desert, destruit et desolé; Fuir m'en fault, ma demeure est doubteuse, Se je ne sui d'aucun reconforté; Ainsi seray de mon lieu rebouté, Comme essilliez, dolereux et meschans, Se mes seigneurs n'ont de mon fait pitié: J'aray desors a nom Brûlé des Champs. (Deschamps, 2014: Ballade 120)[22]

> (Woe, my land is destroyed, ruinous, I am deserted, destroyed, desolate; I have to flee, my residence doubtful, I am comforted by no one. So it is that I am kicked out of my own place, an exile, sad, and bad-spirited. My lords do not have pity for my situation. From here on out I'll have the name Burnt in his fields.)

Deschamps' lamenting voice creates a persona forced to watch his homeland's destruction. He speaks of his suffering in the countryside, just as devastating as that of inhabitants starving inside the city. The poet's rural persona is reduced to having nothing.

Through his grief, he gives voice to the thousands of "Have-nothing" in and around Calais. His ballads are often dialogues. A debate builds between rural people and city merchants, between women and men; in other words, between those less often recognized by court writers who know the pastoral genre.

These poetic debates are remarkable as well because they take place in that extra zone created by the besieged enclave.

> Entre Guynes, Sangates et Callays
> Soubz une saulz, assez pres du marcage
> De pastoureaulx estoit la en grant plays … (Dauphant, 2015: 299, Ballade 60)

> (Between Guînes, Sangatte and Calais
> Under a willow tree, close to the marsh
> Shepherds were deep in discussion …)

In such a place, Deschamps captures individual reactions to the terrible effects of siege and scorched earth warfare.

> Dont l'un disoit que c'estoit grant dommaige
> Qu'il convenoit laissier le pasturer
> Pour les treves qui devoïent cesser …
> Encore me dist cilz pastoureauls aprés
> Que trop envix lairoïent ce passaige,
> Et qu'en traittant [ils] pourchacent adés
> Vivres et gens, et autre cariage…
> Que se le roy veult faire bon visaige
> Et mettre sus gens contre les Anglés
> Et assieger Calais et le riviage … (Dauphant, 2015: 299, Ballade 60)

> (One of them was saying it was a great pity
> That we have to abandon the pasture
> Because the truce should be coming to an end …
> The same shepherd said more to me;
> They won't give up this passage easily;
> And even during negotiations they continue to seize
> Livelihoods, people, other merchandise …
> If the king wishes to resist,
> And raises an army against the English
> To lay siege to Calais and the coast …)

This ballad constructs a pastoral network of talk relaying what needs to be heard and expressed. Through a refrain, it links rural opinions to a no-win, anti-war position in the enclave: "this year we'll have no peace with the English" (*"Nous n'arons paix aux Anglois de l'annee"*) (Dauphant, 2015: 299).

Deschamps' ballads widen the network. The rounds of debate among different inhabitants of the enclave speak of other countries. In ballad 337, for example, two women on the coastal road along the Channel, exchange their views:

> Nous sommes bien trompé
> Aux Anglais n'avons paix n'alongne …
> Car, en Guyenne et en Gascongne …
> En Espagne et en Castalongne
> Et en France ou ilz on grapé
> Escoce et Galles le tesmoigne … (Deschamps, 1893: I, 478)

> (We're tricked again
> With the English we have neither peace nor pause in fighting …
> As in Guyenne, Gascony …
> Spain, Catalonia,
> And in France where they've pillaged,
> Scotland and Wales are witnesses to it …)

Deschamps' people see their predicament in a context larger than a French–English stand-off. They compare what they are enduring to the plight of many others; in the North, in Scotland, as in the South, in Mediterranean kingdoms. They are worldly wise. The exchange signals their participating in extensive dialogue.[23] It also associates Calais' risks under siege with others elsewhere that they cannot see but have heard about.

Out of the experience of grueling war on the home front, Deschamps' poetry creates a chorus of sorts.[24] Calais is transformed in the process, from an isolated struggling enclave into a place open to many others and connected far and wide. The forecast is still grim: "You'll not get peace, if they do not hand over Calais" ("*Paix n'arez ia s'ilz ne rendent Calays* (Deschamps, 1893: I, 63)). The refrain of ballad 344 issues an ultimate warning to the enclave. Little does it matter who is inside, and who is out: all parties are bound together in the same battle for rights to their own livelihood in their place, and freedom of movement.

Deschamps, like Froissart the chronicler, also brings us *into* besieged Calais. Ballad 89 expresses panic: the double bind of being betrayed by his companion, fellow-poet Grandson, and held for ransom.

> J'entray dedenz comme corniz
> Sans congié lors vint .ii. Anglois
> Granson devant et moy apres,
> Qui me prendent parmi la bride:
> L'un me dist: "dogue," l'autre: "ride"
> Lors me devint la couleur bleu:
> "Goday" fait l'un, l'autre "commidre"
> Lors dis: Oil, je voy vo queue (Deschamps, 1893: Ballad 89, V, 79, l. 3–10)

(I entered, went inside like a fool
Without authorization. Two English men approached.
Grandson in front, and I behind,
They seized me by the [horse's] bridle.
One said to me, "dog"; the other, "ride."
Then I turned blue.
"Godday," said one; "come hither," the other.
Then I said, "Yea, I see your tail.")

The poet's persona still gets the last word: an ironic retort from a dog-eat-dog world. He neither surrenders, nor cuts a deal, as Froissart represents the choice. Instead he talks his way out of a dead end. Deschamps outlasts the opposing forces, moving out – as well as – into the enclave. At a time when the English take possession of the city, his ballad transmits the experience of the poet as forced migrant.

Language proves one formidable tool for his survival – the several languages around Calais that writers deploy.[25] In this ballad, the poet plays bilingually to identify himself with some authority. In another, he uses the naming strategy:

Je ne sais qui aura le nom
D'aller par les champs desormais
Un temps vi qu'engles et gascon
Parloient tuit et clers et lais (Deschamps, 1893: I, pp. 217–18)

(I don't know how to call
Those who'll cross the fields from now on.
I've seen a time when everyone, clerks and laypeople,
Spoke English and Gascon.)

Calais' peoples have learned many tongues. The refrain makes clear: "There's always a new language to come" (*"Tousdis vient un nouvel langaige"*). Not only is there English and Gascon, but Breton and Burgundian too. With no break in the impasse, the ballad poses the ultimate question:

Or fais
Demande qui sont plus parfais
A bien raenconner un mesnaige
De ces .IIII. dont je me tays. (Deschamps, 1893: I, pp. 217–18, l. 21–4)

(So I ask
Which of these four
Are the best for ransoming a household,
I'll not say.)

If French is no longer a reliable medium for negotiating, then Deschamps' writing will keep up the talk across languages. In Calais-enclave that is the borderland, this multilingual poetry provides vital material and a creative alternative to its repressive limits. It insures needed personal expression, offering support for dispossessed people holding on.

Today, Deschamps' fellow writer, Patrick Chamoiseau, is alert to this poetic value. His *Brother migrants*, published in spring 2017, expresses his strong feeling of being called to the task of imagining migrants in their desperate situation.[26] Galvanized by thousands of them, known and unknown, who died en route in the years around 2015, Chamoiseau gives witness, and mobilizes support. While he does not share their experience, he adopts poetry's voices to advocate for those forced to abandon their homelands or choosing to leave. His imagining migrants reaches beyond what Deschamps could express: Chamoiseau ranges over "trans-country, trans-nation, trans-world" (Chamoiseau, 2017: 91). The men and some few women he envisages are on the move from sub-Saharan Africa and the Maghreb, attempting to cross the Mediterranean, headed for destinations farther north, including Calais' crossing point. Chamoiseau cultivates a type of poetic cohabitation with them.

Akin to Deschamps, he composes dialogues. His work orchestrates the reactions of a film-maker and a humanitarian volunteer with his own. The multi-vocal essay creates a remarkable network of dialogue:

> Oui … mes chères, déclenche dans les geographies du vent, en étincelles de sel, en étincelles de ciel, une étrange conférence de poètes et de grands êtres humains. (7/127)

> (Yes … [what you say] my dears, brings about a strange colloquium of poets and great human beings in the geographies of wind, in sparks of salt and sky.)

Chamoiseau's network spans land and sea, and shapes an imaginative realm stretching far and wide. It gives people a type of safe place that is still in touch with the outside. De-territorialized, it "spreads across what once were territories, nations, homelands" (Chamoiseau, 2017: 92). In an earlier essay, *Writing in a Dominant Land*, Chamoiseau imagines how such a place is the opposite of a territory; open yet not defined by closed borders, where people express themselves in every possible language.[27]

In just such an imagined place, Chamoiseau calls on poetry to speak on behalf of today's migrants. In one of the most significant declarations:

> Les poètes déclarent qu'aller-venir et dévirer de par les rives du monde sont un Droit poétique, c'est-à-dire: une décence qui s'élève de tous les Droits connus visant à protéger le plus précieux de nos humanités: qu'aller-venir et dévier sont un hommage offert à ceux vers qui l'on va, à ceux chez qui l'on passe, et que c'est une célébration de l'histoire humaine que d'honorer la terre entière de ses élans et de ses rêves. (Chamoiseau, 2017: 132, Déclaration #5)

(The poets declare: Coming and going, taking another route along the banks of the world is a poetic Right; that is, a decency that surpasses all the Rights we know that aim to protect what is most precious about our humanity. Coming and going, taking another route is a form of homage offered to those towards whom you're travelling, those whose homes you pass through. It's a celebration of human history that honors the entire earth in its drives and its dreams.)

Chamoiseau makes freedom of movement a poetic matter. When politics fails, and social action offers a first step, it is poetry that articulates the migrants' human right to move unencumbered. And it does so from the enclave of the imagination that Chamoiseau's notion of poetry creates. The creative energy of this declaration is stunning to sense. It is as sustaining as any statement from the United Nations.

Chamoiseau's sixteen declarations invoke a collective, that "strange colloquium of poets" he spoke about with the film-maker and humanitarian volunteer. These are poets across many times and places. They include François Villon, Deschamps' contemporary whose ballad, "Brother Humans," echoes in Chamoiseau's title, *Brother Migrants*. And it is in this premodern voice that Chamoiseau makes his final poetic declaration:

> Frères migrants qui le monde vivez, qui le vivez bien avant nous, frères de nulle part, ô frères déchus, déshabillés, retenus et détenus partout ... (Chamoiseau, 2017: 136)

> (Brother migrants who live in the world, who have lived in it long before us, brothers from nowhere, fallen, stripped, held and detained everywhere ...)

With all his poetic voices, Chamoiseau solicits a common sense of humanity and launches a call to action to safeguard migrants that is as potent as any political campaign.

*   *   *

Chamoiseau with Deschamps, Froissart with Carrère: these writers, and their inventive work, are a lifeline for thousands of displaced people in search of their place. For all of them and their publics, their fiction is a creative process of coming into awareness. It opens up the sense of being entrapped, held in place, or forced to move. It creates a place of critical reflection. Their writing fosters individual experiments in expressing something freely of the experiences of migrating. The result: a vital enclave of sorts for the hearts and minds of people. While this "imaginative territory" takes various shapes in such premodern and contemporary writing, its truth-claims changing at different times, it demonstrates how fiction is a necessary and invaluable part of composing the centuries-long history of Calais' migrants.

Notes

This chapter, like so much around the globe, was stranded during 2020. I maintain the text as is, updating only the reports and numbers of migrants that continue to increase in 2020–21.

1　See John Le Patourel's pithy résumé of Calais chroniclers by way of the 1930s historians, Calmette and Déprez (Le Patourel, 1951: 228). The chronicles cited: *The Online Froissart* (2013); *Chroniques, Livre I, manuscrit d'Amiens* (1991); Froissart (1978).

2　The "security guard" phrase is found in Nadot and Krimi (2021: 69). Compare this French government report with that of Human Rights Watch (2021).

3　Nadot and Krimi (2021: 70); Human Rights Watch (2021:15); *UN World Migration Report* (2020: 85–91); *Histoire de Calais* (1985: 20). Calais' port, open to the wider world from 1150 on, saw immigrants coming from the Levant. Macé (2017) captures the consternation of many in France, grappling with migrants outside their door, as well as in Calais.

4　David Wallace (2014: 22–73) has long set a standard for interpreting this early Calais chapter comparatively.

5　Sharon Farmer points out how premodern historians are slow to "come to grips with the magnitude … of immigrant communities in France, especially those coming to northern France." See her *Silk Industries of Medieval Paris* (2017: 2). Claudine Billot was a pioneer: "Les mercenaires étrangers pendant la Guerre de Cent Ans comme migrants," (1995: 279–86). See her call, a generation ago, for research for the period 1300–1550 (1980; 1983).

6　*Le Robert Dictionnaire historique de la langue française*, p. 1523; see Dauphant's maps, which trace these limits (2018: 191, 203).

7　*Ex(tra)Territorial* (2014: 9, 25). *Enclaves terrritoriales aux Temps modernes XVI–XVIIIe siècles* (2000: 343).

8　"Le XXIII est De la Clef et de la serrure," *Le dialogue des creatures moralisé*, translated from Latin, p. 2. Thanks to Julie Singer for signaling this work. For the key and lock scene in Calais' camp today, see Evans (2017).

9　"and he who commands the heart took out a small well-made key from his purse … 'at this,' he says, your heart will be closed." "*Qui a le cuer en sa comande … lors a de s'aumoniere treite une petite clef bien feite … A ceste, dist il, fermeré ton cuer,*" *Le Roman de la rose* (1992, v. 1995, 1998, 2000–1).

10　The legend is widespread in the historiography in English and French. For example: Clauzel and Honvault (2014: 11).

11　Bilingual writers working in Latin and French, such as Chartier, use this term; on the *nihil habentes*, see Gauvard (2002: 711); and Kapferer (2014: 109).

12　Figures between 770 and 1200 according to Nadot and Krimi (2021: 119); and 2000 according to Human Rights Watch (2021: 1); Agier et al. (2018), p. 56–7.

13　Rekacewicz (2010); updated April 2014 on the Visionscarto site.

14 *The Online Froissart.* See Besançon, Bibl. mun. 864, fols. 142–145. Following Ainsworth and Croenen, this early fifteenth-century manuscript with Toulouse, Bibl. mun. 511, are my base. See also *Chroniques de Jean le Bel* (1977) / *The True Chronicles of Jean le Bel* (2011).

15 Rodin's sculpture, *The Burghers of Calais* (1889), stands before the townhall; its many castings on public view from London to Stanford, California, has introduced this scenario around the world (Elsen, 2003).

16 Froissart, *Chroniques*, Besançon, Bibl. mun. 864, fol. 142 (Froissart, 1991: 29 ff).

17 Laurence Harf Lancner see this early fifteenth-century manuscript made in France as highlighting the European character of the conflict (1998: 228). Others consider Froissart a transnational (Stahuljak, 2001: 121–42); and an internationalist (Ainsworth, 1998: 15).

18 See the images and commentaries on this series of engravings in the concluding essay, "In Transit."

19 Toulouse, Bibl. mun. ms. 511, fol. 152v, 154v.

20 See also Gauvin's English translation (2016b); the Italian (2016c); and the Spanish (2017).

21 Eustache Deschamps (1893: 6; 2014; 2003). Deborah McGrady draws attention to Deschamps' struggle over his writer's role at the French court, this in the company of Froissart (2018: 171–2); (Butterfield, 2010: 137).

22 Deschamps (2014: 416). See Dauphant (2015).

23 See Denis Clauzel on the question of information circulation in Calais (1992: 204).

24 "Wartime Poetry: Conflict & Identity during the Hundred Years War, a conference organized by Daisy Delogu and Laetitia Tabard in March 2019, treats this subject holistically, including the work of Daniel Davies on Calais.

25 See Butterfield's analysis of this "cross-linguistic use" in her argument about nationalist assumptions (2010: 142). For a more Franco-national one, see Lassabatière (2011: 12). On the crucial, civic function of the diversity of languages in this region, see Hsy (2017: 154); Delogu (2013: 97–112).

26 Chamoiseau (2017). The translations are mine. See also trans. Amos, Rönnbäck (2018).

27 *"Le Lieu est ouvert; le Territoire dresse frontières. Le Lieu vit sa parole dans toutes les langues possibles. Le Territoire n'autorise qu'une langue"* (Chamoiseau, 1997: 205–6).

Manuscripts consulted

Besançon, Bibliothèque municipale, 864
Paris, BNF, f.fr. 840
Paris, BNF, n.a.fr. 151
Toulouse, Bibliothèque municipale, ms. 511

References

Agier, Michel (2018) *L'Étranger qui vient. Repenser l'hospitalité*. Paris: Seuil. Morrison, Helen trans. (2021). *The Stranger as my Guest: A Critical Anthropology of Hospitality*. Cambridge: Polity Press.

Agier, Michel with Yasmine Bouagga, Maël Galisson, Cyrille Hanappe, Mathilde Pette and Philippe Wannesson (2018) *La Jungle de Calais, les migrants, la frontière et le camp*. Paris: PUF. David Fernbach, trans. (2019). *The Jungle: Calais's Camps and Migrants*. Cambridge: Polity Press.

Ainsworth, Peter (1990) "Knife, Key, Bear, Book: Poisoned Metonymies and the Problem of 'Translatio' in Froissart's Later Chronicles," *Medium Ævum* 59:1, pp. 91–113.

— (1998) "Configuring Transience: Patterns of Transmission and Transmissibility in the *Chronicles*, 1395–1995." *Froissart across Genres*, Maddox, Donald and Sara Sturm, eds. Gainesville: University of Florida Press, pp. 15–39.

Aumond, Florian (2015) "De l'enclave à l'entrave territorial: Droits des migrants, frontières internationales," *Revue de la Recherche Juridique* 4, pp. 1815–37.

Billot, Claudine (1980) "Migrants, immigrants: un nouveau fichier documentaire: *Le Médiéviste et l'ordinateur*, p. 20.

— (1983) "L'assimilation des étrangers dans le royaume de France aux XIVe et XVe siècles," *Revue historique* 107: pp. 273–96.

— (1995) "Les mercenaires étrangers pendant la Guerre de Cent Ans comme migrants," in *Le Combattant au Moyen Âge, Actes des congrès de la Société des historiens médiévistes de l'enseignement supérieur public, Montpellier 1987*. Paris: Publications de la Sorbonne, pp. 279–86.

Butterfield, Ardis (2010) *The Familiar Enemy: Chaucer, Language and Nation in the Hundred Years War*. Oxford: Oxford University Press.

Carrère, Emmanuel (2016a) "Lettres à une calaisienne," *XXI*: 34, pp. 30–45.

— (2016b) Edward Gauvin, trans. "That Thing gnawing away at all of us: Calais and the shantytown at its doorstep," *The Guardian*, April 20.

— (2016c) Di Lella, Lorenza and Maria Laura Vanorio, trans. *A Calais*. Milan: Adelphi Edizioni.

— (2017) *Calais*. Barcelona: Anagrama.

Catudal, Honoré (1979) *The Exclave Problem of Western Europe*. Birmingham: University of Alabama Press.

Chamoiseau, Patrick (1997) *Ecrire en pays dominé*. Paris: Gallimard.

— (2017) *Frères migrants*. Paris: Seuil.

— (2018) Amos, Matthew and Fredric Rönnbäck, trans. *Migrant Brothers: A Poet's Declaration of Human Dignity*. New Haven, Conn.: Yale University Press.

Chroniques de Jean le Bel (1977) Viard, Jules and Déprez, Eugène, eds. Paris: Champion, (2011), Bryant, Nigel, trans. Woodbridge: Boydell Press.

Clauzel, Denis (1992) "Terrorisme et contre-terrorisme à la fin du Moyen Âge: le singulier destin de Calais," *Bulletin historique et artistique du calaisis* 127–8: pp. 191–210.

Clauzel, Isabelle and Alain Honvault (2014) *Calais et le pays reconquis en 1584.* Saint Martin Boulogne: Cercle d'études en pays Boulonnais.

Dauphant, Clotilde (2015) *Poétique des Œuvres complètes d'Eustache Deschamps, BnF, ms. fr. 840.* Paris: Champion.

Dauphant, Léonard (2018) *Géographies: ce qu'ils savaient de la France, 1100–1600.* Paris: Champ Vallon.

Delogu, Daisy (2013) "Aucun de ma langue: Language and Political Identity in Late-Medieval France," *Explorations in Renaissance Culture* 39: 2, pp. 97–112.

Deschamps, Eustache (1893) *Œuvres complètes d'Eustache Deschamps, Queux* de Saint-Hilaire, ed. Paris: SATF, vol. 5.

— (2003) *Eustache Deschamps: Selected Poems*, Laurie, I.S. and Sinnreich-Levi, M.D. eds. Curzon, D. and Fiskin, J. trans. New York: Routledge.

— (2014) *Anthologie*, Dauphant, Clotilde, ed. Paris: Librairie Générale Française.

Elsen, Albert E. (2003). *Rodin's Art. Rodin Collection of Iris and B. Gerald Cantor Center for the Visual Arts, Stanford University.* Oxford: Oxford University Press.

Enclaves terrritoriales aux Temps modernes XVI–XVIIIe siècles (2000) Delsalle, Paul and André Ferrer (eds). Besançon: Presses universitaires Franc-comtoises.

Evans, Kate (2017) *Threads: From the Refugee Crisis.* London: Verso.

Ex(tra)Territorial: Reassessing Territory in Literature, Culture and Languages. (2014). Didier Lassalle and Dirk Weissmann (eds). Amsterdam. Rodopi.

Farmer, Sharon (2017) *Silk Industries of Medieval Paris: Artisanal Migration, Technological Innovation, and Gendered Experience.* Philadelphia: University of Pennsylvania Press.

Farran, C. D'Olivier (1955) "International enclaves and the Question of State Servitudes," *International and Comparative Law Quarterly.* 4, no. 2 (April): 294–307.

Froissart, Jean (1978) *Chronicles.* Brereton, Geoffrey, trans. London: Penguin Books.

— (1991) *Chroniques, Livre I, manuscrit d'Amiens, Diller*, George T., ed. Genève: Droz.

The Online Froissart: A Digital Edition of the Chronicles of Froissart (2013) Ainsworth, Peter and Godfried Croenen (eds). Version 1.5. Sheffield: HRIOnline.

Gauvard, Claude (2002) "Le petit peuple au Moyen Âge," in Boglioni, Pierre et al. (eds), *Le Petit peuple dans L'Occident médiéval.* Paris: Editions de la Sorbonne. pp. 707–22.

Guérin, Antoine (2018) "Le traité franco-brittanique de Sandhurst: tout changer pour ne rien changer. Les droits de l'étranger," *La Revue des droits de l'homme*, 14 (February), https://journals.openedition.org/revdh/3772 (Accessed 7 January 2019).

Histoire de Calais (1985) Derville, Alain and Vion, Albert, eds. Westhoek: Editions des Beffrois.

Hsy, Jonathan (2017) *Trading Tongues, Merchants, Multilingualism, Medieval Literature.* Columbus: Ohio State University Press.

Human Rights Watch (2021) "Enforced Misery: The Degrading Treatment of Migrant Children and Adults in Northern France." www.hrw.org/sites/default/files/media_2021/10/france1021_web.pdf (Accessed November 11, 2021).

Jehel, Georges (1994) "Les Relations nord-sud au moyen-âge: voies terrestres et voies maritimes" in Curveiller, Stéphane (ed.), *Les Champs relationnels en Europe du Nord et du Nord –Ouest des origines à la fin du Premier Empire*, Sous l'égide de la municipalité de Calais. Colloque historique de Calais. pp. 59–69.

Kapferer, Anne-Dominique (2014) "Entre les grêves et les trêves, 1339–1505," in Lottin, André (dir). *Histoire de Boulogne-sur-Mer*. Villeneuve d'Ascq: Presses universitaires Septentrion, pp. 99–116.

de Kerangal, Maylis (2015) *À ce stade de la nuit*. Paris: Gallimard.

Lancner, Laurence Harf (1998) "Image and Propaganda: Illustration of Book I of Froissart's *Chroniques*," in Maddox, Donald and Maddox, Sara Sturm (eds), *Froissart Across Genres*, Gainesville: University of Florida Press, pp. 220–50.

Lassabatière, Thierry (2011) *La Cité des hommes: Eustache Deschamps, expression poétique, vision politique*. Paris: Champion.

Le Patourel, John (1951) "Occupation anglaise de Calais au XIVe siècle," *Revue du Nord* 33, pp. 228–41.

Macé, Marielle (2017) *Sidérer, considérer. Migrants en France*. Paris: Verdier.

McGrady, Deborah (2018) *The Writer's Gift or the Patron's Pleasure? The Literary Economy in Late Medieval France*. Toronto: University of Toronto Press.

Nadot Sébastien and Sonia Krimi (2021) "Rapport, Commission d'enquête sur les migrations, les déplacements de populations, les conditions de vie et d'accès aux droits de migrants, refugiés, et apatrides" www.assemblee-nationale.fr/dyn/15/rapports/cemigrants/l15b4665_rapport-enquete (Accessed November 11, 2021).

Rekacewicz, Philippe (2010) "Mourir aux portes de l'Europe: quatres esquisses de cartes sur la question migratoire dans le monde," *Le Monde diplomatique*, cartes (June). Updated April 2014 on the Visionscarto site. https://visionscarto.net/mourir-aux-portes-de-l-europe (Accessed January, 23 2019).

Le Roman de la rose (1992) Armand Strubel, ed. Paris: Livre de poche.

Roubaud, Jacques (1997) "Qu'est-ce-que une forme fixe? Les Formes fixes de la poésie," *Atalaya* 8 (automne), pp. 7–20.

Soto Bermant, L. (2015) "A Tale of Two Cities: The Production of Difference in a Mediterranean Border Enclave," *Social Anthropology* 23: 4, pp. 450–64.

— (2017) "The Mediterranean Question: Europe and its Predicament on its Southern Peripheries," in de Genova, Nicolas (ed.), *The Borders of "Europe:" Autonomy of Migration, Tactics of Bordering*. Durham, NC: Duke University Press, pp. 120–40.

Spiegel, Gabrielle M. (1997) *The Past as Text: The Theory and Practice of Medieval Historiography*. Baltimore: Johns Hopkins University Press.

Stahuljak, Zrinka (2001) "Translation and the Impossible Apprenticeship of Neutrality," in Blumenfeld-Kosinski, Renate, ed. *Politics and Translation in the Middle Ages and Renaissance*. Ottawa: University of Ottawa Press. pp. 121–42.

UN World Migration Report (2020) www.un.org/sites/un2.un.org/files/wmr_2020.pdf (Accessed January, 17 2021).

Wallace, David (2014) *Premodern Places*. London: Blackwell.

— (2016). *Europe: A Literary History, 1348–1418*. Oxford: Oxford University Press.

8

Calais-campscape:
A short history of immigration deterrence
at the French–British border

Vincent Joos (words) with Eric Leleu (photos)

In July 2019, photographer Eric Leleu and I took a drive in the Calais region to document the graves of the migrants[1] who recently died trying to cross the English Channel.[2] Before arriving at Calais, we stopped in Ruminghem, a village where dozens of Chinese indentured laborers who came to France during World War I are buried in a well-kept cemetery. When we arrived at the edge of the wheat field where these laborers rest, we met two men who tend to the flower beds surrounding the cemetery. They work for the British Commonwealth War Graves Commission and take care of the many military cemeteries that dot the region. "These people came to help the English during World War I and lived here, in Calais, and Dunkirk," said one of the workers. "They didn't fight but unloaded munitions, repaired roads or buried soldiers. Not far away from here, many Chinese men died in a train explosion, you can still see a barren area in what is now a field." After our visit to this cemetery, Leleu and I had a conversation with a man who was standing in front of his house and asked him if he knew about the possible location of the Chinese labor camp that stood in the village. While unable to state where the camp used to be, he remembered the location of the train explosion. He pointed to a couple of fields where, supposedly, we could find the barren space. We walked in the tall wheat to no avail. Even though we couldn't find the physical spaces indicating the laborers' life experiences, stories about them were still circulating and their presence continues to be felt.

During World War I, the French government brought approximately 220,000 workers from their colonies and concessions while the allied British government brought around 200,000 indentured workers to help with their war effort in France (Bailey, 2011; Dornel, 2014). These men lived in camps, mostly cut off from local populations, working outside the battlefields. Many of them would stay to help with the rebuilding effort after the war. This massive arrival of non-European and nonwhite laborers would transform

France, as it triggered immigration movements in France and in the UK (Ma, 2012). However, this immigration was not the desired goal of the French or the British states who did everything in their power to deter indentured workers from settling in Europe. For instance, the "French government censored any news that mentioned Chinese-French romances" because these relations could lead to marriages, hence to the settlement of Chinese workers in France (Xu, 2011: 151). Chinese laborers, in particular, became the target of anti-immigrant measures in the immediate post-war 1918–20 period in the Nord-Pas-de-Calais administrative region, where tens of thousands of them lived and worked. This chapter briefly explores the processes and infrastructures meant to deter Chinese indentured workers from migrating to France or the UK, to show the colonial structure of and the continuities between the management of migrants during the first mass influx of non-Europeans between 1917 and 1920 and today's racialized regime of citizenship at the French–British border. I argue that the present anti-immigrant laws and the various practices and technologies of deterrence in the Calais region stem from and reactivate colonial violence against non-European migrant populations. Criminalizing immigration and solidarity, preventing migrants from establishing relations with the local populations through urban segregation, and the racialized administrative processing and management of large groups of non-Europeans are instruments of repression and deterrence that were forged during the French colonial period. As an anthropologist working in the Caribbean, I study how the French and the British empires built their wealth on the plundering of distant colonies where settlers used racial hierarchies, spatial segregation, and conflicts as a means to govern nonwhites and to work them to death. The postcolonial period, in France and in the UK, is marked by an institutional refusal to acknowledge the colonial past and by a series of laws meant to cut off the former empires from their colonial strongholds. With their differential citizenship regimes, which are privileging European immigrants while rejecting and othering former colonial subjects, France and the UK perpetuate a colonial order where physical violence, racism, surveillance, and incarceration are the hallmarks of current immigration politics. By briefly exploring the life of Chinese workers in the Calais region, I aim to analyze the spatial mechanics of immigration regimes and the resistance they engender in order to understand how racism and neocolonialism shape policies and practices that are supposedly non-discriminatory.

Establishing the color lines

In the midst of World War I, in 1916, the French, British, and Chinese governments signed agreements stipulating that young Chinese men could be hired to help with the war effort, with the condition that these men would not fight on the front. As such, China remained neutral in the European conflict. France brought 37,000 Chinese workers who were dispatched to port-cities throughout the country, while the British brought 96,000 Chinese young men who mostly worked in northern France, especially in the Calais region (Bailey, 2011: 36). Most of these men were young peasants from the northern provinces of Hebei and Shandong. Recruited in their native regions, these men sometimes traveled up to three months in gruesome conditions to reach France. In order to avoid German submarine attacks, many of them were first secretly sent to Canada, a World War I ally and a prominent member of the British Commonwealth. They arrived in Vancouver and then went to Halifax or Montreal by train, "herded like so much cattle in cars, forbidden to leave the train and guarded like criminals" (Xu, 2011: 79). From there, the "coolies" – the official British category for indentured Chinese workers – went to France and lived in 17 camps scattered in the Pas-de-Calais region. Disease, lack of nutritious food, inadequate clothing, and generally miserable living conditions in camps killed many of these poorly paid indentured workers. Additionally, they performed dangerous jobs, such as digging trenches, carrying bodies outside the war frontlines and burying them. Most of the Chinese laborers who worked in the Calais region arrived at the beginning of 1917 and were first under the supervision of the British military. At the end of the war in 1918, most of them renewed their contracts and remained in France under the supervision of French civil authorities. From 1918 to 1920, members of the Chinese Labour Corps participated in the post-war effort under the supervision of French regional institutions, helping with the rebuilding of cities, villages, and infrastructures destroyed by the war. The French authorities, like the British, used segregation and deterrence measures to make sure that these workers, whom they described as criminals, would not settle in France.[3] Though the majority of these Chinese men returned to China in 1920, some of them immigrated to Europe, while many others remained in military cemeteries of the Calais region. Yassine Chaïb (2008: 33) estimates that approximately 20,000 Chinese workers died in France from 1917 to 1920. I do not intend to recall the long and complex history of the many indentured workers brought to Europe by colonial forces. Many excellent scholarly works have been published on the subject (Xu, 2012; Ma, 2012; Bailey, 2011). What I am interested in here is the establishment of durable racial hierarchies and the criminalization of nonwhite people in Calais during a mass influx of non-European people there.

In managing military and labor camps, as Tyler Stovall (1998) aptly puts it, the French and the British established a "color line behind the lines." Since 1915, the French government had been recruiting workers from their colonies. These men worked in the fields or in factories, replacing the French men who were fighting on the front. From 1915 to 1918, the French govern-ment recruited around 80,000 Algerians, 35,000 Moroccans, 18,500 Tunisians, 49,000 Indochinese, and 37,000 Chinese men. Thousands of foreign workers from adjacent European countries would also participate in the war effort. In 1916, the government created le Service de la main-d'Œuvre coloniale et chinoise (Colonial and Chinese Labor Corps), a military institution attached to the Ministry of War (Dornel, 2020). This institution was divided into several sections, each of which represented a particular race. For instance, if a private company wanted to hire people from this pool of colonial and indentured workers, it could specify which race it desired. As Laurent Dornel (2020) shows, the colonial and Chinese workers were subjected to surveillance, such as postal control, and were forced to live in camps located at the periphery of the cities where they often worked. In these camps, men were separated by race to limit possible conflicts that could undermine their productivity or subvert the colonial order. Meanwhile, foreign white workers enjoyed much better work and living conditions. These workers were administered by a different institutional entity, the Service de la main-d'Œuvre étrangère (Foreign Laborers Corps). These European workers were relatively free and lived in France on their own terms. There was also the possibility for them to remain in France, while the colonial and Chinese workers had no choice but to return to their country of origin. Starting in 1920, Polish workers, for instance, were encouraged to settle in France after World War I and received advantages from municipal institutions in northern France, such as funding for cultural organizations and administrative help (Genty, 2009: 75). French authorities believed that Polish workers, most of whom were white and Catholic, would better adapt to France and would not pose a threat to its religious conventions. Meanwhile, the Chinese workers who were already in France and who wanted to stay faced many hurdles and often had no choice but to live clandestinely. In other words, through the management of foreign laborers, the French government created new hierarchies of humanity through racial segregation and systemic discrimination. These hierarchies, in turn, shaped the modern French immigration system.

The racial management of colonial and Chinese workers also established a fracture between nonwhite and French workers, as the latter feared being invaded and replaced by Asian workers. Leung Wing-Fai (2014) has shown that the racialist ideology of the "yellow peril" was potent at the beginning of the twentieth century. The "yellow peril" was one of the first iterations of the Great Replacement theory that has made a comeback in political debates recently in Europe and in the US. It fueled European racial debates by blending anxieties about sexual and racist fears with the belief that the "Orientals" would invade the West and replace Europeans. The many xenophobic statements of dock workers' unions in Dunkirk, for instance, attest to these fears of being replaced by a nonwhite, cheaper labor force (Stovall, 1998: 761). As Stovall notes, "during World War I, concepts of racial difference based on skin color became a significant factor in French working-class life for the first time, establishing a discourse of conflict and intolerance that remains powerful today" (1998: 740). These racial hierarchies and social ruptures fashioned an immigration system that served to block nonwhite people from the path to French or UK citizenship.

The French and the British sought to prevent the long-term settlement of indentured workers in western Europe. In order to avoid conflicts with local populations and, more importantly, to avoid cross-cultural contacts that could lead to the permanent settlement of indentured workers, French institutions and the British Army forbade laborers to entertain social relations with Europeans outside of their camps and workplaces (Boniface, 2012). They lived under strict surveillance under a harsh regime of segregation. For example, in July 1918, a military ruling forbade the French population to have friendly relationships with nonwhite workers. A young woman from Boulogne, who had sent a postcard to a Chinese worker she had befriended, was sued by the municipal police tribunal, to be later acquitted (Archives du Pas-de-Calais, 2020). Criminalizing relations between local population and foreign workers sought to deter the latter from migrating and settling in France. The current prohibition against housing or helping migrants and the state prosecution of people who do so in the Calais region, in spirit, does not differ from this 1918 law.

Many Chinese workers managed to create spaces of freedom in and outside their camps. For instance, some of the men under the supervision of the French government managed to gamble, to go to bars and brothels, and sometimes had romantic relationships with young French women who, according to Xu, didn't care about the racial lines (2011: 148). Chinese laborers were never the passive victims of indenture and many of them organized strikes and demonstrations, which often led to violent conflicts with the French police forces (Bailey, 2011). They sometimes acted violently among themselves, with the administrations, and with local populations, using conflict as an expression of presence and agency in a society that largely rejected them (Regnard, 2012). These tensions were important. By opposing the segregation regime and reacting against institutional xenophobia, indentured workers claimed their own rights and autonomy. They interrogated the citizenship regimes of imperial states and created a political space for future immigrants who would confront technologies, processes, and infrastructures of deterrence. If assaults by French citizens on nonwhites were the dominant form of racial violence in France, Chinese workers fought back, as they did in January 1918 in Rouen when a French officer mistreated a Chinese dockworker. Seventy Chinese men took the defense of their co-worker and stormed the Rouen police station where the officer had taken refuge. The commander of this Chinese crew of workers noted that French workers and civilians "whose opinions of Chinese workers are well known" provoked his men (Stovall, 1998: 754). In other words, these Chinese workers stood up against institutional and banal racism and were, like many colonial workers, eager to fight back against race-based oppression. Even though relations between the French and the Chinese were forbidden, a few men settled in northern France and had families, hereby creating the first important settlement of Chinese people in France (Ma, 2012). Obtaining papers, let alone citizenship, was and remains a difficult task.

If the Chinese contributions to the war effort and to the post-conflict reconstruction have only been recently acknowledged by French authorities, many Chinese people who immigrated to France in the twentieth and twenty-first centuries individually and collectively, commemorated them. Individually, Chinese families living in France or even in China come to visit the cemeteries of the Calais region. Collectively, undocumented immigrants, in the recent past, have visited these cemeteries to pay tribute to these indentured workers and to link their present immigration struggles in France to those of the Chinese laborers. In a country where prejudices against people of Asian descent is common, the fate of segregated, otherized, and discriminated Chinese laborers still resonates (Aw, 2019). On July 14, 2000, for instance, a group of 60 Chinese sans-papiers activists (undocumented migrant-activists) and their allies visited the Nolette cemetery to draw attention to the administrative hardships and systemic racism the Chinese diaspora and themselves endured and still endure (Chaïb, 2008). They placed a wreath of flowers with a banner that read:

> Aux travailleurs chinois de 1917–1920
> morts pour la France,
> Les travailleurs chinois de 1997–2000
> rejetés par la France.[4]

The message on the wreath powerfully captures the continuities between current Chinese immigrants and the Chinese laborers who toiled in France but who never got recognition and who, sometimes, struggled to immigrate to Europe. To say that Chinese workers today are rejected would be an understatement. In 2007, when French President Nicholas Sarkozy toughened immigration laws and implemented repatriation quotas, there was a 20% increase in expulsions of Chinese sans-papiers (Korman and Liew, 2009). Moreover, the French Chinese community is the target of police violence. In 2016, the killing by the French police of 56-year-old Liu Shaoyo in his home, while he was preparing dinner for his children, sparked huge demonstrations, led by France's ethnic Chinese protesting against continuing attacks on their community members (Aw, 2019). Moreover, Chinese people who try to immigrate to the UK continue to die at the border.[5] I do not claim that the laws and practices instituted during World War I are identical today. However, I argue that the management of nonwhite populations in France during World War I established a racialized system for the handling of migrants that still endures. The following sections describe some of the colonial legacies that shape immigration in Calais today. Segregation, incarceration, and surveillance, along with the othering and criminalizing of migrants and their allies are not new immigration practices. Along with the externalization and solidification of borders, these practices are the hallmarks of imperial states.

Calais: an English chokepoint?

Before analyzing the forms of criminalization and spatial exclusion of migrants perpetuated by state authorities, I want to describe briefly how and why Calais has become a fortress city over the past twenty years. Politicians on both sides of the Dover Strait touted the construction of the Channel Tunnel (hereafter Chunnel) as a symbol of free circulation in Europe. Calais was supposed to become a "major European crossroads" where people and goods would flow uninterrupted (see ECMT, 1993). However, soon after the opening of the Chunnel, it was clear that Calais was not a crossroads for everyone. When the Chunnel opened in 1994, it increased the legal flows of commodities and people between France and England. Every year, approximately 10 million people cross the 23.5-mile Chunnel, while 1.6 million trucks are carried through the tunnel's rail-transport shuttle. The ferry traffic is even more important: an estimated 4 million trucks and 14 million passengers cross the Strait of Dover by sea every year, making the English Channel the busiest maritime route in the world (Mambra, 2020). Since the opening of the Chunnel, Calais and its periphery have become a chokepoint, a site that "constrict[s] or 'choke[s]' the flow of resources, information, and bodies upon which contemporary life depends" (Carse et al., 2020). The port area of Calais, the train stations, and the Chunnel entrance are today high-security zones surrounded with razor wire and anti-intrusion walls. The French police heavily patrol the inner city, while the tourists of yesteryear do not go there anymore. Calais and its periphery are at once a place where forms of connectivity have increased in the past twenty years, and in the meantime, a place where movements of undesired human traffic have slowed. The Calais chokepoint constricts immigration but, in the meantime, renders it visible and powerful. Calais migrants disrupt the legal traffic of goods and people in the region, and thus thrust to the fore their political claims. If politicians and engineers thought of the Chunnel as a logistical infrastructure, the creation of the tunnel opened a new passageway for people who, very often, were and are fleeing conflicts in former regions of the British colonial empire such as Iraq, Sudan, or Somalia.

In 1999, the influx of refugees in Calais was so strong that the French government asked the French NGO Doctors without Borders to open a temporary camp to offer minimal shelter and services. Up until it was closed in 2002, the Sangatte camp received around 100,000 refugees from the Balkans, North Africa, and the Middle East, many of whom continued to cross the French–English border illegally. The British government forced the closing of this camp with the argument: providing humanitarian help to refugees will create a "magnet" effect and will attract migrants from the world over (Tempest, 2002). Activists and migrants harshly criticized the state-sponsored humanitarian camp, but of course for different reasons. The associations running these types of camps are pressured by French authorities to help with the monitoring and identification of migrants, which blends humanitarian missions with control practices (Van Isacker, 2019). Since the closing of Sangatte, the French government has repeatedly opened camps on the periphery of Calais, cutting off migrants from the solidarity networks of this city. As activists of Calais Migrant Solidarity put it when describing the opening of such camps, "what we are witnessing is the creation of a racial ghetto under the guise of liberal humanitarian concern" (CMS, 2015). It was after the closure of the 2002 Sangatte camp that a forceful institutional assemblage between France and the UK would transform Calais into a city where people would be stopped for identity checks based on their phenotype, and where nonwhite migrants who dared to walk in the city center could be tracked and brutalized by the French police forces on a daily basis (Hicks and Mallet, 2019).

In 2003, while Tony Blair fully engaged his country in the war against Iraq, the French and British signed the Touquet treaty. This treaty, in effect, displaced the English border in Calais. Eight years after the implementation of the Schengen area that dissolved some borders of inland Europe, the French and the British again solidified the border in Calais. In effect, the Schengen agreements allowed for the free circulation of some European citizens, but it made it harder for migrants to circulate in Europe, as the agreements allow police forces to verify the immigration statuses of anyone they stop. Identity checks, in France, continue to generate resentment from nonwhite populations since such controls are mainly made through racial profiling. In other words, if the borders seem to dissolve for some people, mobility within continental Europe was severely constricted upon racial lines. The dream of free circulation in Europe ended with the Touquet treaty as borders on the French–British side of Europe solidified anew. Not only did the British establish immigration checkpoints in Dunkirk and Calais, they were also involved in many aspects of border control in the region.

In December 2016, the French construction company Vinci, one of the largest corporations in Europe, finished the construction of the Great Wall of Calais, a 4-kilometer anti-intrusion barrier built with slippery concrete and topped with razor wire. The Great Wall runs along the port entrance and is meant to deter migrants from entering the loading zones. This anti-intrusion barrier is the most visible element of a flurry of infrastructure constructions funded by British taxpayers' money. These include the creation of a moat around the entrance of the Chunnel, the edification of fences topped with razor wire in the port area, and the installation of surveillance cameras in and around the port. Between 2010 and 2018, the British government spent more than 400 million euros to reinforce security workforces and infrastructure in Calais (Sheldrick, 2018). The British government contributes, in France, to the growth of security corporations, and, in the meantime, to the privatization of border management in Europe. The British rely heavily on private security corporations to filter the entrance of the port and tunnel. British taxpayers' money fund corporations that are doing the job of border agents and are building up a landscape of watchtowers and flooded zones – infrastructures to be considered as agents in the politics of deterrence. For instance, Eamus Cork Solutions, a French corporation, received 90 million euros from the British government for detention and escort services (Populin, 2018). In other words, young uneducated French security guards slowly replace policemen and border agents, knowing that corporate agents regularly bypass state regulations while facing very little backlash (Mermet, 2010). As detailed below, since the implementation of Brexit, these processes of border privatization and of border externalization have drastically increased.

Crimmigration

As the earlier surveillance and control of indentured Chinese workers indicates, and as described above, the British authorities have had a heavy hand in the control of non-European populations on French territory. By investing in security infrastructures and technologies in Calais, the British transformed this city into a fortress. The camp infrastructures such as moats, anti-intrusion walls, and watchtowers dot the Calais coastline, rendering it impenetrable by migrants. These infrastructures and technologies not only deter migrants from entering the city center but also allow for the tracking of relationships between migrants and their allies. In brief, the proliferation of surveillance technology and the permanent harassment of migrants and activists by

French and British authorities create terrible life conditions for non-Europeans by forcing them to sleep in dangerous areas, in the hope that extreme and cruel measures will deter migrants from coming or staying at the border. What we see in these processes briefly outlined here is that immigration is managed through spatial and material practices. Incarcerations, segregation, and surveillance displace and render invisible large groups of migrants.

Trying to render immigration invisible, and contacts between allies and migrants impossible, the French—British institutional assemblage that manages immigration in the Calais region today weaponizes the landscape to deter immigration. During the fieldwork I did in the city of Calais in the summer of 2019, I almost never saw migrants or refugees walking in the city center. Downtown Calais, with its many closed businesses, looks like a ghost town patroled by the French police, private security guards, and British border patrol officers. Refugees are being pushed away from the entry gates to England, namely the English tunnel and the port of Calais. They have no choice but to sleep in temporary tent encampments along the coast. Because of the harsh winter weather of this area, many people have died in these makeshift camps. In November 2019, a 25-year-old Nigerian man died in his tent from smoke inhalation, as he tried to light a fire in a tin to warm up and cook food (Chrisafis, 2019). His death occurred after the city of Calais passed a decree forbidding migrants to come to the city center. For migrants, being visible in Calais is a means of asserting one's presence and of claiming belonging. It is a way of entering in confrontation with French state authorities whose inaction and passivity are also powerful deterrence tools. Hence, removing them from areas where they are highly visible is a spatial, state-sponsored strategy meant to impede claims of belonging and citizenship.

From 1996 to 2015, migrants built large encampments around the port area or squatted in buildings in downtown Calais or Calais-Plage. While, after 2014, squatting in buildings became difficult because of the relentless efforts to criminalize this practice by Calais' right-wing mayor, Natacha Bouchart, many tent encampments – the "jungles" – have reappeared in the region. "Jungle," or *jangle* in Farsi, means wooded area. It is a word many migrants use to describe temporary camps. As Yasmin Ibrahim and Anita Howarth (2017) have argued, French and British descriptions of "jungles" transformed the meaning of the word by adding to it racist connotations. Describing camps as unruly places peopled by "savages" is a strong reminder of the colonial trope of the jungle, and creates a separation between "civilized" city dwellers and people forced to live in camps.

In 2015 there was a large influx of refugees from war-torn regions that formerly belonged to the British empire, namely Afghanistan, Syria, and Iraq. More than one million people arrived in western Europe during this period, and many converged in Calais with the hope of crossing the Dover Strait. From 2008 to 2015, makeshift camps were small and scattered along the coast. However, because of the arrival of so many people in Calais, large migrant camps reappeared in the region. The largest one, called "La Lande," grew in the area adjacent to the port, when French authorities pressured the NGOs and organizations helping migrants to ask people to move next to the newly opened Jules Ferry Day Center. This state-sponsored center run by the large association La Vie Active is meant to shelter women and children during the day and is a place where people can find basic help. In other words, the French state encouraged the creation of "La Lande." Since the Jules Ferry Center is not in downtown Calais, French authorities deemed it an adequate place to concentrate and control migrants. According to the collective Calais Migrant Solidarity, the Jules Ferry Center is more than a state-sponsored humanitarian space. It is also "a place of control, repression and segregation and stands for the racist and neo-colonialist immigration policy of UK and France" (CMS, 2015). Named after Jules Ferry, the center continues its humanitarian mission while it expands the control of migrants' mobility. It is worth noting that Jules Ferry was a nineteenth-century politician who advocated for the colonial expansion of France. In a speech on the colonial empire before the Chamber of Deputies on March 28, 1884, Ferry stated that colonization "is a right for the superior races, because they have a duty. They have the duty to civilize the inferior races." Ferry supervised the colonization of Tunisia, Madagascar and Indochina. If he is remembered for being the education minister who created the public school system in France, the fact that he was a racist and staunch proponent of colonialism did not escape activists and migrants who see the naming of this center as indicative of the current racialized immigration system (CMS, 2015). In 2015, more than 10,000 migrants had gathered around the Jules Ferry Center and lived in "La Lande." The tent camp that grew around the Jules Ferry Center became the focal point of the so-called migrant crisis in Calais.

As it did in 2008, the French state sent policemen and hired private contractors to destroy "La Lande" on October 25, 2016. This destruction marked a turn in the management of the migrants' encampment in the Calais region. This is not a surprise. Since the beginning of Brexit in June 2016, the anti-immigration rhetoric in the UK has become ever more inflammatory. This escalation is reflected in the signing of new treaties that reinforced the British presence in Calais. In 2018, French President Emmanuel Macron and Prime Minister Theresa May signed the Sandhurst Treaty, which allowed the British to process migrants who hope to enter the UK in Calais port. Moreover, the treaty stipulated that approximately 50 million euros would be disbursed to reinforce border controls. To this effect, in the summer of

2018, the British government opened the UK–France Coordination and Information Centre in Calais (Vickers, 2020: 84). British Home Office border officials, National Crime Agency officers and British immigration enforcement personnel staff this coordination center.

The Coordination and Information Center supports and implements a new zero tolerance strategy, which has triggered more suffering for migrants. The UK Home Office statement went on to detail what the work of the center would entail; as it explains, "the centre will see Border Force working closely alongside Police Aux Frontières as part of a 24/7 operation to assist with preventing illegal attempts to cross the shared border, exchange real-time intelligence between UK and French agencies to combat cross-border criminality, work on the prevention of threats to public order on cross-border infrastructure, and provide analysis of cross-Channel traffic flows" (Pyne-Jones, 2018). The center is not only a surveillance tool but also a repressive institution that supposedly prevents threats to public order on French territory. After almost twenty years of strong-arming French politicians, the British Conservatives are efficiently transforming the French immigration system by fostering the privatization of borders and by criminalizing unauthorized immigration. French politicians, when campaigning for election, claim that the Touquet Treaty goes too far and that the UK should receive and process refugees in its own country. For instance, in 2016, while campaigning for the presidential election, Nicolas Sarkozy called for the annulation of the Touquet Treaty. However, Sarkozy signed this treaty in 2003 and his government eagerly implemented the hardline immigration measures the UK government called for – the moat and razor wire fences that surround the Chunnel entrance are the materialization of such politics. During the Hollande and Macron presidencies, UK Prime Minister Theresa May successfully convinced her French counterparts to revise the Touquet treaty. Again, then President Hollande threatened to relax border controls if Brexit went through. However, after the Brexit referendum in 2016, Hollande maintained the Touquet Treaty and reiterated the need for the British to be present in Calais. In 2017, presidential candidate Macron claimed that the Touquet treaty placed a heavy burden on France. Once elected, he and May revised the treaty, enabling the British to clamp down harder on immigration in Calais. As May declared in 2018, "we will reinforce the security infrastructure with extra CCTV, fencing and infrared technology at Calais and other border points" (McCauley and Booth, 2018). In other words, since 2003, French governments have increasingly conceded border control to the British.

The Coordination and Information Centre is the latest materialization of the French–British tough line on immigration. The Center targets both migrants and their allies. Through its impressive surveillance apparatus, it helps French authorities to locate makeshift camps and to carry out the systematic destruction of migrants' temporary shelters (Townsend, 2019). Since 2018, evictions have skyrocketed. Migrants are today forced to change the location of their encampments daily and most of them cannot catch more than a couple of hours of sleep at night, which affects their mental and physical health. As UK reporter Mark Townsend (2018) notes, hundreds of unaccompanied children are forced to walk and hide as well, since the UK ended its program to transfer vulnerable children from France to Britain. Marie-Charlotte Fabié, director of the NGO Safe Passage France, notes that even the family reunification program in the UK is not working anymore. Too many legal burdens, such as proving family ties, have led to what amounts to a closure of this program (Langlet, 2020).

The new zero tolerance policies indicate that the growth in immigration control is accompanied by a criminalization of immigration. Not only do France and the UK make it increasingly difficult to immigrate or to claim asylum, they also frame illicit immigration as a crime. As Juliet Stumpf (2006) has shown, immigration and criminal laws increasingly merge to create what she names "crimmigration." In other words, migrants who are breaking immigration laws are now prosecuted under the criminal law and receive custodial sentences. In France, President Macron has been following a hard-line policy when it comes to immigration. In 2018, his government passed a law that doubled to 90 days the time in which migrants can be detained while their case is being processed. More importantly, illegally crossing borders is now a criminal offense that can lead up to one year in prison and to fines (BBC, 2018). Likewise, in the UK, the government, between 1999 and 2016, created 89 new immigration offence categories, which are mainly targeting a perceived abuse of the immigration system (Bhatia, 2019).

The Dublin regulations that force migrants to apply for asylum in the first European country where they have been formally registered is also a powerful and cruel deterrence tool. Because of the risk of being "dublined," people who are trying to migrate in Europe today have no choice but to hide indefinitely. Louison Mungu Mawu, a 47-year-old agronomist who fled the Democratic Republic of Congo after being detained and tortured by the regime of former president Joseph Kabila, states that the Dublin regulations create great psychological distress for migrants who are forced to live in "an open-air jail" that Europe became for asylum seekers (Pascual, 2020). Being "dublined" or incarcerated are techniques of exclusion that echo the racialized hierarchies of humanity created during the colonial age. As sociologist Monish Bhatia bluntly puts it, "crimmigration is essentially a racial project – an ever expanding system of control that polices and targets immigrants criminalized as 'illegals,' 'bogus' and 'risky'. It is a set of hostile practices designed to manage/filter out racialized 'others' due to their perceived lack of belonging to the (imagined) national community, and involves denigration, punishment and banishment" (2020: 38). The proliferating criminal laws meant to regulate immigration pose a grave danger to certain category of migrants. The French police notoriously use racial profiling when performing identity checks, which puts nonwhite migrants at a greater risk of being incarcerated (HRW, 2020). A hundred years after the end of World War I, the French and the British continue to treat nonwhite people as undesirable bodies. The practice of segregation and racial profiling in Calais show how both states continue to use spatial practices forged during World War I. From 1917 to 1920, while more than 400,000 nonwhite laborers worked on French soil, the French authorities established patterns of mobility echoed in the Dublin regulations and the process of crimmigration. It is during this period that Europeans started to enjoy relatively free circulation in France and the possibility of settling there. In the meantime, nonwhite people lived at the periphery of the cities where they worked, were subjected to extreme surveillance, and were prohibited from circulating freely in the country or to establish social relations with French people.

Spatializing anti-immigration

As Travis Van Isacker has shown, since 2016, the French police, helped by their British counterparts, have practiced systematic domicide, defined here as the willful destruction of one's shelter. Immigration retention centers are no longer the key tool for materializing the racial and ethnic segregation between local populations and non-Europeans. The practice of domicide precisely aims at destroying the solidarity networks refugees and locals have established – by occupying space in the city center of Calais, refugees were claiming basic human rights, they were asserting themselves as political subjects, and they developed solidarities across citizenship categories (Van Isacker, 2019). Domicide is no longer limited to Calais. It is now a key instrument of deterrence along the French northern coast. The French police continue to destroy large camps, such as the Calais hospital camp where more than 800 migrants lived until its forced closing in September 2020. However, while these large-scale destructions make the headlines of newspapers, the daily destruction of tents and migrants' belongings remains invisible to the public. Associations like Calais Migrants Solidarity, L'Auberge des Migrants and Amnesty International keep a thorough record of migrants' deaths and of police brutality. These organizations denounce the practice of domicide as a harmful and cruel technique of immigration management, but to no avail. Documenting police abuse in Calais is a risky activity. For instance, British human rights defender Tom Ciotkowski was assaulted by three French policemen in Calais while he was documenting police abuse against migrants in this city in 2018 (Amnesty International, 2020b). It is not an isolated case. In a thorough and scathing report, association L'Auberge de Migrants states that, from November 1, 2017 to July 1, 2018, the French police had "646 incidents pertaining to the intimidation of volunteers. These intimidations range from systematic identity checks to parking fines and also includes threats, insults and physical violence" (Vigny, 2018). Not surprisingly, police violence against migrants is a daily and systematic occurrence. In October 2017, 92% of migrants living in Calais stated that they had been victims of police brutality (Pope and Welander, 2019).

Because of recurring police brutality and because of systematic domicide, many migrants are condemned to walk along the northern French coast or to risk their lives by crossing Dover Strait by any means. In brief, migrants who are trying to cross the English Channel today face three options: they can go to a French immigration detention center if they accept applying for asylum in France (which will be refused most of the time); they can refuse to ask for asylum in France and go to prison while they are waiting to be deported; or they can hide and try to escape the French and British police forces until they find an opportunity to cross the strait. Many "choose" the third option and attempt to cross the strait on frail boats or by swimming. On a weekly basis, corpses wash up on the shores of the French and Belgian coast. In the summer of 2020, illegal crossings of the strait went up, rising from 1,400 crossings in the summer of 2019 to 5,500 in the summer of 2020 (McLennan, 2020). The British Home Secretary, Priti Patel, pledged to send the Royal Navy to prevent illegal crossing, which drew the ire of right-wing Calais mayor Natacha Bouchart and of the French government. However, Patel threatened to withhold funds meant to secure the border. In a stunning reversal, in August 2020, the French government asked for an extra 33 million euros for its police to intercept people on land (Allen and Hope, 2020). The French government also allowed the presence of UK naval warships in the Strait (Tyerman and Van Isacker, 2020). Beyond crimmigration, the present French and British governments want to militarize their current war with migrants.

Practices of spatial exclusions such as systematic domicide or the military surveillance of the Dover Strait indicate that citizenship is far more than a legal category underlining national belonging. Citizenship is also and primarily a spatialized and racialized regime of exclusion. As Van Isacker (2019) puts it, spatial exclusions need to be thought of in the frame of citizenship "as state exclusionary technology of migration governance and mobility control." The spatial techniques of exclusion remain crude and cruel. In 2020, Home Secretary Patel and her staff studied the possibility of sending asylum seekers to detention camps in Ascension Island, a British territory located in the middle of the Atlantic Ocean. If technologies of surveillance have changed, the colonial nature of immigration management has not. Because sending migrants to an isolated island would be a financial and logistical nightmare, the British Home Secretary instead opted for the reopening of the immigration removal center in Lincolnshire. This camp is run by the British prison service, is located in a remote area of the UK, and offers jail-like conditions for migrants.

Focusing on immigration practices in Calais should not hide another colonial spatial practice: the externalization of European borders. Calais stands at the epicenter of the so-called immigration crisis in France. Repeatedly, French politicians described it as the consequence of the European Union's inaction at the southern European borders. As described here, the British government, through the Touquet treaty, extended its border operations in France. At the European Union (EU) level, the recent process of border externalization reengages relations between Europe, the Middle East, and Africa. The EU's border agency Frontex's budget has gone up by 5.233% since 2005 (Buxton and Akkerman, 2019). In 2018, for instance, Frontex spent 320 million euros to solidify and militarize borders in eastern Europe while reinforcing migration control within the Middle East and the African continent.

The EU has signed border control agreements with 35 non-European countries and does not hesitate to work with authoritarian regimes when it comes to decreasing the flows of migrants coming from continental Africa and the Middle East – especially in regions that Calais migrants stem from. Turkey, for instance, collaborates with Frontex and violently prevents Syrian refugees and Kurdish internal migrants from leaving the country. Many Kurdish and Syrian migrants nonetheless manage to get out of Turkey and to walk to Calais. Likewise, the relations between the EU and Sudan follow this pattern. If the EU maintains international sanctions against the Al-Bashir regime in Sudan, it works with Sudanese governmental agencies to train border police officers who operate in Sudan. The new Sudanese border agents primarily belong to the Rapid Support Forces, an organization that "committed a wide range of horrific abuses, including torture, extrajudicial killings and mass rapes" (HRW, 2019). Buxton and Akkerman aptly note that European border colonialism actually fosters emigration from Africa. "Support for authoritarian rulers, the companies causing climate change, unjust trade relations, corporate impunity, reckless military interventions and the arms trade" are allowing the EU to hold its colonial grip in Africa and the Middle East while transforming entire regions into uninhabitable lands. Most of the people who come to Calais were born in regions formerly colonized by the British. As Mekki Ali, a Sudanese refugee and voluntary refugee worker, declared, the British government should let Sudanese in "because Sudanese were colonized by Britain" (The Telegraph, 2015). The colonial legacies of the current immigration regime at the French–British border does not escape the migrants who are trying to rebuild their lives in the UK, where communities of former subjects of the British empire live and often thrive. The British colonized, or tried to colonize, vast regions in Sudan, Iraq, Syria, Iran, and Afghanistan in the nineteenth century and at the beginning of the twentieth. Today, the French and British armies and through Frontex, the EU, are heavily involved in the conflicts that make these regions unlivable. Now that European crimmigration practices roil African countries that managed newly created internal borders, migrants face cruel treatment beyond the immigration chokepoints of Europe.

By taking a deliberately postcolonial approach to immigration in Calais, I argue that the current management of the French–British border and the externalization of borders through the anchoring of Frontex in Africa show tangible imperial legacies. Moving large numbers of people across oceans, segregating nonwhite people from local populations, criminalizing solidarity and immigration, and using incarcerations and physical violence as means of deterring migrants from settling in the UK are practices inherited from empire states. These practices are not new, and the neutral language of anti-immigrant surveillance and repression cannot hide the racist legacies that sustain the European immigration regime today. On European soil, these racist practices were deployed against the indentured workers who worked for the Allies during World War I. The first mass arrival of nonwhites on French territory, and especially in the Nord-Pas-de-Calais department, fostered the creation of new immigration systems where race and ethnicity opened or closed paths to French and British citizenship. Writing a short history of indenture and immigration in France during World War I allowed me to show that hardline immigration measures are anchored in racialized systems of exclusion. Calais is today a "campscape," a city where the space of the camp overlaps with urban space (Martin, 2015). The "Jungle" of La Lande and other camps that have risen and disappeared since 1994 attest to the encroachment of refugee camp infrastructure in the Calais region. However, another type of camp reminiscent of the labor camps of World War I is transforming the city of Calais today. The watchtowers surrounding the port and Chunnel areas, the anti-intrusion wall, the razor wire fences surrounding industrial sites and parking lots, and the proliferation of surveillance cameras in all corners of the city and of its periphery have transformed Calais into an open-air prison for migrants. The campscape that the city of Calais has become enables the reproduction of the harsh camp life of indentured workers and points to the racist treatment of migrants who overwhelmingly come from former British colonies and/or from regions where the British army continue to attack. As Harsha Walia writes "large-scale displacements and the precarious conditions into which migrants are cast are not coincidental but rather foundational to the structuring of border imperialism" (Walia and Smith, 2013: 41). A postcolonial reading renders visible the colonial nature of the camp and of the forms of segregation used to prevent social and national belonging for people whose regions have been ravaged by the French and British empires.

Even if trapped in the Calais campscape and subjected to crimmigration, the migrants in Calais and their many allies defy the laws or subvert them to create spaces of freedom and autonomy across citizenship statuses. Like their Chinese counterparts in the 1910s, migrants are pushing back against the technologies and practices of deterrence, and are affirming their presence and political subjectivity by squatting in buildings in downtown Calais or by establishing tent encampments in visible areas. Migrants and activists have their own systems of surveillance, which include the systematic documenting of brutality, or the filming of such brutality. Because activists filmed three French policemen beating up activist Tom Ciotkowski, those responsible will soon be prosecuted (Amnesty International, 2020b). The high-profile acquittal of Cédric Herrou, a French farmer who helped asylum seekers and who was charged for "facilitation of irregular entry," proves that the pushback against the criminalization of solidarity is efficient (Amnesty International, 2020a). However, as direct physical violence against migrants crescendoes, many are condemned to languish in the campscape that the Calais region has become, or to die while trying to cross the Channel.

Migrants' and activists' resistance in Calais has never receded, but the violent deterrence practices that one can witness on a daily basis at the French–British border is not a local but a transnational issue, which demands major institutional shifts. As Carolina Sanchez Boe and Darren Byler (2020) put it, combatting surveillance regimes consolidated by the confluence of state power and big tech "require not only an empowered public but also people within governments and companies to regulate and resist harmful forms of surveillance". Reifying borders while surveilling and controlling people's mobilities comes at an enormous financial and human cost. Nationalist leaders who promote hardline anti-immigrant measures and deadly deterrence politics must be held accountable, as much as the corporations that generate profits from the militarization of borders and criminalization of immigration. The struggles of migrant activists and their allies in Calais point to more human means and ends when it comes to dealing with immigration. International organization Calais Migrant Solidarity (CMS) activists know that the freedom of migrants is closely linked to the freedom of Europeans, simply by the fact that big tech surveillance infrastructure meant to track immigrants can also be used against anyone. Standing in solidarity with migrants is a political act, a direct confrontation with a

French state that prohibits and criminalizes acts of solidarity. Standing in solidarity means to refuse to do the work of charity organizations co-opted by the French state to bring a veneer of humanitarianism to their anti-immigrant policies and to track migrants in the Calais region. As the activists of CMS write, "the problems in Calais will not be covered by a million blankets. The violence and misery here are a direct result of the border. As long as the French and British states keep on using razorwire fences, cops, batons, tear gas, media hatred, and other weapons to try and stop people crossing, there will be suffering. The only way to address this problem is to rise up against the border" (CMS, 2016). Standing in solidarity with migrants, instead of offering them charity, means to combat crimmigration and to create social relations across citizenship regimes, as was the case between many Chinese laborers and French people during World War I. The fact that the French state continues to criminalize such relations shows that equal relationships which are indifferent to skin color, ethnicity, or immigration status open cracks in the border. Migrants are not the passive victims of crimmigration. All of them have successfully crossed many danger-ous borders before coming to Calais. Their journeys are a form of resistance to increased border security, not only in Calais but also elsewhere in Europe. Their unnecessary suffering testifies to the need for free circulation in a borderless Europe.

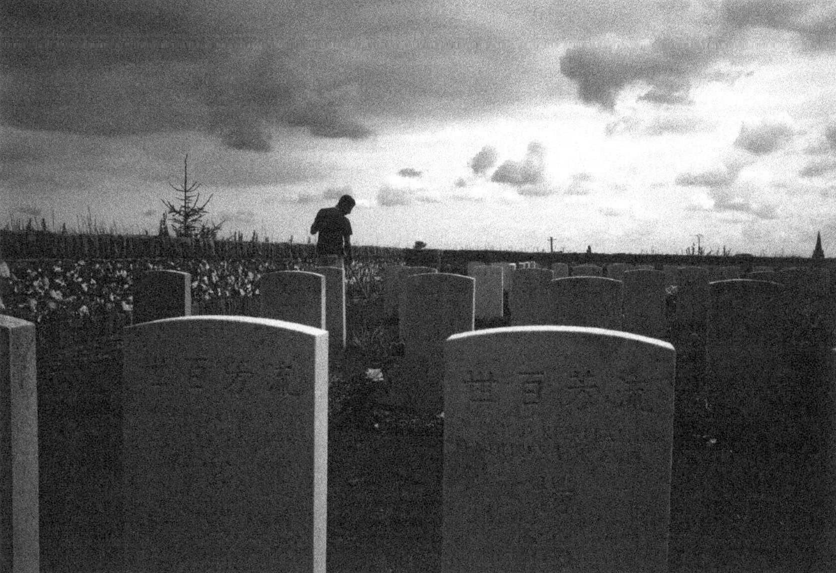

Figure 8.1 Ruminghem Chinese cemetery where indentured workers are buried, July 2019. Photo: Eric Leleu.

 Migrants shaping Europe, past and present

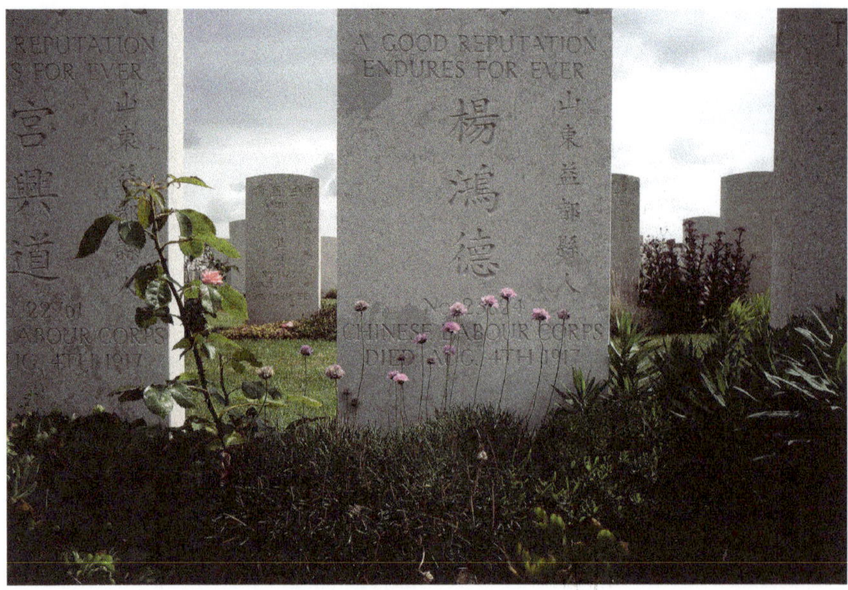

Figure 8.2 Ruminghem Chinese cemetery, July 2019. Photo: Eric Leleu.

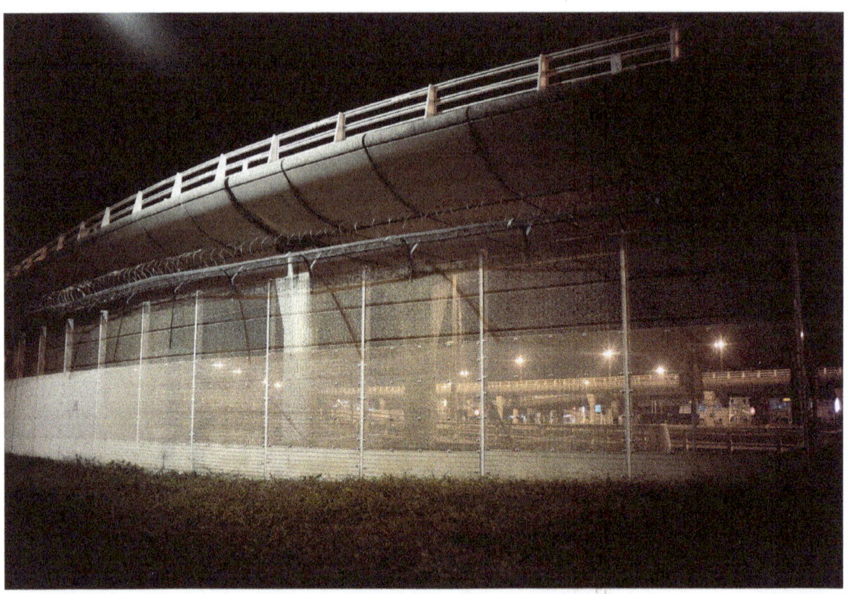

Figure 8.3 Calais, France, 2017. Razor wire fences along the Calais highways. Photo: Eric Leleu.

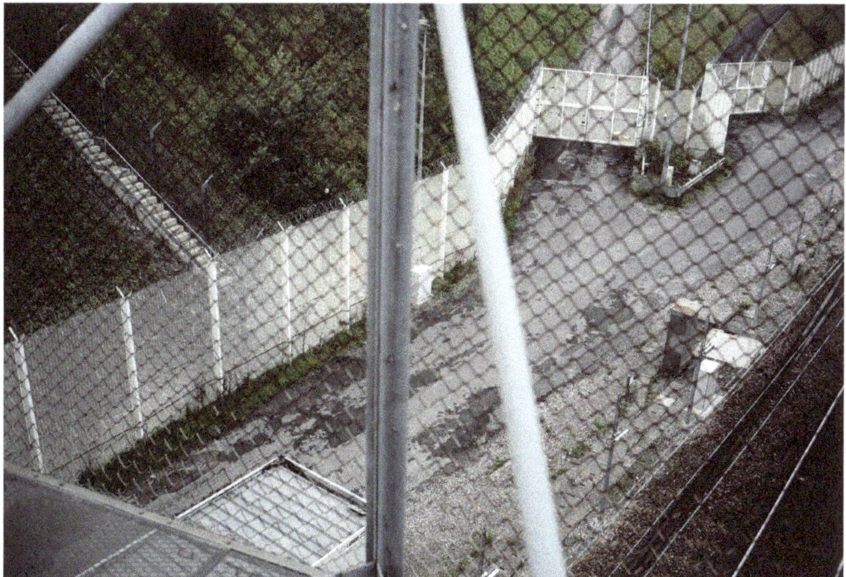

Figure 8.4 Fréthun, France, October 2017. Two hundred meters away from the English Channel entrance. Photo: Eric Leleu.

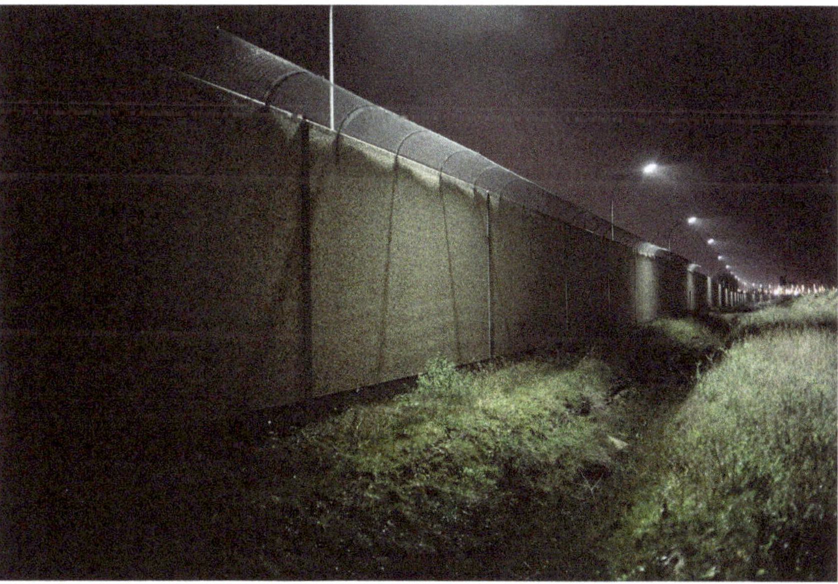

Figure 8.5 Calais, France, June 2017. The Great Wall of Calais: a four-meter high and one-mile long anti-intrusion barrier surrounding the Calais port. The British government funded the construction of this wall. Photo: Eric Leleu.

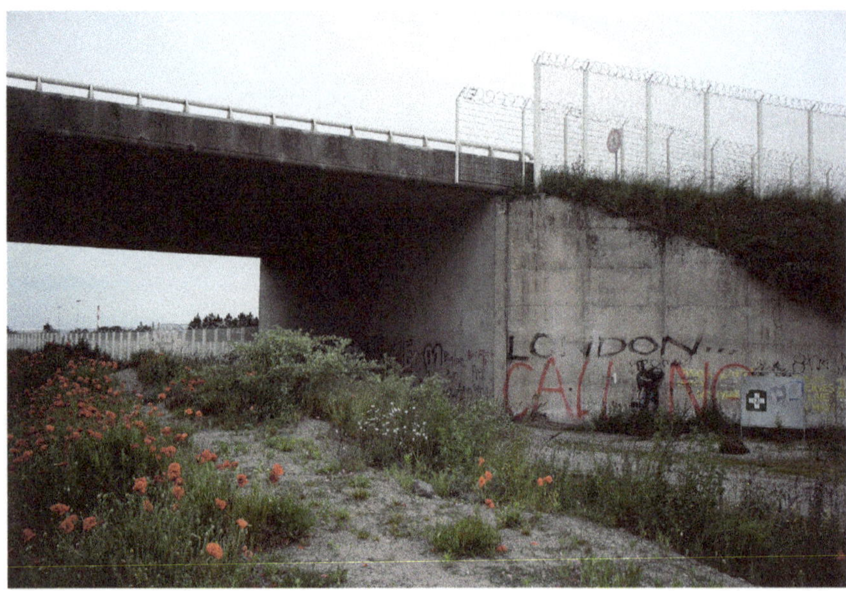

Figure 8.6 Calais, France, June 2017. A Banksy graffiti representing Steve Jobs as a refugee. Located at the exit of the former "Jungle" of Calais. Photo: Eric Leleu.

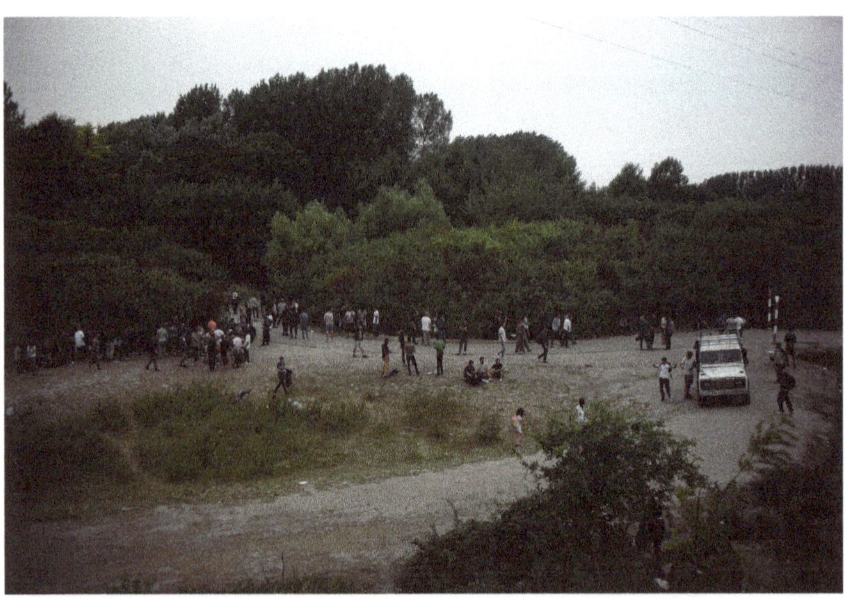

Figure 8.7 Grande-Synthe, France, July 2017. Salaam, a British nongovernmental organization, offers meals to migrants. Photo: Eric Leleu.

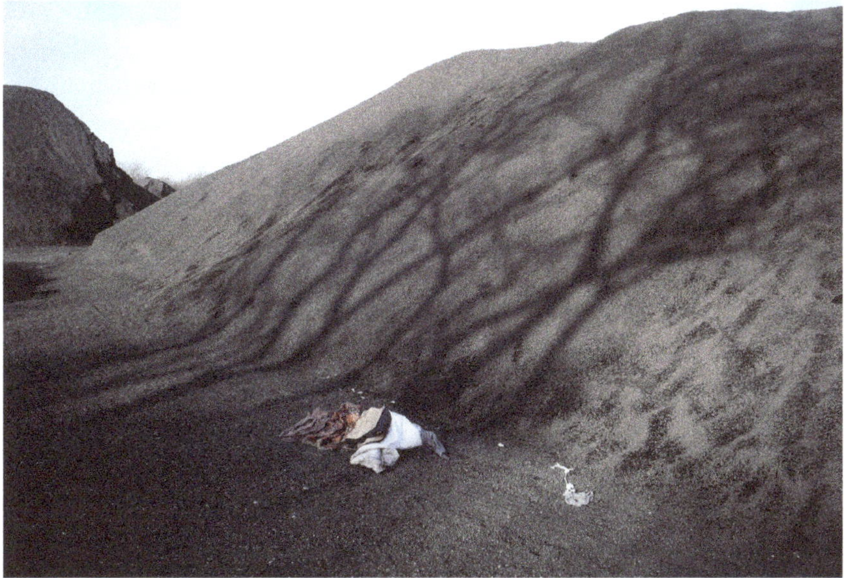

Figure 8.8 Calais, France, January 2018. Blankets left behind by migrants in an industrial site adjacent to the port. Photo: Eric Leleu.

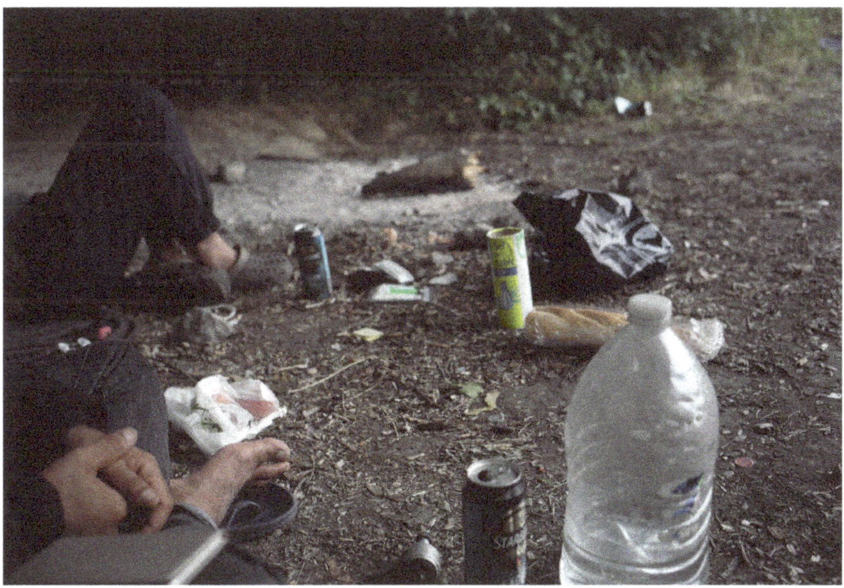

Figure 8.9 Grande-Synthe, France, July 2017. Waiting for the night to come on the shores of Lake Puythouck. Photo: Eric Leleu.

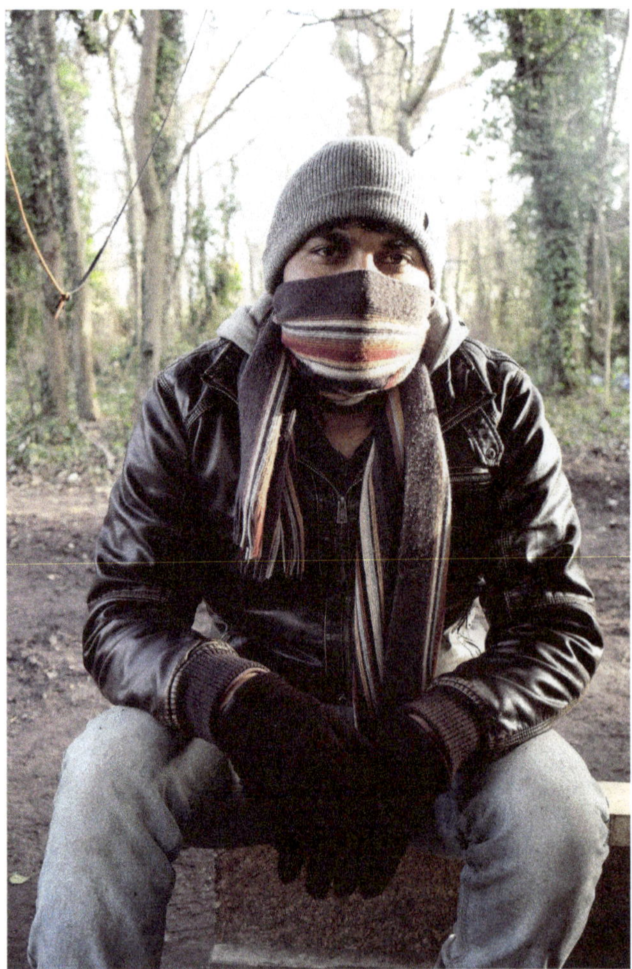

Figure 8.10 Calais, France, January 2018. K., twenty-five years old, walked from Nangarhar Province in Afghanistan and wants to reach England. Photo: Eric Leleu.

Notes

1 In this chapter, I am using "migrants" as a very broad term that encompasses people with different situations, such as asylum seekers, refugees, or so-called economic migrants. Crawley et al. provide an excellent analysis of arbitrary immigration categorizations (2017).
2 Leleu and I have been carrying out long-term fieldwork in Calais since 2018. Our goal is to document the physical changes brought about by the hardening of anti-immigrant policies and Brexit in the Calais region.

3 As Patrice Marcilloux notes (2012), a series of measures taken by local officials show the extent of the xenophobia targeting Chinese workers. For instance, in September 1919, citing the criminal nature of Chinese workers, the prefect Robert Leullier asked the Minister of Freed Regions (Ministre des Régions Libérées), for the removal of all Chinese people in the department of Pas-de-Calais. Many mayors followed this and asked for the departure of Chinese workers. Left-wing elected official Émile Basly denounced the "bad deeds that are customary for Chinese populations [that] terrorize people in northern France." Many other officials asked for more limitations of Chinese mobility in northern France, criminalizing their presence on the basis of xenophobic categorizations.

4 "To the Chinese workers of 1917–1920 who died for France. From the Chinese workers of 1997–2000, who are rejected from France."

5 On two recent occasions, Chinese citizens tried to cross the border by hiding in frigorific trucks. In 2008, 40 people of Chinese descent suffocated in one of these trucks and were found dead, and in 2018, 58 Chinese people died in the same fashion.

References

Allen, Christopher and Peter Hope (2020) "French Demand £30m to Stop Migrants Crossing Channel." *The Telegraph*, August 8, www.telegraph.co.uk/politics/2020/08/08/french-ask-30m-police-channel/. Accessed August 17, 2020.

Amnesty International (2020a) "France: Acquittal of Farmer Who Helped Asylum Seekers Shows That Solidarity is Not a Crime." Amnesty International, www.amnesty.org/en/latest/news/2020/05/france-acquittal-of-farmer-who-helped-asylum-seekers-shows-that-solidarity-is-not-a-crime/. Accessed November 18, 2021.

— (2020b) "France: Prosecution of Police Who Assaulted Calais Camp Volunteer Sends Message against Impunity." Amnesty International, www.amnesty.org/en/latest/news/2020/06/france/. Accessed July 23, 2021.

Archives du Pas-de-Calais (2020) "Les Travailleurs chinois du Pas-de-Calais," https://archivespasdecalais.fr/Decouvrir/Chroniques-de-la-Grande-Guerre/Histoires-de-la-Grande-Guerre/Les-travailleurs-chinois-du-Pas-de-Calais. Accessed August 17, 2020.

Aw, Tash (2019) "Coming out of the Shadows: What it Means to Be French and Chinese." *The Guardian*, November 26, www.theguardian.com/world/2019/nov/26/what-you-hear-about-chinese-people-in-france-feeling-scared-its-true. Accessed August 11, 2020.

Bailey, Paul J. (2011) "An Army of Workers: Chinese Indentured Labour in First World War France". In Santanu Das (ed.) *Race, Empire and First World War Writing*. Cambridge: Cambridge University Press, pp. 35–52.

BBC News (2018) "France Approves Controversial Immigration Bill." *BBC News*, April 23, www.bbc.com/news/world-europe-43860880. Accessed October 3, 2020.

Bhatia, Monish (2019) "Crimmigration, Imprisonment and Racist Violence: Narratives of People Seeking Asylum in Great Britain." *Journal of Sociology*, vol. 56, no. 1, pp. 36–52, doi:10.1177/1440783319882533.

Boniface, Xavier (2012) "Camps Militaires Britanniques et Travailleurs Chinois dans Le Pas-De-Calais Pendant La Grande Guerre." *Les Travailleurs Chinois en France Dans La Première Guerre Mondiale*, CNRS Éditions, https://books.openedition.org/editionscnrs/16986. Accessed August 8, 2020.

Buxton, Nick and Mark Akkerman (2019) "The Rise of Border Imperialism." Transnational Institute, October 18, www.tni.org/en/article/the-rise-of-border-imperialism. Accessed December 7, 2019.

Carse, Ashley, et al. (2020) "Chokepoints: Anthropologies of the Constricted Contemporary." *Ethnos*, pp. 1–11, doi:10.1080/00141844.2019.1696862.

Chaïb, Yassine (2008) "Le Cimetière Chinois De Nolette En Picardie." *Hommes & Migrations*, 1276:1, pp. 30–43, doi:10.3406/homig.2008.4800.

Chrisafis, Angelique (2019) "Outrage in Calais over Death of Nigerian Man in Tent." *The Guardian*, November 3, www.theguardian.com/world/2019/nov/03/outrage-in-calais-over-death-of-nigerian-man-in-tent. Accessed November 29, 2019.

CMS (2015) "Who was Jules Ferry?" Calais Migrant Solidarity, calaismigrantsolidarity.wordpress.com/?s=jules+ferry. Accessed March 6, 2020.

— (2016) "The Calais Wall: Vinci and the Other Profiteers Making a Killing from Building an Anti-Migrant Barrier." Calais Migrant Solidarity, October 4, calaismigrantsolidarity.wordpress.com/2016/10/04/the-calais-wall-vinci-and-the-other-profiteers-making-a-killing-from-building-an-anti-migrant-barrier/. Accessed October 2, 2019.

Crawley, Heaven, et al. (2017) "Unpacking a Rapidly Changing Scenario: Migration Flows, Routes and Trajectories across the Mediterranean." Centre for Trust, Peace and Social Relations, Coventry University, July 11, https://pureportal.coventry.ac.uk/en/publications/unpacking-a-rapidly-changing-scenario-migration-flows-routes-and-. Accessed October 9, 2019.

Dornel, Laurent (2014) "Les Travailleurs Chinois en France Pendant La Grande Guerre." *Hommes & Migrations* no. 1308, pp. 174–8.

— (2020) "L'appel Aux Travailleurs Étrangers, Coloniaux et Chinois Pendant La Grande Guerre." Musée National de l'Histoire de l'Immigration, www.histoire-immigration.fr/dossiers-thematiques/les-etrangers-dans-les-guerres-en-france/l-appel-aux-travailleurs-etrangers. Accessed November 18, 2020.

ECMT (1992) Activities of the Conference: Resolutions of the Council of Ministers of Transport and Reports Approved in 1992: Thirty-Ninth Annual Report (1992), OECD Publishing, Paris, doi.org/10.1787/ecmt_conf-1992-en.

Genty, Jean-René (2009) *Les Étrangers Dans La règion Du Nord: Repères Pour Une Histoire régionale De L'immigration Dans Le Nord-Pas-De-Calais (1850–1970)*. Paris: L'Harmattan.

Hicks, Dan and Sarah Mallet (2019) *Lande: The Calais "Jungle" and Beyond*. Bristol: Bristol University Press.

HRW (Human Rights Watch) (2019) "'Men With No Mercy'." Human Rights Watch, June 26, www.hrw.org/report/2015/09/09/men-no-mercy/rapid-support-forces-attacks-against-civilians-darfur-sudan. Accessed July 18, 2021.

— (2020) "France: Children Face Abusive, Racist Police Stops." Human Rights Watch, October 25, www.hrw.org/news/2020/06/18/france-children-face-abusive-racist-police-stops. Accessed February 6, 2021.

Ibrahim, Yasmin and Anita Howarth (2019) *Calais and its Border Politics: From Control to Demolition*. Abingdon: Routledge.

Isacker, Travis Van (2019) "Bordering through Domicide: Spatializing Citizenship in Calais." *Citizenship Studies*, vol. 23, no. 6, pp. 608–26, doi:10.1080/1362102 5.2019.1634422.

Korman, Rémi and William Liew (2009) "Politics of Invisibility: The Political Underrepresentation of Chinese Communities in France." Humanity in Action, www.humanityinaction.org/knowledge_detail/politics-of-invisibility-the-political-underrepresentation-of-chinese-communities-in-france/. Accessed April 6, 2022.

Langlet, Marianne (2020) "Brexit Défaire Les Familles." Accueil, www.lien-social.com/Brexit-o-Defaire-les-familles. Accessed December 2, 2020.

Ma, Li (2012) "Introduction." *Les Travailleurs Chinois en France Dans La Première Guerre Mondiale*. CNRS Éditions, pp. 19–39.

Mambra, Shamseer (2020) "The Strait of Dover – The Busiest Shipping Route in the World." *Marine Insight*, March 14, www.marineinsight.com/marine-navigation/the-strait-of-dover-the-busiest-shipping-route-in-the-world/. Accessed April 11, 2020.

Marcilloux, Patrice (2012) "Les Travailleurs Chinois et la Reconstruction Du Pas-De-Calais." *Les Travailleurs Chinois en France dans la Première Guerre*, CNRS Éditions, https://books.openedition.org/editionscnrs/17016. Accessed October 21, 2020.

Martin, Diana (2015) "From Spaces of Exception to 'Campscapes': Palestinian Refugee Camps and Informal Settlements in Beirut." *Political Geography*, Elsevier BV, researchportal.port.ac.uk/portal/en/publications/from-spaces-of-exception-to-campscapes(00082165-f190-43c8-af98-6211d90d9fb6).html. Accessed April 6, 2022.

McCauley, James and William Booth (2018) "Pressed by France, Britain Agrees to Do More to Stop Migrants in Calais." *The Washington Post*, January19, www.washingtonpost.com/world/europe/pressed-by-france-britain-agrees-to-do-more-to-stop-migrants-in-calais/2018/01/18/c06373ac-fb9a-11e7-9b5 d-bbf0da31214d_story.html. Accessed November 14, 2020.

McLennan, William (2020) "Channel Crossings: Why Can't the UK Stop Migrants in Small Boats?" *BBC News*, August 20, www.bbc.com/news/uk-england-53650537. Accessed April 18, 2021.

Mermet, Daniel (2010) "Les Charognards de L'immigration (Suite)." # *Numéro Lambda* #, September 12, https://numerolambda.wordpress.com/2010/09/10/les-charognards-de-limmigration/. Accessed March 1, 2020.

Pascual, Julia (2020) "En France, 'Des Gens Sont Devenus Fous' à Cause Des Accords de Dublin Sur Les Réfugiés." *Le Monde*, September 23, www.lemonde.fr/societe/article/2020/09/23/en-france-des-gens-sont-devenus-fous-a-cause-des-accords-de-dublin-sur-les-refugies_6053230_3224.html. Accessed 12 June, 2021.

Pope, Stephanie and Martha Welander (2019) "The State of Refugees and Displaced People in Europe." *Refugee Rights Europe*, September 21, refugee-rights.eu/wp-content/uploads/2018/12/RRE_SummaryReport_2017-18.pdf. Accessed April 4, 2020.

Populin, Eugénio (2018) "2018: Calais + 40 Millions d'Euros, Frontex 1 Milliard Depuis sa Création en 2004." *Mediapart Club De Mediapart*, January 22, blogs.

mediapart.fr/eugenio-populin/blog/220118/2018-calais-40-millions-deuros-frontex-1-milliard-depuis-sa-creation-en-2004. Accessed 12 June, 2021.

Pyne-Jones, Louise (2018) "Refugees Turn to Illegal Channel Crossings after Forced Evictions from Calais in France." International Observatory of Human Rights, December 3, observatoryihr.org/news/refugees-turn-to-illegal-channel-crossings-after-forced-evictions-from-calais-in-france/. Accessed March 3, 2020.

Regnard, Céline (2012) "Réflexions sur les conditions de vie des travailleurs chinois en France pendant la Première Guerre mondiale." *Les Travailleurs Chinois en France Dans La Première Guerre Mondiale*, CNRS Éditions, pp. 285–302, https://books.openedition.org/editionscnrs/16986. Accessed August 7, 2020.

Sanchez Boe, Carolina and Darren Byler (2020) "Tech-Enabled 'Terror Capitalism' is Spreading Worldwide. The Surveillance Regimes Must Be Stopped." *The Guardian*, July 24, www.theguardian.com/world/2020/jul/24/surveillance-tech-facial-recognition-terror-capitalism?fbclid=IwAR0-KF4FDCTGRmkDTXc_vKQVS-nOz6YKwEcS2NrOvLzQrtSBONMp80ua-lq8. Accessed July 26, 2020.

Sheldrick, Giles (2018) "Calais Migrant Crisis Has Already Cost UK Taxpayers over £360m." iWxpress, January 19, www.express.co.uk/news/uk/906716/calais-migrant-crisis-360million-british-taxpayers-theresa-may-emmanuel-macron. Accessed August 26, 2020.

Stovall, Tyler (1998) "The Color Line behind the Lines: Racial Violence in France during the Great War." *The American Historical Review*, vol. 103, no. 3, p. 737–69.

Stumpf, Juliet P. (2006) "The Crimmigration Crisis: Immigrants, Crime, and Sovereign Power." SSRN, October 9, papers.ssrn.com/sol3/papers.cfm?abstract_id=935547. Accessed July 4, 2020.

The Telegraph, August 3, 2015 ("Calais Migrant Crisis"), https://www.youtube.com/watch?v=AsTTTbYT1NU (accessed March 15, 2021).

Tempest, Matthew (2002) "Sangatte to Close." *The Guardian*, July 12, www.theguardian.com/uk/2002/jul/12/immigration.immigrationandpublicservices. Accessed April 8, 2020.

Townsend, Mark (2019) "Record Refugee Evictions at Camps in France to Halt Channel Crossings." *The Guardian*, June 22, www.theguardian.com/world/2019/jun/22/refugee-eviction-peak-in-france-bid-halt-channel-crossings. Accessed June 28, 2019.

Tyerman, Thom and Travis Van Isacker (2020) "Border Securitisation in the Channel." Oxford Law Faculty, October 9, www.law.ox.ac.uk/research-subject-groups/centre-criminology/centreborder-criminologies/blog/2020/10/border. Accessed November 18, 2020.

Van Isacker, Travis (2019) "Bordering through Domicide: Spatializing Citizenship in Calais." *Citizenship Studies*, vol. 23, no. 6, pp. 608–26, doi:10.1080/13621 025.2019.1634422.

Vickers, Tom (2020) *Borders, Migration and Class in an Age of Crisis: Producing Workers And Immigrants*. Bristol: Bristol University Press.

Vigny, Eleonore (2018) "Calais: The Police Harassment of Volunteers," helprefugees.org/wp-content/uploads/2018/08/Police-Harrassment-of-Volunteers-in-Calais-1.pdf. Accessed July 4, 2020.

Walia, Harsha and Andrea Smith (2014) *Undoing Border Imperialism*. AK Press.

Wing-Fai, Leung (2014) "Perceptions of the East – Yellow Peril: An Archive of Anti-Asian Fear." *The Irish Times*, August 16, www.irishtimes.com/culture/books/perceptions-of-the-east-yellow-peril-an-archive-of-anti-asian-fear-1.1895696. Accessed November 11, 2020.

Xu, Guoqi (2011) *Strangers on the Western Front: Chinese Workers in the Great War*. Cambridge, MA: Harvard University Press.

PART V

Arts of migration

9

In Transit

The In Transit Collective: Ellen Raimond, Marianne Wardle, Elvira Vilches, Alán José, Pedro Lasch, Raquel Salvatella de Prada, Shreya Hurli, Helen Solterer

How to compose a cultural history of migration around Europe through the visual and material arts? The following ensemble of artwork offers one experimental answer developed by a group of faculty members and students at Duke University. It presents a portion of a small installation on view at the Nasher Museum of Art during the autumn of 2018. This was the fruit of a collective debate that also engaged colleagues from the Americas, Europe, and Africa. Historian Pierre-Olivier Dittmar brought his thinking on premodern attitudes of tolerance and xenophobia to bear on our question. Art historian Laura Weigert introduced tapestries as a key model of mobility in early modern cultures. Michael Gerli focused attention on the visual evidence of the early modern banishment of Spanish Muslims, and their diaspora in North Africa; while curator Sara Raza spoke to the range of contemporary art in that region and the Middle East. Sociologist Piotr Plewa enriched our project by examining questions of migrant labor with us. Writer Hisham Matar offered his inimitable voice relaying Bedouin poets and his sharp eye on Jacques Callot's engravings. Students in seminars on migration taught in Spanish and French contributed their translations and critical view. Over some three years, In Transit drew on various vantage points to identify who and what represent migrant art, to delineate "Europe" as one constantly changing human field of migration – in the twelfth century, when men of science traveled between the Maghreb and the Iberian peninsula, and in the current-day when activist-artists move between West African and European communities.

Selecting objects began to answer our question in concrete form, and in a variety of media. Barthélémy Toguo's artwork was chosen because of the politically provocative ways it represents routes between Cameroon and France today, and Annette Messager's textile installation linked closely to the region of Pas-de-Calais. We chose the engravings of Jacques Callot in North Carolina collections because they delineate a precise, early modern picture of men and women in flight from war in northern Europe. Pedro

Lasch, a globally engaged artist in our midst, joined our collective and contributed his video work. All these pieces began to trace a widening scope of "Europe" that migration creates.

"In Transit" was designed as a small installation. The eight pieces are laid out in a way that tests a technique developed by curator Jean-Hubert Martin. His notion of *carambolage*, from the effect of billiard balls hitting off one another, creates encounters between objects rarely seen side-by-side. Such unexpected contact between things can give viewers a sudden shock. Does this trigger a change in outlook? The technique that has become familiar now is often combined with a historical *carambolage*, one placing objects of different times side-by-side. In one room, we spatialized the diptych that structures this comparative volume as well.

The portion of the "In Transit" installation that follows juxtaposes early modern artwork with that of contemporary artists. Callot's engraved *Bohemians* encounter Messager's fabric *Replicants*. Toguo's *New World Climax* woodcuts from 2011 are set across from Muhammad ibn al-Fattuh al-Khama'iri's astrolabe from Al-Andalus in Spain, which are paired with the fourteenth-century Catalan Atlas, one of the earliest maps drawing on Muslim science and accurately representing the Sahara. Furthermore, the sequence of artwork serves to accentuate the creations of Arab and Black artists in the history of those migrating around Europe. In this way of seeing, history and human geography are deepened.

Each piece is accompanied by a brief commentary. Together as a group, they cover the areas examined in the volume: from regions identified today with the global South, and from cities and countryside associated with northern Europe. Through visual languages, they express something of the range of migrant cultures explored in the chapters. The early and premodern pieces visually "translate" the long critical view of contributors. The contemporary pieces respond to the movements of today's migrants in multiple directions south and north, across "Europe." As a whole, the set of eight works offers a visual counterpoint to the chapters.

Cornered, the installation of Raquel de Salvatella de Prada, was first exhibited with the Nasher installation, in the Rubenstein Arts Center nearby. De Salvatella de Prada depicts West African migrants on their way to Spain via Melilla in Morocco. Visitors who came to see it moved back and forth between the artwork in the two venues, mimicking the motion of many migrants. Together the two installations stand as a fitting conclusion to the volume as a whole.

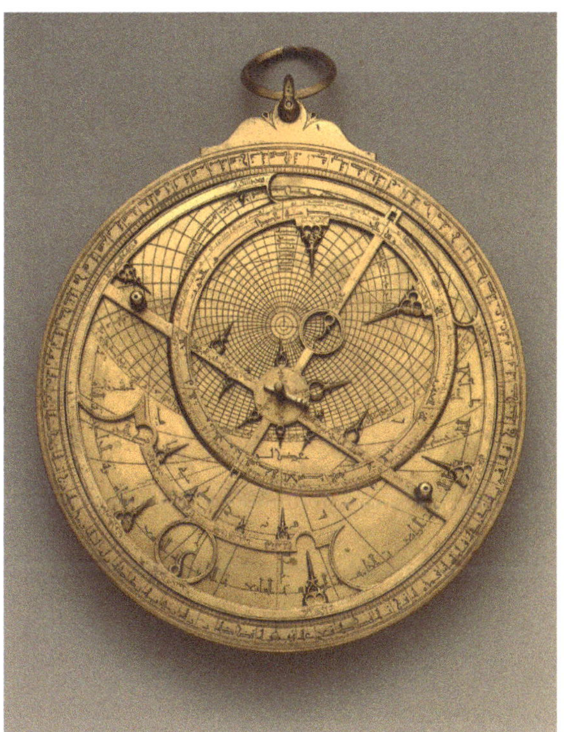

Figure 9.1 Muhammad ibn al-Fattuh al-Khama'iri (Spanish, active 1200s), Astrolabe, 1236–37. Brass. Adler Planetarium, Chicago, Illinois, M-35.

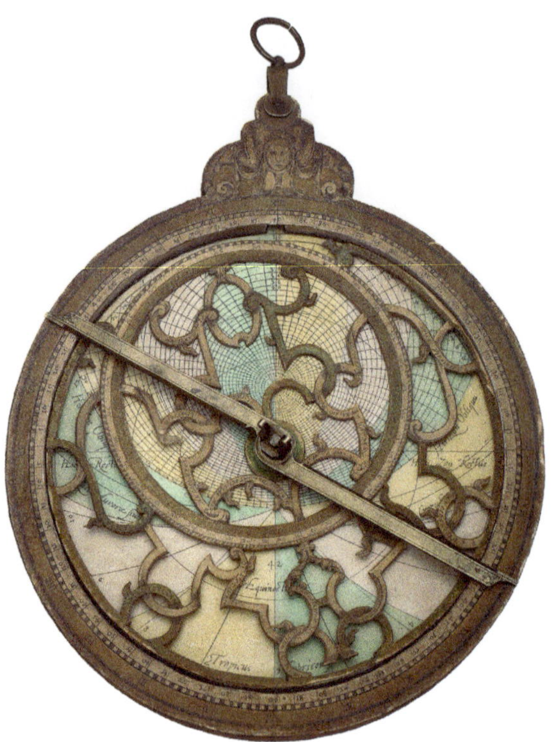

Figure 9.2 Philippe Danfrie (French, active 1500s), Jehan Moreau (French, active 1600s), Astrolabe, 1584 (designed) and 1622 (printed). Wood, paper, brass. Adler Planetarium, Chicago, Illinois, W-98a.

These intricate instruments are called "star-taker," astrolabe, in Arabic and all Romance languages, including English; they enable users to locate celestial bodies and tell time by measuring the angles of an object's elevation in relation to gravity.

The thirteenth-century astrolabe, made by Muhammad ibn al-Fattuh al-Khama'iri was used in Al-Andalus, the Muslim caliphate on the Iberian peninsula. Its Arabic inscriptions engraved on the edge of the main disk offer a user's manual in miniature: how to determine Islamic prayer times; how to locate the direction of Mecca, Islam's holiest city, as well as other places significant to the Muslim world across southern Europe, the Maghreb, sub-Saharan Africa, and the Levant.

The model of an astrolabe, fashioned out of paper and wood as well as metal, in a sixteenth-century Parisian workshop substantiates the wide circulation of the instrument. Translated through Latin as well as Roman numerals, and given a human face, this instrument was taken up by other European cultures. In this hub of scientific experimentation, the object was put to use by astronomers and navigators.

Together this pair of astrolabes display the technological ingenuity of early modern inventors in the Arabo-Muslim south moving northwards, responding to the necessity people felt to place themselves in maps of time and space.

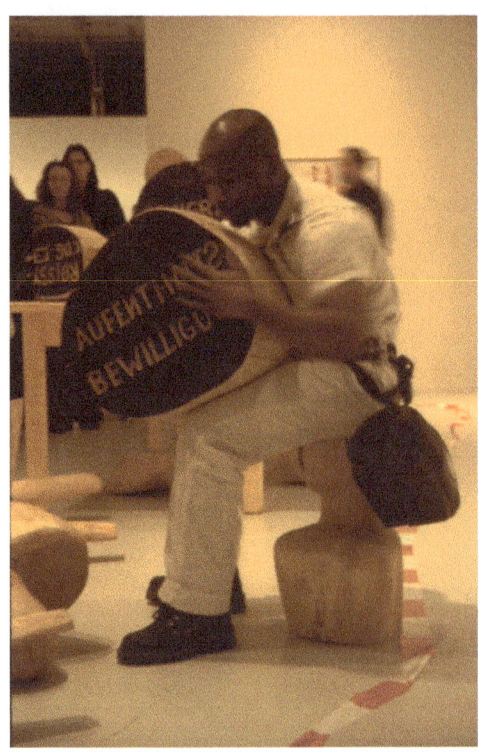

Figure 9.3 Barthélémy Toguo, *The New World Climax*, performance, 2011. Courtesy of LeLong Gallery, Paris.

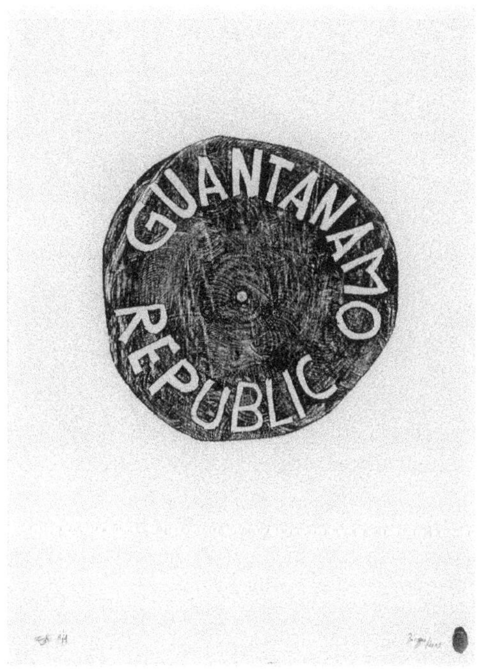

Figure 9.4 Barthélémy Toguo (Born in Mbalmayo, Cameroon, 1967), *The New World Climax – Guantanamo Republic*, 2011. Woodcut on paper. Edition 1/1. Nasher Museum of Art at Duke University 2014.25.1. © 2021 Artists Rights Society (ARS), New York / ADAGP, Paris.

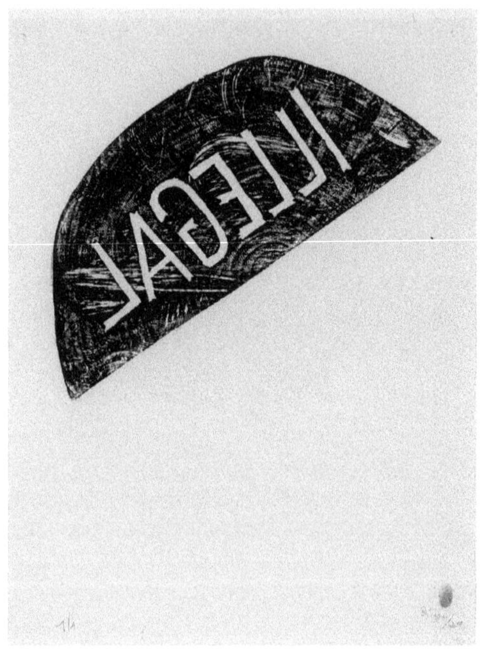

Figure 9.5 Barthélémy Toguo, *The New World Climax – Illegal*, 2011. Woodcut on paper. Edition 1/1. Gift of Tom and Elizabeth Caine, 2014.25.3. © 2021 Artists Rights Society (ARS), New York / ADAGP, Paris.

Barthélémy Toguo, a Cameroonian artist working in France, carved the wooden stamps for these prints by hand over many hours. The stamps are enlarged replicas of the ones used by customs officials, with one difference – the stamp handles are faceless and featureless human busts. When they are used to make prints, the human-stamp hybrids imprint judgements and designations in permanent ink.

The carved stamps allow easy replication of the prints. And yet Toguo prints just one copy of each, putting his toeprint in the lower right corner much like the thumbprints on travel documents.

Guantanamo Republic designates Guantanamo Bay Detention Camp, a military prison established by America in Cuba in the wake of 9/11, an independent republic. Suspected terrorists are brought to the detention center to be imprisoned, and are sometimes tortured for information. Like America's banana republics, Guantanamo Bay operates on its own terms, under its own laws. Guantanamo Bay has also been imprinted with another, *Colonization Imperialism*.

Illegal, unlike these two, is a reversed print. The word "illegal" is printed backwards, as though it is stamped on the viewer. In rough, simple ink, it mechanically designates the viewer as "illegal," just as immigration officials might. Its stamp works in several languages.

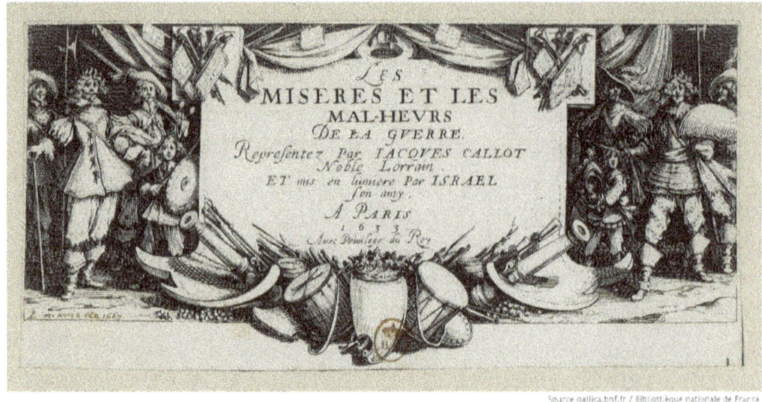

9.6 *Frontispiece / Frontispice*

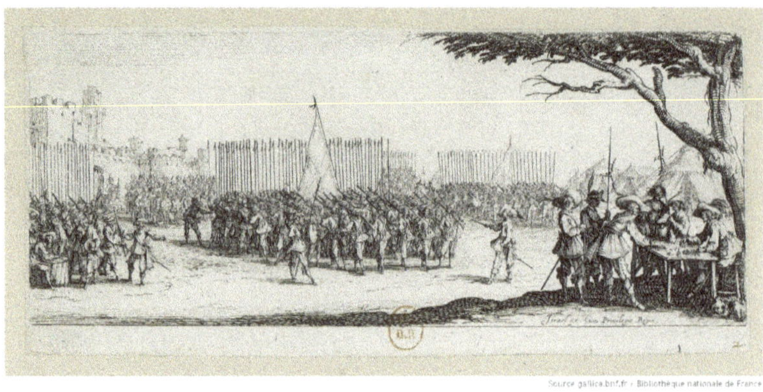

9.7 *Recruiting Troops / L'Enrôlement des troupes*

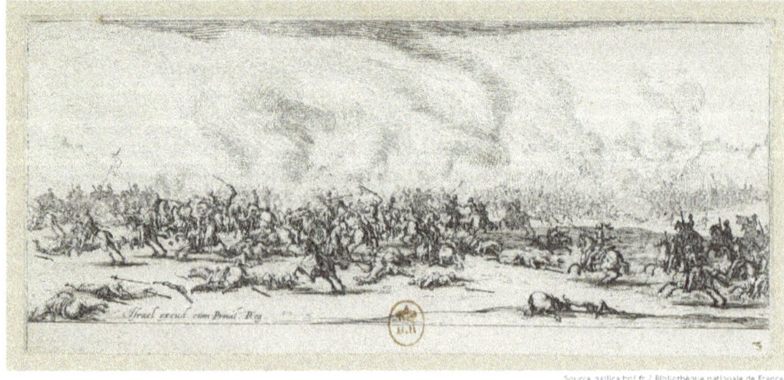

9.8 *A Battle / La Bataille*

Figures 9.6–23 Jacques Callot (French, 1592–1635), *Les Grandes misères de la guerre / The Miseries of War*, 1633. Etchings on paper. The Ackland Art Museum, The University of North Carolina at Chapel Hill 2004.15.1.1–18 and Bibliothèque nationale de France. Courtesy of gallica.bnf.fr.

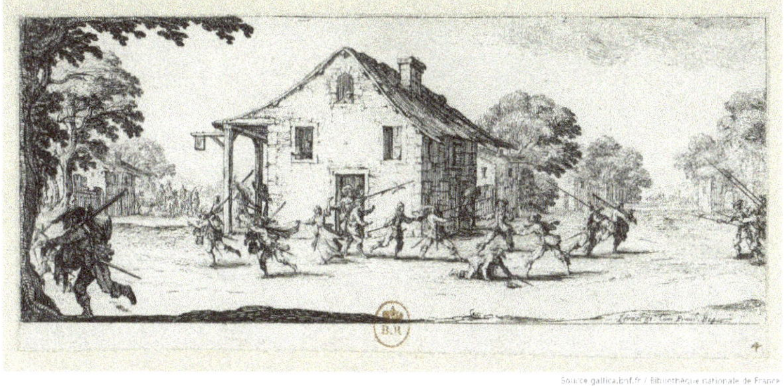

9.9 *Foraging: Stealing Food from an Inn / La Maraude*

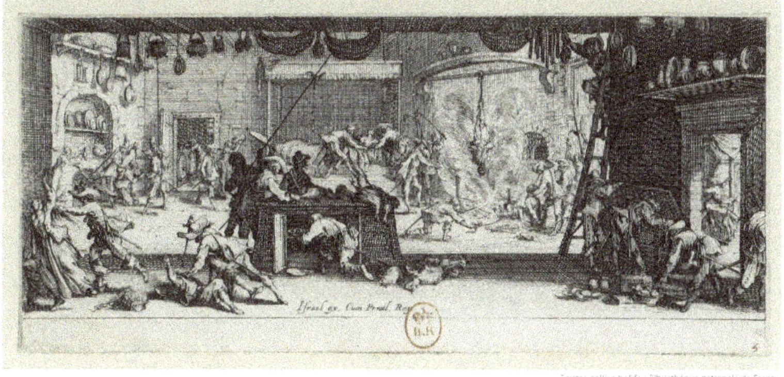

9.10 *Pillaging a Country House / Le Pillage d'une ferme*

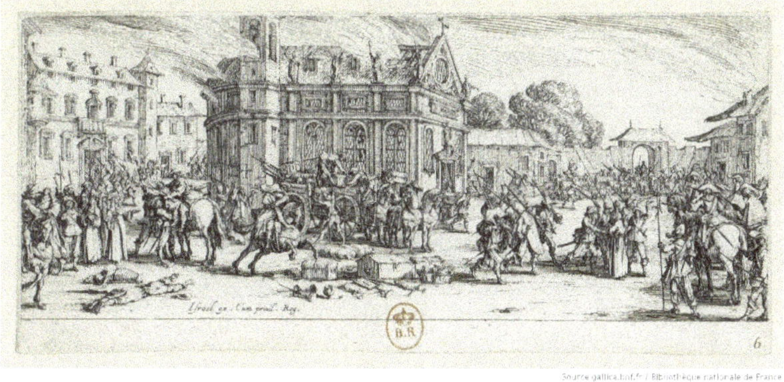

9.11 *A Convent: Looting, Arson, and Rape / Dévastation d'un monastère*

Figures 9.6–23 (Continued)

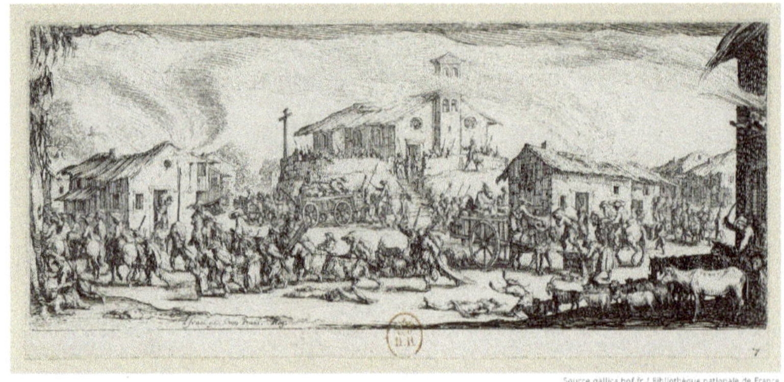

9.12 *Looting a Village / Pillage et l'incendie d'un village*

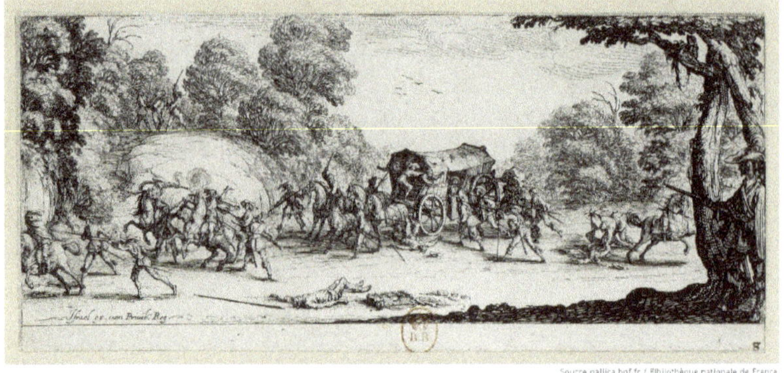

9.13 *Soldiers Turned Bandits / L'Attaque de la diligence*

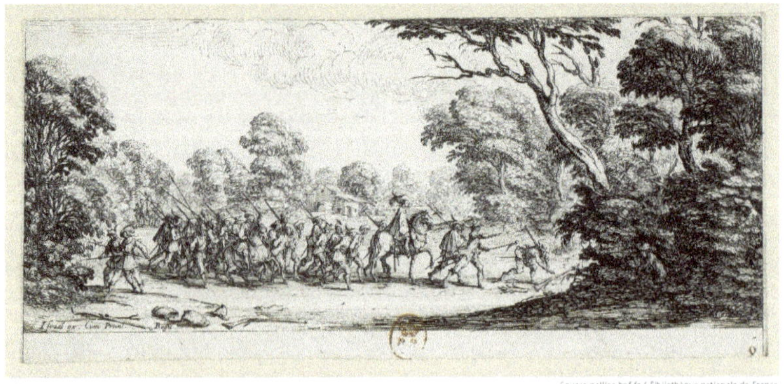

9.14 *Capture of the Bandits / La Découverte des malfaiteurs*

Figures 9.6–23 (Continued)

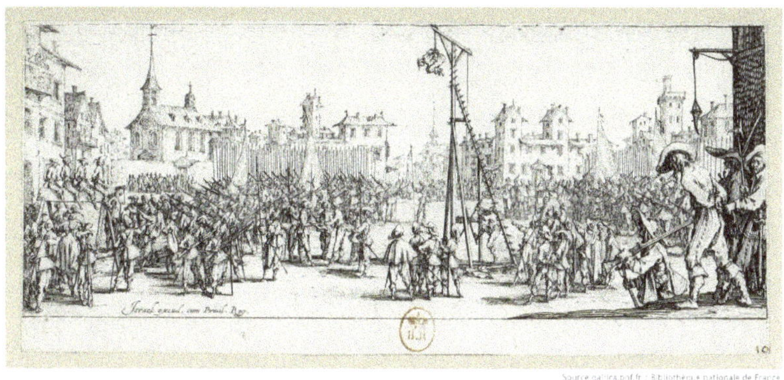

9.15 *Various Military Punishments / L'Estrapade*

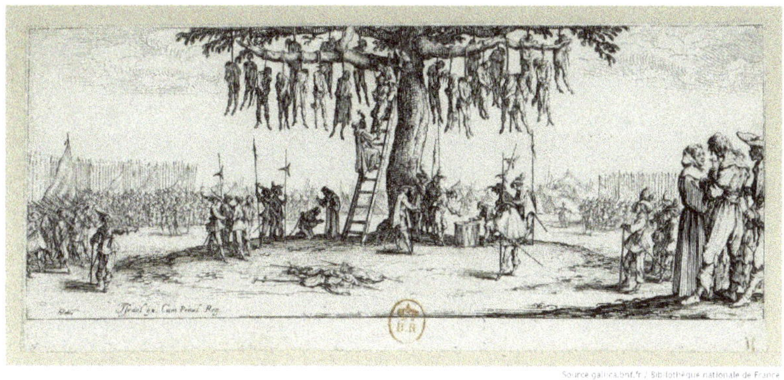

9.16 *Execution by Hanging / La Pendaison*

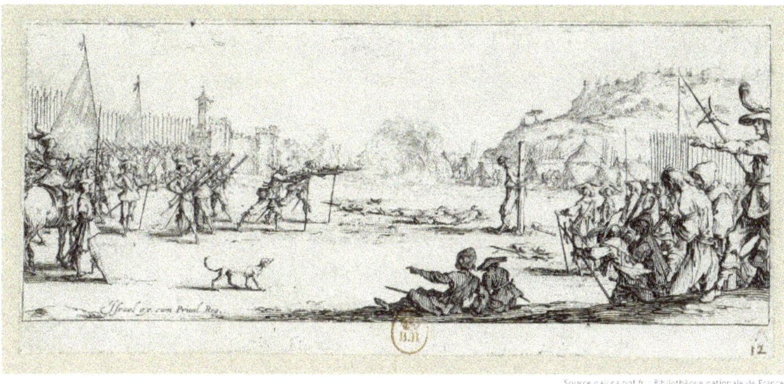

9.17 *Execution by Firing Squad /L'Arquebusade*

Figures 9.6–23 (Continued)

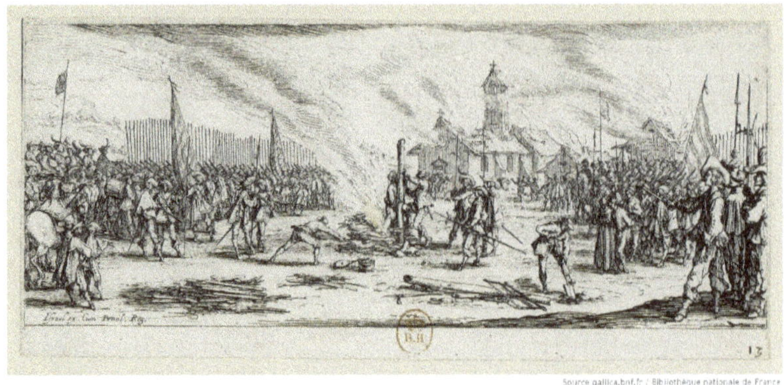

9.18 *Punishment for Sacrilege: Burning at the Stake / Le Bûcher*

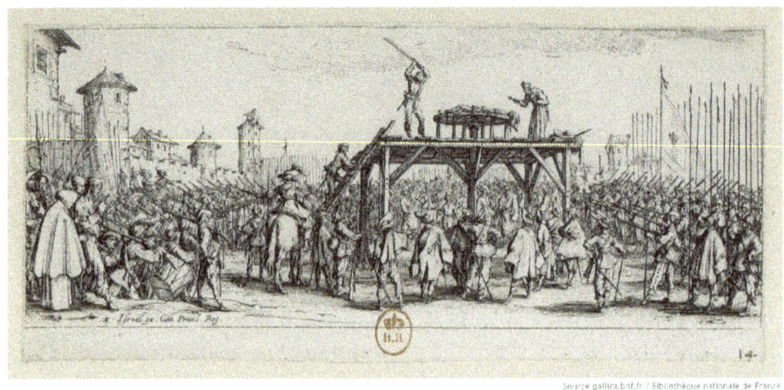

9.19 *Punishment: Breaking a Man on the Wheel / La Roue*

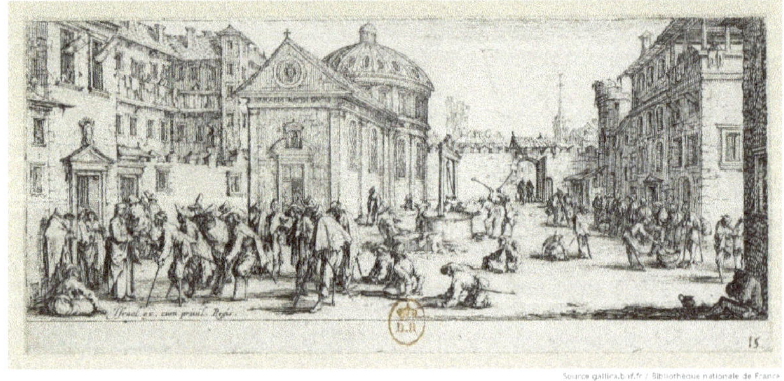

9.20 *Crippled Veterans in the Hospital / L'Hôpital*

Figures 9.6–23 (Continued)

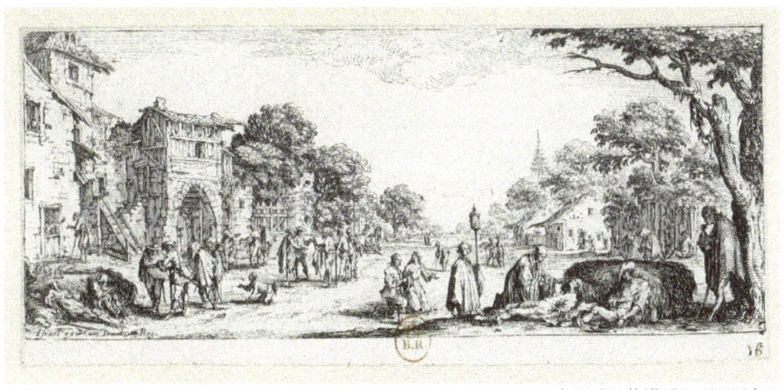

9.21 *After the War: Veterans Beg on the Street /*
Les Mourants sur le bord des routes

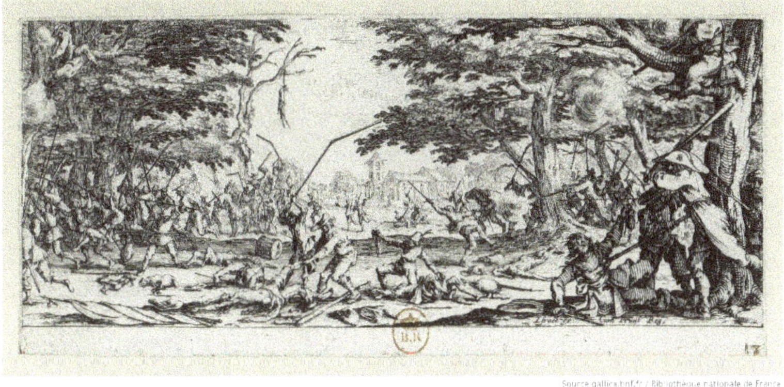

9.22 *Peasants Take Revenge on Soldiers / La Revanche des paysans*

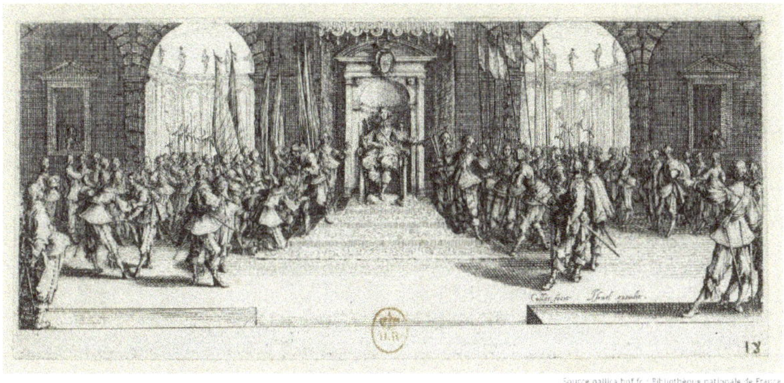

9.23 *A Good King Punishes Evildoers and Rewards Good /*
Distribution des récompenses

Figures 9.6–23 (Continued)

Jacques Callot returned home to the Thirty Years War raging across France, Flanders, and Germany. He created this series of etchings in response to this conflict that pitted mercenaries hired by France against his own people in Lorraine. Callot drew what he saw, etching a graphic short story in a sequence of episodes, on copper plates. In the first ones, his vertical lines of soldiers' pikes raised and spirals of gun smoke draw us into the chaos of battle. He focuses his drawing on all those victimized, expulsed from inns and churches, violated in their homes. His etching spares nothing: panoramas of towns ransacked, miniatures of individuals suffering at the hands of mercenaries run amok. During this time, the public viewed the assault on clergy, women, children, and travelers as particularly vile. Callot pioneered an art of representing ordinary people caught in the crossfire of political conflict. His friend, the printer Israël Henriet, who had his name etched on the series, produced multiple series of prints. These small works on paper migrated far and wide, transmitting scenes that depict why so many in Lorraine had to flee.

The story of their disenfranchisement gains momentum with tableaux of poor country people, deported from villages, assaulted along their get-away routes. In the corner of these scenes, Callot introduces an onlooker – a goat or a spy in the trees whose line of sight directs our own toward the ongoing strife. The military men, drawn spreading destruction wherever they go, are, in turn, rounded up. At the core of the artist's graphic story: these condemned men are no less the victims of war than those they brutalized. Callot's drawings fix our eye on public spectacles of execution. These include a riveting etching of men, "hanging like unfortunate fruit in that tree" that inspired generations of artists and printmakers in many cultures. His figures are recognizable here and now in another more familiar African-American history of violent migration.

Callot represents the devastating consequences for all who endured this war, at the gateway of a town, in the open road. The genre scene of daily life practiced by many artists becomes, in his hands, a portrait of the homeless. The two final etchings reveal Callot's ultimate innovation: an explosive counter attack, "the peasants' revolt," depicting the insurrections across northern Europe, followed by a calm scene of king and loyal men who seem to impose order from on high. The sequence creates an uncommon critical vision. What "Callot does" and "Israel accomplishes" – as the inscriptions say – suggests why countless early modern people were forced to move, dispossessed.

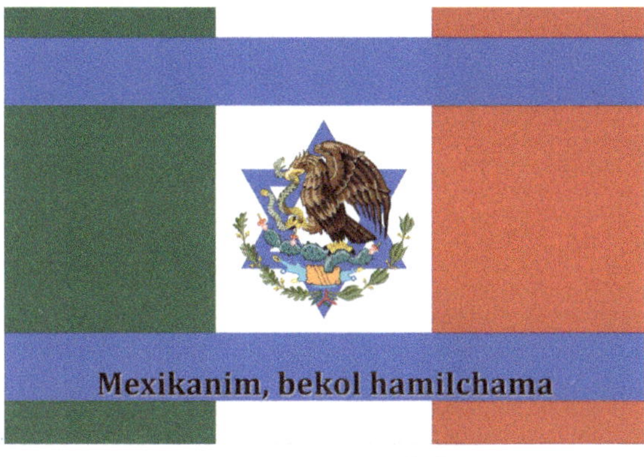

9.24 *Mexican-Israeli flags*

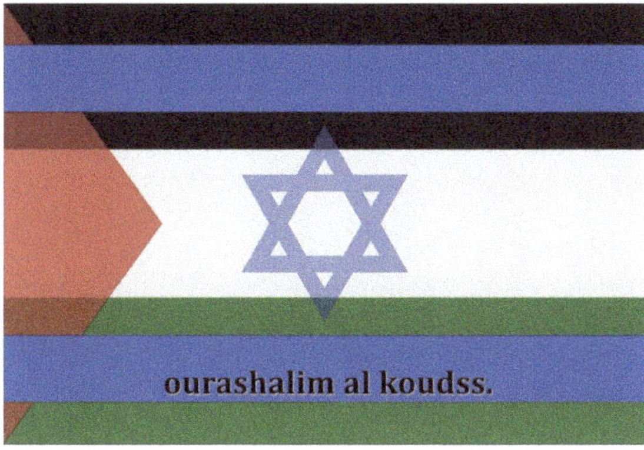

9.25 *Israeli-Palestinian flags*

Figures 9.24–26 Pedro Lasch (American born in Mexico City, Mexico, 1975), *Venice Biennale Sing Along or Karaoke Anthem*, 2015. Video (color, sound), 7:21 minutes. Courtesy of the artist.

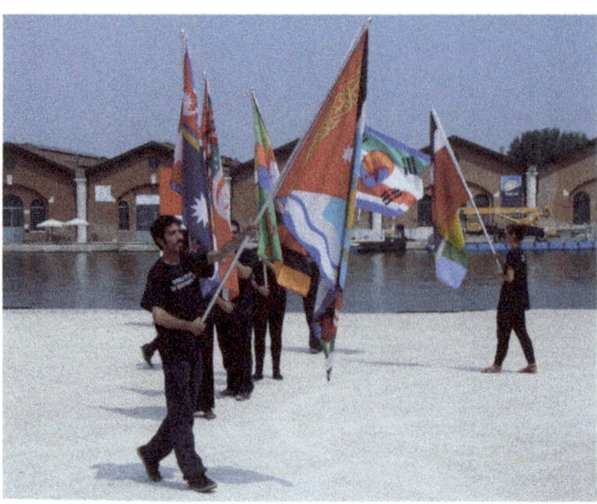

9.26 *Sing Along Karaoke Anthem at the Venice Biennale, 2015*

Figures 9.24–26 (Continued)

For the 56th Venice Biennale & Creative Time Summit (2015), artist Pedro Lasch created *Venice Biennale Sing Along or Karaoke Anthem* as a continuation of his larger *Abstract Nationalism* project (2001–present). The looped video presents five national flags, each representing a different country – the United States, Mexico, Israel, Palestine, Italy, and China – in succession. The stars and stripes of the American flag, for example, appear, transforming piece by piece into the vertical green, white, and red of the Mexican flag. And so on. Each national symbol metamorphoses into another.

Beneath each flag, the lyrics of that country's national anthem also appear in the language of the country that follows – "The Star-Spangled Banner" is sung in Spanish, the Mexican anthem in Hebrew, the Israeli in Arabic, the Palestinian in Italian, and the Italian in Chinese. Subverting easy expectations, each visual/audio transition speaks to the powerful and complicated experience of diaspora, migration, and belonging by drawing from the rich and often contradictory emotional associations each person brings to these anthems. When first exhibited in Italy, audiences sang along to the work's musical track. Here, readers can imagine their own voices raised in song, responding to the anthems sung by a single professional soprano and recorded for viewers at the Nasher Museum.

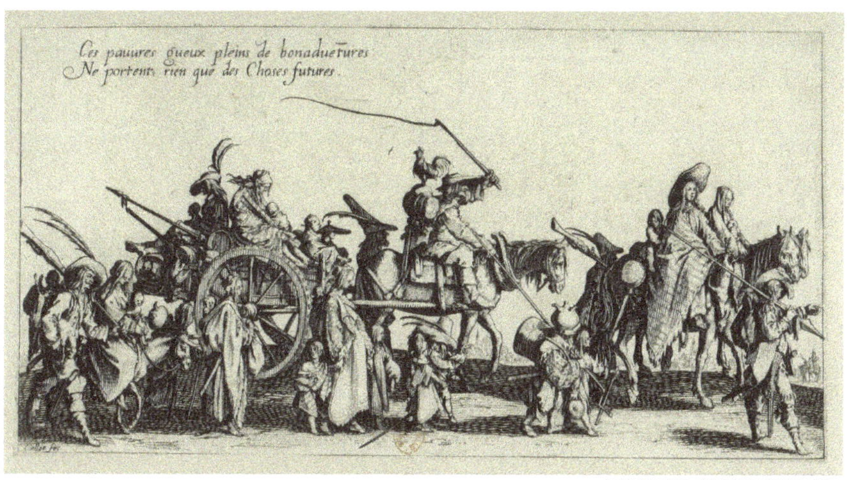

9.27 *Departure / L'Arrière-Garde*

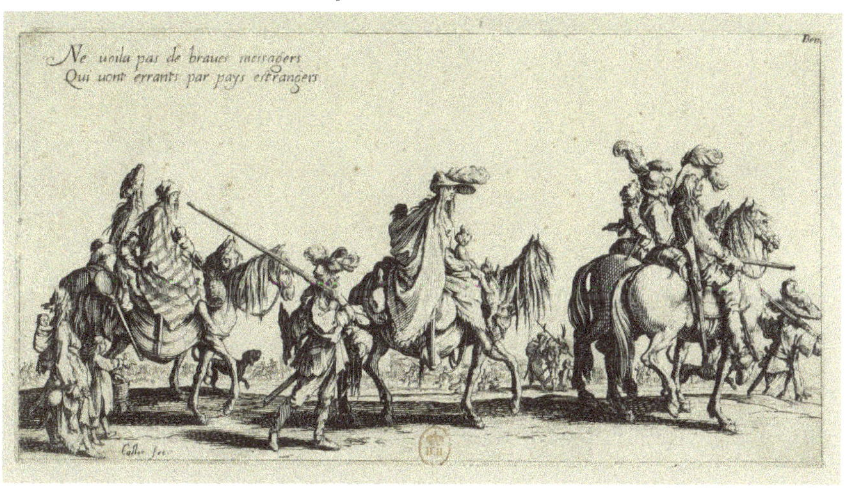

9.28 *The Advance Guard / Les Bohémiens en marche*

Figures 9.27–30 Jacques Callot (French, 1592–1635), *Les Bohémiens / The Bohemians*, seventeenth-century. Etching on paper. The Ackland Art Museum, The University of North Carolina at Chapel Hill, 60.16.17–20. Public domain. Bibliothèque nationale de France. Courtesy of gallica.bnf.fr.

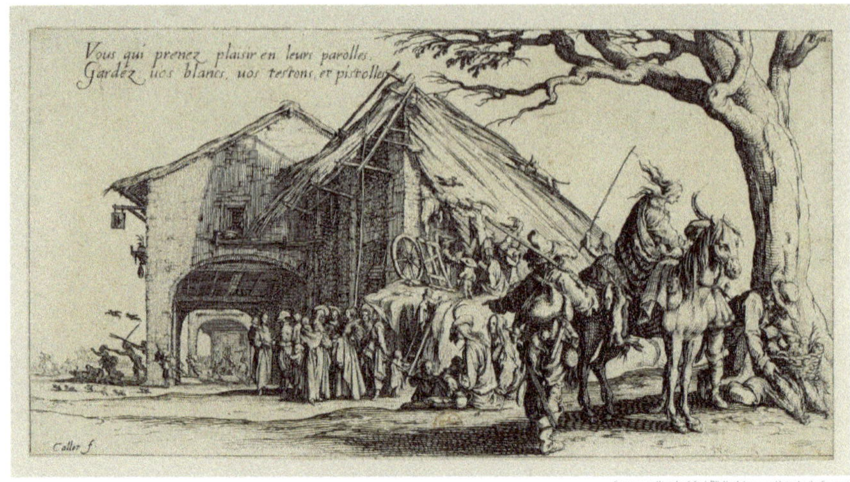

9.29 *The Stopping Place / La Halte des Bohémiens*

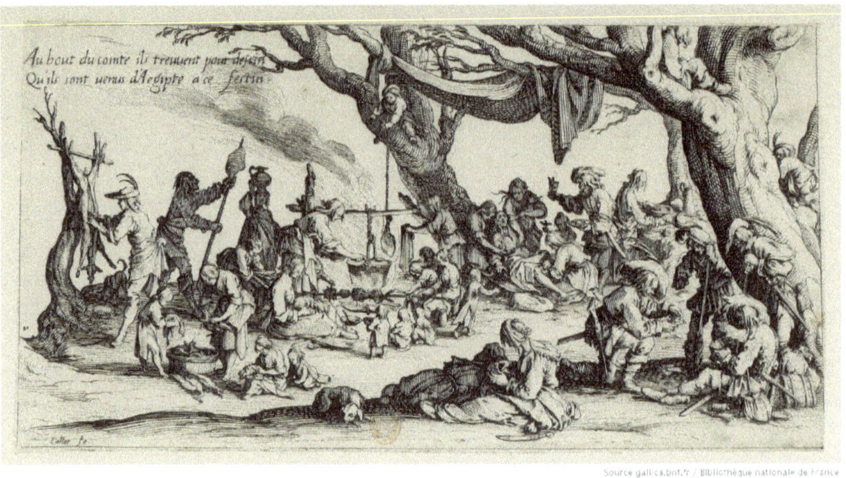

9.30 *Preparations for the Feast / Les Apprêts des Festins*

Figures 9.27–30 (Continued)

Callot devoted this brief sequence to one travelling people: the Roma, who lived in relative freedom across the early modern continent. Other artists, such as Caravaggio, and writers, portray them as exotic men and women – Egyptian fortune tellers, or suspicious, seductive foreigners who would steal your money. Callot, by contrast, depicts them as families in scenes of everyday life on the road. All is movement in the first pair of etchings; neither departure point nor destination of these migrants is visible. The figures carry on, separated from the towns in the background. In the second pair, everyone comes to a halt. Close to an inn, or at a camp site in the middle of nowhere, they shelter; a woman gives birth under a tree; others cook; still others play with their dogs.

Callot offers an unusual collective portrait of Europe's major nomadic peoples, often called Bohemians during his time. The four etchings were so compelling that they drew the attention of an anonymous writer; a poem was added to the sequence, capturing the sense of adventure these nomads embodied. Callot represents a way of life, of those "who carry with them only things of the future." For this artist, who traveled to work in the South, in Rome, as in the North, these etchings highlight his affinity with those who chose not to settle down.

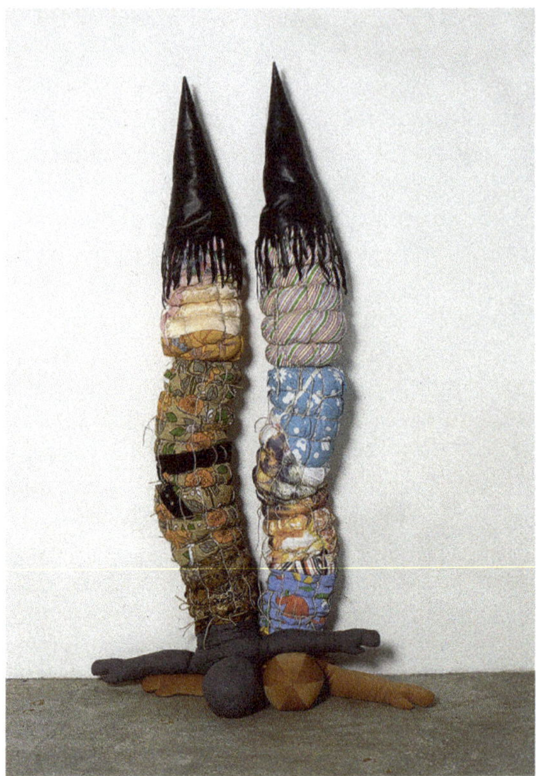

Figure 9.31 Annette Messager (Born in Berck-sur-Mer, France 1943), *Two Replicants Together/ 2 répliquants ensemble*, 2006. Fabric. Courtesy of the artist and Marian Goodman Gallery, New York/London/Paris. © 2021 Artists Rights Society (ARS), New York / ADAGP, Paris.

Two faceless humanoid columns of bound fabric huddle together in this corner installation. The colors and patterns of their "bodies" collide visually – Annette Messager constructed them from scraps. Both ordinary and fantastical, they wear startlingly black witchlike hats with long fringes that mask what could have been their "faces." The pair of figures are thrown together, and lie at their "feet," prostrate, limp and disordered.

The installation's title refers to the replicants from the neo-noir film *Blade Runner* (1982), bioengineered mechanical beings who perform tasks that their human counterparts cannot, or will not, undertake. Messager, a native of the French region Pas-de-Calais, is compelled by the migrants fleeing war and poverty in East Africa and Kurdistan for camps in Calais. Her work calls viewers' attention to migrants in relation to workers in the failing textile industry in northern France and Belgium.

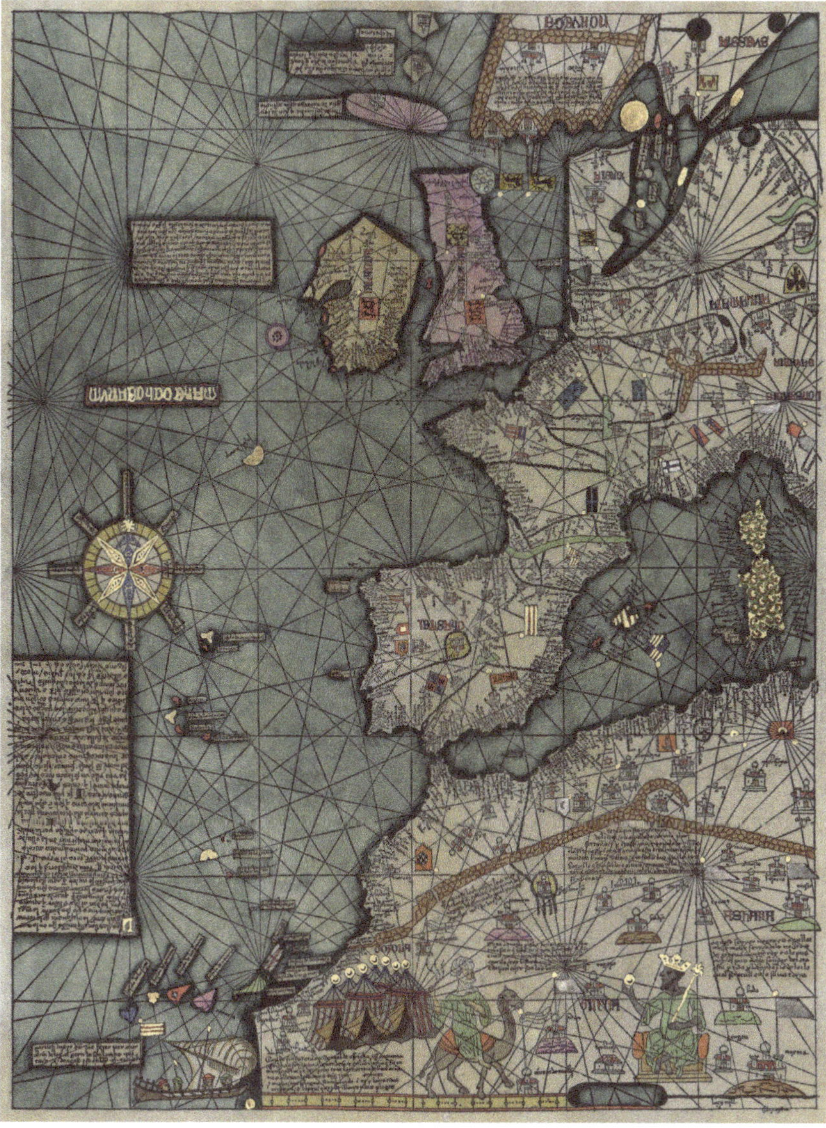

Figures 9.32–33 Anonymous, painting of the *Atlas Catalan*, c. 1959. Abraham Cresques (Majorcan, 1325–87), Paris, Bibliothèque nationale de France, c. 1375. Ink, pigment, and gold leaf on vellum. Collection of the David M. Rubenstein Rare Book & Manuscript Library, Duke University. www.loc.gov/item/2010587630/ (accessed April 6, 2022).

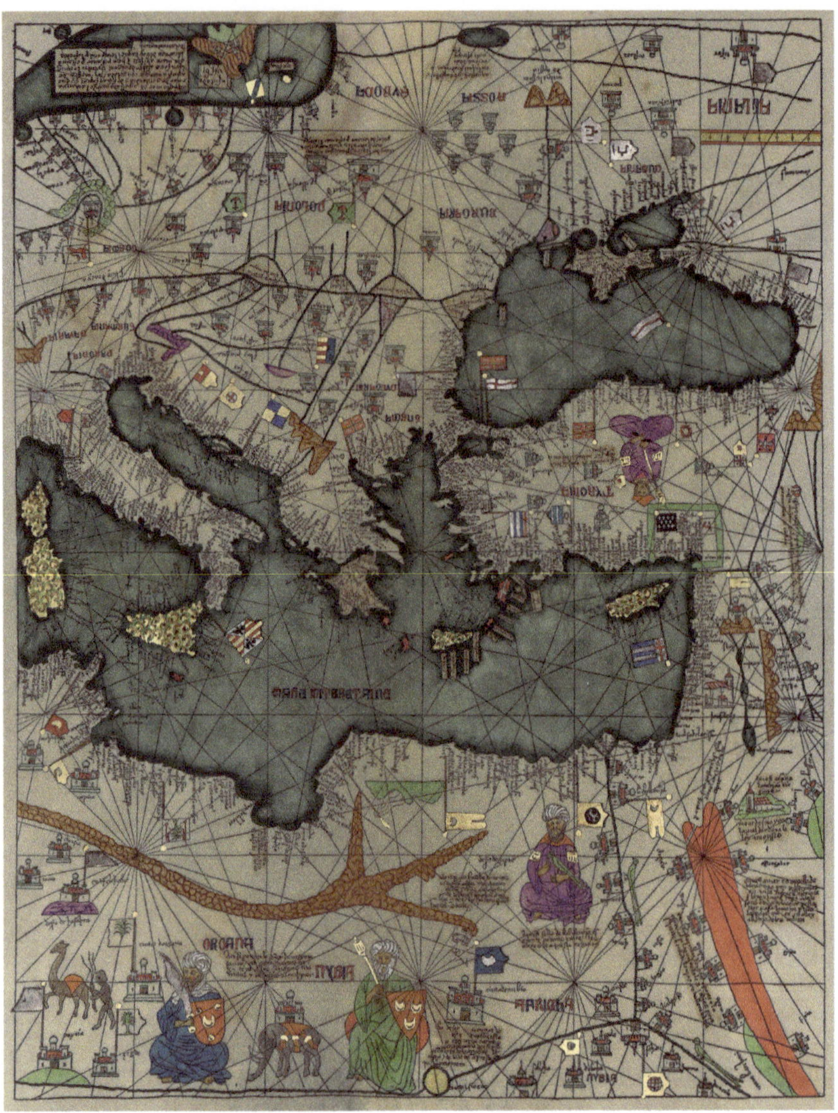

Figures 9.32–33 (Continued)

This anonymous artist, working in Franco's Spain – and against its repressive regime – painted a map drawn by an early modern cartographer working in the kingdom of Catalonia. This Jewish man of science depicted the world as known to him; the first two panels represent a Mediterranean-centered geography in accurate detail. From the Sahara in the South, ringed by the yellow Atlas mountains, to islands and peninsulas in the North, the artist surveys a vast area. The painting builds on geographies in the line of Abu 'Abdallah Muhammad al-Idrīsī, one of the first to trace the contours of land and Mediterranean sea precisely. It shows them to be in closer conjunction with these pioneering Arabo-Muslim traditions of mapping than with Christian ones in Spain, Italy, and France, which configured the known world symbolically with Jerusalem at its center. Cresques also depicts human geography. The coastlines teem with port cities, the interiors with pennants flagging political strongholds, the Muslim Al-Madina, as well as Granada facing off with the Catalan kingdom in Valencia, and further north and east, the French court in Paris, and the papacy in Rome. The map plots pathways for merchants, suggesting considerable contact southwards. Several well-defended cities with turrets and high walls were destinations; if they were not yet reached, they were sought after.

The atlas takes the form of a portolan chart, a navigational map based on compass directions. When its long panels are placed flat on a surface, the map has no single orientation. Approached from multiple vantage points, it signals varying paths and gives multiple perspectives.

The two panels, out of six, represent African, European, and Levantine regions. The only human and animal figures represented are placed south of the Mediterranean, in Guinya [Ghana]. The atlas introduces rulers such as Mansa Musa, reigning over the Empire of Mali in Tembuk [Timbuktu] with golden crown, scepter and orb. Since the Majorcan monarch had commissioned it as a gift for the French king, it was intended to expand his perception of human culture. For many viewers, it outlines the routes that were opening up for early modern peoples.

Works consulted for the 2018 installation

Butler, Judith and Athena Athanasiou (2013) *Dispossession, the Performative in the Political*. Cambridge: Polity Press.

Berzock, Kathleen Bickford, ed. (2018) *Caravans of Gold, Fragments in Time: Art, Culture and Exchange across Medieval Saharan Africa*. Chicago and New Jersey: The Block Museum and Princeton University Press.

Dittmar, Pierre-Olivier (2018) "Peoples from the East, Monstrosities from the West." www.youtube.com/watch?v=bE2E7GX6R2Y (Accessed September 18, 2018).

Faegre, Torvald (1979) *Tents: Architecture of the Nomads*. New York: Anchor Press.

Fancy, Hussein (2016) *The Mercenary Mediterranean*. Chicago: University of Chicago Press.

Farley, Helen (2009) *A Cultural History of Tarot*. London: Palgrave Macmillan.

Fauvell-Aymar, François-Xavier (2013) *Le Rhinocéros d'or: histoires du moyen âge africain*. Paris: Alma.

Gerli, Michael (2017) "The Expulsion of the Moriscos," *The Routledge Companion to Iberian Studies*. New York: Routledge, pp. 184–200.

History of Cartography (1987–2015) J. B. Harley and David Woodward, eds. Chicago: University of Chicago Press.

Il Libro dei vagabondi (2003) Camporesi, Piero, ed. Milan: Garzanti.

Images de pensée (2011) Marie Hau de Caraës, ed. Paris: Musées nationaux.

Images et Révoltes dans le livre et l'estampe (2016) Yann Sordet, ed. Paris: Éditions des Cendres.

"Insecurities: Tracing Displacement and Shelter" (2016–17) New York: MOMA.

Martin, Jean-Hubert (2016) *Carambolages*, Paris: Grand Palais.

Matar, Hisham (2016) *The Return: Fathers, Sons, and the Land In Between*. New York: Random House. (2017). *La Terre qui les sépare*, Agnès Desarthe, trans. Paris. Gallimard.

McIntosh, Gregory (2000) *The Piri Reis Map of 1513*. Athens: University of Georgia Press.

Messager, Annette (2015) *Dessus Dessous*, Paris: Éditions Dilecta.

"Persona grata; L'art contemporain interroge l'hospitalité" (October 2018). Exposition, Le Musée d'art contemporain du Val-du-Marne, et le Musée national de l'histoire de l'immigration, Paris.

Plewa, Piotr (2007) "The Rise and Fall of Temporary Foreign Worker Policies: Lessons for Poland. *International Migration* 45, no. 2. pp. 3–36.

Raza, Sara (2016) "But a Storm is Blowing from Paradise: Contemporary Art from the Middle East and North Africa." Exhibition. New York: Solomon R. Guggenheim Museum.

Refugiés, Cinq Pays, cinq camps (2016) Paris: Editions invenit.

Toguo, Barthélémy (2013) *Print Shock*, Milan: Silvana Editoriale.

Weigert, Laura (2015) "Review Essay, *The Interwoven Globe: The Worldwide Textile Trade 1500–1800*." *Art Bulletin* 97, no. 3, pp. 342–5.

10

Cornered

Raquel Salvatella de Prada

Cornered is a video installation about contemporary migrants making attempts, most often failed, to cross the border from Morocco to the Spanish cities of Melilla and Ceuta, the only European enclaves on Africa's mainland.

The visual imagery focuses on the ambitions and struggles of the migrants: their journey from their home country to the Spanish border, and the frustration of the perpetual effort to reach Europe.

Immigration across Spain's southern border

Ceuta (18.5 km^2) and Melilla (13.3 km^2) are situated on the northern coast of Africa and share a border with Morocco and the Mediterranean Sea.

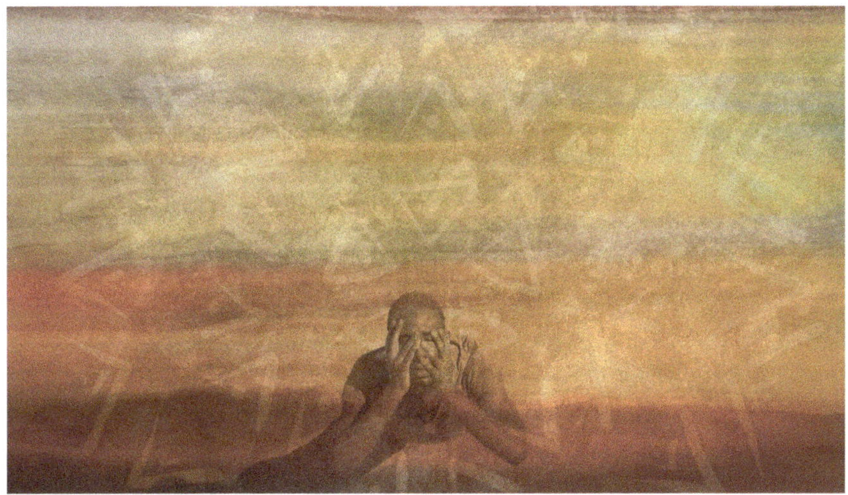

Figure 10.1 Style frame from video animation. Raquel Salvatella de Prada, 2018.

For centuries, these autonomous cities were vital ports that offered protection for Spanish ships. Spain remains a region where people emigrate from, but it is also attracting a growing number of migrants. As was the case with mass expulsions of Jewish converso populations in the fifteenth century and of Moriscos in the seventeenth century, a large number of people who want to be in Spain are excluded by force, marginalized, persecuted, and pushed away towards other borders.

Figure 10.2 illustrates different routes by which people/migrants commonly arrive to Spain. The trip to reach Morocco is often strenuous, dangerous, and thousands of kilometers long; sometimes it involves crossing the Sahara, which migrants call the second sea. Human smugglers regularly take advantage of their "customers" along the way. When migrants reach Morocco, they stay there for a while to earn money and wait for the right time to cross into Europe, often living in makeshift shelters near the borders for months or even years.

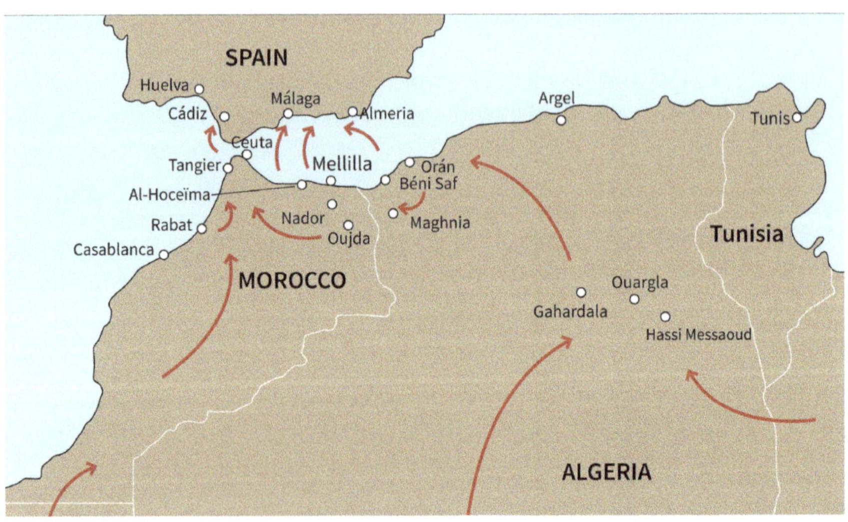

Figure 10.2 Migration routes in North Africa. Source: https://elpais.com/elpais/2014/02/16/media/1392579160_005825.html (accessed April 6, 2022).

These migrants use different modes of transportation to cross the border, including cars, planes, and boats, but the most affordable way to attempt the crossing is by climbing the fence that separates the Spanish enclaves from Morocco. The Spanish erected the first fence between Morocco and Spain in 1971. The Spanish government added reinforcement and fencing over the years. In 2014, 40,000 undocumented immigrants gathered in Morocco to try to enter Europe through Spain. For instance, between January and February of 2014, more than 4000 people tried to cross the fence and 600 made it. Since 2014, migration across Spain's southern border has increased drastically, even as the fences around Ceuta and Melilla have been reinforced. The new fences do not provide handholds for climbing. This has made crossing the border more difficult but not impossible. For instance, migrants now climb the fences with hooks attached to their hands and shoes.

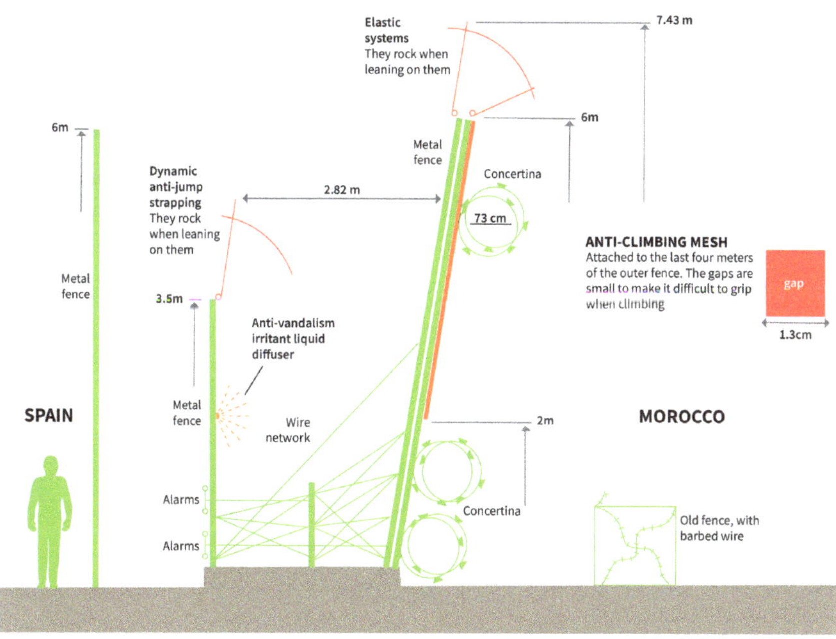

Figure 10.3 Ceuta and Melilla's border wall. Source: Ministerio del Interior. https://elpais.com/elpais/2014/03/07/media/1394187503_458548.html (accessed April 6, 2022).

When migrants fail to cross the fence, they are often beaten and have their papers taken away. Then they are deported hundreds of kilometers away, to Rabat, Fes, or Casablanca. Soon they try again and fail, and try and fail, as if in an infinite loop. They are trapped in Morocco. Without papers, they cannot go to Spain or go back to their home countries. They are trapped in the forest where each day, they hide and run away from the police. They are trapped, as they appear to be inside the dome created for this installation. They are trapped, but still they have hope.

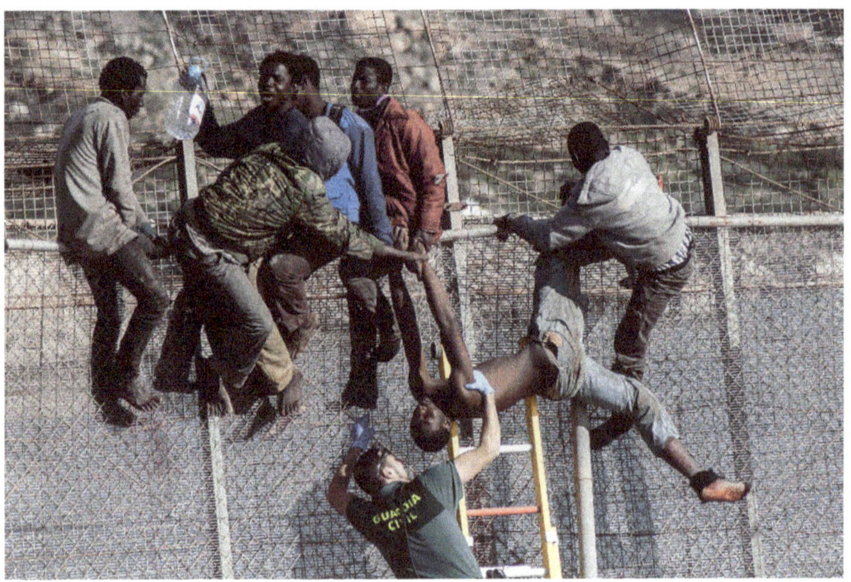

Figure 10.4 Border wall between Morocco and Spain. Photo: Jesús Blasco de Avellaneda, 2014.

Installation

Part sculpture, part light installation and video animation, *Cornered* provides an immersive visual experience that takes an emotional and atmospheric approach to describing migration at the southern border of Spain.

The installation projects an original dance performance interlaced with stylized visuals on an intricately patterned and light filled structure, which is reminiscent of a carved Moroccan table, covered on top by a screened dome. The interior of the structure contains a short throw projector, with the dome as a rear-projection screen. The visuals and the original scores are experienced by walking around the structure, immersing the viewer in the light patterns that emanate from it to cover floors and surrounding walls.

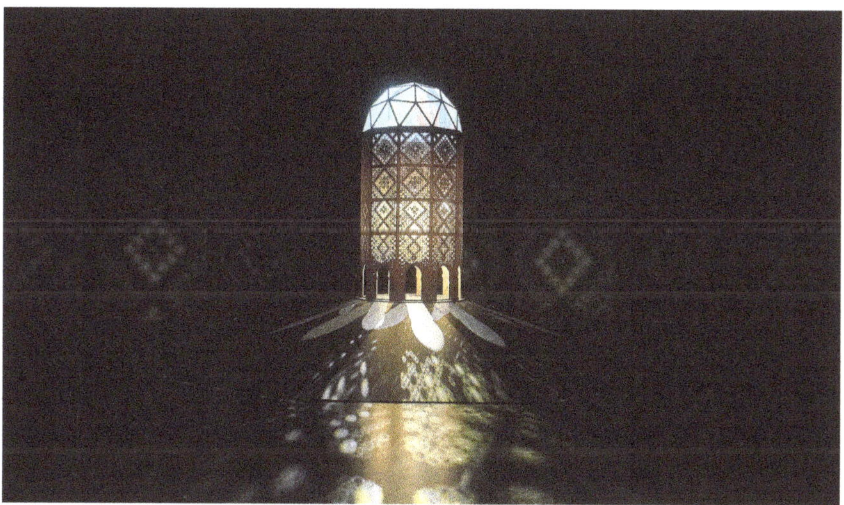

Figure 10.5 "Cornered" Photo: Robert Zimmerman, 2018.

The visual style of the video projection is based on African art from countries where migration via Morocco often originates. The color palette focuses on silhouettes that are placeholders for the many human beings in a similar situation. These silhouettes represent the darkness and frustration of the journey and at the same time reflect the physical beauty and skilled craftsmanship of African peoples. They are contrasted by incorporating vibrant colors that are familiar from African fabrics, patterns, and paintings.

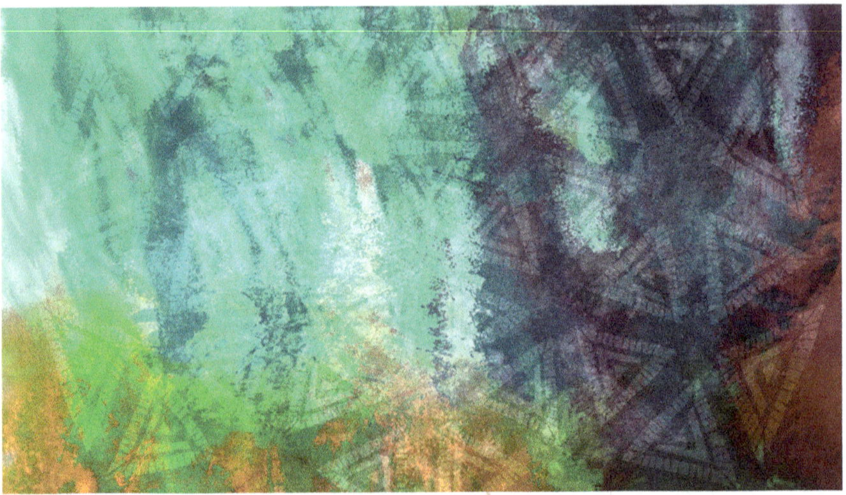

Figure 10.6 Style frame from video animation. Raquel Salvatella de Prada, 2018.

The video combines real footage and animation, and the projection scale varies by using different numbers of screens (the dome is framed with triangles). Sometimes, only one animation covers the entire projection surface. Other times, the multi-video utilizes each individual facet or just a few at a time. While the projection is playing, the light from numerous LEDs shines through the structure to paint the walls around the viewer with geometric light patterns. In this way, the installation inhabits the entire space it occupies. Jonathan Henderson and his music group Diali Cissokho & Kaira Ba composed the musical score for the installation. Henderson is a North Carolina-based multi-instrumentalist, composer, and producer currently pursuing a PhD in ethnomusicology at Duke University. Diali Cissokho & Kaira Ba's music is steeped in ancient West African griot traditions combined with the impulses of a rock band.

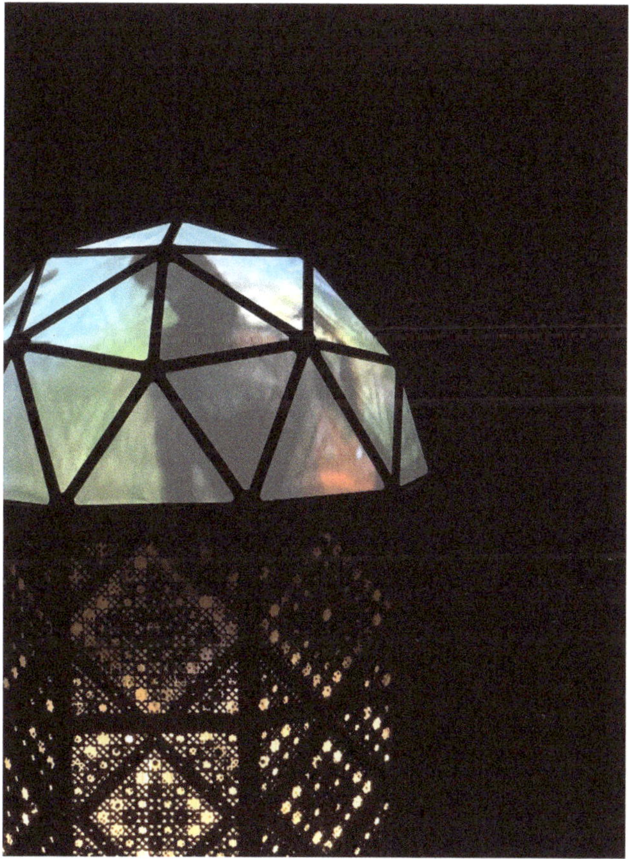

Figure 10.7 "Cornered" Close-up of wooden structure and video projection. Photo: Raquel Salvatella de Prada, 2018.

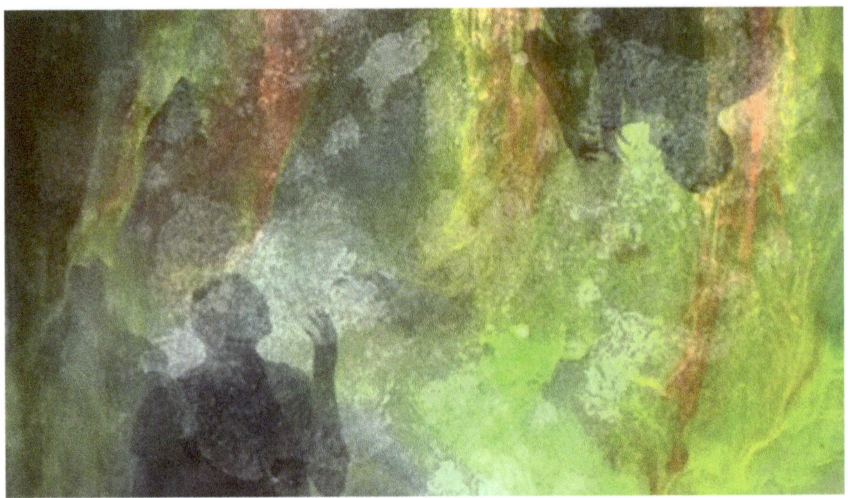

Figure 10.8 Style frame from video animation. Raquel Salvatella de Prada, 2018.

Cornered creates an ambivalent atmosphere of frustration and hope. Through the video of dancers, and through Diali's voice and words in his native Wolof, *Cornered* provides an emotional perspective on the migratory issue, leaving the viewer with an impression of determination, deliberateness, and desperation. The intensity and mood of the audio track and the video rise and fall, reflecting the back and forth between emotional highs and lows. The 8-minute animation then repeats itself, further mirroring the repeated failed attempts to cross the border.

Cornered was first shown on September 27, 2018 at the Rubenstein Arts Center at Duke University as part of an experimental exhibition about migration in and around Europe, "In Transit", which was held at the Nasher Museum from September 2018 to January 2019. It has since been shown nationally and internationally. *Cornered* contributes to a broader awareness of the humanitarian crisis at Spain's southern border.

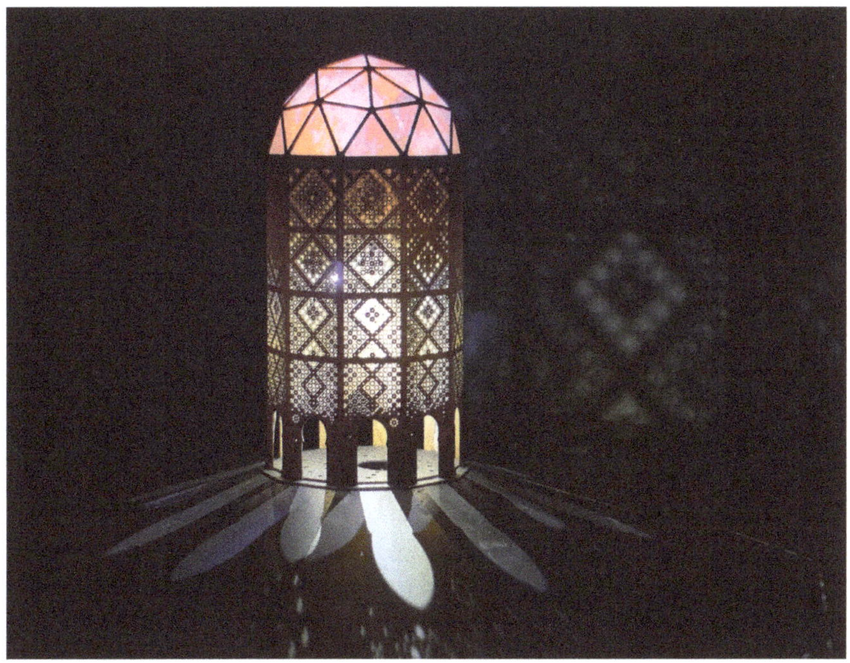

Figure 10.9 "Cornered" Photo: Robert Zimmerman, 2018.

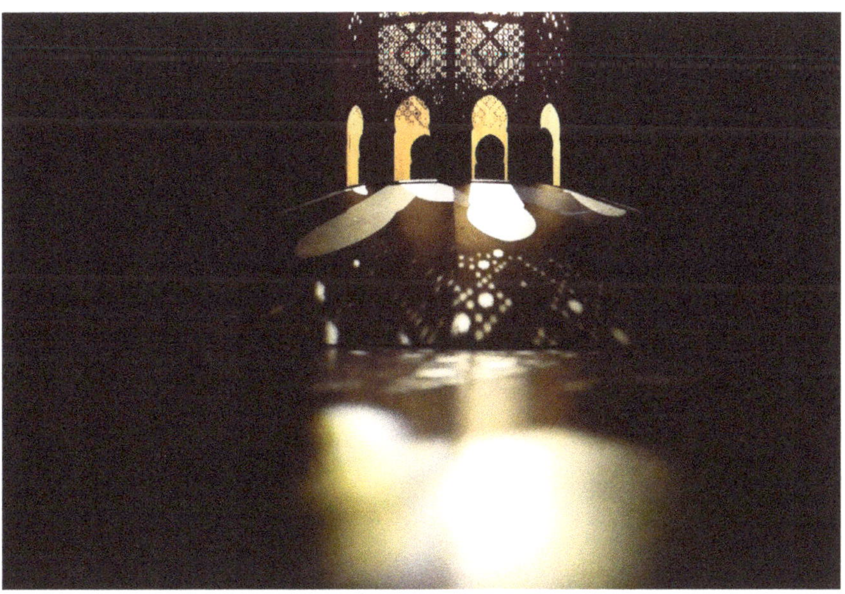

Figure 10.10 "Cornered" Photo: Raquel Salvatella, 2018.

The process

In researching the material for *Cornered*, I traveled to Morocco, as well as Melilla in 2016 and 2017 to see the location and regional art, and to talk to aspiring and successful migrants and the people with whom they regularly interact. I interviewed Omar (fictitious name), a Senegalese man now living in Dahkla, in southern Morocco. He had already made four attempts to cross the border near Nador. In his first attempt, Omar waited for a month before he tried to cross. While camping in the Gurugú forest, he and others were chased frequently and had to run and hide. In one of his later attempts, Omar was on the top of the fence for one hour before being captured and sent to Rabat (300 miles away). He then found employment in Dakhla, where he worked for about 3 months to earn some money to try again. In his last attempt, Omar was so badly beaten that he went back to Dahkla to recover. In spite of his comparatively comfortable position in Dakhla, Omar does not feel at home there because he experiences racism and discrimination. His will to migrate to Europe remains unbroken.

For the first iteration of the installation, the dome structure was created using a 3D-printable geodesic connector system with hardwood dowels. Trace paper was used as the rear projection screen. The second iteration was created using plywood, and the final piece was built using oak, often used in Moroccan woodwork. To reduce the possibility of fire hazards, a professional rear screen projection film was chosen that is reminiscent of silk, which is an often-used fabric in Morocco.

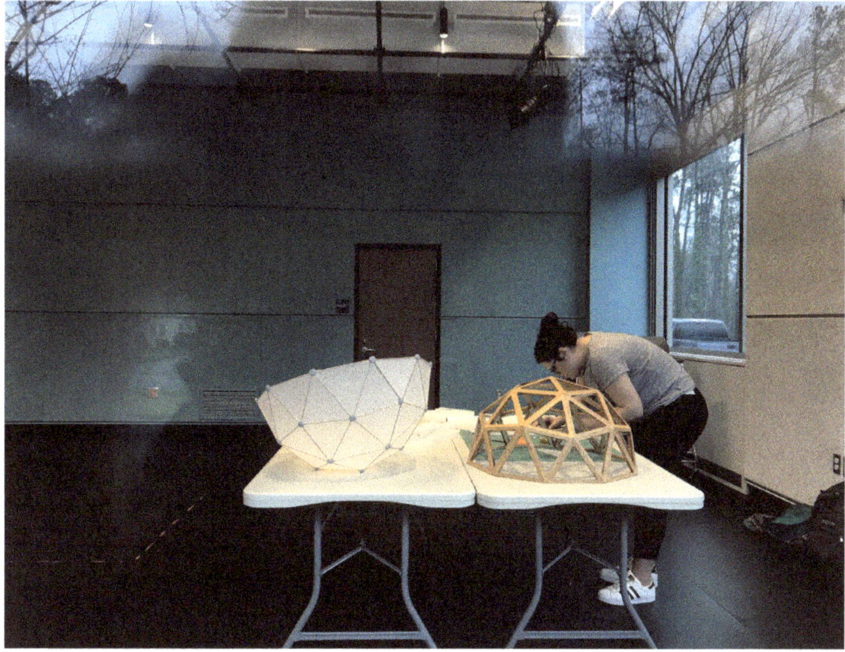

Figure 10.11 Artistic assistant Lexi Bateman. Photo: Raquel Salvatella de Prada, 2018.

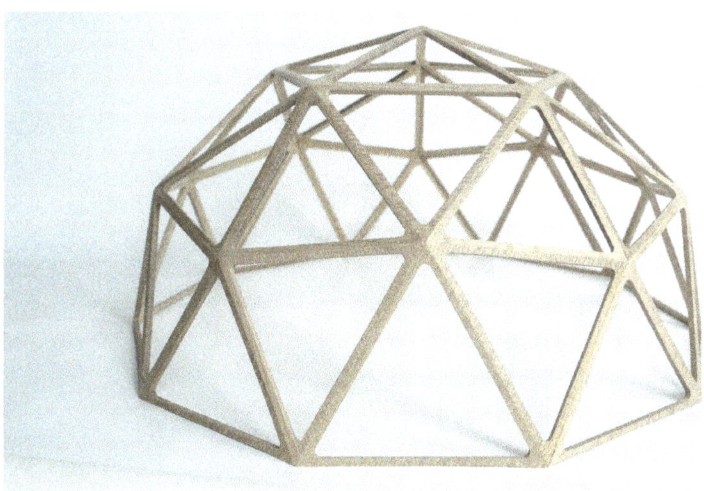

Figure 10.12 Geodesic dome created by Dimitri Titov. Photo: Lexi Bass, 2018.

After finding a projector that could throw the image at a sufficiently short distance, one of the biggest technological challenges was to keep the image from becoming distorted by the shape of the projection screen. The process I used to achieve this is called UV Mapping, which is a technique borrowed from applications where a 2D image is mapped to a 3D model's surface for texture mapping. UVs are two-dimensional coordinates that correspond to the vertex information of the geometry of a 3D object.

They are basically marker points that control which pixels on the image/texture correspond to which vertices on the 3D mesh, thereby providing the link between a surface mesh and the application of images to the surface.

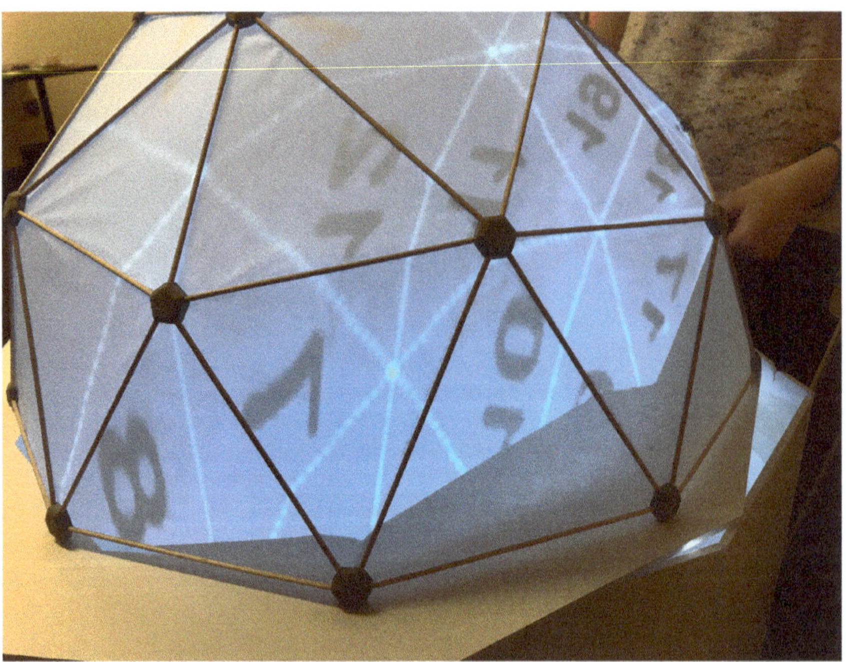

Figures 10.13–15 Projection tests on a mockup geodesic dome, 2017. Photos: Raquel Salvatella de Prada, 2017.

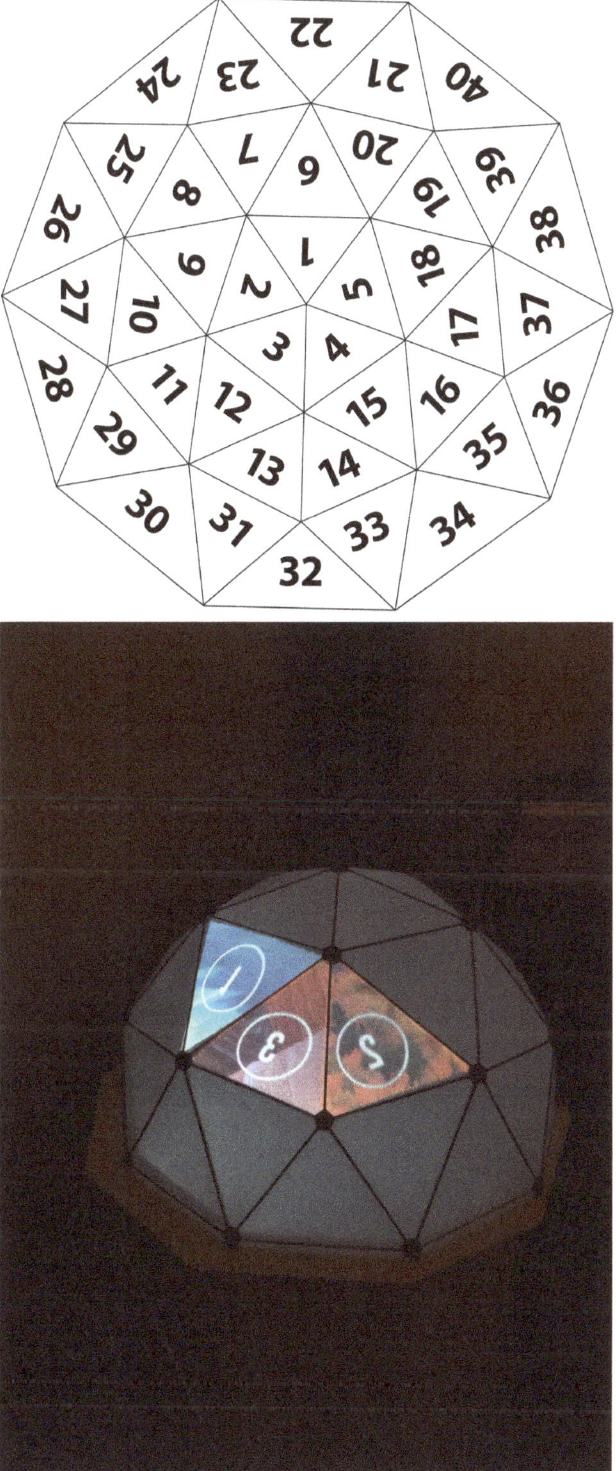

Figures 10.13–15 (Continued)

The process begins by laying out the UVs by creating a 2D representation of the 3D object, as if it were unfolded and flattened out. Then, working with a software such as Isadora, which is mostly used in theater for projection mapping, the original flat image is deformed to align with the triangular segments of the flattened dome. That way, when projected onto the actual 3D dome, the image does not appear deformed anymore.

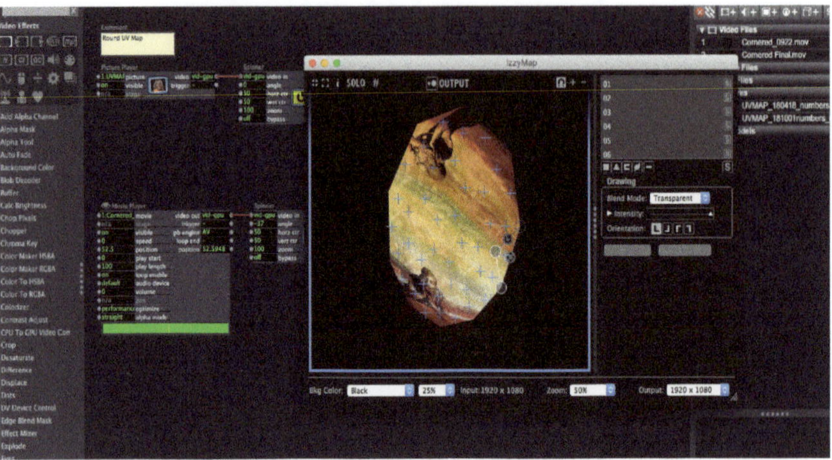

Figure 10.16 Screenshot of graphic programming environment software Isadora, from Troikatronix.

The geometric patterns engraved on (into) the body of the structure are an original design that takes inspiration from patterns frequently found on Moroccan doors and furniture. In particular, the design is a variation of one that can be found on a wooden door in Madrasa Bou Inania, an educational institution founded in 1351–56 in Fez. This design repeats a regular 8-pointed star polygon, one of the most common regular polygons and fundamental elements in Islamic art design. It lends itself to variations as part of a more contemporary aesthetic that complements the traditional African patterns shown in the animation. On the one hand, this blend of styles reflects the mingling of cultures that results from migration.

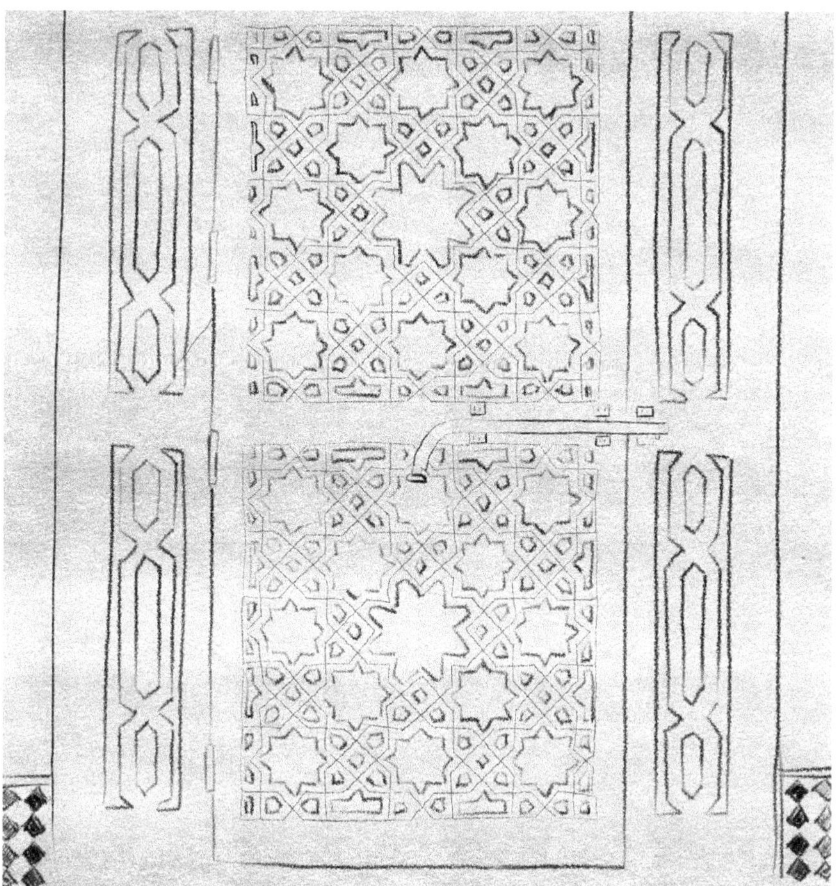

Figure 10.17 Sketch of wooden door. Raquel Salvatella de Prada, 2018.

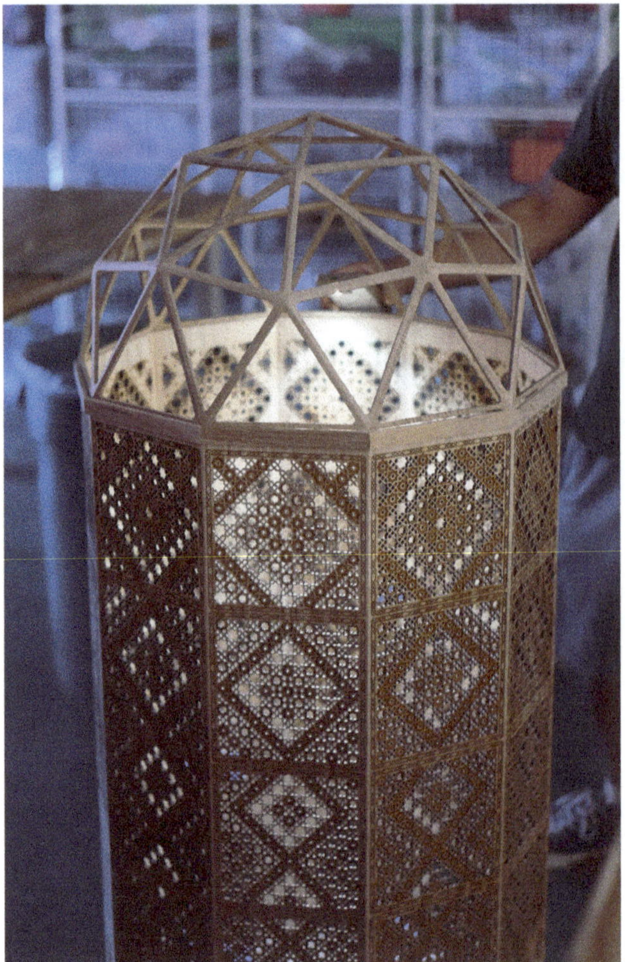

Figure 10.18 Wooden structure. Photo: Robert Zimmerman, 2018.

On the other hand, stacking up intricate variations of the original pattern gives the impression of changing size, thereby emphasizing the projection dome atop the structure. Fading of the pattern towards the bottom of the installation further strengthens this emphasis. I created the pattern using Adobe Illustrator, a vector graphics software.

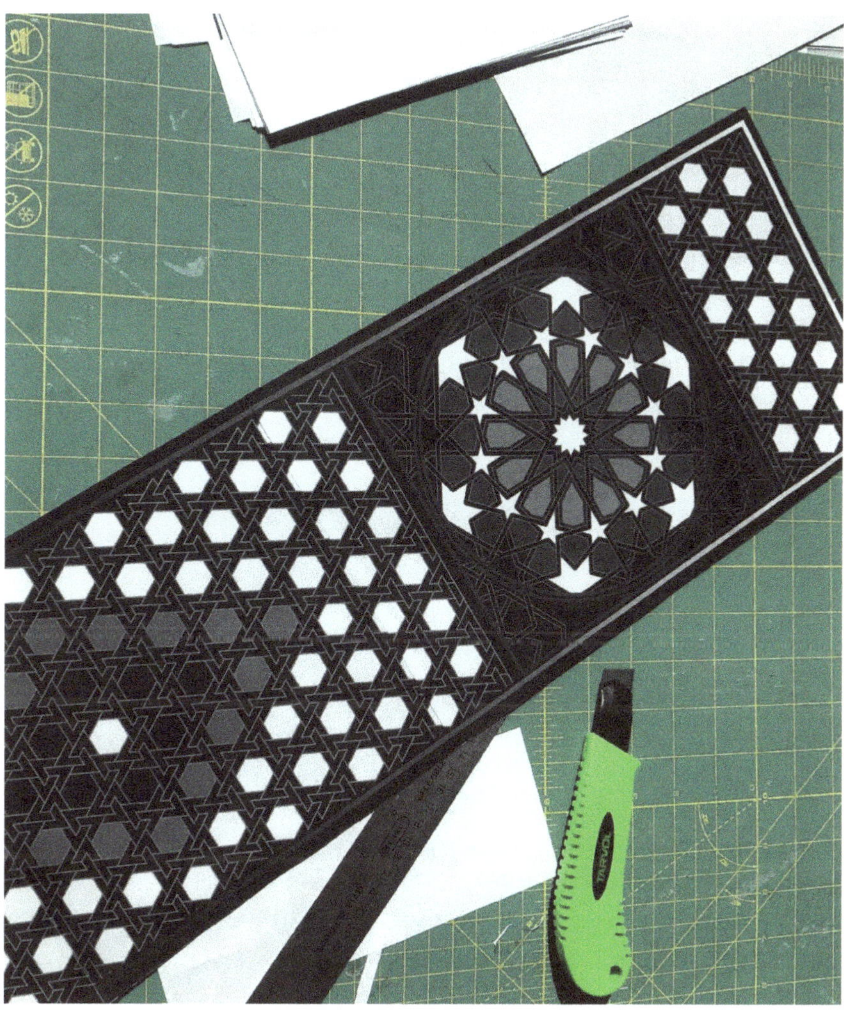

Figures 10.19–21 Multiple alterations of the designs. Raquel Salvatella de Prada, 2017–18.

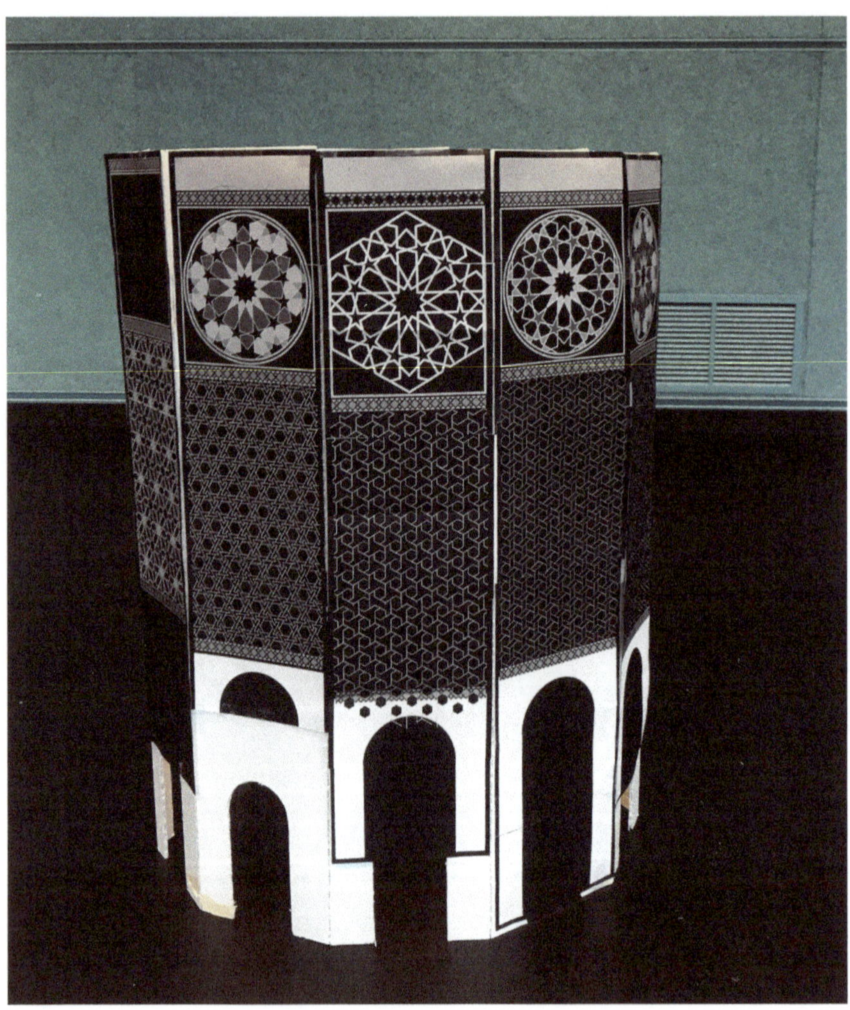

Figures 10.19–21 (Continued)

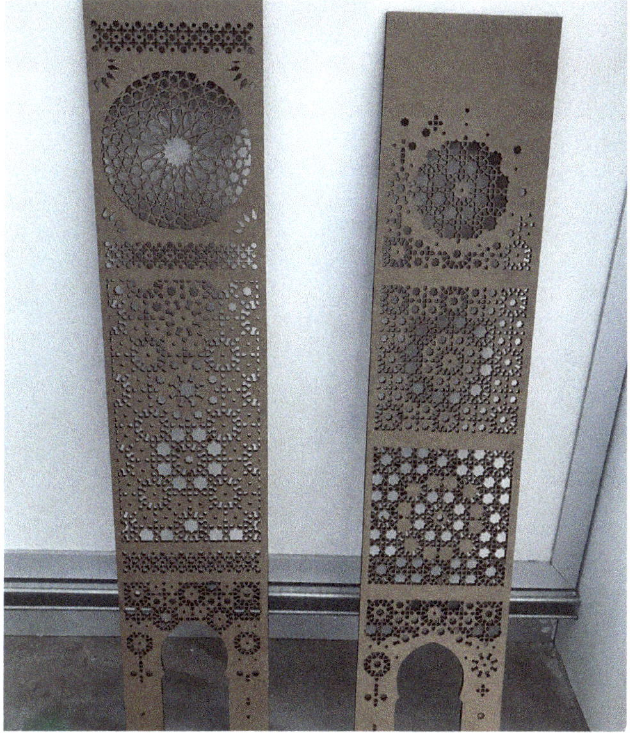

Figures 10.19–21 (Continued)

Engravings were created using a laser cutting process. First, many different design drafts were printed on paper. Second, a small selection of drafts was laser cut in cardboard for more efficient experimentation. Finally, the engraving of the final design in wood was finetuned in many iterations.

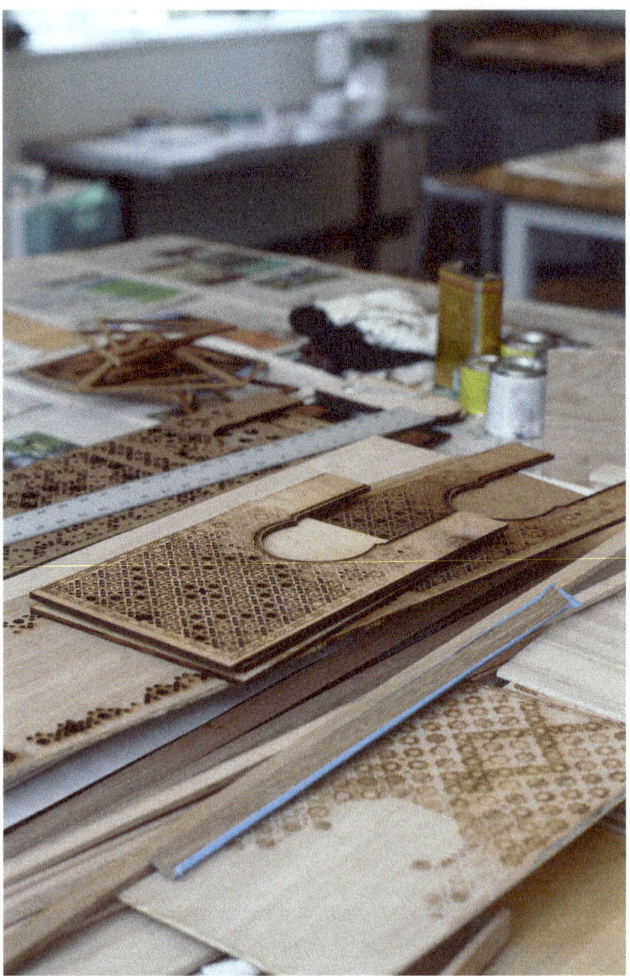

Figures 10.22–24 Test engravings, construction, and set-up of the wooden structure. Photos: Robert Zimmerman, 2018.

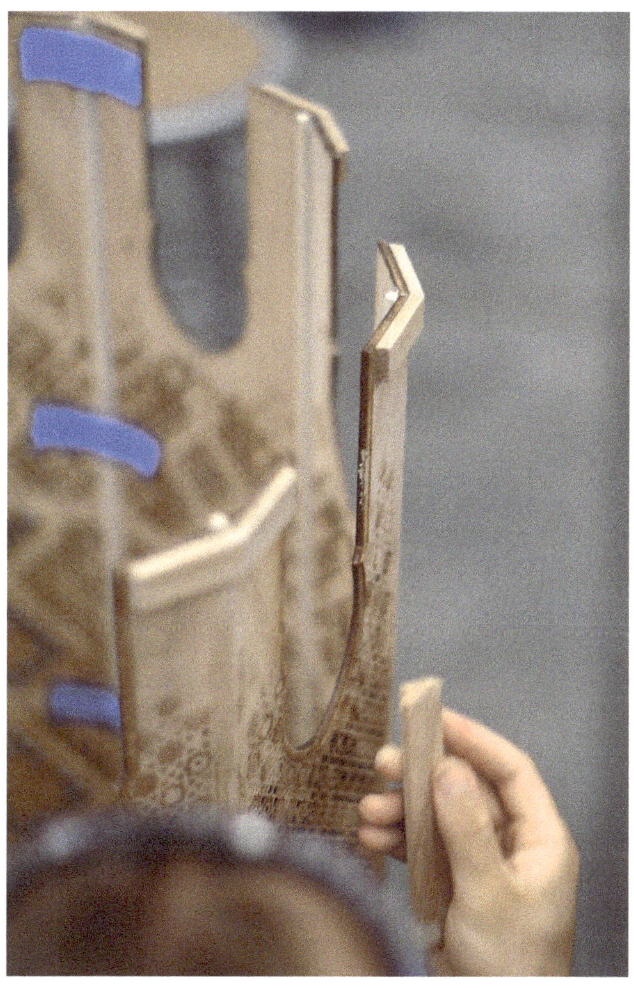

Figures 10.22–24 (Continued)

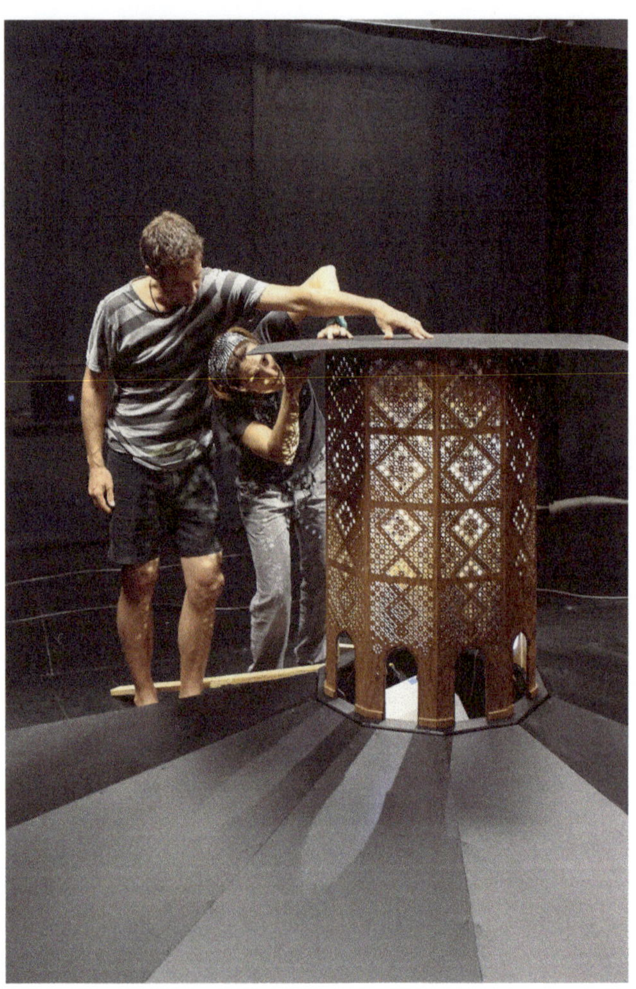

Figures 10.22–24 (Continued)

To fill the structure with light, LEDs were placed inside it. Each LED was behind a covered lens to reduce the amount of stray light that would otherwise diffuse the visuals projected on the screened dome. The light shines through the engravings to create patterns of light and shadow on the floor and walls surrounding the structure, enveloping and drawing in viewers so that they themselves become part of the installation, helping them to become emotionally engaged rather than just observant.

Swirling patterns of bright colors are an integral part of the video animation. They were generated by filming ink billowing and sliding in water. Video of the swirling ink was merged with patterns inspired by African fabrics to create a contrast to black and faceless human silhouettes. To create the silhouettes, dancer Tristan Park was filmed against a white background, and the video was composited with the rest of the visuals in post-production. The sequencing of colors and evocative body language work together to reflect on the migrant's journey, where the color palette follows the course of a day, from bright blues to the deep reds and oranges of sunset.

The video was shot as footage that would later be fragmented and reassembled to create the story line and a mood oscillating between hope and desperation. This process was crucial in integrating video and soundtrack.

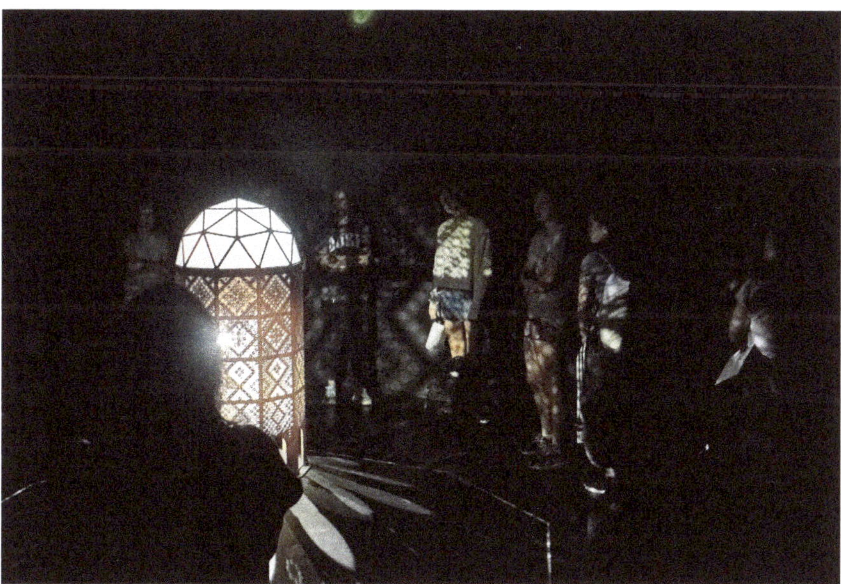

Figure 10.25 Opening Day at the Rubenstein Arts Center, Durham, NC. Photo: Robert Zimmerman, 2018.

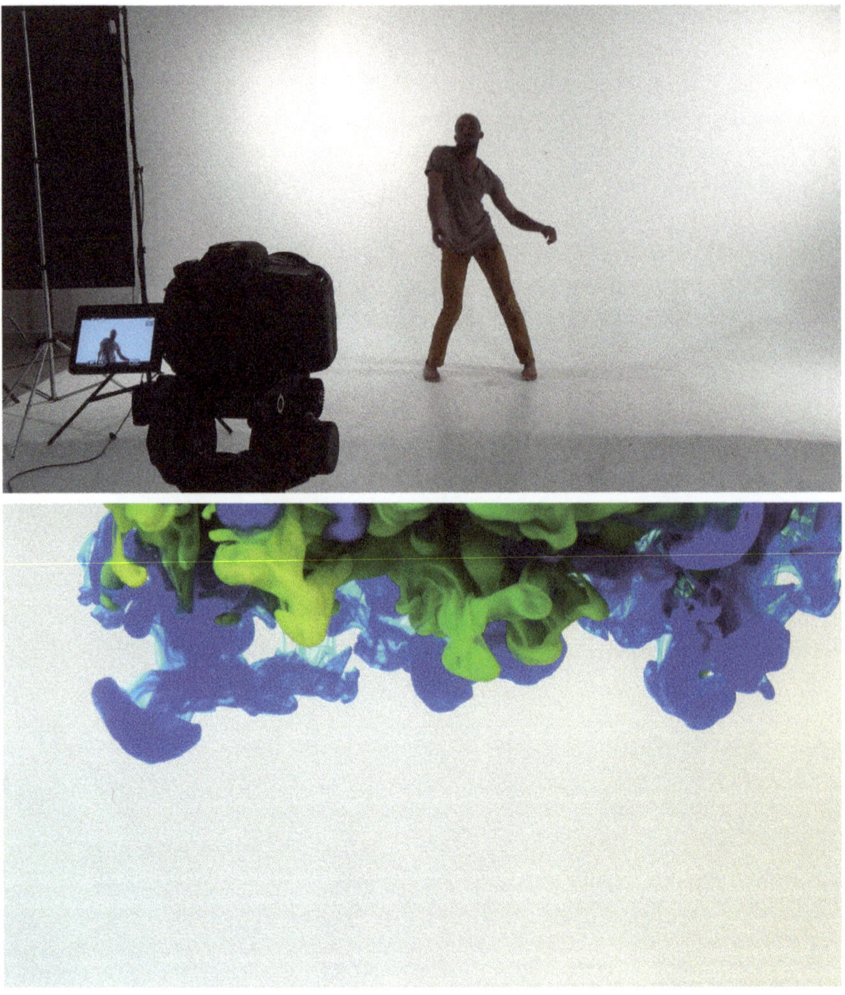

Figures 10.26–27 Watercolors in water – tests for video projection. Filming dancer Tristan Park. Photos: Raquel Salvatella de Prada, 2018.

In fact, the soundtrack was created by Henderson before the post-production of the video took place, constrained only by the need to capture the increasing emotional tension experienced by migrants, as well as the geographic distance between the places where they began their journey and the Moroccan forest where they take their last stand before attempting to enter Spain. The audio begins with sounds of the forest, such as voices, crickets, running steps and the wind, which Henderson recorded in Senegal. These sounds are blended with North African instruments and melodies, followed by a variation of

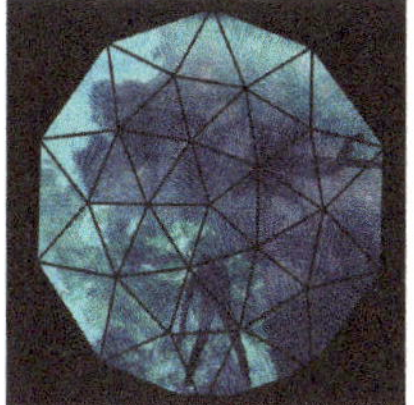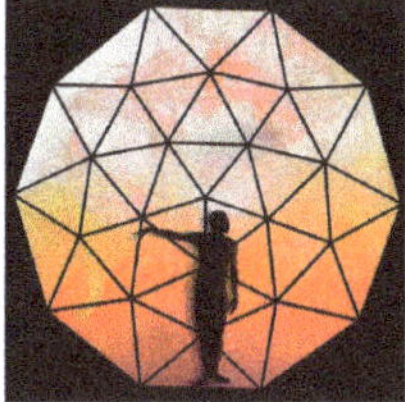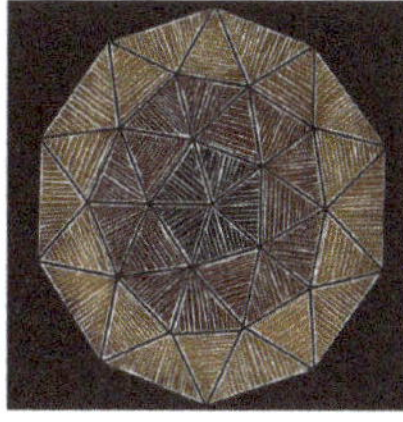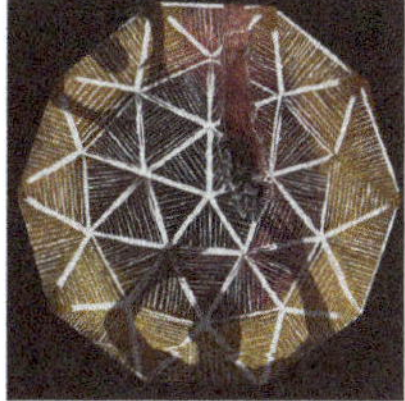

Figure 10.28 Style frames from video animation. Raquel Salvatella de Prada, 2018.

a traditional Senegalese song and the recorded voice of Diali Cissokho, a Senegalese musician. The different musical styles reflect the cultural differences between the migrants and the local Moroccan population. Diali has family members that attempted the crossing and speaks about their experience in his native tongue. Matching the video to the finished soundtrack allowed the mood to be changed, not only via images, colors, and the body language of the dancer, but also by creatively cutting, duplicating, and blending video footage in the rhythm of the music.

Collaborators

Jonathan Henderson (Music)
Tristan Park (Dance)
Dimitri Titov (Geodesic Dome)

Acknowledgments

Valuable assistance was provided by Lexi Bateman, Diali Cissokho & Kaira Ba, Katy Clune, Michael Faber, Philip Moss, Mark Olson, Gabriel Pelli, Victor Ribet, Austin Powers, Philipp Sadowski, Yuchen Zhao, and Robert Zimmerman.

Cornered was supported by Duke Africa Initiative, Duke Arts, the Josiah Charles Trent Memorial Foundation, the Arts & Sciences Council, Art, Art History & Visual Studies at Duke University, and the Puffin Foundation.

Index

Milton Keynes UK
Ingram Content Group UK Ltd.
UKHW051434080124
435668UK00012B/161